RUSSIAN RESEARCH CENTER STUDIES 1

PUBLIC OPINION IN SOVIET RUSSIA

A STUDY IN MASS PERSUASION

PUBLIC OPINION
IN SOVIET RUSSIA

A STUDY IN MASS PERSUASION

By ALEX INKELES

HARVARD UNIVERSITY PRESS
CAMBRIDGE · MASSACHUSETTS
1 9 6 7

The Russian Research Center of Harvard University
is supported by grants from the Carnegie Corporation,
the Ford Foundation, and the Rockefeller Foundation.
The Center carries out interdisciplinary study of Russian institutions and behavior and related subjects.

This volume was prepared under a grant from the
Carnegie Corporation of New York. That Corporation
is not, however, the author, owner, publisher, or
proprietor of this publication and is not to be understood as approving by virtue of its grant any of the
statements made or views expressed therein.

DISTRIBUTED IN GREAT BRITAIN BY
OXFORD UNIVERSITY PRESS · LONDON

PRINTED IN THE UNITED STATES OF AMERICA

FOREWORD

It is particularly appropriate that the first volume of the Russian Research Center studies should be by a sociologist. Dr. Inkeles has brought to his research upon the working of mass communication in the Soviet social system his knowledge of social systems in general. He has made excellent use of the generalizations which have been developed by students of social psychology and the sociology of public opinion in the United States. In turn, he has refined their theory by testing it in a different social system and a different culture. His book is, then, equally important as a contribution to the understanding of Soviet society and to the general theory of the social role of mass communication.

From the point of view of pure science as well as from that of practical importance, a detailed institutional analysis of public-opinion mechanisms in the Soviet Union is a peculiarly inviting research undertaking. The institutions concerned were created almost entirely *de novo* after the 1917 Revolution and on such a scale that the complicating factors of historical tradition and cultural lag, although present and exerting real influence, had less impact than in many older social systems. Moreover, Soviet society is based upon the explicit assumption that all social institutions should be adapted to the goals defined by the elite who determine the tactical and strategic objectives of the Soviet Union. In other words, the social system in this case is truly a system. There is legitimate expectation that it can be analyzed with consistency and clarity, since it is dominated by centralized, known purposes that have a certain constancy rather than by the shifting currents that characterize non-authoritarian states.

Dr. Inkeles effectively demonstrates that public opinion is a factor of real importance in Soviet society and that the leaders take account of it, even though they are not oriented toward following it. In fact, this book constitutes the most sophisticated analysis yet available for any society of the intimate and intricate inter-

relationships and interdependences between a system of communication and a social system. A splendid example is the treatment of the social role of the agitator and the diverse ways in which his activities gear in to support the economic, political, and social structure, and yet constitute an element of strain in the total system. Equally subtle and exciting for social-science theory is the case of the radio, where the convergent demands created by both a shortage of regular sets and the party's desire to control listening have produced the system of wired radio reception, which in turn has its positive and negative impact on the functioning of the society as a whole.

Another striking theme is Dr. Inkeles' discussion of the importance which the initial Leninist conception of the relations of the elite to the masses and of the consequent role of communications in Communist society had on the actual working out of the details of structure and function in the particular media as they developed. This conception of Lenin's, Dr. Inkeles shows, decided not only general questions of how much freedom there was to be, and freedom for whom to do what, but also determined the development of such concrete features of Soviet communications as the system for indoctrinating the "opinion leaders" in Marxist-Leninist thought and the organization of the newspapers into distinct groups designed to reach different strata of the population. This case history and analysis is a highly instructive contribution to the study of the role of ideas in political and social action.

Communist means of persuasion (and of communication in the broadest sense) must be as well understood as those of coercion. Dr. Inkeles helps us enormously to grasp the distinctive Soviet conceptions of freedom of the press as access to the means of expression; of the press, in Stalin's words, as "a transmission belt between the masses and the Party"; of freedom as the spokes of a wheel bound together by responsibility. To understand is by no means necessarily to agree. Understanding, however, is essential both for prediction and for avoidance of hasty judgments and actions on our part which could all too easily grow out of the unconscious conviction that the underlying Soviet premises are identical with our own. It is of tremendous importance that we should be able to see the world in general and what is going on in the Soviet Union in particular as they see it. We are then the better prepared to appraise the distortion of that particular lens from the point of view of our own and possibly even of more universal values.

Although Dr. Inkeles is fully aware that no social scientist can escape completely from evaluations, and although he makes himself and his readers conscious of certain value judgments on his part, his relative detachment is a special merit of this book. No sensitive reader can fail to have a sense of getting at least part way inside the Soviet mind. This detachment plus first-rate theoretical sophistication plus rigorously gathered data make the Russian Research Center proud to present this first substantial account of the relations between the structure of the media of communication and the structure of the social system in the Soviet Union.

CLYDE KLUCKHOHN

AUTHOR'S PREFACE

This book neither pretends nor seeks to be a "definitive" investigation of the media of mass communication in the Soviet Union. The complexity of the Soviet communication system is such that a really exhaustive study of the techniques and institutions utilized for propaganda and agitation would have to be several times the length of the present work. At the same time, it should be recognized that this book is not an analysis of Soviet public opinion as such. It does not describe what the Soviet people think of the regime and the Communist Party, or about the United States, international relations, and the chances for peace. Although those questions are extremely important, the answers to them can be obtained only through direct contact with the Soviet people. Unfortunately, such contact is not now possible, nor is it likely to become more feasible in the immediate future, although research investigations among the numerous Soviet citizens who decided not to return home after the recent war may provide partial answers to many questions about the state of public opinion in the Soviet Union.

Accepting these limitations, I have sought to present an adequate, up-to-date description and analysis of the functioning of the media of mass communication in the Soviet Union. This study attempts to explain how Soviet mass communication works, and why it has the particular characteristics it possesses. But it is by no means intended primarily as a technical discussion of the Soviet press, radio, and film. On the contrary, I hope that this work will promote a more adequate evaluation of the implications of the Soviet system. Since exposure to a steady flow of propaganda and agitation is a major facet of the daily life of every Soviet citizen, no assessment of his life situation can be complete if it does not take account of that fact. Furthermore, Soviet philosophy and practice in the realm of public opinion are important indexes to the nature of the regime. This book is therefore addressed not merely to students of the Soviet Union and to public-opinion specialists, but to all who wish to increase their understanding of contemporary world affairs.

The material presented here is intended neither as a polemic nor as a political tract, but rather seeks to take the form of a scientific investigation. I have earnestly striven to report the facts as objectively as possible. The field of Soviet studies is such, however, that failure explicitly to condemn is viewed by some as tantamount to approval, and failure explicitly to praise is taken by others to be equivalent to criticism. Such misunderstanding may be avoided, or at least minimized, if the reader will keep in mind the distinction between a political and moral evaluation and a scientific judgment. The failure to accept the principle that such judgments are distinct would make it impossible to obtain a realistic picture of the nature of Soviet society, and particularly of its strengths and weaknesses.

Some comment is also in order about the sources used. Just as a study of the media of communication in the United States would have to utilize American sources predominantly, so it has been necessary to rest this investigation primarily on Soviet sources. The use of such "official" Soviet sources poses special problems of interpretation, faced by all analysts of Soviet society, which cannot be discussed here. It must suffice to note that in working with these materials I have sought to draw on the accumulated experience of Western students of the Soviet Union, and on my own years of work with government and university research organizations engaged in collecting and interpreting such data. In regard to the adequacy of my efforts, the text must in the last analysis speak for itself.

There remains, nevertheless, a major difference between this study and any equivalent investigation about the United States, which lies in the fact that a person doing research on mass communication in the United States can check his information and conclusions within the country. Obviously, such field research is not possible in the case of the Soviet Union. As a result, the investigator of mass communication in the U.S.S.R. is at the mercy of his sources. Even if the published information is reliable, a great deal of equal or greater importance may be left unsaid, and much of what happens left undescribed.

It would be misleading not to indicate that these facts constitute a serious limitation upon this study as upon all studies of the Soviet Union. Indeed, in the face of such restrictions it might be argued that scholarly research on the Soviet Union should not be attempted. But it is patently impossible to accept such a decision. If we are to make effective progress in comprehending and dealing with the force represented by Soviet Communism, we are under obligation to make the best of our available resources for studying that phenomenon. Clearly, one would not seriously attempt to state what the people of the U.S.S.R. are actually thinking on the basis of official Soviet assertions on the subject. On the other hand, we have real confidence in our scholarly studies on the Soviet economic and political systems, although they are based almost entirely on Soviet sources. It is my hope that this book will demonstrate that it is possible to achieve the same degree of knowledge about and insight into a social phenomenon like the system of mass communication.

My work naturally owes a great deal to all the men and women who as teachers and later as colleagues stimulated and helped sustain my interest in social science, but a special place is held by Lauriston R. Sharp, Philip Weintraub, and Julian L. Woodward, who introduced and first wedded me to the study of social relations. In addition, I am deeply indebted to Leonard S. Cottrell, Jr., who at a crucial point helped me to decide on a career in sociology and has always shown a friendly interest in that career. Specifically in connection with this book, mention must be given to Paul F. Lazarsfeld and Robert K. Merton, who urged me to undertake the first exploratory investigation of Soviet radiobroadcasting; to Robert S. Lynd, whose warm encouragement, wise counsel, and firm criticism guided the study through to completion; and to Clyde Kluckhohn, whose vigorous support was a major factor in bringing the book to final form for publication.

Bernard Barber, Raymond Bauer, Isaiah Berlin, Kingsley Davis,

Merle Fainsod, John Hazard, Bernadette Inkeles, Philip Mosely, Talcott Parsons, Geroid Robinson, and Hans Speier read the manuscript in various stages of its development and made many useful suggestions and pointed criticisms, all too few of which I was able to take account of in the end product. Amy Wright was a constant help in preparing the manuscript for the press, and Mary Conley and Helen Constantine were devoted and patient typists. To Arnold Horelick, who prepared the index, I owe a special debt of gratitude.

During the greater part of the time spent in gathering the material and preparing the early drafts for this book, I was a Demobilization Fellow of the Social Science Research Council. Great assistance was also rendered by Harvard University's Russian Research Center, of which I was a Research Associate during the later stages in the preparation of the manuscript. Grateful acknowledgment is hereby made to both organizations. Harper and Brothers were kind enough to grant permission for the use of my material on Soviet radiobroadcasting, which originally appeared in slightly revised form in *Communications Research 1948-1949*, edited by Paul F. Lazarsfeld and Frank N. Stanton.

ALEX INKELES

Cambridge, Massachusetts
March 1950

Note on the Third Printing

A chapter, ADDENDUM: 1950–1960? has been added in this printing, September 1958.

Contents

PART 3

THE SOVIET PRESS

PART 4

DOMESTIC BROADCASTING
IN THE U.S.S.R.

PART 5

THE FILM IN SOVIET SOCIETY

PART 6

CONCLUSION

TABLES

CHARTS

PART 1

IDEAS OF PROPAGANDA
AND THE PROPAGANDA OF IDEAS

1

THE STUDY OF
MASS COMMUNICATION

L ENIN ONCE DECLARED THAT THE SOVIET REGIME RESTED
on a balance of coercion and persuasion.[1] This
formula of Lenin's, repeated in various forms by
Soviet leaders, is a master key to the understanding
of Soviet society.

All societies rely to some degree on coercion and persuasion. But
by coercion we ordinarily mean the exercise of force by constituted
authorities against individuals who violate the law, and by persuasion the effort to convince individuals through personal contact
to act in accord with social values. In contrast, Lenin used coercion
to mean the application of force against whole segments or classes
of the population, including the very working class on which the
regime rested.[2] And by persuasion he meant organized, systematic,
concerted campaigns to change the attitudes and influence the
actions of large social groups.

Traditional Western liberalism has held up as an ideal and has
striven, however imperfectly, toward the establishment of a society
in which coercion is at a minimum. It has sought to rely instead
on so structuring the individual's life situation that he is personally
motivated to act in accord with socially defined expectations. In addition, it has sought to rely on a stable group of widely accepted
social norms, manifested in the individual as personal conviction
about what it is right and proper to do. Campaigns of mass persuasion by government, except in time of crisis, have been viewed
with suspicion.

In many older and well-established societies the smooth functioning of the social system can be secured with a minimum of coercion and organized persuasion. But in the Soviet Union the revolution has meant a program of rapid and forced social change, and the regime has been attempting to promulgate and secure acceptance for an unstable, markedly new, and shifting set of social norms. Under these conditions large-scale coercion and mass persuasion came to the fore as instruments for controlling human action.

Yet in the Soviet Union the need for such measures is not based on the demands of the current situation alone. It is embodied in the theory of government itself. Indeed, one of the persistent paradoxes posed by the Soviet Union is that it combines to so high a degree simultaneous emphasis on coercion and persuasion. The theory of Bolshevik leadership presents one of the most Promethean, if not Utopian, approaches to man that the world has witnessed. For it assumes that a small group of men, acting not on the basis of selfish interest but as the representatives of social forces, will bring to the rest of mankind consciousness and enlightenment, and will, behind this torch, lead it toward infinite human perfectibility and toward a state of society—in the form of communism—which is a most literal representation of the conception of paradise on earth. Yet this same group of men, as the whole history of the Soviet Union gives ample testimony, has shown an extraordinary capacity to sacrifice, if not ignore, human liberty, well-being, and life, on a prodigious scale in the name of man's greater good. And this was done not merely under the trying conditions of active revolution, war, and self defense, but with equal intensity in a period which the leaders themselves labeled as one of "peaceful construction."

A major portion of the recent studies of the Soviet Union have emphasized these coercive aspects of Soviet society. Such studies have been stimulated by the high degree of tension between the U.S.S.R. and the Western powers, and have been fortified by evidence drawn from the personal experience of many displaced persons who were directly affected by that coercion. In the light of past experience, when so many of the books on the Soviet Union tended to ignore or gloss over the regime's use of force, these more recent investigations represent a positive development.

But in so far as the emphasis on the part played by coercion leads to the neglect, in some cases even to the denial, of the role of persuasion in Soviet society, our net gain will be a small one. For an adequate assessment of that social system must take account of both factors. And a picture of Soviet society which dealt only with the aspect of force would be inadequate, indeed misleading. Whether the U.S.S.R. is approached in a spirit of friendliness, neutrality, or hostility, such a description can form a sufficient basis neither for effective government policy nor for an informed public opinion.

This study of public opinion in the U.S.S.R., therefore, focuses its attention on the role of persuasion, on the efforts of the Soviet regime to facilitate the tasks of leadership and to mobilize the minds and efforts of the population by means of propaganda and agitation. The choice made is intended neither to deny the role of force in the Soviet Union, to minimize it, nor to suggest that it is of lesser importance than persuasion. But it is intended, by filling in a major and neglected gap in our knowledge, to serve as a contribution toward fuller understanding of the dynamics of Soviet society.

We live in an age of simultaneous mass communication. Following the appearance of mass newspaper and book publishing, the development of the radio and moving picture effected a revolution in human communication. Men now have available possibilities for communication which were absolutely unparalleled, indeed which were almost beyond conception, fifty years ago. The voice of one man may be heard, the same news read, by millions at the same moment. Even a play, transferred to the screen, may be seen by a nationwide audience. And since communication always has potentialities for influencing human attitudes and actions, mass communication implies mass influence.

Where there is a relatively free flow of public information, the influences of the different mass-communication media may to some degree cancel each other. Even when there is a high degree of uniformity in the direction of all of these media, so long as face-to-face communication is left relatively unfettered, the influence of the mass media may be counteracted by personal influence.[3] Furthermore, when the media do not serve any single concerted goal, but have varying purposes and ends which they serve simultaneously—to advertise goods, to spread news, to present human-interest stories—the effect of their concentration may be muted. But in the Soviet Union the free flow of public information is sharply restricted, and an individual can exert personal influence which runs counter to the main tenor of government policy only in relative secrecy and frequently at the risk of losing personal freedom. All of the media of communication, including the personal address in face-to-face contact with small audiences, are part of a political monopoly, precisely controlled, backed by the force of state and law, geared in directly with broader political purposes, and oriented in a specific and centrally determined direction which dictates a high degree of uniformity in form and content. The potentialities of mass communication for exerting an influence on human attitudes and actions in the Soviet Union are thus greatly magnified. And the operations of this apparatus are governed and given real impetus by an explicit theory which places prime importance on a conscious and planned effort to exert just such influence on the thoughts and actions of men.

The growth of mass communication has been accompanied by the development of a special field of investigation devoted to analyzing the formation and change of public opinion.[4] An understanding of the role of mass persuasion in Soviet society should, indeed it must, utilize the methods and findings of that discipline.

The development of the scientific study of public opinion may be viewed as having been fostered by three major groups. The first of these, composed predominantly of people of liberal persuasion, was stimulated by an apparent "failure of communication." They sought to discover its causes and to learn what could be done to make mass communication provide not only greater contact but also greater understanding and sympathy between men. A second major source of interest in, and the prime source of financial assistance for, the analysis of communication came from industry and trade. Founded on the study of advertising and "public relations," this interest led to the development of elaborate techniques for market research and extensive empirical systems for testing the content and effectiveness of various phases of mass communication—Hooper ratings, readership indexes, and so on. A third source of support came from government agencies, whose interest was given particular impetus during the recent war. This led, in particular, to elaboration of the study of domestic, foreign, and counterpropaganda techniques.[5]

This account neglects, of course, the role of the academicians, whose interest was stimulated primarily by scientific curiosity, the desire to explore, grasp, and perhaps control the phenomenon of mass communication. To a significant degree, however, they were influenced by much the same forces which affected the other groups. And since the scientific and systematic study of public opinion is an exceedingly expensive operation, they tended to investigate those problems regarded as most pressing by the sponsors who financed their scientific endeavors.

The predominantly quantitative analysis of mass communication and public opinion which has developed under these auspices in the last two decades has produced a very considerable literature.[6] And the studies completed—ranging from investigations of the reading habits of children to the recording and exploration of voting behavior and political opinions—have done much to increase our understanding of what goes on in mass communication and to push back the boundaries of our knowledge of opinion formation and change. But all of the groups engaged in and sponsoring this research had one thing in common, in that their approach and emphasis was primarily psychological. Their chief interest was either in the *content* of communication, which led to the investigation of images, symbols, stereotypes, and so forth; or their interest lay in the *effects* of communication, seen as a process of manipulating thought and feeling, changing attitudes, creating certain predispositions to act, and so on. Almost all of the work done has been guided by the formula "who says what to whom with what effect."[7]

The priority given to answering these questions has meant that our public-opinion research has very largely neglected systematic investigation into the dynamic interrelations between the structure and functioning of the media of communication and the social system in which those media operate. In brief, little has been done to determine what is the *social role* of mass communication, either on the most general level or in regard to the particular societies in which it appears. And it is precisely this social role of mass communication which must form the basis for an assessment of the place of mass persuasion in Soviet society.

The difficulty can be fruitfully illustrated from Soviet experience. For example, in the Soviet Union personal oral agitation, conducted everywhere throughout the country by Communist Party members working in face-to-face contact with small groups of the population, ranks with the newspaper and radio as one of the major organized forms of mass communication. Yet a search of the voluminous American and British literature on mass communication yields little more than a half dozen items that even take cognizance of such agitation.[8]

Furthermore, in so far as attention is paid to this form of communication within the framework of the predominant approach to public-opinion studies, prime emphasis is placed on the investigation of differences in the effectiveness of various forms of agitation as methods of changing attitudes. This is undoubtedly a problem of first importance. But it is equally important to ask what special needs of the Soviet system, and what characteristics of the role of the Communist Party in that society, account for this tremendous development and elaboration of personal oral agitation in the U.S.S.R. The answers to such questions can be provided only by an approach to mass communication which focuses attention on the changes in the structure and functioning of the media which result from changes in other parts of the social system.

An equally neglected type of problem concerns the impact that the media themselves may have on the social system in which they operate, and in particular the ways in which they enter as elements of strength or weakness into the effective functioning of that system. For example, radio reception in the Soviet Union is not predominantly dependent on ordinary radio-receiving sets, but rather relies primarily on a network of wired speakers linked in small receiving networks joining all the listeners in a given area. This enables the party and government, in seeking to mobilize the population for particular tasks, to adapt their appeals and directly to orient them in terms of the composition of the particular group of workers, farmers, or housewives in any given locality. This network of wired receivers acts in a variety of other important ways as both a functional and dysfunctional element in the performance of the Soviet system as a whole. And once again, this is precisely the type of problem that is likely to be overlooked by an approach to the field of public opinion principally oriented toward investigating the content and effects of communication.

These examples should suffice to indicate that an understanding of the role of persuasion in Soviet society depends upon utilization of a sociology of mass communication to supplement the psychological work already done in the field. This study seeks to present a detailed institutional analysis of mass communication in the U.S.S.R., and to accomplish that end it is to some degree necessary to forge new tools. Thus, this investigation offers a double opportunity, both to increase the understanding of Soviet society and to contribute toward meeting the pressing need for a sociology of mass communication.[9] It will not be primarily concerned, therefore, with the psychological analysis of Soviet communications, with the images used, the stereotypes developed, or the characteristic patterns of expression that are manifested. Nor will it be predominantly concerned with the "effects" of mass communication in the Soviet Union, that is, with the problem of the ways in which that communication acts to affect attitudes, changes predispositions to act, and so on. These elements will certainly not be ignored. But the analysis will concentrate mainly on the impact which a given kind of social system has on the structure and functioning of the media of communication, and on the reciprocal impact which those media have on that social system.

Within this general framework, four major tasks will serve as points of orientation. In the first place, this study seeks to make available in English under one cover the basic facts about the formal structure and operations of the principal media of mass communication in the Soviet Union. This involves what is primarily a task of description, but it is obviously a worth-while task both because of the general importance of mass communication as a major element of Soviet society, and because valid analysis of the subject depends initially on an adequate grasp of the basic facts.

This study attempts, in the second place, to answer the question of what has been the impact on the organization and operation of the media of communication resulting from their functioning in the complex of political, economic, and social conditions that constitute the Soviet system. When the Bolsheviks came to power in 1917 they inherited from the old regime only a minor and fragmented system of public communication. The major media of communication in the U.S.S.R. have been almost entirely shaped and developed to meet the changing needs of the party and government. The Soviet Union provides, therefore, an opportunity to study the impact on the media of the social definition of their functions and the influence of their total social setting. And this is a rare opportunity, for it is seldom that either history or contemporary societies supply adequate data for the study of so significant a variable in a total process of dynamic social change.

A third problem will be to answer the question: What is the social role of the media of communication in Soviet society? For the Soviet propaganda and agitation apparatus furnishes a unique opportunity to examine the use of the media of mass communication as a definite instrument of public or government policy, designed to mobilize large numbers of people for the attainment of social goals, to disseminate new values, to mold patterns of motivation, and to assist in the process of social control.

Finally, it must be recognized that, even if such a procedure should be desired, it would not be possible to treat this material in an absolutely abstract manner. Both his methods of research and the nature of his material constantly bring the social scientist to the very edge of evaluation. Quite apart from the question of whether or not such social material can be treated without evaluation, either implicit or explicit, there remains the problem of the responsibility of the social scientist toward his subject and his audience. If for no other reason, the social scientist is obliged to make known his own judgment of his data lest someone else make it for him. Wherever the need is evident, therefore, an effort has been made to point out the implications of the findings for an evaluation of the Soviet system.

2

LENINIST THEORY
AND PUBLIC OPINION

THE COMMUNIST PARTY IS THE HARD CORE OF THE Soviet system. And the party is more than Stalin, it is more than a massive monolithic organization, more than six million members and a history of three decades of rule in Russia. However large these elements loom in the description of the party, the picture which includes them alone is incomplete. For the party is also and in the first instance the embodiment of a set of ideas, of a theory. One aspect of that theory is of fundamental concern here, namely, the Leninist conception of the basic relationship between the masses on the one hand, and the revolutionary workers' party and the government through which it operates on the other. Most Marxists prior to Lenin were inclined to identify party and masses as a unity. It is a distinguishing characteristic of Leninist thought that it treats them as a dichotomy. This led Lenin to an interpretation of the role of the masses in the revolutionary process which was markedly different from that of other Marxists in Russia and Western Europe, including Rosa Luxemburg, leader of the German Communist uprising of 1919. Yet it was that conception of Lenin's which largely shaped the course of development of Soviet policy in the sphere of public opinion.[1]

THE PARTY · THE MASSES · AND THE REVOLUTIONARY PROCESS

There are two major strains in Lenin's thinking about the working classes. As a Marxist, and thus as one who drew a significant part of his intellectual tradition from rational Western liberalism, he had faith in the virtually limitless perfectibility of mankind. He held to the essentially utopian position, most clearly expressed earlier by Engels, that a new type of man, the like of which had not been seen on earth, could be developed under socialism. In Lenin's view, even under the bondage of capitalism the masses moved, however uncertainly, in the right direction. Thus he declared that, "according to their instinct, their feeling, their inclination, the majority of the population of Russia is sympathetic to a revolution against the capitalists."[2]

But for Lenin this did not suffice. For he was first and foremost the practical revolutionist, and when he assessed the conditions and the forces which would be required to effect a revolution in Russia he found the masses lacking in two indispensable qualities: class consciousness and organization.

Lenin asserted that the history of the working class in all countries revealed that through its own efforts alone the working class could develop only what he termed "trade-union consciousness." By this he meant that the workers could recognize the need to form unions, to struggle with their employers, and even to engage in some political agitation to force the government to enact labor legislation. But a trade-union consciousness was not the kind of revolutionary class consciousness which Lenin insisted was essential if the working-class movement were to progress beyond agitation for "mere" economic reform to a program of revolutionary political action.[3]

The second major gap in the equipment of the working class which Lenin noted was the absence of revolutionary organization. It was true that there existed a broad working-class organization in the form of the trade unions. But Lenin held it to be a fundamental error, and one of which he accused many social-democrats of his time, to confuse such an organization with an organization of revolutionists.[4] He felt that a working-class movement which was restricted to trade unions must of necessity lack the coherence, direction, and purposiveness to lead the masses toward the revolutionary goal of overthrowing the old and building a new society. Instead of moving in this direction its actions were governed by a principle he termed "spontaneity." And to Lenin, in contrast to other Communists like Rosa Luxemburg, the word spontaneity was not a term of approbation.[5]

Lenin stressed the fact that any ordinary organization of workers like a trade union was immersed in and affected by the capitalist society which surrounded it. Consequently, he found such organizations to be wavering, characterized by unthinking confidence, prey to demagogues, and subject to a form of mass frenzy or "petty-bourgeois ebullience" during the time of mere reformist revolutions. Even the proletariat, defined as the more advanced and important segment of the toiling masses, was in Lenin's view frequently permeated and corrupted by the atmosphere which surrounded it, and thus subject to "constant relapses . . . into petty-bourgeois spinelessness, disintegration, individualism, and alternate moods of exaltation and dejection."[6]

If the toiling masses living under capitalism possessed neither the necessary class consciousness nor the organization to effect the overthrow of the old social order, how were these qualities to be attained? Lenin made it absolutely clear that through its own resources alone the working class could not be expected to achieve this end. He stated expressly that the essential class consciousness, a revolutionary social-democratic consciousness, *"could only be brought to them from without."*[7] And when Lenin said from without he meant from a revolutionary party, specifically from that segment of the Russian Social Democratic Party which was known as the Bolshevik faction, later to become the Communist Party.

It was Lenin's view that the social-democrat should "concern himself first and foremost with an organization of revolutionists, capable of guiding the *whole* proletarian struggle" against Tsarist absolutism and the whole of the then existing social-economic system. This organization of revolutionists was not intended to supplant a mass workers' movement such as the trade unions. It was indeed to be intimately linked with it, inextricably interwoven with it, and in many respects dependent on it. Yet this organization of revolutionists, in Lenin's view, had to be distinct from the trade-union type of mass movement, with its own peculiar form of organization, with an entirely different conception of eligibility for membership, and with a precise and unique set of functions.[8]

Lenin insisted that this group, particularly because it had to operate under conditions of Tsarist autocracy, must be a secret, concentrated, restricted, and extremely highly organized group. Its members, whether drawn from the workers or the intelligentsia, had to be professional revolutionaries, men who were carefully trained, schooled, and experienced, and capable of working in perfect harmony to carry out a consistent and integrated program of action. This group of professional revolutionaries, which was to exercise the function of leadership, earned its right to that role by virtue of its mastery of Marxist philosophy and its knowledge of the direction of the road to socialism and the class forces leading to it.[9]

Such an organization was for Lenin the *sine qua non* of revolution, and he declared that without it "no class in modern society is capable of conducting a determined struggle."[10] He asserted that no mass movement could be durable unless it had a stable organization of leaders to maintain continuity. The broader the mass participation in the movement, the more necessary such an organization became, the more stable it had to be. And in order to insure this stability Lenin insisted that the party be strongly centralized, "built from the top downwards."[11]

Lenin was, in brief, interested in an elite, what he referred to as a "dozen tried and talented leaders," and he warned that such talented men were not born by the hundreds.[12] But it was obvious to Lenin that this organization of professional revolutionaries could not alone effect a successful revolution. A basis of mass support was indispensable, and to think of acting without it mere political "adventurism." What then were to be the relations between this organized revolutionary vanguard and the mass movement on which it depended? What, in effect, is the Bolshevik conception of leadership?

The leadership of a political organization may regard itself as being primarily an instrument for attaining the goals arrived at by the rank and file, or it may seek to determine the goals of the movement itself and attempt to carry the masses along with it. The choice made determines the character of the movement as a political party. Lenin and Stalin were fully cognizant of the necessity to make such a choice. Each gave essentially the same unequivocal answer.

They determined to act as would the general staff of an army. Lenin frequently spoke of the party as being the "general staff" of the working class.[13] Stalin has, in turn, shown a particular fondness for this expression. He concluded that just as no army could go into battle without an experienced general staff to direct its activities, so neither could the working class, for "the working class without a revolutionary party is an army without a general staff." It was to be this party, functioning as a general staff, which would put the proletariat on the offensive when conditions warranted, and which would withdraw it from the fight when the course of events called for a retreat.[14]

The use of the term general staff to describe the revolutionary party was no mere figure of speech. For Bolshevik theory admits the possibility of, and indeed, as many of Lenin's comments indicate, it recognized the existence of, differences between the self-determined goals of the rank and file of the workers and those of its organized revolutionary vanguard.[15]* In Lenin's view the self-determined goals of the working-class movement as represented by the trade unions were concerned with "mere" economic gains, whereas the organized vanguard, the party, was oriented toward a fundamental revolutionary struggle.[16] And for Lenin the "interests of social development," that is, the revolution and the building of socialism, "are above the interests of the proletariat."[17]

It was precisely because of their alleged confusion of these two aspects of the broad working-class movement, because of their "muddlement" about the relations between the "material" and the "ideological" elements of the movement, that Lenin most severely criticized the social-democrats in the early 1900's. He charged that they not only tended to follow but even to worship the spontaneous urges of the masses. Borrowing an apt phrase from Plekhanov, Lenin declared that these social-democrats were "gazing with awe upon the

---

*The gulf between the party's goals and those of the masses was most marked, in Lenin's view, in the "April days" following the "bourgeois" or February Revolution. Disturbed by the popular sentiment in favor of this revolt and the apparent lack of mass interest in proceeding to a more fundamental social upheaval, Lenin called on the party "to resist [this] 'mass' frenzy rather than 'wish to remain' with the masses." We must, he declared, "pour vinegar and bile into the sweetish water of revolutionary democratic eloquence." Lenin, Collected Works, XX(1), 129, 135.

'posteriors' of the Russian proletariat."[18] Such people were not worthy of the name ideologist, he asserted, for to be an ideologist one must march ahead of the spontaneous movement, pointing out the road, and solving in advance of the rank and file those theoretical, tactical, and organizational problems which the spontaneous movement runs against. One must, he declared, seek "to *elevate* spontaneity to consciousness."[19]

The tendency to drag at the tail of the masses, or *khvostizm** as it was called by Lenin, was an equally favorite target for Stalin. If the party were content simply to follow where the mass movement led, he declared, it would reveal itself as not fit to take over the functions of leadership. It would be no "true Party," Stalin continued, "if it limits its activities to a *mere registration of the sufferings and thoughts of the proletarian masses.*" The true party should lead the proletariat, not lag in the rear, he concluded, and this meant that it should see further than the working class as a whole and be able to "rise superior to the transient interests of the proletariat."[20]

The Bolsheviks, of course, maintain that their program is designed to achieve the long-range, or, as they repeatedly phrase it, the "true" interests of the working masses. But it is also perfectly clear that Bolshevik theory as formulated by Lenin and Stalin did not conceive of the workers' party as simply a vehicle for expressing the workers' day-to-day economic aspirations, nor as an instrument for attaining such limited goals.

It is equally clear, however, that the Communist leaders were not naïve adventurers who would lightly jeopardize the success of their movement by acting without careful consideration of the state of mass thinking. Both Lenin and Stalin repeatedly insisted that one could not make a revolution "by decree," nor effect fundamental social change simply by giving orders to the masses.[21] The first step in the Bolshevik program of action was ideologically to capture the vanguard of the proletariat, to win it over to Marxism. But Lenin warned that to throw this vanguard alone into the battle "would not merely be folly, but a crime." It was necessary, prior to accepting a decisive challenge for power, to be certain that the broad masses had

---

*From the Russian *khvost*, for tail.

taken up a position "either of direct support of the vanguard, or at least of benevolent neutrality toward it."[22] The communist position was very aptly summed up by Lenin when he said that "the art of politics (and the Communist's correct understanding of his tasks) lies in correctly gauging the conditions and the moment when the vanguard of the proletariat can successfully seize power, when it will be able, during and after this seizure of power, to obtain adequate support from sufficiently broad strata of the working class and the non-proletarian toiling masses, and when, thereafter, it will be able, to maintain, consolidate, and extend its rule."[23]

But what course of action was the revolutionary vanguard to follow while it was gauging the existing conditions to determine whether or not they met the criteria for the correct moment to open the fight? Obviously, it was not in keeping with the whole spirit of the Bolshevik movement to adopt a policy of watchful waiting. As early as 1902 Lenin had given an unequivocal answer to this question when he stated that the working class must be pushed on from the outside, and declared "there has never been too much of *such* 'pushing on from outside'. . . We professional revolutionaries must continue, and will continue, *this kind* of 'pushing,' and a hundred times more forcibly than we have done hitherto."[24] It was, in brief, necessary to go beyond a policy of mere testing of the state of mass thinking to an active policy of *"influencing* the mood of the masses."[25]

How this influence was to be achieved is summed up in the words to persuade or to convince (*ubezhdat'*). Again and again this term appears in the discussion of the basic relation between the party and the masses as conceived by Bolshevik theory; it runs like a thread through the writings of Lenin and Stalin on the subject. One must recognize, said Lenin, that "the whole task of the Communists is to be able to *convince* the backward elements";[26] and Stalin defined leadership as the "ability to convince the masses that the Party policy is right; ability to issue and to act upon slogans that will bring the masses nearer to the Party standpoint."[27]

The learning process which inhered in the relationship between organized vanguard and masses was not conceived of as strictly a one-way affair. Lenin and Stalin repeatedly spoke of the masses learning from their own experience,[28] and on at least one occasion

Stalin went so far as to say that the party must be ready "not only to teach the masses, but also to learn from them."[29] What was to be the nature of this learning?

When Lenin and Stalin spoke of the masses learning by experience, they apparently meant that as a result of their spontaneous activity, and with the aid of the party in pointing up the lessons, the masses would in their own way come to accept the principles which the organized leadership knew to be correct all along. With this realization, the masses would presumably come to recognize that the party was indispensable to the achievement of their "true" interests and to accept it as guide, leader, and teacher. As Stalin put it, "The Party is able to convince the masses by their own experience that its policy is sound, thus ensuring the support of the working class and inducing the broad masses of the workers to follow its lead."[30]

Furthermore, the learning which the party could do was severely circumscribed. For even in making his often-quoted remark that it was nonsense to claim that Marx and the Marxists knew the road to socialism in all its completeness, Lenin at the same time did affirm that Marx defined the general goal of communism and that Marxists knew both the direction of this road and the class forces leading to it.[31] Two things remained that the party might learn from the masses: first, the correct time and place at which to strike the revolutionary blow, and second, new forms and techniques for conducting the revolutionary struggle which would be brought forward on the initiative of the masses.[32]

The problem, therefore, was clearly defined more as a matter of tactics than of educating the party. The party is not under obligation to base its goals on the popular sentiments of the masses. But it is under obligation to take account of those sentiments in its planning, the key principle being that it is equally as bad to rush ahead of the masses as it is to lag too far behind. If the party moves too rapidly, Lenin and Stalin warned, it may find itself isolated from the masses, without close contact, and hence without the necessary support.[33] Consequently, the theory holds, the party must have "a good ear" for the voice of the masses, testing its policy against the measuring stick of their readiness to support the party's policy.[34] Such appears to be the chief "teaching" of the masses from which the party must learn. And in fact, one could hardly expect Bolshevik theory to take a different position, in so far as it assumed that Marxism is the only correct science of society and that the leaders are better qualified to interpret that science than the rank and file.

The Bolshevik theory described above was largely developed to guide the actions of the party in its efforts to effect the revolutionary seizure of power. What then did the theory anticipate would be the relations between the organized vanguard and the masses after the seizure of power?

In the long run, of course, with the transfer of the means of production to the people and the freeing of man from "wage slavery," it was assumed that a new type of man would appear.[35] But while this new generation was being raised, the old generation was still the chief material with which the party had to work. Hence the task might be long drawn out, for the struggle would then be against what Lenin called that "terrible force," the force of habit of tens of millions of people, brought up under the old regime and, even in the new generation, affected by the "bourgeois remnants" of the past. Consequently, Lenin conceived of the Soviet regime as a kind of enormous school, which he spoke of as the " 'school' of communism," in which the workers and even the peasants could study to rule so that in time they might take into their own hands the direction of the entire national life.[36]

But while the masses were to be at school after the revolution, the Communist Party was still to be the teacher. The party, Stalin declared, "is not only indispensable to the proletariat for the establishment of the dictatorship. It becomes even more necessary after the seizure of power."[37] And following this seizure the party was not expected to be able to abandon that "pushing" of the masses from without of which Lenin had spoken. When he spoke of this pushing he meant teaching the fundamentals of Marxism to the masses.[38] But this by no means excluded the possibility of the application of force on the masses, or at least some segment of it (as opposed to the use of force against the ruling classes, which was assumed automatically). Lenin asserted that the work of persuasion prior to action could not wait until the last worker with craft union prejudices had been converted,[39] and he declared: "We must convince first and keep force in reserve. At any cost, we must convince first and not use force till afterwards."[40] Thus, the application of force on the masses was placed in reserve but not disavowed.

In elaborating on this theme Stalin asserted that the prime reliance on persuasion not only does not exclude the use of compulsion when necessary, but as a matter of fact presupposes it. Such compulsion was permissible, he indicated, if applied to a minority, subject to the condition that the majority of the working class supported the action of the party. From another remark of his in the same context, one additional condition may be inferred under which the party was likely to go beyond persuasion to compulsion: namely, when the masses were not yet ready to accept an essentially sound party policy, "and the Party will not and cannot wait until the masses have a chance of learning by their own experience that the Party policy is right."[41] Stalin did warn that such action could destroy the essential state of "mutual confidence" between the vanguard and the masses, but here again force was not disavowed. It is true, of course, that in time the leading role of the organized vanguard is expected to become superfluous and, like the state, wither away. But the deadline for this event is set in the rather indefinite future, and it appears continuously to recede as it is approached.[42] Meanwhile, the masses must continue to learn, and one of the most important lessons, we gather from Lenin and Stalin, is that the masses must regard the party, the disciplined and conscious vanguard, as trusted leader.

Thus, it is assumed that for an unspecified (although theoretically limited) period of time after the revolution, the party will continue to function as a tightly organized, elite formation, which is the real locus of power in Soviet society. As such it will continue to play its self-defined role of organizer, teacher, guide, and leader of the masses. As in the prerevolutionary period, what the masses can teach the party will be restricted to suggesting new methods and techniques, like socialist competition or Stakhanovism, rather than new socialist goals.

Recognition of this principle is of the greatest importance in understanding much of what has occurred in the course of development of the Soviet regime. To a striking degree the Communist Party in the Soviet Union has operated in the post-revolutionary period with essentially the same type of structure and with virtually the identical conception of its social role that had been developed to guide its earlier operations as an ironclad instrument for the revolutionary seizure of power. This is attested to, in the most general way, by the whole pattern of the party's operations since the period of the New Economic Policy. It is evidenced in a more subtle way by the widespread tendency to quote Lenin's strictures on the organization and functioning of the party without any genuine effort to indicate or determine whether he meant these instructions to apply primarily to a party seeking to seize power or to one already in control of the reins of government in a country with socialized means of production.[43] This uncritical extension to the post-revolutionary era of those ideas devised to guide the activities of a revolutionary organization seeking to take power has largely shaped the whole course of development of Soviet society as we know it today. It has particularly determined the pattern of Soviet policy toward public opinion.

SOME IMPLICATIONS OF BOLSHEVIK THEORY FOR PUBLIC-OPINION POLICY

Ideologies may be altered or reinterpreted under the impact of the harsh realities of the existing social situation, and such shifts may also be brought about by changes within the revolutionary group which bears the ideology. Nevertheless, when men wielding great power are oriented toward a precise body of doctrinal principles, which is the case with the Soviet leaders, that body of doctrine will enter significantly into the actions of the men concerned. Certainly a knowledge of their fundamental beliefs is hardly sufficient for the explanation of men's actions in the real world. But in so far as these actions reflect a mutual adjustment between ideology and social realities, an understanding of the ideology becomes a necessary condition for an understanding of the action. And this study is primarily oriented toward examining the working out of such an adjustment between ideology and social forces in the realm of mass communication in the Soviet Union.

It is therefore appropriate at this point to ask: What are the implications of the party's theory for public-opinion policy; and, what major lines of public-opinion policy may we anticipate after the coming to power of men who hold such a conception of their role?

The theory clearly requires that responsibility for and control of the media of communication must be concentrated in the hands of the party. The Soviet government, for example, does not include any agency which serves the functions of a ministry of public information.[44] The organization which fulfills those functions in the U.S.S.R., known as the Department of Propaganda and Agitation, is a part of the Communist Party apparatus under the direct and immediate supervision of the Central Committee of the party.

The party's control of public communication follows from the fact that it has assigned itself the role of teacher, guide, and leader, and from the assumption that the party must influence the psychology of the masses and win them over to its side. Thus, Lenin and Stalin frequently spoke of the press, the radio, and other forms of mass communication as a "tool" or "instrument" in the hands of the party, and as a "driving belt" between the party and the masses. In Bolshevik thought, to surrender this control of communication would be to invite the conversion of these media into mirrors for that "mere registration of the sufferings and thoughts" of the masses which Stalin had rejected. Bolshevik theory must regard the absence of such party supervision of communication as an invitation to *khvostizm* or "tailism."

It would be an error, however, to assume that this insistence on party control is based solely on such negative considerations. The Bolshevik position is also based on the general assumption that all social institutions should be adapted to and utilized for the attainment of the goals toward which the society in which they operate is striving. When extended to the media of communication, this principle leads to the conclusion that the flow of public intelligence should be organized to support the values of the society and to contribute to the attainment of its goals. In Soviet society, of course, it is the party, acting in the name of the masses, that selects the values and determines the goals to be pursued by the society as a whole.

A second major area for which Bolshevik theory has important implications is that of the physical development and structure of the media of communication. The defined functions of the media in the Soviet Union are to make effective the efforts of the organized vanguard, to tie the masses to it, and to mobilize the entire population in the attainment of the goals set by the party for the whole society. Such a task demands that the means of public communication be elaborated and extended up to the full limits of the physical resources of the party and the national economy. Consequently, under the Soviet regime, as shall be seen in detail, there has been a marked growth of the regular means of public communication; and new forms of contact between the leaders and the population have been developed, such as the extensive network of individual Bolshevik agitators. The growth of the media of communication in the Soviet Union, although frequently only modest in absolute figures, is certainly impressive when viewed against the achievements of Tsarist Russia; for in the case of the latter, the government frequently appeared to feel little need for any apparatus to facilitate communication with the population, and some of its prominent members actually viewed the high rate of illiteracy as a political asset.

Apart from the physical extension of the media, it is important to recognize that the Bolshevik conception of the role of communications demands a high degree of differentiation between and within each medium to fit it for the particular contribution which it is expected to make to the over-all national goals. Bolshevik theory assigns to the various segments of the population distinct roles which they are expected to play in the process of building the new social order. And since the party is regarded as a kind of general staff, it is assumed that it should have special lines of communication to each group, to the party membership, to the workers and peasants, the intelligentsia, the women, the youth, and so on. But such differentiation increases the problem of control and therefore encourages the development of a high degree of uniformity in the organization of public communication and in the media's patterns of operation.

A third aspect of public communication for which Bolshevik theory has major implications is content. The Communist Party determines the content of the radio, press, and films on the familiar grounds that it has the clearest view of the common goals, and as teacher and guide is best able to select that content which will most advance them. And since the goals are so distinct, it may be assumed, as indeed we shall see, that such familiar criteria for the choice of content as newsworthiness and the "effectiveness" of communication will have a profoundly different meaning in the Soviet Union. This is equally true of the methods for reckoning the "costs" of the process of public communication. For in the U.S.S.R. that cost is largely figured in terms of the contribution the media are able to make to effective party leadership. In that sense the propaganda and agitation carried by the Soviet media are the functional equivalent of advertising in the United States; both pay the way for the operation as a whole.

A fourth problem that merits attention concerns the extent to which the state of public opinion is taken into consideration when communication policy is decided upon. Loose thinking on this subject has led to the widespread, facile assumption that Bolshevik theory expects, and in fact requires, that the party operate without regard to the state of public opinion, simply relentlessly pursuing its revolutionary goals. Our discussion of the position taken by Lenin and Stalin on the subject should make it clear that this assumption is inaccurate. Bolshevik theory does not disregard public opinion. Its emphasis, however, more or less completely rejects following public opinion and stresses the prime need to shape and mold it. This implies that one studies public opinion primarily to determine the pace and speed of his own actions. The goal is not to cater to public opinion, but to move it along with you as rapidly as possible without undermining your popular support. But one cannot determine his own pace, according to this formula, unless he knows the state of mass thinking. This, as we shall see, has important implications for the place of public-opinion testing in Soviet society, for the definition of the effectiveness of mass-communication materials, and for a series of related problems.

There is, finally, one additional point which should be mentioned here, which has to do with the attitude toward mass psychology reflected in Bolshevik theory. It is relevant to note, in this connection, that in the Soviet literature on public opinion and in the practical journals and handbooks for propagandists and agitators, surprisingly little attention is given to problems of method; the importance of content is stressed infinitely more than questions of how, by what devices and mechanisms, one can influence attitudes and change opinions. The assumption which is explicitly stated in Soviet public-opinion theory is that only personal conviction on the part of the agitator and the essential "truth" of his message can effectively serve to convince the masses. By the same token, one cannot find any open avowal of a cynical approach toward mass psychology in the practical discussions of propaganda and agitation in the voluminous Soviet literature on public opinion.* Indeed, there are in the Soviet literature some vigorous attacks on propagandists and agitators who were no more than suspected of manifesting such an approach.[45] In this respect, Soviet theory is radically different in its attitude toward mass psychology from the type of theory epitomized by Hitler's *Mein Kampf.* And this strongly suggests the inadequacy of hasty generalizations about Soviet public-opinion policy on the assumption that anything which applied to public-opinion policy in one totalitarian system automatically applies to all other systems so defined.

*To state that there is no open avowal of a cynical approach to mass psychology in Soviet public-opinion theory is not to deny that in Western eyes much of Soviet practice appears to be grounded on such an approach.

3

THE ADMINISTRATION OF PROPAGANDA AND AGITATION

THE BASIC PRINCIPLES OF BOLSHEVIK THEORY LEAD inevitably to the conclusion that control of the media of communication must be concentrated in the hands of the party. This means, of course, that the party structure must include some special apparatus to fulfill this function, and indeed throughout most of its history in power the party has had a particular administrative unit to meet this responsibility. In its present form this unit is known as the Department of Propaganda and Agitation of the Central Committee of the All-Union Communist Party of Bolsheviks. Understanding the activities of this organization requires some knowledge of its place within the total party structure. Since some familiarity with that structure is in fact basic to an understanding of a great deal of the material which follows, it is appropriate at this point to turn to a brief examination of the party organization as a whole.[1]

THE PARTY STRUCTURE

The Rules or Bylaws (*ustav*) of the All-Union Communist Party[2] are prefaced by a general section which incorporates many of the basic conceptions of the role of the party elaborated by Lenin and Stalin. The Rules declare the party to be the organized vanguard of the working class of the Soviet Union, a unified, militant, disciplined, and coherent organization. The party is affirmed to be the central element in the leadership of all organizations of the toiling masses, both public and governmental,[3] leading the Soviet people in the task of strengthening the dictatorship of the proletariat, developing a socialist system, and building a communist society. The party is guided in this activity, the Rules affirm, by the theories of Marx and Lenin.

The party constitutes an elaborate hierarchical structure within which three major levels may be distinguished. At the base of the triangle stand the "primary" party organizations, known in the West under their old name of communist "cells," located in factories, villages, collective farms, offices, military units, and so on. Membership in the party is to be had, with minor exceptions, only through membership in a primary organization. The primary units are joined into intermediary units—district organizations—which in turn form regional, territorial, and union-republic organizations. The highest echelon of the party, the central or all-union organs in Moscow, determine both general policy and specific courses of action, and control their execution.

The basic principle that underlies the functioning of the party apparatus is known as "democratic centralism." It involves four elements: (1) the process of election is to be applied in the selection of all so-called directing bodies, from the executive bureau of the primary organization to the Central Committee of the All-Union Party; (2) these directing bodies are periodically accountable to their respective organizations; (3) strict discipline, involving the subordination of any minority to the will of the majority; and (4) the rule that all decisions of higher bodies are absolutely binding on all lower units. Clearly, the first two elements represent the democratic aspect of the principle of democratic centralism, and the second two the centralist aspect.* In practice, particularly in the later stages of the party's development under Stalin's control, the democratic elements have been by far the least honored, and in fact the intensive application of the principle of centralism has to a large extent negated the meaning of the democratic provisions.

Local organizations have autonomy in deciding local questions, but this is sharply limited by the provision that such action will not

*On the surface, the third principle concerning subordination of a minority to the majority might appear to be one of the democratic elements. This principle, however, is interpreted to mean that the majority alone decides when even the mere open discussion of any policy is permissible. Consequently, this provision is in its effect more centralist than democratic. *Eighteenth Congress,* p. 680.

be in conflict with any decision of the party as a whole. Local autonomy is further limited by the "territorial-production principle," which provides that a party unit serving any area or branch of work as a whole is regarded as superior to the unit serving only a part of that area or branch of work. The effect of these limitations has been to make the intermediary sections of the party essentially administrative organs of the central leadership, designed to execute the policy of the top leadership in any given area and to report back to the top the state of affairs in the subordinate primary organizations.

A local party body or member may, at least theoretically, always go "outside channels" to appeal to the highest party authorities over the heads of intermediary units. And the central authorities maintain a special agency or control commission which not only does general checking on the execution of policy, but is expected to see to it that tyranny between the intermediary and lower echelons is kept to a minimum. With the centralization of authority this is, of course, only very imperfectly achieved. It is clear, therefore, that from a sociological point of view the most important elements in the party are the central organs which control the entire structure, and the lower echelons in which members participate directly and which are the party's major point of face-to-face contact with the population.

The supreme body of the party is stated to be the All-Union Party Congress, made up of delegates apportioned according to the size of the local units. A congress has the broadest powers, including the authority to revise the party Rules and to determine the general line of the party on all principal questions. The Rules provide that a congress shall be called not less than once in three years, but congresses have actually met infrequently and with progressively greater intervals between sessions.* Even if the congress anticipated for

---

*An interval of only one year separated the congresses from the Eighth in 1919 through the Thirteenth in 1924; a year and a half elapsed before the Fourteenth, and two years separated it from the Fifteenth. The interval then increased to two and a half years before the Sixteenth, three and a half before the Seventeenth in 1934, and rose to five years before the Eighteenth Congress in 1939. Similarly, the Komsomol or Young Communist League did not convene one of its congresses for about thirteen years, between 1936 and 1949.

early 1950 is held, more than ten years will have elapsed since the preceding Eighteenth Congress in 1939 and about five years since the end of the war.

The significance of this growing gap between congresses is highlighted if it is recognized that a congress is normally called by the permanent or standing Central Committee of the party, which is elected by each congress. For it is this All-Union Central Committee which is authorized to act for the party as a whole in the interval between congresses. Its authority includes the general right to govern all the activities of the party, and such specific powers as the right to establish party institutions and guide their work, to appoint or confirm the selection of editors, to distribute the forces and resources of the party and to manage its funds, and to direct the work of governmental and public (for example, trade-union) organizations "through the party groups in them."

Even on the few occasions when congresses have met in recent times, their sessions have been brief, the discussions cursory and carefully kept within the limits set by the leaders, and the action taken largely restricted to approving the previous decisions of the Central Committee and the new course suggested by it to the congress. In effect, this has meant that the supreme body of the party has been not the congress but its Central Committee. This is a manifestation of the general tendency in the U.S.S.R. toward the concentration of power in the hands of small bodies of men, which has its counterpart in the government structure, where final power is nominally in the hands of the Supreme Soviet but is actually exercised by the Presidium of the Supreme Soviet and by the Council of Ministers.

The Central Committee, however, is itself a large and somewhat unwieldy organization currently including some seventy members and about the same number of alternates or candidates. Real power has therefore been still further concentrated. The Rules provide that the Central Committee is to establish an Organizational Bureau, which has general guidance over the functioning of the total structure; a Secretariat, which acts as an administrative office; a Commission of Party Control, which sees to the fulfillment of party decisions on lower levels; a Central Auditing Commission; and a

Political Bureau, whose function is cryptically defined as "for political work."[4]

It is in the hands of this Political Bureau or *Politburo* that actual political power in the Soviet state is centralized. It generally numbers about fourteen members and alternates, although its size is not fixed by the Rules. Composed of Stalin and his chief lieutenants such as Molotov, the *Politburo* is a locus of concentrated power whose membership has been remarkably stable since the absolute consolidation of Stalin's position in the middle thirties.[5] In the initial stages of the party's development under Lenin, such concentration of power was neither planned nor anticipated. In fact, even the Rules now in force give no indication of the overwhelming importance of the *Politburo*. It exercises a *de facto* rather than a *de jure* authority, its influence being a manifestation of the informal contrasted with the formal structure of power within the party.

In addition to the major units mentioned above, the Central Committee incorporates several administrative departments that are supposed to perform the practical work of carrying out party decisions. The 1939 Rules provided for five of these units. Administrations were established for propaganda and agitation, and for cadres or personnel; and three departments were created for organization-instructional work, agriculture, and schools. Lower party organizations down through the city and district committees have a similar but more limited array, corresponding to the departments of the Central Committee.

EVOLUTION OF THE DEPARTMENT OF PROPAGANDA AND AGITATION

The Department* of Propaganda and Agitation of the Central Committee is charged with general responsibility for molding and mobilizing public opinion in the Soviet Union so that it will most effectively support and facilitate the achievement of those long- and short-range ends which the party leadership has defined as the goals of the nation as a whole. It unifies and gives central direction to the vast and multiform activities designed to influence public opinion

*The title of the organization was changed in July 1948 from administration (*upravlenie*) to department (*otdel*), and the title of its subdivisions from department to sector (*sektor*). The more recent usage of "department" and "sector" is followed here whenever appropriate.

which are carried on by the party, and by the government and public agencies under the party's supervision. Its crucial importance for the over-all success of the party's leadership is indicated by the fact that Andrei A. Zhdanov, who stood very close, if not equal, to Molotov in the line of succession after Stalin, had for many years taken personal responsibility within the *Politburo* for the correct functioning of the Administration of Propaganda and Agitation, and acted for several years as its formal head in addition to his other party duties.

Within the framework of the basic policy decisions adopted by the *Politburo,* the agit-prop department determines both the general line and the specific course of action in all matters directly affecting Soviet public opinion on all its levels. It must bring the decisions of the party and government to the people, explain them, win popular support for them, and effect the mobilization of the population to secure their fulfillment. Not only is the department the chief channel of communication from the party to the people, but it is the chief instrument through which mass attitudes are conveyed to the leaders.* It is both funnel and siphon, and its directors must see that the lines of communication are, as the party journals often phrase it, always "open from the top to the bottom and from the bottom to the top." Its activities range all the way from handling difficult and sensitive questions on the interpretation of Marxist texts, to explaining to an ordinary worker why his work norms have been changed; and from selecting the nationwide slogans for the celebration of the anniversary of the Revolution, to the detailed criticism of some obscure handwritten wall newspaper in an outlying factory or farm.[6]

Despite the range of its responsibilities, however, the department is not primarily an operational agency. It does not do any major publishing; it does not operate the Soviet radio or make films. It is devoted to setting policy and to securing the execution of that policy by the party, government, and public organizations which actually

---

*The MVD (formerly NKVD), or secret police, apparently also has the responsibility of informing the top officials about the state of mass thinking. This activity is of course carried on in the manner of secret police, and very little is known about it. In all probability the MVD restricts itself to reporting on serious tensions and potential trouble spots.

operate the media of communication. Its function, of the broadest scope, is exercised at a national level, yet its impact is felt at the lowest reaches and in the smallest matters.

The agit-prop department, since it encompasses so important a sphere of the party's work, has in one form or another long been an essential segment of the total party apparatus. The history of its development cannot be traced here in any detail, but the high lights are sufficiently important to warrant brief comment.

In the period before the Bolshevik seizure of power, when the party concentrated on solidifying its organization and was oriented toward the unitary goal of effecting a revolution, there was relatively little differentiation of function within the party. Every Bolshevik was expected to be a more or less full-time agitator and propagandist, and in a sense the entire party apparatus served what was later to become but one function among many.[7] To a considerable extent this absence of specialization carried over into the period of the Revolution and Civil War. In 1918 and 1919 a number of so-called "agit-points" were established, particularly in the armed forces,[8] and several special agitation trains and agitation steamers toured the countryside and the rivers, but these efforts were fragmentary and diffuse.[9]

Toward the end of the period of foreign intervention, as the party turned its attention to the tasks of reconstructing and building up the shattered economic and political structures of the nation, a much greater differentiation of function within the party became necessary. As part of this general trend, a special Department of Propaganda and Agitation had been created by 1920 in the Secretariat of the Central Committee of the national organization, along with corresponding units in the regional party establishments. This arrangement was formalized by a special regulation in November 1921, which set forth the organization and tasks of the agit-prop department. This agit-prop department was defined as the instrument through which the Central Committee was to unite and direct all of the party's efforts in the realm of oral and printed propaganda and agitation.[10] It was assigned general responsibility for guiding the party's ideological work within and outside the party's ranks, and for directing and controlling the educational activities of governmental, trade union, coöperative, and other organizations. Its mandate was very broad and called for the general political education and development of the masses to prepare them for conscious participation in building the new social order, which involved activities ranging from those of Communist academies to simple schools for the elimination of illiteracy.[11]

In connection with the general reorganization of the party apparatus late in 1929, the Propaganda and Agitation Department was divided into two units, a Department of Agitation and Mass Campaigns, and a Department of Culture and Propaganda.[12] These departments retained both their form and duties without substantial change until 1934. But the Seventeenth Party Congress, which met in that year, criticized the party organization for being ridden by "functionalism." The Propaganda and Agitation Department was held up as an example of this functionalism, because it conducted agitation on all questions and in all branches of the national life, in industry, in transport, in the villages, and so on. The Rules were therefore revised to eliminate all of these "functional" departments, replacing them with "integral industrial-branch" departments. This meant that the newly created Agricultural Department, for example, would control all activities bearing on agricultural production, including mass agitation and production propaganda in rural areas. Other new departments, such as those for industry, transport, and trade, were also given charge of agitation and propaganda work in their spheres of competence.

What remained of the old Propaganda and Agitation Department was now named the Culture and Propaganda of Leninism Department. Of its original responsibility for all forms of agitation and propaganda, it retained the control of little more than Marxist training within the party, although it was authorized to supervise the work of such government agencies as the Commissariats of Education and Public Health.[13] Stripped of so many of the functions of its predecessor, the new department, abbreviated as *Kultprop,* was something of an administrative anomaly, and it had a short life. In 1935 the Central Committee decided to replace *Kultprop* with five separate departments: schools, science and scientific invention, the press and publishing, cultural-educational work, and propaganda and agitation. Thus restored in name, the Propaganda and Agitation Department was, nevertheless, but a shadow of its former self, since control of the press, science, schools, libraries, and mass agitation in production work remained with the industrial and other departments.[14]

The pitfalls created by a dispersion of responsibility for propaganda and agitation soon manifested themselves, however, and overlapping, confusion, and contradiction in the work became an obvious handicap to the party in its efforts to mold and mobilize public opinion. The party's work in this realm came in for a critical reëxamination from Stalin and Andrei Zhdanov at the plenary session of the Central Committee in March 1937.[15] Then, in 1938, as part of the fundamental decision on party propaganda issued in conjunction with the publication of the new official *History of the Party,* the Central Committee ordered the unification of the Department of Propaganda and Agitation and the Department of the Press and Publishing in order to effect "a radical improvement in the party's direction of propaganda."[16] The Eighteenth Congress, meeting in 1939, finally abolished the troublesome industrial branch departments* and gave formal approval to the earlier action of the Central Committee. It resolved that the Central Committee should have a powerful apparatus for propaganda and agitation in the form of a new administration in which would be concentrated all phases of printed and oral propaganda and agitation.[17] Thus, the powers of the former department were largely restored to their original form. Those powers continue to be exercised at the present time.

One point brought out by this brief review, relating to the centralization of responsibility in matters affecting public opinion, deserves special mention. The party's experience with the division of authority over matters affecting public opinion was not satisfactory. Public opinion, the party discovered, is a unity, and if it is to be effectively harnessed in the support of social, political, and economic action, policy must be centrally determined and action centrally administered.

---

*The Agriculture Department was excepted because of the special problems that continued to manifest themselves almost a decade after the beginning of forced collectivization.

The present department and its equivalent units on the local level concentrate in their hands all work on the printed and oral propaganda of Marxism-Leninism and all mass agitation activities. This involves either direct responsibility for or control and supervision over the party press, the publication of propaganda and agitation literature, the organization of printed and oral Marxist-Leninist propaganda, the ideological content of propaganda work, the selection and assignment of propaganda personnel, the political training and retraining of party personnel, and the organization of mass political agitation.[18]

To fulfill its responsibility for these activities, the central department is divided into a series of sectors, each of which has a distinct sphere of operations.[19] The Propaganda Sector deals primarily with the party membership and the non-party intelligentsia, and is concerned with their education in the principles of Marxism-Leninism and their ideological "correctness." It is, to paraphrase a popular Soviet expression, the guardian of the sacred Bolshevik word. Political education for the broad masses of the working class in the spirit of communism is the responsibility of the Mass Agitation Sector, which also has charge of mass agitational activities designed to mobilize the population to meet the tasks set for it by the party. A third unit, the Sector for Cultural Enlightenment, supervises the activities of village reading huts, libraries, district "houses of culture," museums, and related institutions. These institutions are principally staffed, operated, and financed by the commissariats of education of the various republic and lower territorial governments and by the trade unions, but their work is guided by the party's Sector for Cultural Enlightenment to insure their contribution to the advancement of the general party line on public opinion.

Control over the work of newspapers and journals, supervision of book publishing, and the training and replacement of press personnel were in the hands of a unified press department within the administration down through the war years. It has now been divided into series of smaller and more specialized units. Control of newspaper work, and presumably of nonliterary journals, is apparently carried out by three sectors: for the central press; for republic, territorial, and regional press activities; and for the local press. Responsibility for the control of books and magazines in the field of literature lies with a separate Literature Sector.

The film industry and radiobroadcasting are directly administered by governmental agencies: the Ministry of Cinematography, and the All-Union Committee on Radiobroadcasting; but those media are also represented by special sectors in the Department of Propaganda and Agitation. Mention should also be made of the Sector on Art, which supervises the activities of dramatists, writers, musicians, painters, and other groups whose work is more directly administered by the government Committee on Art of the Council of Ministers. Finally, there is a Science Sector and a School Sector.

This review of the structure of the Department of Propaganda and Agitation reveals two central features. Most obvious is the scope of the department's interest. There is no realm of intellectual endeavor, no form of organized activity which might conceivably influence public opinion, which the party exempts from scrutiny and control. Secondly, the structure of the department highlights the division of function between the party and the Soviet state. The day-to-day management of affairs is left largely in the hands of government agencies. But in each sphere the operating government organization has its parallel unit in the party responsible for the constant supervision and direction of that agency.

The head of the department has the title of director and is assisted by a group of three or four vice-directors. Each vice-director apparently supervises one related group of sectors, such as the four or five units dealing with the press and publishing. Each sector also has a special administrative chief. The director and vice-directors are appointed by the Central Committee of the party. Just prior to the recent war, Andrei Zhdanov turned over the directorship of the administration to Georgi F. Alexandrov, although he continued until his death in 1948 to take general responsibility within the *Politburo* for the ideological activities of the party.[20] Mr. Alexandrov, a philosopher and political scientist by profession rather than an ordinary party career man, held his post with apparent success until the middle of 1947, when he fell into disfavor because of alleged leanings toward bourgeois philosophy manifested in his Stalin-prize *History of Western European Philosophy.* Mr. Alexandrov was replaced by Mikhail A. Suslov, a regular party career man.

Each of the lower territorial divisions of the party hierarchy, from the republic down to the city and district committees, has its own department of agitation and propaganda corresponding to the department on the national level. Primary party organizations merely have a special secretary charged with responsibility for the propaganda and agitation activities of his organization.[21] The personnel of each of these local departments is selected by its respective party organization, with the approval of the next higher party unit in the case of the appointment of more responsible officials. Each local department of propaganda and agitation serves the same function for its corresponding local party unit as the national department serves for the Central Committee and the party as a whole. At the same time, each of these local departments is supervised by the department next above it in the territorial hierarchy, until the top of the pyramid is reached in the central administration.[22] Thus, the absolute control of all matters affecting public opinion is concentrated and centralized in the hands of the Department of Propaganda and Agitation, whose lines of authority reach out to include the lowliest secretary for propaganda and agitation in the smallest executive committee of some remote primary party organization in factory or village.

4

COMMUNIST PROPAGANDA: THE SCHOOLING OF OPINION LEADERS

DEFINITIONS OF PROPAGANDA AND AGITATION

AMERICAN AND, IN GENERAL, WESTERN SCIENTIFIC LITerature on public opinion and the related phenomena of propaganda and agitation tends to give rather slight treatment to "agitation" in contrast to "propaganda." *The Encyclopedia of the Social Sciences,* for example, devotes almost ten times as much space to the article on propaganda as to that on agitation,[1] and the most exhaustive current bibliography on public communication does not even include the word agitation in its index to over twenty-five hundred books and articles.[2] Frequently, no effort is made to distinguish propaganda from agitation, and where the attempt is made the results are generally far from revealing and the distinctions hardly precise. Harold D. Lasswell, probably the best-known and most-quoted authority on the subject, says that, although agitation specifies a method of collective influence, there is no consensus in distinguishing the term from propaganda, nonviolent coercion, and other expressions.[3] American and British writers are inclined to use the word propaganda to include all efforts aimed at influencing public opinion; thus, Lasswell has defined propaganda as "the manipulation of symbols as a means of influencing attitudes on controversial matters."[4] In so far as a distinction is made between propaganda and agitation, it tends to follow dictionary definitions of propaganda as the spreading of doctrines or ideas, and of agitation as inciting or arousing people to spontaneous action.

Bolshevik theory and practice, on the other hand, go to great pains to distinguish carefully between propaganda and agitation, and there are a great many discussions of the problem in communist literature. The basic Bolshevik position on propaganda and agitation derives from the classic definition of Plekhanov, who stated: "A propagandist presents many ideas to one or a few persons; an agitator presents only one or a few ideas, but he presents them to a mass of people."[5]

Lenin accepted this distinction as fundamental. To illustrate the difference between the two roles, he took the problem of unemployment. A propagandist dealing with this question, Lenin suggested, would have to explain the capitalist nature of economic crises, show why such crises are inevitable in modern society, and then describe the ways in which contemporary society must inevitably be transformed into socialist society in order to eliminate the possibility of continued crises. In short, he would treat the question by presenting a complex of ideas, so many indeed that only a comparatively few people could understand him. An agitator discussing the same subject would operate differently. He would select as a starting point, Lenin stated, some striking and widely known fact, for example, the death from starvation of some worker's family, or the general increase in impoverishment among the workers. He would then utilize this simple illustration to drive home a single point to his audience, namely, "the idea of the senseless contradiction between the increase of wealth and increase of poverty." This single idea would then serve as a basis for an attempt to arouse the discontent of the masses. A more complete explanation, Lenin concluded, should be left to the propagandist.[6]

For Lenin this distinction between the presentation of many ideas about a subject to a small number of people and advancing a single idea to a mass of people remained the fundamental basis for distinguishing propaganda and agitation. He vigorously rejected the notion that propaganda was primarily the elucidation of a problem, and agitation chiefly a call to action. The theoretician who writes a research paper on tariff policy, he insisted, "calls" for a struggle for free trade no less than the propagandist writing in the periodical press and the agitator making speeches. The last stage in the process may be the act of signing petitions by large numbers of people, but the call to action, Lenin held, came as much from the theoretician and the propagandist as from the agitator who carried the petitions.[7]

Later Soviet discussions of this question have been largely based on the analysis of Plekhanov and Lenin. The idea that the presence or absence of a "call to action" can be used to distinguish agitation and propaganda has been strongly rejected. The related proposition that agitation is primarily incitement, an effort to excite and arouse, has also been criticized. Finally, the idea that the distinction may be based on the medium utilized has been found equally unacceptable. Lenin had said that the printed word was the chief tool of the propagandist, the spoken word the main instrument for the agitator. But this is by no means a necessary condition, and Soviet theory and practice hold that both propaganda and agitation may be printed or oral. Thus, a lecture on the Leninist theory of the state is regarded as being no less propaganda than a journal article on the subject, and a newspaper article calling for an increase in labor productivity no less agitation than the personal appeal of a party agitator in some machine shop.[8]

Apart from the basic distinction sketched above, Soviet usage recognizes a general and a specific meaning of both terms. Adapting the term propaganda from the expression early used by the Roman Catholic Church, Soviet source books define it as the dissemination or preaching of any idea or doctrine, along with the recruiting of supporters for the idea disseminated. As such, it may be a means whereby any class or social group seeks to spread abroad ideas which will support and justify the social position and demands of the group concerned. Agitation is seen as equally subject to use as an instrument in the political struggle of parties and classes, and may be used by any political party to organize in support of its goals the forces of its own class and to attract allies from other classes.[9] This approach, of course, derives directly from the fundamental Marxian conception of the social and ideological "superstructure" which is built up on the basis of any given economic system or basic mode of production.

Since the terms propaganda and agitation could be used in this general sense, it was obviously necessary to make a distinction between types of propaganda and agitation according to the class or social group utilizing these instruments. Soviet writers, therefore, tend to use these expressions in a carefully restricted manner. They speak of *bourgeois* propaganda and agitation, and *communist* propaganda and agitation. Religious propaganda, for example, is defined as one of the more important aspects of the ruling classes' political activity carried on through churches, missionaries, and public education institutions as a means of spiritual subjugation of the masses. Similarly, bourgeois agitation is defined as a form of political deception of the masses, a method of throwing sand in their eyes to blind them to their state of oppression and exploitation.[10]

In the hands of the Bolsheviks, however, propaganda and agitation are supposed to become something quite different. Communist propaganda is strictly defined as the intensive elucidation of the teachings of Marx, Engels, Lenin, and Stalin, and of the history of the Bolshevik party and its tasks. As such, it is regarded as one of the most important standard components of party activity. It is through the propaganda of Marxism-Leninism that the party members are "armed" with requisite theory and with knowledge of the Marxian laws governing the development of society and of political struggles. Communist propaganda is therefore directed primarily toward the more "advanced" segments of society, the party members and the non-party intelligentsia, to leaders, directors and responsible officials in all spheres of the national life.[11]

Communist agitation, in turn, is defined as the chief means for the political education of the broad working-class masses in the spirit of communism. It is therefore primarily directed toward the broad masses and seeks to acquaint them with the party's slogans and decisions, to explain the policy of the party and government, and to mobilize all the workers for active and conscious participation in the building of the new social order.[12]

It is appropriate at this point to ask why it is that the Bolsheviks' treatment of propaganda and agitation, of which only a brief indication has been given above, is so much more thorough and elaborate than the efforts of Western writers on the subject. The difference is, of course, not due to the fact that communist thinking is generally more precise than that of non-communist political writers and public-opinion experts. The difference is directly related to and derives from the fundamental Bolshevik theories about the relations between the organized vanguard of the working class united in the Communist Party and the masses, whose teacher, guide, and leader the party is to be.*

In Bolshevik thought Marxism and Leninism are defined as a philosophical system and a body of scientific principles which provide an explanation of the development of social systems and a guide to revolutionary action and the building of a communist society. In effecting this revolution and in building the new society, a small group of advanced men with a highly developed class consciousness united in a close-knit organization is expected, as we have seen, to exercise the function of leadership. The actions of these men are to be governed by the body of doctrine that is Marxism. They must study and understand, or, as the Soviet phrase has it, "master" Marxism. This learning process is represented by the expression "the propaganda of Marxism-Leninism," and the men who do the teaching are the propagandists.

Obviously, the great mass of people cannot be expected to grasp fully the principles of Marxism, and Stalin has declared that even among the party members by no means all of them can be expected actually to "master" the party program.[13] Bolshevik theory does demand, however, that the broad masses be imbued with the "spirit" of Marxist doctrine in so far as their general level of development permits. The leadership concept, furthermore, requires that the actions taken by the leaders be known to the masses and "explained" to them. This teaching and explanation among the masses is the task of the agitator. But if he is to teach the masses and explain the party's actions to them, the agitator must himself have an understanding of these problems and a grasp of the basic principles of Marxism. The agitator and organizer, therefore, while he is the teacher of the masses, is also himself a student who studies under the guidance of the propagandist. The circle is thus closed: propaganda develops the more advanced members and natural

---

*This is by no means to say that the Bolshevik distinction between propaganda and agitation is a matter of "mere ideology." The distinction is a useful one and could be applied outside of the Soviet context.

leaders of the masses, the agitators and organizers, who in turn bring the party's message to the people through agitation.

Consequently, the formation of public opinion on any important question in the Soviet Union involves two distinct phases: the formation of opinion among the directing personnel and associated groups, and the subsequent formation of mass public opinion by these opinion leaders or opinion makers. The three tasks of the party sketched by Lenin, namely, propaganda, agitation, and organization, form a natural sequence, each stage being a necessary precondition of the next.

THE FUNCTIONS OF PROPAGANDA

Propaganda serves two distinct functions, one of which is of importance primarily for the relations between the party and the population at large, the other being crucial for the internal operations of the party as such. The simplest and most easily discernible function of propaganda is to serve as a precondition for successful agitation and consequently for the general leadership of the masses by the party. Agitation is not a sporadic and momentary phenomenon in the Soviet Union, but rather is a continuous and highly organized activity carried on by men whose role as agitators is persistent and thoroughly formalized. Agitation is the province not only of the regular Bolshevik agitator, with whom the next chapter will deal, but is also regarded as the task of newspaper editors, writers, radiobroadcasters, film makers, artists, and others. Since all of these people are charged with responsibility for the general "political education" of the populace and are expected to explain the policy of the party to the masses, it is assumed that they themselves must be well educated politically and must have an excellent understanding of the policy of the party and government and the reasons lying behind that policy. Consequently, the party propaganda apparatus is to a large extent directed toward the general Marxist education of these groups, and toward keeping them abreast of current developments. Journalists, for example, attend the same school for their ideological training as do those people who are specifically preparing for careers as propagandists.[14]

The role Marxist propaganda plays in the net of relationships which is internal to the party is more complex. Stalin has declared that one of the reasons for the Bolsheviks' success has been their ability to distinguish leadership of the masses from leadership of the party, to recognize that these represent distinct problems, and to act accordingly.[15] A central element in this leadership of the party is control over the propaganda of Marxism-Leninism. To a large extent the Communist Party of the Soviet Union bases its claim to legitimacy on the grounds that it is operating according to the scientific principles of Marxism. In the U.S.S.R. any action may be justified or condemned on the basis of the assertion that it adheres to or departs from Marxist doctrine.* Despite the repeated protests of both Lenin and Stalin that Marxism is not an inflexible dogma but simply a guide to action,[16] it constitutes in fact a kind of orthodoxy. And in so far as this is the case, it manifests the features that are characteristic of orthodoxies.[17]

There is, for example, the problem of conflicting interpretations of the basic doctrine. The priests of any orthodoxy may not permit the free and independent interpretation of the basic doctrines, since the interpretations arrived at may challenge the correctness of the action and eventually the very position of the priesthood. The party, it is clear, must and indeed does maintain in its own hands a monopoly of the right to interpret Marxism, and this monopoly is in the last analysis exercised directly by the top party leadership. There is, as well, the problem of adjusting the doctrine to meet new conditions and to justify new courses of action. This again requires concentrated effort and firm control, and provides one of the most difficult tests of leadership, as exemplified by the party's internal difficulties at the time of Lenin's "retreat" to the New Economic Policy in 1921. A third problem arises from the necessity to indoctrinate those new members who are accepted into the circle of the elite. It is this task of indoctrinating new members that is most closely related to our more general problem of opinion forming.

From the time of the fall of the Tsarist regime in February 1917,

---

*It is true that although policies were justified or condemned in terms of their orthodoxy, the issues were in the last analysis settled on the basis of who had the most power. But it is important to recognize that both sides in the great party controversies felt it necessary to defend their own policy and criticize the opposition on the grounds of adherence to or deviation from the articles of the faith.

when the Bolsheviks numbered only slightly more than twenty thousand, the membership of the party increased rapidly. Following the Bolshevik rise to power in October, this trend was intensified, and by the end of the Civil War the party numbered more than a half million members. But while the party concentrated its energies on effecting the Revolution and fighting the Civil War and the foreign intervention, it was able to spare very little effort for the ideological indoctrination of its new forces. With the end of the Civil War, however, the party turned its attention to this task and issued a series of important decisions on the Marxist training of its membership.[18]

The party had taken a large bite, however, and had some difficulty digesting it. The great number of new members sat like something of a hard lump in the party's insides. Either from conviction or because they sought to ride out this new wave, many members of the old intelligentsia and other elements regarded as unreliable had joined the party's ranks. There was a consequent reduction of the proportion of workers in the total membership, which was disturbing to the party's leaders. The situation was further exacerbated by the disillusionment and even disaffection which spread through the party's ranks as a result of the adoption of the New Economic Policy in 1921 and the associated partial restoration of capitalism.

The party's leaders met this situation in part by a "cleansing" of its ranks, through a series of extensive purges designed to eliminate persons regarded as untrustworthy or wavering.[19] The main emphasis, however, was placed on a policy of drawing into the party ordinary workers from the bench. Thus, the so-called Lenin draft drew about two hundred thousand workers into the party in 1923 and 1924, and another hundred thousand were attracted to the party on the tenth anniversary of the Revolution in 1927. In large part, these people were of low quality in the sense that they were poorly educated and in many cases actually illiterate. But from the point of view of the party they had the prime qualification of being from the working class, since this was felt to insure the absence of that ideological wavering and vacillation manifested by the intellectuals. The working-class origin of these members was especially important at the time, since the party needed greatly enlarged forces who could take the lead in the task of national reconstruction that was in progress, and it was assumed that once trained these workers would conduct agitation for the party among the rank and file in industry.[20] The party, therefore, set about giving these new members as much Marxist training as their educational preparation and capacities permitted, beginning where necessary with their general education and even with instruction in the ABC's. Many of them proved very capable, in fact, and were not returned to the factories as agitators, but were given further training and assigned to responsible posts.

The introduction of the First Five Year Plan in 1928 placed much heavier demands on the personnel resources of the party than had been experienced up to that time. The success of the Plan depended very strongly on the mobilization of the energies of great masses of the population who were swept into construction and industrial work, and agitators were needed in large numbers to give support to this effort. In addition, the Plan had as one of its goals a profound change in the consciousness of the masses and the elimination of what was called the remnants of capitalist thought which persisted in their minds. This also required an intensification of agitation activities, a precondition of which was the training of new agitators through the party's propaganda system. Finally, the struggle between Trotsky and Stalin, which resulted in Stalin's victory and the expulsion from the party of Trotsky, was followed by the great purges of 1928 and 1929. The resulting gaps in the ranks had to be filled and the loyalty of the new members to the Stalin faction had to be assured.

All of these forces were reflected in the growth of the party membership to almost two million by 1930, and of course the total number of new members taken in since 1920 was actually greater than a million and a half owing to the great rate of internal replacement. These new members again presented an indoctrination problem, but the basic approach to their indoctrination did not vary greatly from that practiced earlier. The new members were predominantly workers, although frequently better prepared than their opposite numbers of a decade earlier, and their training in Marxism was not always very deep.

Although qualitatively the same, quantitatively the party program of communist education presented a quite different picture. It was no longer dealing with a mere matter of a hundred thousand or so in its "student" body. By 1930, for example, there were fifty-two thousand party schools and study circles, including over one million students, and by mid-1933 the number of schools had risen to two hundred and ten thousand, and the number of students to four and a half million. It is an indication of the wide net which the party was casting at this time that just under half of these students were not party members at all. They were, as the Soviet expression has it, "non-party Bolsheviks," promising workers who identified themselves with the party and whom the party was training and advancing to positions of responsibility and trust.[21] Many became party members in time, of course, and their participation in party schools was regarded as a step in that direction. A further indication of the extent of the party's efforts to spread basic Marxist education in the early thirties is to be seen in the large number of party propagandists working at the time. In 1934 there were one hundred and thirty thousand people reckoned as party propagandists, more than five times the number so engaged in 1928.[22]

While the party was thus throwing wide its net of Marxist schooling, the economic development of the Soviet Union under the Five Year Plans was progressing apace. A corollary of that development was the appearance of a new, large-scale, Soviet-trained technical intelligentsia, which rapidly came to represent a major social force in Soviet life. In the period of the First Plan, as in the earlier period of reconstruction, the party relied heavily on the remnants of the old technical intelligentsia. These technical specialists worked under the supervision of trusted party members, frequently former workers who had been given ideological and some technical training by the party. At the same time, the party sought to provide its own specialists by giving party men who had managerial experience or high skills special training in technical schools characterized by extreme specialization and short-term, speeded-up courses. These men were known as the Red Specialists.[23]

The defects of this system rapidly manifested themselves, however, and in 1932 steps were taken to stabilize and improve technical training. The speed-up system was eliminated, and more extensive educational preparation was demanded of applicants for advanced training. This resulted in an improvement in the general level of technical education, but it was accomplished only by decreasing the emphasis on and preoccupation with the working-class origin of the students.

By 1936 this new crop of technical experts began to make its weight felt in Soviet industrial management. They differed considerably, however, from the Red Specialists whom they supplemented and to some extent replaced. The Red Specialists tended to be older men who had formerly been industrial workers and were later given some technical training under party auspices. Generally their ability as technicians was limited by the type of training they had received, and their prime qualification was their worker's background and the loyalty to the party they were felt to have. The new group was composed primarily of younger men who had gone directly through adequate secondary-school education on to technical colleges. Although many of them had been "brought up" by the Young Communist League, they were oriented more toward problems of a professional and technical nature and less toward political questions than the Red Specialists. They owed their position in the first instance to their technical competence, and their party status was a secondary consideration so long as they fulfilled their tasks adequately and effectively.[24]

These engineers and other industrial experts were only one major segment of the broader social stratum of the Soviet intelligentsia, which as a whole was undergoing a similar internal development. The tremendous expansion of industry and the marked development of all phases of the national life under the Five Year Plans produced an extremely rapid increase in the size of this social group at a rate which exceeded the rate of growth of the industrial labor force. By 1937 the industrial technicians and managers mentioned above, along with agricultural specialists, teachers, members of the various professions, administrators and government officials, and related white-collar groups (exclusive of clerks and ordinary office employees) numbered ten million persons.[25]

The growing importance of this social group to the successful functioning of the total social system forced a change in the party's attitude toward the intelligentsia, a change facilitated by that group's altered composition. In the early years of the regime the intelligentsia was subject to suspicion and distrust and was the object of constant attack and all manner of legal restriction and disadvantage. The first major break in this situation came in 1931, when Stalin called for a new policy of enlisting the support of the engineers and technicians and of showing them solicitude. This referred primarily to the old intelligentsia, and in the interim Stalin called for the development of a new Soviet intelligentsia.[26] Despite repeated setbacks, trials of specialists, and other upheavals, the position of the intelligentsia continued to improve from this time forward, and the whole process was hastened along as the ranks of the intelligentsia filled up with young people trained under the Soviet system. The Constitution adopted in 1936, for example, eliminated all aspects of legal discrimination against this "social stratum," as it was defined, and Stalin, commenting on the Constitution, declared the intelligentsia to be "an equal member of Soviet society" along with the working class and the peasantry.[27]

Although the intelligentsia was gradually integrated into the total social structure, its relationship to the Communist Party posed a more difficult problem. The expansion of Soviet industry, the elaboration of State functions, and the growing complexity of the total system brought the intelligentsia to a point where it was absolutely indispensable to the party in directing Soviet society. Because of its crucial importance, however, the intelligentsia was winning for itself a fairly distinct way of life which was both different from and often richer than that of the bulk of the population. A basis for the development of the intelligentsia into an effective and independent social force was provided not only by the higher standard of living, but also by the common background and experiences, the similarity of interests, and the unity of the general social and economic goals of its members. The intelligentsia, in short, began to show signs that it might possibly become a potential locus of power outside the party and conceivably might eventually compete with the party for power. Obviously, the possibility of such an independent locus of power could not be permitted to develop if the party were to continue absolutely secure in its position. At the same time, it was clearly neither advisable nor feasible for the party to take action against this group, both because it was essential to the party and because it had, as a group, in no way challenged the party or given any concrete evidence of disloyalty.*

Nevertheless, this locus of power could not be left outside the party, but had to be integrated and subordinated to the existing power structure. This required that larger elements of the intelligentsia be incorporated into the party, an undertaking that was gradually accomplished after 1936. But prime emphasis was placed on imbuing the intelligentsia with the doctrines of the Bolshevik faith as the most certain means of preventing their development as a potentially divisive force.

Thus, at a special plenary session of the Central Committee in 1937 devoted largely to ideological questions, Stalin set the party on a new direction in its propaganda efforts. The major problem up to that time, Stalin stated, had been the mastering of technique, but that problem had been solved for the most part and the slogan outlived. A new slogan was required which would stress the need for the political education of cadres, for the mastering of Bolshevism and the liquidation of political complacency.[28] At the same plenum, A. A. Zhdanov complained that the party's propaganda had become scholastic and separated from current practical problems. It had to be transformed from being an end in itself to an instrument for developing active propagandists for the party's cause.[29]

As a result of the decisions thus reached by the Central Committee, a new history of the party was prepared. This new *History of the All-Union Communist Party (of Bolsheviks)* was issued in 1938 along with what was probably the most important decision on party propaganda to appear during the party's life span.[30] That decision left no doubt that from that time forward the chief goal of party propaganda was to be the inculcation of the intelligentsia with the principles of Marxism-Leninism as interpreted by the party leaders.[31]

---

*Large numbers of the intelligentsia were indeed victims of the purges in the mid-thirties, but the attack was on individuals rather than on the intelligentsia as a group. It was the supposed "opposition" within the party that was under attack as a group.

Party propaganda, the decision noted, had in the past placed its emphasis on scope, on the extent of its coverage, and had given priority to the indoctrination of workers from the bench. This had resulted in neglect of political preparation and "Marxist-Leninist hardening" for the members of the Soviet intelligentsia. Yet, the decision warned, it was chiefly with the aid of such personnel, the trained cadres in party, government, industrial, coöperative, trade, trade-union, agricultural, and military institutions, that the working class and the peasantry effected their rule of the Soviet Union. This educated group had special significance in a country like the U.S.S.R., the decision continued, because the government was responsible for all branches and phases of economic and social life. Hence, every government worker, if he were consciously and successfully to meet his responsibilities, had to understand the basic policy of the government and the tasks it and the party faced. This understanding could be obtained only by political indoctrination, and consequently the Soviet intelligentsia as a whole had to be imbued with "the spirit of Marxism-Leninism." It was therefore necessary, the Central Committee asserted, to put an end to the "absurd, anti-Leninist" attitude which slighted the needs of the intelligentsia for political education. However advanced and productive they were in their practical work, it was stated, the directing cadres were seriously behind in the realm of theory, and this backwardness had to be liquidated. The new *History of the Party* was, therefore, to be addressed *"in the first instance* to the directing cadres of Party, Komsomol, economic and other workers, to all Party and non-Party members of the intelligentsia in the city and in the village."[32]

The shift in the party's focus of attention from the workers to the intelligentsia necessitated certain changes in the form and content of the party's propaganda activities. The basic form for conducting propaganda had been the small group or "circle" for the study of Marxism-Leninism, and at large plants there might be tens and even hundreds of such groups. The chief method of study had been through oral propaganda, based on instruction by one of the large body of party propagandists and involving extensive discussions in a classroom manner. Many of the local party organizations had on their own initiative made attendance at these study circles compulsory for party members, and had developed formal examinations to test and evaluate the progress of those studying.[33]

While such methods might have been well adapted to propaganda work with relatively untrained and frequently unsophisticated workers, they were not equally suited to work among the intelligentsia. The study circle provided an intimate and relatively free atmosphere of discussion. Clearly, if such discussion were left to the better educated and more independent thought of the intelligentsia, the result might be interpretations of the Marxian texts and conclusions which would be unacceptable to the party leadership. It must be remembered, in this connection, that the party's decision came at the end of the period of the great purges and the Moscow trials. The party had been shaken by a severe internal crisis, probably the most extreme it has experienced. Stalin was apparently of the opinion that the party was permeated with a network of opposition, and he must have viewed the Marxist study circles as a focus of this opposition, for he spoke of the necessity of rooting out "the infatuation for the system of propaganda through study circles."[34]

The party met this situation by declaring self-study to be the basic method for Marxist indoctrination. This meant that each student of Marxism would read the party history and basic Marxian texts not as part of a classroom program, but rather would read from the originals, and would be guided in his studies by standard and official commentaries and interpretations provided by the party publishing houses and the party press. As the slogan adopted at the time declared, "in the propaganda of Marxism-Leninism the chief, decisive weapon must be the press . . . and oral propaganda should occupy the place of a secondary aid." The press, it was said, was more powerful than oral propaganda because "it gives the ability to make one or another truth simultaneously the possession of all."[35] The implication, of course, is that if one relies on discussion groups, which cannot be controlled as well as the written word, there may be more than the "one" truth. Thus, Stalin had at last effectively succeeded in putting an end to real discussion within the party ranks, in keeping with views which he had made perfectly clear as early as 1925. For in his struggle with the Kamenev-Zinoviev opposition he had then declared: "We are opposed to the idea of a special press organ for discussion... *Discussion must not be driven too far.*"[36]

THE LEVELS OF MARXIST-LENINIST PROPAGANDA

The special apparatus that was developed as a result of the party's reëxamination of its propaganda activities in the late thirties has persisted relatively unchanged for over a decade. In the light of the general trend toward the stabilization of social forms in the Soviet Union since 1936, it may be assumed that the present approach will be more durable than those that preceded it. Currently, propaganda is conducted by the party at three different levels, and at each level relatively distinct goals and methods of instruction apply. The three groups concerned are the intelligentsia, the rank-and-file party members, and the cadres, or officials of the party and government functioning in all the major spheres of the national life.

The universal characteristic of the intelligentsia's membership, of the lawyers, doctors, engineers, economists, teachers, and so on, is advanced schooling. And it is, therefore, primarily at the point of their attendance at higher schools of learning that the party seeks to secure the Marxist training of the Soviet intelligentsia. Stalin has laid down the dictum that "there is one branch of science which Bolsheviks in all [other] branches of science are in duty bound to know, and that is the Marxist-Leninist science of society."[37] This applies equally well to medical specialists and physicists as to economists and political scientists, to party members and to non-party members. All higher educational institutions in the Soviet Union, therefore, must provide as a minimum instruction based on the *Short Course on the History of the Party*. A general course on the "Foundations of Marxism-Leninism" is a prerequisite for students in faculties of all types; and in universities and institutes which include a faculty of history, philosophy, or literature, courses in dialectical and historical materialism are also required of all students. The men who teach these courses are selected on the basis of consultation between the Department of Propaganda and Agitation and the government officials responsible for higher education, and are trained in the Higher School of Marxism-Leninism operated by the Central Committee of the party.[38]

Although it represents the party's major effort, the Marxist indoctrination of the intelligentsia does not end with one or two courses at the level of the higher school. From time to time, when the party undertakes one of its periodic campaigns of ideological retraining, large numbers of the intelligentsia are swept into special schools like the evening institutes of Marxism-Leninism which have developed so rapidly since the end of the recent war. Before the war there were only about forty of these schools, but by September 1948, 188 were in operation with a student body of about one hundred thousand. These evening "universities," located in the major cities, offer a two-year course leading to a certificate. From twenty to twenty-four hours per month are required of each student, and the study program is under one of three faculties—historical, philosophical, and economic—or a special art division. The student body is made up predominantly of the intelligentsia—engineers, technicians, scientific workers, teachers, artists, and so forth. Attendance is defined as voluntary, and it has been reported that of those enrolled generally no more than 65 to 80 per cent attend the lectures, 40 to 50 per cent the seminars.[39]

In the "postgraduate" indoctrination of the intelligentsia, heavy emphasis is also placed on a system of public lectures which seek to keep this group abreast of current party thinking on political, economic, and social questions. The party maintains special lecture bureaus for this purpose, which in conjunction with related governmental organizations enlist prominent university professors, and frequently high party officials, to deliver these public talks. It seems worth noting that although there is a small admission fee, the lectures appear to be very heavily attended. They are given primarily in the major centers, such as Moscow or Kiev, where the bulk of the intelligentsia is concentrated, and are open to the general public.[40] Finally, it should be noted that the Soviet daily press devotes considerable attention to the ideological "needs" of those of its readers who are members of the intelligentsia, and even the specialized and technical professional journals have a responsibility in this respect.[41]

The goal of this indoctrination, as has already been seen, is chiefly to forestall the development of an independent and potentially threatening ideology among the intelligentsia. The objective is negative rather than positive. Despite apparent utterances to the contrary, the party leaders can hardly seriously assume that a man will be a more inventive physicist or even botanist by virtue of his Marxist indoctrination. Were this really the case, the indoctrination of specialists would certainly be more extensive than it is. In general, a technical specialist is treated as such, unless his work is felt to have serious implications for the basic body of Marxist doctrine. The field of genetics has such implications, and it has been the center of a long-lasting ideological storm, in which *Pravda* and the Central Committee of the party have fully participated. And as the ideological campaign against the "kowtowing" to the West and "cosmopolitanism" has risen in intensity in the postwar years, ever wider areas of scientific and technical endeavor have come under criticism or attack for "ideological deficiencies." The actual effect of these campaigns on science is yet to be determined. Their effect on art and scholarship is unmistakable.

It is difficult to determine how deeply imbued the majority of the intelligentsia is with the Marxist spirit as interpreted in the Soviet Union. Clearly every specialist must know enough to avoid— or to have a fair chance of avoiding—the sin of heresy or deviation. For the social scientist, say an economist or historian, this requires rather more knowledge and greater caution than for a physicist or botanist, although the latter are by no means immune against attack. For the average technical specialist, however, the problem infrequently arises; so long as formal obeisance is paid to the "parent science" of Marxism, he is free—within the limits on political freedom which exist in the Soviet Union—to enjoy the benefits of a superior social and economic status. It is not demanded of him that he be a fervent believer in the faith; it is required simply that he not utter any heresies.[42]

The second major level toward which the party directs its propaganda efforts is the rank and file of the party membership. The

Rules of the party declare that it is the first obligation of every member to strive without letup in order "to master the principles of Marxism-Leninism."[43] The task of providing the necessary indoctrination was greatly complicated by the tremendous increase in the party membership, which rose from a prewar level of under four million to 6,300,000 after the war. Because of the rapid rate of internal replacement due to wartime losses, two thirds of the entire membership in 1946 was made up of people who had joined during the war years.[44] These members had received only the most superficial indoctrination during the war. To meet this condition the party adopted special measures to reorganize and revitalize the system for instructing and training new party members.[45]

Candidates and party members whose general education is inadequate must attend evening general-education schools operated by the primary party organizations, in which they are taught the Rules of the party and the Constitution of the U.S.S.R., and are assisted in improving their general educational background. Beyond this the primary party organization maintains three levels of training for the candidate and rank-and-file member.[46] Basic training is given in the *politshkol* or political school for communist education. The course lasts for nine months and requires about one and a half hours of classroom time per week from the student. It is divided into three basic subjects: the social and state structure of the Soviet Union, including the Constitution; problems of the postwar Five Year Plan; and the Rules of the party. Instruction is provided by propagandists sent from the city and district party organizations and by qualified leaders and members of the intelligentsia in the primary organization.[47] In the "school year" 1948-1949 there were well in excess of one hundred thousand such schools, attended by eight hundred thousand party members.

Graduates of the *politshkol* and similarly qualified members are enrolled in "study circles," in which they study the *History of the Party* in accordance with the plan set down by the Central Committee at the time of the *History's* publication in 1938.[48] The study circles are also instructed by propagandists, and during 1948-1949 they included approximately eight hundred thousand party members.

Despite this effort at systematic schooling, however, the Party continues to affirm, in accord with its basic decision of November 1938, that self- or individual study of the Marxist-Leninist classics is the best and most important form of political indoctrination.[49] Graduates of the study circles and other qualified members are therefore urged to undertake such individual study, following the program set out by the Department of Propaganda and Agitation and the Central Committee. To assist these members engaged in self-study, enormous numbers of the works of Marx, Engels, Lenin, and Stalin, along with standard commentaries and interpretations, are printed and sold at low cost.*

In addition, both central and local newspapers have a regular department or special column that discusses material designed to aid those engaged in the independent or self-study of Marxism, and that is in general expected to facilitate the ideological education of party members. The regular party journals, such as *Partiinaya Zhizn'* (Party Life), are also expected to make an important contribution in this respect. There are, finally, the Party "cabinets" or consultation rooms serving as specialized libraries for the membership and staffed by propagandists who are supposed to give aid and advice to the students.

The current objectives of the party's propaganda work with its rank-and-file members are much more limited than those which obtained during some of the earlier phases of the party's development. It is no longer a precondition of party membership that the candidate for admission have actually "mastered" the party program. Stalin declared in 1937 that one who had mastered the party program could be defined as "a tested and theoretically trained Marxist." There were actually very few people in the party who met this criterion, Stalin continued, and he asserted that if the principles were strictly applied there would be left in the party only intellectuals and learned people. His response to this possibility was: "Who wants

---

*Within about a year of its publication the *History of the All-Union Communist Party*, which is defined in the Soviet Union as a basic work of Marxism, had "sold" twelve million copies in Russian and four million in other languages. From 1917 to 1947 there were about 737 million copies of books and pamphlets described as "classics of Marxism-Leninism" printed in the U.S.S.R. *Sovetskaya Pechat' v Tsifrakh* (The Soviet Press in Figures; Moscow, 1948), p. 53; and *Tsifry o Pechati S.S.S.R.* (Figures on the Press of the U.S.S.R.; Moscow, 1940), p. 43.

such a Party?" [50] Finally, Zhdanov made it clear in 1939 that accepting the Program and Rules of the Party, paying membership dues, and working within some party organization were the only conditions of party membership. The mastery of Marxism is an obligation of the member to be met by study, but it is not regarded as a condition of membership.[51]

Party theory and practice indicate that currently the chief tasks of the average member are to assist in securing the execution of policy arrived at by the leaders and to set an example for the rest of the population. The party school for the rank-and-file member is defined as a school for training in militant loyalty to the party and in Bolshevik discipline. Its main goal is to shape the "communist world-view" of the member, which means to give him "knowledge of the laws of social development and of political struggle, assist him in correctly orienting himself in life, to make his activity purposeful, [and] to aid him in fulfilling his role as leader and organizer of the masses." [52]

It is clear that to fulfill his functions the rank-and-file member has need of only a minimum grasp of actual Marxist theory. His first need is a clear understanding of the goals of the party and the energy and devotion to work for their attainment. Consequently, it becomes more important to study party policy, to stay abreast of party decisions, than to study Marxist doctrine as such, and this is reflected in the ideological indoctrination which the party gives its rank and file. One of the most important activities of party members is to serve as agitators among the general population, carrying and explaining the decisions of the party to the people, and mobilizing them for the execution of these decisions. To meet this task a certain minimum comprehension of Marxist doctrine is naturally a prerequisite, both for the general orientation of the agitator and to enable him to answer questions intelligently. But the agitator's chief need is for familiarity with the party's decisions, the goals toward which party policy is focused, and the basic approach of the party to the questions concerned. And it is largely toward the provision of such background and information that the propaganda activities of the party among the rank and file of its membership are actually oriented.

The third level of the party's propaganda activities, and in recent times the most important, concerns the ideological training of the party cadres, that is, party officials and functionaries in the hierarchy and those representatives of the party working in the government, in industry and trade, in the trade unions, coöperatives, military, and other organizations. It is taken as axiomatic in the U.S.S.R. that "the art of Bolshevik leadership requires a knowledge of theory, *i.e.*, the laws of the development . . . of the proletarian revolution . . . and the ability of utilizing these laws in the practical work of directing socialist construction."[53]

The party leads and directs the Soviet Union through a vast and complex apparatus of state and public organizations in which its members are strategically located. Elaborate channels of communication have been developed between the center of planning and decision-making in Moscow and the party's representatives in all the territories of the land and branches of the national life. But any apparatus of such size and scope is subject to errors, confusions, and occasionally to breakdowns. Nor can it, even when working smoothly, take account of every situation that may arise. Those on the periphery must have an adequate understanding of the general goals and methods of thought of those in the center, as well as knowledge of specific policies and decisions. They must be able to orient themselves in new situations as they arise, and to make decisions without receiving specific instructions before each action.

It is only in this context that we are able to grasp the full significance of Stalin's remarks to the Eighteenth Party Congress on the subject of party propaganda. It would not suffice, he declared, to regulate the composition of the party, to improve the communication between the higher and the lower units, and carefully to select and allocate personnel. With all this, he continued, if there were deficiencies in the Marxist-Leninist training of the cadres, if they "cease to understand the truth of our cause and are transformed into narrow plodders with no outlook, blindly and mechanically carrying out instructions from above—then our entire state and Party work must inevitably languish." It could be accepted as axiomatic, Stalin asserted, that the greater the knowledge of Marxism-Leninism possessed by the personnel in any sphere of state or party work, the more fruitful and effective the work would be, and vice versa. It could be stated with confidence, he concluded, that if the party's propaganda could succeed in developing party cadres into "mature Marxist-Leninists capable of solving the problems involved in the guidance of the country without serious error, we should have every reason to consider nine tenths of our problems already settled." [54]

An important factor which lay behind Stalin's call for an intensification of the ideological indoctrination of the party's cadres was the great turnover in the ranks of that group which accompanied the purges of the middle thirties. As a result of the general election of the party's governing bodies in 1938, the proportion of officials who held their posts for the first time ranged from 35 per cent in the case of the executive committees of primary party organizations to 60 per cent in the case of republican, territorial, and regional committees.[55] A similar situation was created by the great changes in the party membership during the war years. To secure the Marxist training of such new cadres, and the retraining of the old, the party has always maintained an extensive schooling system. This system was reorganized and greatly expanded in 1938, and was once again extensively overhauled in the years following the recent war.[56]

The first stage in the party system for training its responsible personnel is the district party school. These schools, of which there were about six thousand in 1948 with two hundred thousand students, are operated by the district and city party organizations for the training of personnel working at lower levels. The student body consists mainly of the secretaries of primary party and Komsomol organizations, but it also includes workers in the local government apparatus. Courses are held in the evening, with one or two sessions a week over an eight-month period. The program requires 160 hours of classroom work and outside reading divided between the history of the party (80 hours), the geography of the U.S.S.R. and the rest of the world (42 hours), the Fourth Five-Year Plan (14 hours), and the structure of the party and the Soviet state (24 hours).[57]

The officials of district and city party organizations are themselves trained in schools operated by the regional, territorial, and union-republican party units. The basic course offered by these schools is a two-year program for training party and Komsomol secretaries, propagandists, newspaper editors, and government officials for positions at the district and city level. The curriculum includes the study of the history of the party and the Soviet Union, general history, political economy, dialectical and historical materialism, Soviet foreign policy and international relations, the economic and political geography of the U.S.S.R., the bases of the Soviet economy, and the party structure. Course work is supplemented by practical work experience in managing economic enterprises. There are two faculties, one for Soviet officials and one for party personnel.

In addition to the two-year courses, a nine-month refresher course along the same lines is offered for similar groups of students already holding administrative posts in the district and city organizations. The schools are held in the larger cities where professors, senior editors, and other qualified teaching personnel are available. In 1947, 178 of these schools with a student body of thirty thousand were in operation.[58] Finally, to supplement this system of formal schooling, ten-day seminars are held for these intermediary officials to keep them abreast of developments in Soviet internal and foreign policy, the progress of the Five Year Plans, and problems of ideology and culture, and to permit the exchange of practical experience in party work on the district and city level.[59]

To train party and Soviet officials, propagandists, and journalists who will work at the union-republican, territorial, and regional levels, there is a Higher Party School under the Central Committee. This school offers a three-year course in both its party and Soviet faculties, as well as a nine-month refresher course for persons already holding positions of responsibility at the designated level. The curriculum is similar to that of the schools at the regional level, with the addition of such subjects as logic and law. Candidates for admission must have at least completed their secondary education or must pass equivalent examinations, and must have had considerable experience at practical administrative work with the party or government. A general examination is required upon completion of the course, which leads to a diploma equal to a certificate from a regular higher educational institution. In 1947 there were almost a thousand students enrolled in the three-year and refresher courses.[60]

In addition to the Higher Party School, the Central Committee of the party currently maintains an Academy of Social Sciences which began functioning in November 1946. In contrast to the Higher School, the Academy will train primarily workers in theory for the central, union-republican, and regional party organizations, including teachers of Marxism-Leninism at higher educational and scientific-research institutions, and writers and editors for scientific and political journals. The regular curriculum lasts for three years, the third year being devoted to preparation of a thesis, but there are also nine-month refresher courses. Students at the Academy must have the equivalent of a higher education. The number of candidates for the degree is only about one hundred, but several hundred are enrolled in the refresher courses. The instructing staff of the Academy as well as the Higher Party School is made up of high-ranking party officials, and the foremost professors, theorists, and newspaper and journal editors of the Soviet Union.[61]

Clearly these schools cannot be thought of as being devoted simply to the study of Marxist-Leninist classics. They are not solely schools for Marxist indoctrination, but are in the broadest sense schools for training party and government cadres, that is, official personnel. For this reason the curricula include not only classes in Marxism-Leninism based on the fundamental political texts, but also include a large proportion of practical courses ranging from administrative procedures to methods of economic accounting, and from the history of the party to the development of Soviet foreign policy. Thus the party, through the ideological schooling of its cadres, does not seek simply to make more thorough Marxists of them, but rather seeks to make them more effective party officials by virtue of their Marxist indoctrination.

The changes in the propaganda policies of the party that have taken place over the last two decades reflect the increased specialization, stabilization, and, to some extent, stratification of the total social system in which those policies developed.

In the late twenties and early thirties Marxist indoctrination was regarded as a value or end in itself. The emphasis was therefore on the broadest possible scope, and an effort was made to secure the Marxist indoctrination of the widest segments of the population as evidenced by the four and a half million students in party schools in

1933. The subordination of Marxist training to immediate practical ends was limited, since the ideological schooling of the ordinary worker from the bench, who made up the bulk of the student body, could be expected to enter only most indirectly into his efficiency as a worker. The lines of demarcation between the various levels of schooling were not rigid, and a worker who showed talent could move freely through the continuous levels of indoctrination from the lowest to the highest.

The early thirties witnessed the virtually complete concentration of power within the party in the hands of Stalin and the small group associated with him. At the same time, the Five Year Plans brought about important social changes, and in particular the greater need for specialization which accompanied the increased complexity of administrative tasks. The rise of the intelligentsia, and of the party official who was at the same time a technical expert, was a product of this development. With these changes in Soviet society there were corresponding shifts in the pattern of party propaganda. Ideological indoctrination came to be treated very specifically as means to an end, the end being more effective party control of the national life: and the valuing of Marxist training in and of itself came to be labeled a "scholastic" approach. Marxist schooling was sharply restricted in scope, limited to those whose ideological training could be viewed as promising practical returns. The average party member was no longer expected to master Marxism; it was enough that he understand the party's program and policies and work to secure their attainment. The intelligentsia, which had developed as a potential locus of power outside the party, replaced the ordinary worker from the bench as the chief subject of propaganda efforts. The party officials, the cadres, were provided with a special school system which was distinct, rather than merely being one higher stage in a continuous and general system for Marxist indoctrination.

Hence, it may be said that the present organization of the party's propaganda apparatus is in keeping with the letter of the original Leninist interpretation of agitation as being for the masses and propaganda for the few, the elite. Whether or not the present pattern is equally in keeping with the spirit of the earlier position is another question.

PART 2

PERSONAL ORAL AGITATION
AND OPINION LEADERS

5

THE BOLSHEVIK AGITATOR

THE PERSISTENCE OF PERSONAL ORAL AGITATION

LTHOUGH THE MECHANICALLY UNAIDED VOICE UN-doubtedly accounts for the bulk of all human communication, the mass media such as the newspaper, the radio, and the film have radically altered the whole pattern of public communication. The impact of these mass media on modern society has been so marked that students of public opinion have concentrated their attention on them almost exclusively. As a consequence of this concentration, the study of direct personal communication has been neglected, and there has been some tendency to undervalue its significance for the formation of opinions and attitudes.*

In contrast, Bolshevik thought and practice continue to place the heaviest emphasis on daily face-to-face contact between the masses and representatives of the party, as a fundamental instrument of public communication and as a method of influencing opinions and shaping attitudes. In the U.S.S.R. such communication is referred to as "personal oral agitation." Agitation, as has been noted, is defined as the dissemination of a single simple idea to a large number of people. In that sense agitation may be printed in newspapers and magazines or on posters. Or it may be oral. In communist thought oral agitation is further differentiated. *Mass* oral agitation is conducted primarily by the radio, but speeches at mass meetings also fall in this category. There are two other important forms of oral agitation: that conducted with a few people in face-to-face contact, known

---

*Fortunately, this is not universally applicable. The late Kurt Lewin and his associates, to name but one group, largely concentrated their research efforts on the study of face-to-face contacts and their role in shaping attitudes.

as *group* agitation, and that involving only one person besides the agitator, known as *individual* agitation. This section is concerned with such group and individual agitation, referred to above collectively as "personal oral agitation." [1]

The following remarks of G. F. Aleksandrov, wartime head of the party's Administration of Propaganda and Agitation, are characteristic of the party's evaluation of the importance of personal oral agitation:

> The correct explanation of the contemporary state of affairs . . . is the great and worthy task of the agitator, for on his explanation depends in significant measure the clear understanding by the workers of the U.S.S.R. of the urgency of their duties . . .
>
> The agitator develops iron discipline and the devotion of the Soviet people to the motherland, great firmness in their struggle with the Germans, and flaming hatred of the enemy. By his work the agitator contributes to the great moral-political unity of the Soviet people.[2]

The extent of the party's interest and faith in personal agitation is probably best reflected in the size of the army of agitators it has mobilized and organized to carry its message to the people. Thus, at the time of the election campaign in February 1946, the party was able to draw on the services of approximately three million agitators.[3] This figure does not represent the size of the regular corps of agitators, since at election times the party usually makes especially strenuous agitation efforts and many people are drawn into that work on a short-term basis. Evidence available on a large number of republics and regions of the U.S.S.R. indicates that the party regularly maintains a force of approximately two million agitators. Assuming a population of about two hundred million, this would yield a ratio of one agitator for each one hundred of population, or one agitator for every sixty-five persons over the age of fifteen.[4]

This ratio is, of course, not uniformly maintained throughout the territory of the Soviet Union. The concentration is higher in the more densely settled and economically important areas. In the Ukrainian Republic in 1949, for example, there were 764,000 agitators, yielding a ratio of one agitator to approximately every fifty persons in the population.[5] The concentration in the urban areas is also much greater than in rural areas. Thus, the capital city of Moscow, with a population of about five million, had 160,000 agitators in 1946, or a ratio of one agitator for every thirty individuals in the population.[6] In contrast, in some rural areas there are many collective farms, incorporating several hundred people, which do not boast a single agitator, and which may be visited by a district agitator only two or three times a year.[7] These are the Soviet equivalent of the famous "deaf corners" of Tsarist Russia.

In the face of the great territory and population of the country, the formal media of communication in the Soviet Union are inadequate to the tasks set for them by the party. But whatever these inadequacies, they cannot serve as a satisfactory explanation of the continued emphasis that the party has placed on personal oral agitation. The expansion of the system of personal agitation has not only kept pace with the growth of the formal media, but has, if anything, exceeded the rate of growth of the press, radio, and film. For example, the *Agitator's Guidebook*, a semimonthly handbook of information, advice, and instruction for local agitators, increased in circulation by more than eighteen times between 1925 and 1939, and between 1935 and 1939 alone it increased sixfold. Its circulation of 650,000 copies in 1939 made it the largest magazine and journal of any type in the Soviet Union. The journal, furthermore, is printed only in Russian, and non-Russian speaking agitators are served by native language equivalents of the *Agitator's Guidebook*. There is one in each union republic and territory, in nine of the autonomous republics, and in thirty-six regions, with a combined circulation of 800,000 copies per issue in 1947.[8]*

The party's continued emphasis on personal oral agitation is based on the assumption that this form has certain special qualities which particularly suit it to the party's needs and interests. The party may, of course, fulfill its self-assigned functions as a leader, teacher, and guide of the masses from a distance. But the party recognizes that

*The total circulation of the agitators' guidebooks should not be assumed to be the same as the total number of agitators. The paper shortage makes it impossible to provide every agitator with a copy of these journals, and they are therefore directed largely to reading rooms set up by the local party organizations. There several agitators may utilize the same copy of the magazines along with other related materials.

the kind of effort and sacrifice which it expects and requires on the part of the population depends upon some intimate contact between it and the masses. The existence of any real gulfs between the party and the people renders ineffective the leadership principle. For this reason Lenin, Stalin, and other Bolshevik leaders have insisted that, at least in this respect, the party must make it an inalienable principle of its tactics to stay "close" to the masses.[9] The party, in brief, cannot expect discipline and sacrifice from the masses unless it is itself a model of these virtues. This approach is characterized by the party's conception of "agitation by example," and it is indeed regarded as the first responsibility of the individual agitator that he set his group a shining example of effort, discipline, and sacrifice.

It is clear that personal oral agitation is much better suited to giving concrete meaning to the party's conception of "agitation by example" than are the radio or the press. In addition, group and individual agitation are ideally suited to the resolution of the party's ever-pressing problem of mobilizing the people for greater agricultural and industrial production. But the greatest importance of this type of agitation lies in the fact that it provides a direct channel of communication between the masses and the otherwise distant party leaders. For the Bolshevik agitator is in daily, intimate contact with small groups of people whose problems he knows at first hand and whom he meets in a relatively free atmosphere of discussion.* He is thus able to provide the party officials at all levels with a constant flow of information on the state of popular thought. He can report the desires and interests of the people, and advise the party leaders of trends in public opinion which they may effectively exploit or which they must counteract.[10]

The Bolshevik agitator is, in the last analysis, the figure on whom the success of the party's oral agitation depends. Of all the representatives of the party it is the agitator who has the most frequent, regular, and intimate contact with the industrial workers, the collective

*The atmosphere of discussion at a Soviet agitation session would not be regarded as "free" by Anglo-American standards. Any man who persistently asked questions which indicated underlying opposition to the party's program would soon be exposed to police investigation. But by Soviet standards, the agitation sessions apparently involve more open criticism and a broader range of questions than are permitted at comparable Soviet public gatherings.

farmers, and the rest of the Soviet citizens. He is the individual through whom the party daily "talks things over with the people," as the writers for party journals are fond of putting it. Before or after the change of shift or in the rest period in the plants and on the farms, and even in the workers' dormitories or at their apartments, he meets with small groups to conduct his agitation. Whether he reads aloud some article from the daily press, describes some important recent decision of the party or government, leads a critical discussion of the work performance of his group, or exhorts them to greater effort, he speaks in each case as the voice of the party. He is a major link between the party leadership and the masses.

THE SELECTION AND TRAINING OF AGITATORS

Traditionally, every Communist has been expected actively to propagate the views of the party in his daily work and contacts, and a provision to this effect is embodied in the party rules as one of the first duties of a Bolshevik.[11] The party is not inclined, however, to provide for so important an activity as agitation solely on the basis of a blanket responsibility of the total party membership. Consequently, the executive committees of primary party organizations are instructed to designate specific agitators from among the best party and Komsomol members and from among the non-party Bolsheviks (those sympathetic to the party's aims although not members).[12] These agitators are selected from among the regular personnel in the industrial enterprises, collective farms, Machine-Tractor Stations, State Farms, and other establishments and institutions at which the primary party organizations are located.

This "designation" of certain individuals as agitators derives from the conditions of party membership. In addition to his regular occupation, every member is expected to perform some special work for the party. Service as an agitator is one of the most common and, from the point of view of the party, one of the most acceptable methods for the discharge of this obligation. Such service is officially regarded as the prime party responsibility of those performing it, and they are supposed to be freed of other party duties.[13] Party members who prefer agitation to other party duties may volunteer for service as an agitator. Similarly, persons who are not members but are classified as party "sympathizers" may volunteer or may be invited to work as agitators. The proportion of such non-party agitators is not great. For example, less than one fourth of the agitators in Moscow during the 1947 election campaign were non-party,[14] and generally during elections the number of such agitators is much higher than at other times.

The party member, having been selected or having volunteered for agitation work, and having been confirmed for the job by the local party executive committee, is usually assigned to a kind of agitators' seminar known as an *agit-kollectiv*. The first agit-collectives were set up in 1923, following a decision of the Twelfth Party Congress which stressed the need for a specialized apparatus for instructing local agitators and working out the details of local campaigns.[15] In the succeeding years the party issued instructions from time to time governing the operations of these groups, and in 1938 a formal set of "Model Rules for Agit-Collectives" was adopted. Those rules are apparently still in force.[16]

Agit-collectives are established, and their work is supervised, by the primary party organizations at industrial establishments, governmental offices and institutions, collective farms and Machine-Tractor Stations, and so on. An agit-collective should number not less than fifteen and not more than thirty agitators. For this reason, major establishments and particularly large industrial plants, which may have as many as fifteen hundred agitators,[17] will usually have several agit-collectives. There may be one for each shop in the plant, and the same shop may have a different collective for each of the shifts. In moderate-sized plants there will usually be only a few agit-collectives. At most small plants and establishments there will usually not be enough agitators to form a collective. This is especially true on collective farms and in Machine-Tractor Stations, and as late as 1940 it was reported that there were many collective farms that did not have a single agitator.[18]* In the case of such plants and farms

*The availability of agitators on the farms is limited by the small number of party members in the rural areas. Less than 10 per cent of the party membership is made up of collective farmers, and the rural areas as a whole include only about 20 per cent of the membership, even though they contain 65 per cent of the total population. In 1939 there was on the average only one party organization for every twenty collective farms. See A. A. Andreev's report in *Eighteenth Congress*, pp. 108-09.

the individual agitators will usually be enrolled in an agit-collective operating under the supervision of the district or county party organization.[19]

The secretary of the local primary party organization is expected to serve as the chairman of the agit-collective, conducting the meetings and personally instructing the agitators in their duties. In larger plants where the primary party organization is broken down into shop committees, the agit-collective in each shop will be supervised by the head of the party shop committee. In such cases, the secretary of the parent primary party organization will direct a factory-wide agit-collective made up of the heads of the shop agit-collectives and of the more experienced or strategically located agitators. The party secretary, or the man he deputizes as director of the agit-collective,* is expected to report back to the executive committee of his party organization at least twice monthly; he then gives an account of the work of his group of agitators and receives instructions for the future. The executive committee of the primary organization is, of course, itself subject to instructions from higher party authorities, in particular from the Department of Propaganda and Agitation of the Central Committee.

The agit-collective is expected to meet once every ten days. At these meetings a plan of work is drawn up to cover the next period, and this plan is supposed to be approved by the executive committee of the primary organization. The subjects discussed at these meetings include current events; major aspects of current party policy; mass political campaigns, such as those associated with forthcoming elections; questions of special interest to the workers at the local plant, such as the application of recent government decisions; and most important, the practical economic or political tasks facing the given plant, farm, or organization. The members are expected to review and discuss their experiences, obtain advice from the best agi-

---

*The "Model Rules for Agit-Collectives" provide that the secretary of the primary party organization may turn over the task of supervising the agit-collective to a deputy. Although this procedure is not encouraged by higher authorities, many of the harassed local secretaries take advantage of this provision. In the Stalingrad Region in 1941, for example, only twenty out of 487 agit-collectives were headed by their local party secretaries; the remainder were served by deputies. *Agitator's Guidebook*, no. 11 (1941), p. 18.

tators and the director, and learn not only what to agitate about but also how to approach each subject.

The immediate and chief purpose of the agit-collective is to prepare the agitator to carry on agitation on a specific subject of importance, such as reducing waste in the plant, during a specified campaign period. But the agit-collective is also supposed to improve his general qualifications as a representative of the party who goes before the workers. The agit-collective will, therefore, also discuss general subjects like geography, economics, and cultural or political questions. Through the collective, the party makes available to the agitator books, newspapers, maps, visual aids, and special literature of all kinds. The agitator is also served by the local *partkabinet* (party cabinet.) At the *partkabinet* the agitator may consult individually or in groups with a party official about some question of theory or about the correct way to answer certain questions of the workers. The *partkabinet* also provides the agitators with analyses of important speeches and decrees, and prepares digests of the press for them on important political and economic problems in both internal and international affairs.[20]

In addition, the party has from time to time ordered special short-term schools established for agitators at the district or county level. These courses usually last ten days or less, and are generally given in the evenings so that the agitator need not leave his regular job in the factory. On occasion, these courses will be on a special subject of particular importance at the time, such as foreign affairs. Most of them are general, however, and the student will divide his time between lectures and self-study or reading. The courses are designed to improve the general preparation of the agitator, and usually include lectures on Soviet and world geography, on "conditions" in capitalist countries, and on the economic and political policies of the Soviet regime.[21] They are not supposed to duplicate the services of either the regular schools for adult education or the regular party schools for Marxist training, but are expected to orient themselves specifically to the task of improving the effectiveness of the agitators as the voice of the party among the rank and file of the working population.[22]

CHANGING CONCEPTIONS OF THE MODEL AGITATOR

In the years following the Revolution the party was faced with a vast problem in seeking to mobilize a great population against heavy pressure from all sides in a period of extreme social disorganization, and with the instruments of communication lacking or in a state of disrepair. The weakness of the formal means of communication which had been inherited from the old regime increased the burden on oral agitation, and this at a time when the human resources of the party were most limited. Lenin, commenting on what he called the party's "great shortage of forces" in mid-1918, called for a broadening of the party's oral agitation and urged: "Comrades who are capable of doing anything at all must not be kept in office jobs."[23]

Under these conditions the logical and inevitable course for the party to adopt was to make maximum use of its available resources for contact with the masses. Lenin provided the slogan "Every Bolshevik an agitator," the Eighth Party Conference (1919) called on members of the party to school themselves in mass agitation work, and the Thirteenth Congress in 1924 urged as a goal that every rank-and-file party member, whether a workingman or woman, be an active agitator for the party.[24]

The conception of the ideal agitator that emerged in this period was that of the ordinary Communist, an activist and a man of deep personal convictions, who by means of direct contact with the populace in the course of his everyday affairs, and by means of his own shining example, brought the masses around to the side of the Bolsheviks. For example, Lenin said to a gathering of factory committeemen in April 1919: "Less than gatherings and meetings, there is a need for personal agitation."[25] Later that month, speaking to a conference of railroad workers, he said: "And we are sure, comrades, that this mobilization would be incomparably better . . . if besides those agitators who appear before gatherings, each of you and each of your acquaintances turned yourselves into an agitator, went to your comrades, factory workers, and railway men, and explained to them, simply, clearly, why it is necessary to strain all our forces."[26] A similar note was sounded by the Thirteenth Congress in 1924, which resolved: "In chance groups and personal contacts with workers—during breaks, at the workbench, at home and so on—these comrades must conduct agitation for the Party about the more important political events and on all questions which move the workers."[27]

Many of the agitators who were well adapted to the sloganeering and more inflammatory style of the prerevolutionary period apparently found it difficult to move over to the relatively more subdued, practical, and mundane type of agitation required of a party in power. In his criticism of the newspapers in 1918, Lenin complained that there was too much of "political fireworks," and too little concern with workaday problems, with helping the masses by careful explanation and concrete examples from everyday life.[28] And again in his comment on the work of the Commissariat of Education in 1921, he insisted:

> Lessen the political chatter; let us have less of the political haranguing and the abstract slogans in which the inexperienced and those who do not understand their tasks as Communists take delight—let us have all the more propaganda about production, and a more active study of actual experience so as to facilitate and expedite the development of the masses.[29]

Although the rank-and-file Communist carrying the word of the party to the people in his daily contacts represented the ideal in agitation during the first period of Soviet development up to the introduction of the Plans, he was not in fact the dominant figure. The party forces were neither so numerous nor so well distributed as to reach anything but a small part of the population with oral agitation. And the more capable rank-and-file members who would have been qualified to carry on this work were quickly drafted to meet the pressing needs of administration and management. Consequently, agitation was placed largely in the hands of a small number of semi-professional agitators,[30] mobilized at the centers of party strength, who traveled about on party orders delivering speeches. These men were primarily orators, experienced in public speaking and capable of arousing popular enthusiasm.[31] They concentrated on explaining to the people in popular language the aims and goals of the new regime.

But with the introduction of the Five Year Plan in 1928, the party concentrated all of its energies on the factory shop and the task of getting out production. With this shift of emphasis to the shop, these professional agitators had largely outlived their usefulness. The days of the "tourist" agitator who spoke to many occupational groups without knowing the work of any was over. The man who could not tell wheat from rye, or one bean from another, was no longer considered useful as an agitator.[32]

Thus, by 1928 the idea of the agitator as a *popularizer* of the party line was being rooted out and replaced by the conception of the agitator as *organizer* of the masses.[33] This meant that the agitator did not simply talk about the importance of higher production, for example, but personally directed the workers in better organizing their work processes. All other agitation was termed the agitation of windbags. The "agitator-lord" who stood off from his audience, the "depersonalized" campaigners, the "noisemakers," in short, all those who could not bring their work fully to bear on practical fulfillment of concrete tasks were to be eliminated from agitation.[34]

What were the characteristics of the ideal agitator in this period, beyond his quality as an organizer? In these early years of the Plan, of extra-human effort, the ideal agitator was himself a foremost *otlichnik* (exemplary) or *udarnik* (shock) worker, who showed by personal example what was the right way to work and how to overcome deficiencies. By this example, through his work and initiative, the model agitator rallied the other workers around him and brought them into the campaign for socialist competition and for outstanding work. He led his brigade, through his agitation, in concrete programs such as those for lowering production costs and improving the quality of output; and he did not simply pose the question but showed the way in person and by presenting the experience of the best workers and the best brigades in the plant.[35]

The model agitator in the early thirties, we are told, was not like the man who came to the plant with an inflexible scheme for a speech, fixed his eyes on some point on the ceiling, and monotonously rolled out his slogans and abstractions about "surplus value" without realizing that many of his listeners were fresh from the village and were falling asleep under his measured phrases. Nor was he supposed to be like a second type of agitator who did not think too much of his audience or their ability to understand matters of "policy," who did not really talk but "lisped," and slapped the workers on the back. The third type, the model, worked hard at improving his own ideo-political level. He was "systematic," and before each appearance he prepared thoroughly, thought over the question, and utilized live facts and concrete examples. He carefully considered the general political situation in the shop and the cultural-political level of his audience, and he tried to answer the questions that interested the workers.[36]

This ideal was not easily come by, however, for many of the best workers, no matter how great their devotion to the cause of building socialism nor how high their production record, were not personally equipped to conduct agitation. A constant theme in the early thirties, therefore, was the demand for an improvement in the general level of the average agitator, many of whom were described as knowing little more than the workers to whom they were supposed to explain things.[37] Throughout the period, agitators were urged to improve their political knowledge, their grasp of geography and economics, to read newspapers and books regularly, on the grounds that they were supposed to be better informed than their audience.[38]

The particular adjustment problems which many agitators experienced under the conditions of this shift in emphasis to production problems should easily be anticipated. The crucial question was whether or not the agitator could adjust himself to the new practical level of agitation, to production propaganda, and what frequently amounted simply to direct instruction of the mass of new workers who flowed into industry. Many could not make the adjustment. Some, who persisted in being "popularizers," were charged with separating mass work from practical work, of making cultural work "apolitical," of divorcing agitation from organization.[39] Others, who apparently tried at least to simulate the period's dominant pattern of "special efforts," were charged with triteness and routinization in their work.[40] At the same time, many agitators were castigated for not being sufficiently vigorous in their criticism of those who lagged behind and in their attacks on disrupters of labor discipline and other "hostile" elements.

After 1935 the model agitator soon developed into the well-informed Stakhanovite worker.* In the shop the model agitator set a personal example by his outstanding work, but he also gave help and instruction to those lagging behind his production record.[41] He strove to raise his own cultural and political level, attended the party school and adult classes, and sought to master Marxism-Leninism.[42] He did not wait around for the workers to gather for a meeting, but went directly to them; he would talk with them in any place or at any time. He did not dodge their "difficult" questions, and he was patient and friendly in his explanations because he realized that the business of communist education is a slow affair.[43] At the same time, this model agitator did not hesitate, when the going was rough, to be vigorous in his criticism of those who lagged behind or disrupted production and to carry the fight to those who showed themselves hostile to the regime.[44]

Even while the Stakhanovite stood as the model Bolshevik agitator, another type of man came increasingly into the center of attention, particularly in the period following the Eighteenth Party Congress (1939) and the adoption of the Third Five Year Plan. As part of the campaign to increase the authoritativeness of agitation, which previously had primarily meant getting local party leaders personally to participate in agitation, there was now a call for the wider attraction of the Soviet intelligentsia to agitation work.

In particular, this meant engineering-technical personnel and representatives of plant management.[45] Among the lists of active agitators and directors of agit-collectives began to appear regular mention of titles virtually unknown before: the director of the plant, the chief engineer, the shift engineer, the chief technologist, the foreman of the shop, and similar titles.[46] There was, we are told, a significant "bringing closer" of the managerial cadres to agit-mass work. In mid-1940 there were said to be few plants where the plant director, his assistant, and the managers or foremen of the various

---

*Stakhanovism was a "movement from below," fostered by the party, which sought to achieve an increase in labor productivity by replacing the earlier stress on mere extra-personal exertion with an emphasis on individual and group improvements in particular work processes. It was a movement for the greater rationalization of labor supposed to be introduced by the workers themselves.

shops and departments did not personally participate in agitation work along with the secretary of the party committee and the secretary of the trade-union committee.[47]

This attraction of the managerial personnel was held to have significantly improved the quality of agitation, its ideological level, and its effectiveness.[48] When the question was raised whether the shop chiefs could be expected to conduct agitation in the face of their other responsibilities, the answer was in the affirmative both on the basis of experience and of necessity; they were held to be necessary to agitation because of their authority in the shop, their better intellectual preparation, their superior training, and so on. It is not surprising, therefore, that on the eve of the war a report from Stalinsk Region indicated that after a restructuring of agitation work in one city, 620, or more than a third of the total of 1,837 agitators, were directors of party organizations and managerial personnel.[49] The situation was much the same in the rural areas.[50] Wartime production demands, and especially the influx of new workers into industry to replace those drafted, gave added impetus to this movement. In the Moscow Region's industries in 1942, more than half of all agitators were reported to be foremen or brigade leaders, and in some plants they accounted for 70 to 80 per cent of the agitators.[51] This trend continued unabated into the postwar period.[52]

Thus, as the Soviet Union passed through each of the major periods of its development, the party sought to adjust to changes in its own composition, in the social structure of the nation, and in the problems facing it, by significant shifts in its conception of the model agitator.

THE SOCIAL ROLE OF THE BOLSHEVIK AGITATOR

The Bolshevik agitator is the most constant and direct personal link between the party leaders and the mass of the people. It is said of him that he "fulfills the most important Party responsibility and is one of the most important figures of the proletarian revolutionary movement."[53] But the lot of the agitator is not a happy one, buffeted as he is by the pressures from both above and below. It is the efforts of agitators to evolve for themselves a stable, satisfying, and satisfactory role in this total situation that must now be considered.

If one were to make a list of the specific tasks and functions which the party has assigned to its agitators, it would more than fill this page.[54] These duties range from leading the workers to maintain a high level of cleanliness at their workbenches, to eliminating the remnants of capitalist thought in men's minds and inculcating a new "socialist consciousness." For the purposes of this study the responsibilities of the agitators may be regarded as divided into two related categories, the practical and the political. Both types of agitation have their roots deep in the Soviet system.

The practical tasks of the agitator are concentrated at the level of industrial and agricultural production, in the shop and the brigade. The success of the Plans, on which the success of the regime has largely rested, depend on extra-human effort, or, as Stalin put it, on the willingness of the people to work in the new way. The whole industrial order has been in an almost continuous state of flux, with millions of new workers entering industry from the rural areas, with new processes, techniques, and procedures being constantly introduced. In the midst of all this the Bolshevik agitator has been expected to be both a stabilizer and an innovator. He has been expected to introduce the new workers to the industrial order, and by his steadiness and personal achievement to act as a model for all. At the same time he has been expected to be first in every new movement, pushing the workers on to new goals, training them in new methods, urging them to combat waste or to increase productivity, criticizing their failures and deficiencies.

On the political side, the agitator has to carry "the word" of the party to the people. He must introduce and explain the new decrees, expound and justify the party's policy. He is expected to persuade and convince, to mobilize opinion in support of the party's leadership and its actions, to criticize those who are defined as enemies and praise those who are defined as friends. He must keep the "revolutionary spirit" alive among the masses, educate them in communism, rally them to the support of the party and the Soviet motherland.

The needs of the party are constant, and the pressure it exerts on the agitator is correspondingly regular. But the agitator must reckon not only with the party officials who instruct him, for he daily faces a live audience of people with whom he has other relations than that of agitator. If the agitator had only good news to bring the people, of course, his most serious problem would be limited to that of maintaining audience interest. But the practical and political tasks of the agitator are not always such as will arouse an enthusiastic response in his audience. Most of the time the content of the agitation is such that it places new demands on the people who listen—more production, less waste, greater cleanliness in the shop and in the living quarters, better work discipline.

The workers have questions to ask, furthermore, and frequently these queries are what are termed "difficult" or even "painful"; but the party insists that they be answered, and it is the agitator who must make the reply, lest they be answered by "hostile" elements who have their own answers, not those of the party.[55] The agitator may be asked, for example, why it is still necessary to queue up at the stores despite the supposed improvement in consumers' services.[56] Or he may be asked why the pay of directors is so much higher than that of some workers.[57] And sometimes he must introduce measures, such as the increase in work norms or the lengthening of the work day, which arouse the "temporary displeasure" of particular groups of workers. Such problems are considered to be tests of the agitator's "Bolshevik tempering," and he is told: "Do not hide from a puzzling, trenchant, or even hostile question, but, on the contrary, give an answer that is straightforward and full of the stuff of the Party spirit."[58]

So, in hard times and times of extra effort, the task of the agitator as he faces his audience grows more difficult. There are people, he is told, "who not only do not understand us [the Bolsheviks] but oppose us."[59] The agitator must carry the fight to these people.[60] When the labor discipline laws are tightened and the work day increased, the party will not tolerate a "liberal" attitude on the part of agitators in their dealings with drifters and disorganizers of production.[61] The agitator must be ever on the alert for such manifestations: "In an occasional conference, in a private chat, in the trolley, on a train, in a dormitory, wherever the Communist hears the agitation of the class enemy . . . he must there, on the spot, meet the enemy with fixed bayonet and oppose him with the agitation of the Bolshevik word."[62]

Such is the situation of the agitator as he is pressed forward by the party; yet he must reckon on the response of his audience with which he must live and work during the hours when he is not acting in the role of agitator. One possible resolution of the problem would be to have agitation conducted by professional agitators sent out from a central point to speak in some shop or on some farm and then to move on to their next assignment. Such a procedure would have the virtue of facilitating that type of direct control of agitation content to which press, radio, and film lend themselves quite naturally. But the party rejected this course. It did so not only because of the organizational, financial, and manpower burden it would have imposed, but also because it would have meant putting oral agitation on a mass basis rather than on a group and individual basis. For in the view of party officials, group and individual agitation have marked advantages over other forms of oral agitation, at least for the purposes and ends to which the party's oral agitation is primarily oriented.*

Consequently, the average party member is likely to find himself, if he is selected to conduct agitation, assigned to agitate in his own shop or his own farm brigade. It is largely from this fact that there arise certain persistent difficulties for the agitator, which manifest themselves in two ways that are closely related.

In the first place, the socially defined role of the agitator involves inconsistent expectations which can easily produce a conflict situation for the men who agitate. The party emphasizes the selection of agitators from the rank and file of the workers because it knows that such an agitator will have the same general interests as his audience; indeed, his effectiveness as an agitator is presumed to

---

*The specific advantages of individual and group over mass agitation have been stated as follows: they (1) are more systematic, in that they can be conducted from day to day; (2) provide broader coverage, since they can deal with problems that really concern the workers; (3) allow deeper penetration, since the agitator comes from the same shop and can talk face to face and meet people eye to eye; (4) permit greater homogeneity in the audience; (5) provide greater opportunity to verify the effectiveness of the agitation; (6) have greater ability to link agitation with concrete production problems. Perchik *Agitation*, p. 83.

depend in good part on this similarity. At the same time, the party expects these agitators to be spokesmen for other, different, interests which are passed on to the agitator from the higher reaches of the party hierarchy. These other interests may be broader, larger, national interests, but they are still different interests. And frequently these larger interests may not be perfectly coördinated with the immediate interests of the agitator, for example, when he must agitate for a speed-up system which national interest requires even though he personally may be lukewarm or even hostile to the idea of exerting still more "extra" effort. Thus, there is potential strain which is structured by the several conflicting expectations of the agitator's role, and which is in this sense internal to the role itself.

In the second place, a man's role as agitator may conflict with other roles which he plays as a member of society. In particular, it may conflict with the agitator's personal relations with his audience of fellow workers, personal relations toward which he has a real emotional commitment. Because the men who are his "audience" when he acts as agitator are often, during the rest of the day, simply his fellow workers, men with whom he eats in the factory lunchrooms, rides home on the trolley in the evening, and whom he perhaps sees socially and reckons as friends after working hours. And in some situations, in so far as the agitator consolidates his party position by fulfilling his agitation instructions, he may at the same time be disrupting his relations with his fellow workers.

Our problem, therefore, is to explore the alternatives which his situation presents to him, and to attempt to discover that form of the role of agitator which provides the fullest resolution of the difficulties inherent in the agitator's situation.

One solution of their dilemma which many agitators have apparently adopted has been to dodge their responsibility, in one way or another to get out of agitation. Certainly all of the turnover in the ranks of the agitators, and it appears to be considerable, cannot be attributed to the personal difficulties faced by the agitator, but a significant percentage of the total may safely be traced to this factor.

In one way or another virtually all of the various party decisions on agitation and innumerable articles and editorials in the *Agitator's Guidebook* have complained of the instability of the corps of agitators.[63] The so-called "paper" agitators, carried on the roles but not actively conducting agitation, have been a continuous problem. In a Dnepropetrovsk plant in 1939, for example, agitators failed to hold twenty-three scheduled sessions in a short period; and in six election districts in the same city, of a total of 704 scheduled agitation sessions in September and October, 312 were not held owing to failure of the agitators to meet their obligations.[64]

The problem of keeping agitators on the job and preventing this dodging of responsibility was highlighted by the party's experience in connection with the first election campaign under the new Constitution in 1937. "Hundreds of thousands" of new faces were reported to have joined the agitators' ranks as the party prepared for the election campaign. Presumably, the party intended to retain these new agitators after the election for agitation among the general population. But the defections from the ranks after the election campaign were apparently as impressive as the initial gains. In one district of Vladivostok, for example, the number of agitators fell from three thousand to seven hundred, and of those who remained it was charged that less than half actually did any work.[65] And in the Kharkov Region the majority of the agitation "circles" for work on the elections had fallen apart by mid-1938; in one district only seventy-four of six hundred circles remained, in another not a single circle was left of the initial group of two hundred.[66] There were similar reports from other regions.[67]

A considerable proportion of these new agitators were not party members, and to a large extent the party journals explained their abandonment of agitation by declaring that they were not "tempered" or "hardened" in the same way as real Bolsheviks. There is, however, a good deal more that can be said on this subject of Bolshevik tempering. The defection from the ranks suggests, in the first place, a considerable disillusionment with the actual effect of the new Constitution on political freedom, as contrasted with the expectations of many Soviet citizens. This was apparently particularly true among the Soviet intelligentsia, who bulked large among the new agitators.

A second point which this defection highlights is the difficulty of maintaining a stable corps of political agitators who are nonprofessional, and in particular the difficulty of doing this under Soviet conditions. For agitation is a time-consuming affair and is likely to meet competition from the demands made by the other obligations of the nonprofessional agitator, such as those to his regular job, his family, his recreational interests, and so on. This raises the question of what immediate rewards are available to the nonprofessional political agitator. Unlike the agitator in a two- or multiple-party system, the Bolshevik political agitator operating under a one-party system does not have a positive, rewarding goal such as taking power; and operating with a single slate of candidates within that one party, he cannot hope for the satisfaction of having his group win over some competing group. The only "external" reward * is the praise of the party director and the associated knowledge that one may in this way secure and perhaps advance his position in the party. Thus, it is to be expected that non-party political agitators, faced neither by the pressure of their membership obligation nor by the promise of reward, would tend to drop out of agitation as their other role obligations continued to make demands on their time.[68]

The situation is not quite the same in agitation which has to do with production. Here both the party and the non-party agitator is working for visible goals, since he may test his success by watching the production record of his group; and that success may mean tangible economic advancement. Here the type case is the managerial agitator who may benefit both immediately, through bonuses, and in the long run, through promotions, if his agitation is successful in inducing higher production in his shop or factory. All of this suggests that while the nonprofessional political agitator can be sustained in his role by personal zeal alone, this places a most important function on a very unstable base. The agitator's enthusiasm may run out, his ardor may be dampened by disappointments and disillusioning experiences, or he may simply find himself too busy to agitate

---

*All rewards are, of course, internal in the last analysis. It seems desirable, however, to distinguish "external" rewards for agitators, like the promise of advancement, from "internal" or ego and status rewards of the type discussed in the summary in Chapter 8.

and still take care of his other obligations and responsibilities. The result is that the agitator either gives up or continues to perform his duties, but does so haphazardly.

To shirk his responsibilities as an agitator, although it might get him relieved of the duty, can hardly serve the party member in good stead so far as his party standing is concerned. There is a second, safer, alternative. It is the course of action which the party has often labeled the "routinization" of agitation, or "formalism," or "bureau-cratic-clericalism" in agitation work.[69] This is the charge leveled against those who stick to agitation "in general," who are alleged to avoid troublesome questions, who concentrate on the revolutionary dates and agitate according to the calendar, who wait for the people to come to them and who read prepared speeches instead of seeking out the people, who look the other way when they see shirkers on the job or hear hostile remarks made against the regime. These are the people, it is said, who distorted the 1935 party decision about the importance of using literary materials in agitation,[70] and who thought that thereafter they could fulfill their agitation obligation solely by reading aloud from *War and Peace* and *Don Quixote*.[71] These were the people accused of being interested only in the figures they could turn in to the party committee on the number of talks they had given and the number who attended, but whose agitation was hackneyed and had no real impact on the organization of the mass.

Although this kind of "routinization" of agitation solved some of the personal problems of the agitator, it could not be a permanent solution of either half of his dilemma. For he could not long hope to retain his audience if he kept his agitation work on a continuously abstract level, and in any event the party was unwilling to have its agitation turned into a simple adult-education program. These first two courses of action, dodging responsibility and "formalism," are not really resolutions of, but rather are unstable compromises with, the problem faced by the Bolshevik agitator. The crux of the problem lies in the defined role of the agitator. He must be capable of criticizing the work of his fellow workers, of introducing them to measures which they may find objectionable, and of defending the party and government against criticism. Yet he cannot escape at the end of the session, for he speaks to workers he knows and sees every day, frequently on intimate personal terms. The crucial problem becomes one of recruiting as agitators individuals of sufficient authority among the people to carry this off without later suffering such social ostracism or rebuff at the hands of their audiences as would thereafter discourage them from further agitation, or which would reduce their effectiveness as agitators. Such authority can be based either on the personal qualities of the agitator or on his social status.

The need for agitators with personal authority among the men with whom they worked came forcefully to the fore when the party put its agitation on a really large-scale basis after 1930, by taking it out of the hands of the "narrow circle of specialists" and turning it over to a large number of men in every plant and shop. As one writer stated the problem, the authority of the agitator in the pre-revolutionary period was never in question because the workers knew the agitator for what he was—a man of convictions who came to speak to them at great personal risk, a revolutionary devoted to their interests. But at the present time, the writer continued:

> The group agitator comes from the rank and file, shoulder to shoulder with other workers just like himself. And if he does not possess political and moral authority he will not stand above the average man, and the workers will not believe in him; and for success in agitation it is necessary that there be great faith in the agitator on the part of the mass.[72]

How was he to obtain this authority? In part, he could win it by the outstanding quality of his own fulfillment of production and social responsibilities,[73] so that no worker could properly say to him "you are always agitating to me, but you never make a move yourself."[74] But in the last analysis, it would be the general personal respect in which the man was held by his co-workers that would determine his success as an agitator.

The successful agitator is, therefore, currently described as the man who knows not only how each person in his shop works, but also how he lives, what his family is like, what his living conditions are, and whether or not he needs advice on one or another personal problem. The agitator is told that "only in the event that the agitator stands in close contact with the people does he actually win for himself authority and respect."[75] Again and again in descriptions of the experience of model agitators, there are examples of such personal contact between the agitator and the members of his group. Sometimes it is the case of an agitator who assisted some worker to improve his qualifications and his earnings.[76] Another time he helps a man, whose work was poor because his quarters were inadequate, to find a room,[77] or he helps another man with some difficulty he was having in collecting his pay.[78] He may help the men who share his dormitory room with their reading and evening study,[79] or he may help another man solve a family problem.[80]

In every case, the fact of central importance is that the agitator is establishing a relationship of social solidarity with the members of his work group; or, as one man who had been given personal assistance by the agitator is reported to have put it, the agitator had developed the feeling that the shop and the working group in it was a sort of family, with close ties, and that each man had certain responsibilities toward it.[81] Reports on the personal experiences of agitators working on collective farms or with the general population, and particularly with housewives, indicate that there too the successful agitator bases his success largely on the same type of personal relationship with his audience.[82] This general role of the agitator in relation to his audience was well summarized by the *Agitator's Guidebook* as follows:

The Bolshevik agitator cannot be a formalist in his relations with and approach to people. He must give consideration to the questions of the masses, must be closely tied to them, and may not wave himself off from the living needs of the workers, but must show them attention, struggle for the improvement of their life, and always and everywhere show himself truthful, never making unfulfillable promises, and not lagging behind with outmoded viewpoints.[83]

Thus, one solution of the agitator's dilemma has been to develop agitators whose personal standing with their audiences has been very high. The party literature indicates that this type of relation, based on the social solidarity of agitator and audience, was developed independently by individual agitators who sought a satisfactory solution to the problem, and was also sanctioned and encouraged by the party. It was and remains, nevertheless, only a partial solution and an unstable compromise.

One of the difficult tasks of the group agitator is to exhort and constantly to urge the workers on to greater efforts. This he can do more effectively if he has the esteem and personal respect of his co-workers. Even more difficult, however, are his tasks of criticizing workers whose production records are poor or who violate labor discipline, and of introducing and carrying into effect new government measures such as increases in the work norms. These tasks he can also perform more effectively if he has close personal relations with his audience. But the very element that gives him this increased effectiveness also acts as a real limiting factor on that effectiveness. For at times when the agitator is being pressed most by the party for more intensive criticism of lagging workers, or when he has to introduce measures which meet the displeasure of the workers, his personal relations with those workers will then most induce him to temper his criticism or to soft-pedal the measures as much as it is within his power to do so. Furthermore, in so far as he behaves as a good party man at such times and carries out the instructions of the party to the letter, then he runs the risk of losing that close contact with his fellow workers which was the basis of his authority in the first place.

Thus, the personal standing of the agitator is clearly but one means of giving him the authority he requires to fulfill his function successfully. Another means is to select for agitation people of high social status, in particular the managerial personnel of the plant. From the point of view of social distance, the field here is completely reversed, for in the first case it is precisely the absence of social distance that makes possible the success of the agitator, whereas in the case of management-agitators it is the very fact of social distance that accounts for their authority.

It would be a mistake, in evaluating the increase noted earlier in the number of agitators who were from the managerial category, to overlook certain changes in the general status of that social group.[84] The shake-up which attended the purge trials in 1936 was accompanied by a great turnover in the ranks of industrial managers, and large numbers of young men came into positions of authority. They were largely men brought up under the Soviet regime, products of Soviet schools and training, frequently from the ranks of the Young Communist League, and often members of the party. In general, after 1937, the ranks of managerial and administrative workers contained more people—with the fairly complete overshadowing of the remnants of the older type of prerevolutionary technician—of the type the party would be inclined to call on for agitation work. But this simply accounts for the greater availability of potential agitators in the ranks of the managerial group; it does not account for the new emphasis which the party placed on getting these people to participate in agitation. It is important to recognize this point, for it throws additional light on the social role of the agitator.

Managerial personnel as agitators also have authority, but it is authority based on their social status, their standing in the hierarchy of positions in the productive process, and not on their purely personal relations with the audience. The foreman, shop director, engineer, or plant director are not like the traveling jack-of-all-trades agitator of earlier years. They know the plant and its production problems, and they have regular contact with the workers whom they know and who know them to varying degrees. Since the agitator is supposed to criticize errors and to explain the reasons for new processes, the managerial personnel is clearly suited to carry on agitation. For the manager-agitator possesses the authority of technical competence, which, it may be assumed, would frequently enable criticism of a man's work with less resentment than might be aroused by such criticism coming from an agitator who is just another worker. At the same time, the managerial personnel is generally better trained and is frequently well educated and well informed, which adds to its general standing and to its qualifications for agitation.[85]

Thus, pressing managerial personnel into agitation largely overcomes the two major sources of conflict that inhere in the situation of the agitator who is a rank-and-file worker. In the first place, the internal conflict of duties is not so apparent in the case of the manager-agitator, for very few of his interests are the same as those of the workers with whom he agitates. If the national interest demands extra effort for higher production, he can freely agitate for that goal, since it does not conflict with his immediate interests as a manager.

Indeed, it is frequently very much to his interest in general to agitate for higher production and greater effort. In the second place, service as an agitator by the representative of management is less likely to involve conflict between different roles. For there is a secure social distance between him and his audience. Once having completed his agitation work, he is not obliged to continue on an intimate personal basis with his audience, working shoulder to shoulder with the other workers. He is free to withdraw, not only to his own special work, but to the company of other people of managerial rank. Since he has only limited cause to fear loss of the personal good will of his audience as a threat of real social deprivation, he is better suited to conduct agitation in those hard times when the need for the agitator is greatest. It may well be true, therefore, that "when the director of the shop or establishment is able to combine politics with economics, the success of affairs is assured," as one agitation official declared in urging that every plant director be first among the agitators in his establishment.[86]*

But there are also limits on the effectiveness of the managerial agitator, and again these limits arise from the very source of his strength. Despite official assertions that there is no antagonism between the managerial personnel and the workers in the Soviet Union, and the conclusion of some serious scholars that such antagonism between managers and workers may indeed be less in the U.S.S.R. than in the industrial order in capitalist countries,[87] it cannot be safely assumed that there is no longer a considerable gulf between the two groups, or that there is no longer any antagonism, resentment, or suspicion between the mass of workers and management. In so far as such social distance persists between the two groups, then the representative of management who comes forward in the role of agitator must expect his effectiveness as an agitator to be reduced by the feeling he generates as a representative of management. Further-

*Robert S. Lynd has suggested, in a personal communication, that the use of managerial agitators may also have been part of a general prewar move toward the equivalent of "labor-management" coöperation in the Soviet Union, in an effort to "close the ranks" and increase solidarity on every level in anticipation of the shock of war. Certainly, the Soviet emphasis on drawing management into agitation bears striking resemblance to the current emphasis on better "communication" between management and labor manifested in American industrial sociology.

more, in so far as there is at all widespread among the workers a feeling that management receives a disproportionate share of the total plant income (witness the question about managers' salaries cited above), then the presentation of any demands by managerial agitators for higher production or new processes must become suspect in such a way as to reduce seriously the effectiveness of their agitation.

It may be anticipated, therefore, that in the future the party will continue to draw upon both the rank-and-file and the managerial groups for its agitators, seeking through their combined efforts to achieve that mobilization of the mind, will, and energy of the working masses which it finds necessary to its purposes.

6

THE ROLE OF THE LOCAL PARTY ORGANIZATION

THE RESPONSIBILITY FOR EXECUTING THE AGITATION policy decided upon by the superior organs of the party such as the Central Committee falls chiefly upon the primary party organizations. It is one of their main duties to conduct "agitational and organizational work among the masses in order to carry out the Party slogans and decisions."[1] Within the primary organization, administrative work is concentrated in the hands of a small executive committee, and in particular in the hands of the secretary of the organization, who is usually a full-time party official. In the case of these officials, no less than in that of the individual agitator, an understanding of their role in the conduct of oral agitation depends upon full recognition of their other obligations and of the total situation in which they find themselves. There are two major characteristics of the position of these men that must be taken into account.

In the first place, it must be recognized that these men are assigned duties which are exceedingly varied and complex. The primary organization is not, strictly speaking, an agency either of government or industrial and agricultural management. In many rural areas, however, it is more or less equal to, if not synonymous with, the local government; and in industrial plants it has heavy quasi-managerial functions to perform. In the course of the party's development, through many upheavals and purges, there has been a progressively stronger emphasis on the economic, administrative, and managerial skills of the members of the primary organization's executive committee. This has been particularly true of the secretaries. They are men with difficult and widespread responsibilities, and tend to be what we know as "practical" men. Their general success and their specific continuance in office depend largely on the economic performance of the establishments at which they are located. They are expected to "get out the work," and if their plant fails to meet its plan or their farm its quota, the responsibility is largely charged to them.

In the second place, account must be taken of their position in the party hierarchy. The primary organization stands at the base of the party structure. Above it towers a long series of superior organizations: first the district. above that the regional, and then the republican organization. Finally, at the apex in Moscow, there are the highest organs of the party like the Central Committee and its Department of Propaganda and Agitation. The directors of the primary organization may receive instructions and orders from any one of these levels of the hierarchy, and such orders come in great profusion. Frequently, to the man at the bottom of the structure, harassed by the practical demands of everyday life in his own plant or farm, these orders may seem contradictory or impossible to fulfill. Yet his official position requires, and the rigors of party discipline demand, that he carry out his instructions. It is inevitable, under the circumstances, that to the people at the top it will often seem that the local secretary is executing his orders very poorly, if at all.

One persistent source of complaint on the part of the central authorities has been the failure of local organizations to give proper attention to the selection of adequate agitators, a problem mentioned earlier. A reading of the decisions of the Central Committee on the subject might lead one to believe that this was a product of either willful neglect or lack of interest in agitation on the part of the local officials.[2] The matter appears in a different light, however, when viewed in terms of the position in which those local officials found themselves. The party forces available to them were always limited, whereas the demands made on those forces under conditions of great political, economic, and social change were virtually unlimited. Especially after the introduction of the Plans, when the party made it unmistakably clear that building factories and getting out production was the prime consideration, it was natural for the party secretary to direct his best members to economic problems. If there were any members left unassigned when these needs were taken care of, the secretary might begin to think about sending some into agitation work. But frequently there were no members available by that time, and often those remaining were not well equipped for agitation.[3] Hence, the central authorities found it necessary to repeat their charges of neglect; but so long as the situation of the local secretaries remained the same, there was little possibility of improvement.

Another aspect of the agitation work of the local party organizations that the central authorities found consistently unsatisfactory was the degree to which local party officials personally participated in agitation. The Central Committee had many times reiterated its demand that the secretary and other officials of the local organizations participate directly and in person in the agitation activities of their organization. In the first years of the Plan, when factory-wide mass meetings were the order of the day, the secretary was expected to address these meetings himself rather than send a deputy. Later, when special question periods were established for the workers, the secretary was directed to appear in person with the plant managers to respond to the workers' questions. And from the earliest origins of the agit-collective, the secretary was expected to take personal charge of it, and to instruct and guide the local agitators in their duties.[4] But it was hardly to be supposed that these secretaries, with their exceedingly practical interests and responsibilities in the plants, would be able to find time to give to agitation. Consequently, in this matter of personal participation of local party secretaries in agitation work, as in the matter of proper selection and training of agitators, the central authorities found it necessary repeatedly to castigate the local officials for their failure to give "proper" and "correct" attention to agitation work.[5]

Only by bearing in mind the special position in which they found themselves, can one understand those activities of the local party officials which produced such consistent charges of inertia, disinterest, and neglect from the central authorities.[6] Thus, when the *Agitator's Guidebook* charged in 1931 that "despite . . . repeated and categorical directives of the highest Party organizations, the great majority of . . . committees . . . at the factory-plant level have up to now shown a completely unsatisfactory attitude towards the organization and establishment of group agitation in the enterprises," [7] the charge cannot be accepted simply at its face value. For frequently the criticized behavior of the local officials was not so much the reflection of any given "attitude" toward agitation, but rather was a product of the total situation in which those officials found themselves. In a way, the *Agitator's Guidebook* recognized this fact when it asserted that local deficiencies in establishing mass agitation work were an outgrowth of a "preoccupation with running things" which characterized the local officials. [8] It is only proper to inquire whether or not a preoccupation with running things was not precisely the characteristic that the party expected of its local officials if they were to fulfill the many responsibilities placed on them.

In addition to this problem of fitting in the organization of agitation along with their other duties, the local party secretaries have often had difficulty in correctly interpreting the instructions they received from on high. In 1934, for example, the Rules of the party were amended to provide specifically that every Communist must act as a Bolshevik agitator. [9] In the following years the party placed progressively heavier emphasis on political agitation than on agitation for higher production, which in the early years of the Plan had excluded virtually all else. At about the same time, the scope of agitation was widely extended to reach out beyond the factory and farm to the homes of the workers, to the schools, and to other areas. [10] Furthermore, in those years following the first successes of the Five Year Plans, the official party journals were full of assertions from the highest quarters to the effect that the people were indeed firm and steadfast in their support of the Soviet regime and the stewardship of the party. This new feeling was highlighted by the introduction in 1936 of the so-called Stalin Constitution, which was the center of elaborate discussions about the "new Soviet democracy."

Under the circumstances, it should not be a surprise that some local party officials interpreted this new atmosphere to mean that specialized agitation was no longer needed. Some party officials ceased to select agitators, and in a few cases they disbanded the agit-collectives. [11] They also interpreted the new situation as indicating the advisability of turning over their agitation responsibilities to non-party public organizations, which seemed to them to have a more direct relation to the new type of agitation. Thus, in some regions, the local party organizations transferred the task of directing the agit-collectives to the village governments (Soviets) and to the trade unions. Some local party committees went so far along the road of the "new democracy" that they permitted the general membership meetings of the collective farm, and the work brigade in the factories, to elect their own agitators.[12]

The higher authorities in the party did not take kindly to these manifestations, and the local party groups responsible for them were sharply criticized. The Central Committee, in a major decision adopted in 1935, warned that although it was correct to state that the masses had come to have unlimited faith in the party and the Soviet regime, it was incorrect to draw from this the conclusion that political agitation among the masses could be reduced.[13] And in the succeeding years, whenever this view cropped up again—and it did—it met the same hostile reception as a "mistaken conception," as "the idea of political fools," and as "a stupid and anti-Bolshevik theory."[14]

However strong the language of the central authorities in condemning these manifestations, it seems likely that many of the local officials were acting in good faith when they discontinued agitation or turned it over to other groups. This is not to say, of course, that the actions of local officials were solely the result of a naïve interpretation of the general pronouncements of the party leaders. Those pronouncements may have served for some simply as a convenient excuse to unload one of the many burdens they were carrying. But many of them undoubtedly read the signs of the time to mean that the party no longer had any need to conduct agitation, and believed that such activity could at least be given to popular organizations like the trade unions or even be put into the hands of the people themselves. The fact that such tendencies met a sharp rebuff from the higher authorities of the party, highlights the problem which the local officials had in interpreting the flood of directives that made their way from the center to the localities through the many stages of the party hierarchy.

In a hierarchical organization as strongly centralized as the Communist Party, however, local officials must inevitably meet the demands and conform with the directives of higher authority, or suffer removal and possibly more serious punishment. Consequently, the Central Committee has in time secured conformity from the local party officials in the matters just discussed. But even in seeking to act strictly in accord with instructions from above, the local officials have been affected by the conditions under which they operate. And this has markedly conditioned the quality of the results they achieved.

The higher officials of the party, as has been noted, have been unrelenting in the demands they have made on local officials for more and better oral agitation. But at the same time, these higher authorities have not reduced the other heavy responsibilities of the local party secretaries. In so far as they were able, most of the local officials have apparently sought to meet the party's requirements for oral agitation. But to the extent that meeting those requirements has been beyond the means of the secretaries of primary organizations, they have had to seek for other ways of placating their superior officers in the party. In this situation they were, in a sense, provided an "out" by the Central Committee itself.

Over the years, the party had been pressing hard for "systematic" and "planned" programs of agitation in the localities, and procedures had been established for a periodic accounting to higher authorities on the agitation work done by the local organizations. Taking advantage of this fact, many local secretaries spread their agitation forces as thinly as possible, often neglecting quality, in order to be able to present the central authorities with impressive records about the "100 per cent coverage" they had achieved. Thus, Lazar Kaganovich, a member of the Central Committee, charged in 1935 that there were many organizations which put all of their revolutionary spirit into making graphs showing the number of conferences held and the number of workers who attended, but that frequently there was little concern about the effectiveness of the agitation so conducted.[15] For example, it has been reported that in supervising their agitators many local organizations did not ask about the manner in which the agitation session had been held, or what was said. Their only interest was in how many sessions were called and how many people attended, so that these figures could be incorporated in reports to the higher authorities.[16]

The central authorities were not long in discovering this watered stock, and they indicated to the local secretaries that such an approach to agitation was more fitting for a statistical clerk than for Bolshevik officials. But once again, since their basic situation did not change markedly, the actions of the local secretaries did not change greatly either. And despite the strictures of the party, charges of "formalism" and "bureaucratic manifestations" in agitation, as these tendencies were labeled, were still very much in evidence in the *Agitator's Guidebook* when the Soviet Union entered the Second World War. These charges continued, furthermore, into the post-war period.[17]

It is a truism, of course, that as a policy passes down through the various levels of a hierarchical organization it often undergoes changes in form and content as it is interpreted, applied, and sometimes openly adapted to the needs and the concrete life situation of the people who are executing that policy. The Communist Party is such a hierarchical organization, and we might therefore expect to find that the agitation policy as put into effect at the base was not always precisely the same as that adopted at the top of the hierarchy.

It was not the purpose of this study, however, to use the execution of the party's agitation policy as simply another illustration of this principle of large-scale organization. On the contrary, this material was presented to demonstrate that the "resistance" offered by lower organizations and the policy "distortions" created by local officials were not inevitable "natural" phenomena, but were meaningfully related to the total situation in which those organizations and individuals found themselves. And in this light, the deficiencies which the higher authorities noted in the performance of local officials may be seen not so much as manifestations of neglect or caprice, but as the product of the conflicting demands made by the other roles which local officials were obliged to play at the same time that they served as the local executors of party agitation policy.

7

THE DEVELOPMENT OF ORAL AGITATION POLICY

THE AGITATION POLICY OF WHICH THE BOLSHEVIK AGITATOR and the primary party organization are the local executors is passed down to them by the central authorities of the party. Just as the execution of that policy is affected by the situation in which the agitator and the secretary of the local organization find themselves, so the over-all agitation policy is largely determined by conditions in the country as a whole. As the Soviet system moved through the several stages of its development, the party set different tasks and goals for the population. In each of these stages the party changed its conception of the functions of oral agitation, its content and forms, to adapt it to new conditions and make it a more effective instrument of party leadership. The development of Soviet agitation policy, therefore, provides an interesting example of the impact on a major medium of communication of some of the other forces operating in the social system.

The initial Bolshevik conception of the function of oral agitation included two elements that were apparently conceived of as being in no way incompatible.* The first element was political agitation, thought of as being primarily a process of political indoctrination and education of the masses. The content of political agitation varied significantly from period to period. For example, in the time of the New Economic Policy it meant a combination of teaching the

---

*Lenin set this pattern from the outset when he declared: "Every agitator must be a governmental director, a leader of all the peasants and workers in the affairs of economic construction." Lenin, *Sochineniya*, XXVII, 45.

illiterate to read and write and at the same time transmitting to them the rudiments of Marxist thought; and in the late thirties it meant explaining the foreign and internal policies of the party and government. But whatever the variations in content, this political agitation is not to be confused with the second element, or practical, "production" agitation. This production agitation was designed to make some contribution toward the resolution of the immediate, concrete, economic problems facing the party at any given time. In content it varied from such general efforts as encouraging the workers to engage in "socialist competition" for higher production during the first years of the Five Year Plan, to the most detailed instructions and advice on how to rationalize some labor process in the late thirties. But no matter what the content, this agitation on production tended to be extremely practical, circumscribed in its interests, and oriented toward directly mobilizing the workers, urging them on to greater effort, criticizing their deficiencies, introducing new work techniques, and so on.

It can readily be seen that it is no simple matter to maintain a system of agitation that simultaneously serves as a means of political education and as an instrument for getting out more production. This involves a balance that is by nature precarious, and that could be preserved only under the most stable social conditions—a state which in the past has hardly characterized the Soviet Union. For once the initial commitment is made permitting the utilization of agitation for immediate practical ends, the possibility is thereby created that under the pressure of strong need the educational emphasis, whose results are not nearly so immediate or tangible, will either be displaced by or subordinated to the practical emphasis. And when this happens, agitation loses its political character and becomes simply a phase of the industrial process, an adjunct of management, an aspect of the total system for the organization of the labor force.

This is not to say that political and production agitation are polar types which may only be seen as being opposed to each other. The question is primarily one of the balance between the two elements, and this balance is best judged by examining the content of agitation. For example, political agitation is no less political if the agitator concentrates on explaining to a group of workers the reasons why greater effort and higher production are necessary to the national welfare. But when the party says in effect, as it did at one point, that the good political agitator is not the man who simply explains why higher production is necessary, but rather is the one who concentrates on directly organizing his work group to achieve that higher production—then production agitation may fairly be said to have absorbed and displaced political agitation.

EARLY DEVELOPMENT: THE SEIZURE OF POWER AND WAR COMMUNISM

The development of the propaganda and agitation policies of the Russian Communist Party did not begin with the seizure of power by the Bolsheviks in 1917. Behind it lay almost twenty years of experience, the bulk of it in illegal and underground activities, in propagating its ideas and agitating for its program among the industrial workers of Russia and in the ranks of the intelligentsia. Throughout the greater part of this period, the party placed its main emphasis on propaganda, designed to build up the kind of professional revolutionary party that Lenin had envisioned.[1]

Agitation was, of course, also conducted by the party to bring the masses to that "position either of direct support of the vanguard, or at least of benevolent neutrality toward it" which Lenin had held to be a precondition of open action by the revolutionary workers' party.[2] But the party's ability to conduct agitation was severely limited by the fact that many of its activities were illegal throughout most of the prerevolutionary period. Consequently, the party's agitation was conducted only sporadically and was largely restricted to occasional mass meetings, with heavy reliance placed upon the utilization of popular slogans. The content of the agitation was on the whole simple and direct, as expressed by such slogans as "Peace and Land" or "All Power to the Soviets," which were designed more to shake the existing regime and facilitate the Bolshevik accession to power, than actually to mobilize the people for concrete organized action.

When the Bolsheviks seized power in October of 1917, they were quickly obliged to recognize how different were the problems and tasks of a party actually in power from those of one simply seeking to take power. As the Eleventh Congress later noted in a resolution, the whole party had been devoted to propaganda and agitation before the Revolution, but now this work had to be relegated to but one department among many others devoted to economic and political affairs.[3] For now the party had the responsibility of administering all aspects of the national life, and had available little more than the disintegrating administrative apparatus inherited from the Tsarist regime. Furthermore, the Bolsheviks were vouchsafed only a few months of relative calm to grapple with the collapse of virtually the entire economic and political structure of the old society before they found themselves fighting for the very existence of their regime against Civil War and foreign intervention within the borders of Russia.

Under these conditions, oral agitation did not flourish, and it certainly fell far short of expectations. In the first place, the party found itself compelled by the course of events to act as the needs of the moment dictated, and such action was not always what would have been suggested by a wise agitation policy. Thus when the Bolsheviks, under pressure of the struggle for survival and spurred on by overzealousness in establishing communism, came to make their requisitions of grain in the villages, they relied more on force than on agitation. The persuasion of the word was largely replaced by the persuasion of the armed group of city workers who came to requisition the grain. There was, consequently, a certain shriveling of true political agitation in this period, and the party admitted that the line between agitation and coercive administrative measures had become very thin.[4]

The second great difficulty which the party experienced in this period was an acute shortage of adequate personnel. The most capable party members were drawn into administrative work or were dispatched to the fighting fronts to stiffen the Red Armies. Many of the remainder were not suited by temperament or background to function successfully as agitators among the ordinary workers and peasants who had to be mobilized for many tasks they had little desire to perform. The average party official was most interested in running things. And it was the preoccupation with administrative problems, coupled with the acute shortage of hands, that led Lenin in 1918 to charge that the local party nuclei were displaying too little initiative in seeking to influence the broad working-class masses.[5]

But although political agitation was not greatly advanced in the period of War Communism, the party did make a statement of intentions and drew up a blueprint for its future agitation activities in the form of an extensive resolution on political propaganda and cultural educational work in the villages. In general, the party's resolution viewed agitation as a process of political education, which aspired not merely to teach but to change the very consciousness of the population.[6] It was primarily in the next phase of Soviet development, however, that a concentrated effort was made to carry this plan of agitation into effect.

A NEW ECONOMIC POLICY AND A NEW AGITATION POLICY

In March 1921 Lenin called for a new economic policy. The need for immediate changes in policy was indicated by a political crisis which included peasant uprisings and the Kronstadt rebellion, and by a state of economic collapse which Lenin referred to as "a more serious defeat than any previously inflicted on us by Kolchak, Denikin, or Pilsudski."[7] This New Economic Policy, designed to replace War Communism, essentially meant the restoration of capitalism in no small degree.

It was clear that in making this retreat the party had committed itself not only to an organizational struggle on the economic front, but to an ideological struggle on the political front as well. No one realized this more fully than Lenin. A political revolution, he warned the Soviet political education workers, could not be effected merely through "declarations, statements, manifestoes, and edicts." To assume this, he declared, was merely "Bolshevik conceit," an attitude which he indicated had been characteristic of the party's approach to political education up to that point. A political revolution, he continued, had to be carried into life among the masses, and this was a "cultural" task that it might take many years to complete. The Soviets were entering on a new struggle, he affirmed, that was to be more bitter than the previous military struggle. And the final source of power and victory in that struggle, Lenin asserted, was to be found in the *consciousness* of the masses of workers and peasants.[8]

To meet the challenge posed by Lenin the party turned sharply in the direction of broad popular political education. In keeping with the "cultural" task that Lenin had set it, the party sought through its agitation to affect people's basic social attitudes. This included such things as trying to change their patterns of personal and communal hygiene, the attitudes of men toward women, the drinking habits of the men, and so on. General adult education and political agitation were closely linked. On the more directly political front, the party sought to popularize the doctrines of Marxism.

Words like "illumination," "explanation," and "clarification" appeared with increasing frequency in the party's deliberations, and political education workers were instructed to discuss the most important international and internal events, the major measures adopted by the Soviet government, and important aspects of local life such as the operations of local organs of government, the trade unions, coöperatives, and so on. The keynote which was sounded was the call for a "deepened agitation," and the party went so far as to suggest the need for a change-over from mass agitation to mass propaganda.[9] If one keeps in mind the distinction that the party has always made between propaganda and agitation, the magnitude of the shift suggested will be clear. This proposal represented, in fact, the high point of the party's emphasis on the direct political education of the population through the medium of oral agitâtion.

To secure this effort, the party undertook an administrative reorganization, consolidating the organizations responsible for agitation and political education, and subordinating those outside the party to its control. Within the party a more precise differentiation of function was demanded. Each of the larger local party organizations was instructed to establish a special agitation department to be headed by a responsible official well trained in Marxism, who was to be freed from other party obligations. At the same time, the party took measures to increase the number of agitators and improve their quality. It called for mobilization of the best agitators in the cities, and ordered them directed to work in the districts, villages, and local factories. To insure more thorough instruction of agitators, the Twelfth Party Congress in April 1923 called upon regional and district party committees to establish the "collective of agitators" (*agit-kollectiv*) which has already been discussed. Perhaps the most important action taken was the decision to train the two hundred thousand new members, drafted into the party from among the "workers of the bench" in 1924, so as to fit them for service as individual and group agitators in industrial enterprises.[10]

The changes in the content of agitation made necessary certain corresponding changes in the forms used. It was felt that mass meetings, which had been the predominant form for agitation in the period of War Communism, were not suited to the more serious, comprehensive, and objective* discussion of basic issues that was now aimed at. Emphasis was placed on smaller and less formal gatherings and discussion groups, and the party called for the training of speakers who specialized on certain subjects such as the trade-union movement or problems of economics.

Thus, in the period of the New Economic Policy, political agitation was clearly predominant. Although its forces were limited and agitation was therefore primarily in the hands of a small group of specialists, the party sought to popularize Marxist doctrine and explain its policy to the population. Agitation was, as a result, carried on in small groups and was closely linked with general adult education.

THE INITIAL PERIOD OF INDUSTRIALIZATION: 1927-1934

The reconstruction program under the New Economic Policy was largely completed by the end of 1926, and new construction was progressively undertaken. In the last quarter of 1928 the First Five Year Plan was launched, and the Soviet Union embarked on a course of action that was to have a profound impact on all aspects of the national life. The Five Year Plan was mainly financed by means of a program of enforced savings at an extremely high rate, which initially produced a marked decline in living standards. It also required sharp improvements in labor productivity, which at first could be secured only by the exertion of extra-human effort on the part of the workers.[11] Both of these courses of action had in common the

---

*The word "objective" is far from being favored in the Bolshevik lexicon. Its frequent use at this time is an indication of the relatively liberal attitude of the party toward agitation in the period of reconstruction.

fact that they increased the sacrifices the party was asking the people to make. This increased the party's need for an effective instrument with which to mobilize the people in support of its policy and in the execution of their assigned tasks. At the same time, millions of new workers were being drawn into industry, under the most difficult conditions of rapid social change and in the face of extreme scarcities of housing, food, goods, and other necessities. The problem of integrating these workers into the new and changing industrial order emphasized the need for a more effective instrument for mobilizing the collective efforts of the population.

The party felt that the needs created by the industrialization program could not be met by agitation of the type dominant under the New Economic Policy with its prime concentration on cultural development and general political education. The great demand from 1926 on was for agitation that was concrete and practical. This shift affected the party's agitation policy in two major respects.

In the first place, agitation was decisively geared in with the needs of production. As early as 1926 the *Agitator's Guidebook* warned that it could not safely be assumed that in order to get higher quality work it was sufficient "to explain, to persuade, to appeal." Although this had been taken as an article of faith in earlier years, it now came to be viewed as a mistaken notion. In the words of the *Guidebook*, there were "unfortunately . . . still many comrades who continue to think that the masses may be educated by books, by speeches at meetings, but not by practical communal work."[12] Local agitators were told that it was especially important "to root out the conception of agitation as the *popularizer* of the line of the Party . . . and to sharpen the role of agitation as the *organizer* of the masses."[13] And this new trend was given sanction in the highest quarters when Stalin warned the party that unless it stopped talking about things "in general" and came to work on practical measures for getting those things done, it stood in danger "of drowning in empty chatter."[14]

The party formalized this new policy in a basic decision laying down the tasks of agitation during the period of industrialization, in which it declared: "Under the conditions of reconstruction of the entire economy, political agitation must mobilize the widest masses of the working class for active and conscious participation in socialist construction, directing the energies of the masses to overcoming the difficulties of that construction."[15] The key words in this statement are active and conscious, for they reflect the fact that the party still sought to have its agitation serve a dual purpose, simultaneously exerting an ideological influence and serving to improve the organization of the work process on farms and in factories.

Thus, along with his more practical tasks of striving to secure order and cleanliness in the workers' barracks, of urging the workers to eliminate waste and increase productivity, and of organizing and spreading the socialist competition and shock-worker movements, the agitator was still expected to undertake a great deal of general political agitation. This was, of course, given a more practical emphasis. For example, agitators were told that rather than attempt to explain the complicated questions of economic and political policy which underlay the Plans, they should seek to familiarize the worker with and clarify the many practical decisions being adopted by the party and government to regulate wages, hours of work, the rationing system, and so on.[16]

But during the first years of the Plans, the rise of labor productivity was not fully satisfactory. The party also faced a serious deterioration in the quality of the goods produced, and an extraordinarily high rate of labor turnover. Under those conditions it became even more insistent after 1930 that agitation be directly geared in with the needs of production. The party charged that there was too much emphasis on the "superficial explanation" of the measures adopted by it and the government, and not enough effort at organizing the workers to fulfill the demands placed before the country.[17] Lest there be any doubt in the minds of the agitators, they were told that "it is perfectly clear that production agitation is a composite part of political agitation and by no means opposed to it."[18] Agitation which failed to result in this better organization of the masses, which was not filled with material bearing directly on improved production, was termed the agitation of windbags.[19]

The second major effect of the plans was on the forms and the patterning of oral agitation activities. The small face-to-face group became the standard form, and the conduct of agitation was regularized and systematized.

Initially, the tremendous influx of new workers into the plants and the shortage of agitators combined to encourage a trend away from the classroom atmosphere that was prevalent during the New Economic Policy. Mass meetings were prescribed as the best agitation form, and these tended to range from shop meetings of about eighty persons to factory-wide meetings of several thousands of workers.[20] So long as the emphasis was on the explanation of the measures adopted by the party and government, these large meetings were fairly well adapted to their purposes. But they encouraged agitators to judge the success of their efforts by the number of meetings held and the size of the audience which attended,[21] a manifestation of the tendency to equate quantity with quality which was widely prevalent throughout Soviet life at the time.* And they were characterized by the fact that intimate contact between speaker and audience was not possible.

After 1930 agitators were instructed to give less attention to the size of their audience and to concentrate on visible results in the form of greater production records and higher quality.[22] And in order to achieve this they were advised to abandon mass meetings and to expand agitation conducted on a face-to-face basis with small groups. In effect this meant an end to factory-wide meetings and a shift in the focus of attention to the individual shop or work brigade, where the agitator could know each worker in the group, could orient himself toward particular problems, and could concentrate on concrete production tasks. It was felt that in this way it would be possible to have an immediate index of the success of agitation, and quickly to take measures to correct any deficiencies in agitation that were revealed.[23]

In addition, the mass meetings of the early years of the First Plan were conducted irregularly and sporadically. Agitation was conducted only at the time of special campaigns, which were largely geared in with the special efforts to "storm" the heights of production at the end of each quarterly plan period in order to meet the quotas. Just as this practice in production came to be called the

*As a prominent economist has somewhat dryly phrased it: ". . . enthusiasm for quantitative achievement was prevalent in the early years of the Plan." Baykov, *Development of Soviet Economic System*, p. 162.

"storm-craze," so in agitation it was labeled the "campaign-craze." But the party was interested in a smooth flow of production, day in and day out. Agitation was, therefore, henceforth to become a "daily" function in the plant, a continuous process carried on without being harnessed to the quarterly periods or restricted to special occasions such as the revolutionary holidays.[24]

The party's action on these and related matters brought oral agitation in industry to the highest peak in a course of development which had begun with the first efforts of over-all planning in the late twenties. A formal and systematic pattern for conducting agitation had been evolved, and it was a steady and regular, if not actually a daily, component of factory life. Agitation activities were concentrated at the shop and work-brigade level, and in this way it was possible to utilize agitation directly in improving the flow of work and the production process in general. In content, agitation was concerned primarily with concrete and practical problems relating to production, techniques of work, labor discipline, the reduction of waste, and labor productivity. The forms used were adapted to these prescribed functions and to the required content. The mass meeting was largely replaced by agitation in small groups, in which the agitator personally knew the work of each member of the group and could therefore effectively criticize, praise, advise, and exhort. Thus, in 1934, the *Agitator's Guidebook* was able to declare that more than in any earlier period it was clear to all that the basic responsibility of the Bolshevik agitator was to tie in his activities with concrete production problems so that "the result of agitation must without fail be the organization of the masses."[25]

The overwhelming emphasis on problems of production in oral agitation which was thus developed did not mean the formal abandonment by the party of the conception of agitation as having a dual role, responsible both for political "education" and for facilitating the solution of the country's economic problems. On the contrary, the instructions to agitators continued to speak of the necessity of explaining such things as the causes of the class struggle. Agitators were still charged with responsibility for the development of a "socialist consciousness" in the rank and file of the working class, and for the elimination of the remnants of "capitalist consciousness" among the people. Under the pressure to get out more production and to advance the economic development of the country, however, the interpretation of these directives did not produce real political agitation, but simply another variation of the agitation already directly geared to the needs of production. Thus, in practice, the efforts to eliminate the remnants of "capitalist consciousness" among the workers were translated into a campaign against people who disrupted labor discipline, against industrial "saboteurs," and others similarly labeled as "class enemies."[26] To a large extent, therefore, one of the two functions of agitation, that having to do with assisting in the resolution of economic tasks, had absorbed the function of political education. Political agitation had lost its character as such and had become essentially a mere phase of practical economic agitation.

THE STABILIZATION OF SOCIAL RELATIONS: FROM THE END OF RATIONING TO THE WAR · 1935-1941

At the close of 1934 the first steps were taken to bring rationing to an end, and this event marked the beginning of a new phase of development in the Soviet Union. During the years of the First Plan a prodigious expansion of industry had been achieved, although at great material cost and with immeasurable human sacrifice. Once this industry had been established, however, it was necessary to concentrate on its effective exploitation. And after great numbers of new workers had been swept into industry, it was necessary to train and to equip them technically. The party recognized that in significant measure the success of these efforts depended on the mental state and the "quality" of the available human material. As Stalin phrased it in 1935, "we have . . . emerged from the period of dearth in technique . . . [and] we have entered a new period, a period . . . of a dearth in people, in cadres [skilled labor]."[27]

At the same time that the party sought to consolidate the gains made in the industrialization program, it undertook a reëxamination of policy in the political and social spheres. The country had for a long period been running more or less on its nerves, pushed on by pressure from without exerted by the party. An effort was now made to get the system thus established to operate more efficiently and naturally under the impetus of its own internal dynamics. This required a program of social and political legislation ranging from changes in the family law to the introduction of the "democratic" Stalin Constitution.

Meanwhile, there was a major change in the nation's external situation. The rise of Hitler and the subsequent events in Spain left the Soviet leaders with little doubt that the Soviet regime might before long be engaged in a military struggle for its very existence. And it was clear that whatever the economic capabilities of the nation, the Soviet regime could not undertake a successful defense against a powerful onslaught without the support of widespread patriotism and loyalty to the regime throughout the mass of the population.

All of these developments led the party in the same direction. Each of them suggested the need for a return, in some degree, to agitation which was broader, more political and educational, than the agitation which had been predominant during the first years of industrialization and collectivization. Under pressure of an overwhelming drive to organize and to build industry, the party had concentrated on measures to control men's actions and to exhort them to greater effort. But the changed conditions that the party now faced led it to seek measures to strengthen its influence over men's minds and to encourage them to greater productivity through their own initiative. It is significant that early in 1935 *Pravda* found it appropriate and necessary to prepare a special editorial entitled "Agitation is a Great Art," in which it declared that recent developments had posed the problem of agitation in a new light and had increased the importance of persuasion. Whereas previously coercive administrative measures had been indicated, said *Pravda,* the basic approach should now be talking to people and explaining things to them.[28]

The party sought to broaden the scope of its agitation by giving more attention to political questions, and by extending agitation to include more discussions of social developments, foreign affairs, and other previously neglected areas. Words like "explanation," "clarification," and "education" reappeared with increasing frequency in the pages of the *Agitator's Guidebook*. The Central Committee reviewed the agitation activities of the local party units in 1935 and found their work in the realm of political explanation inadequate and unsatisfactory. Political agitation, the Central Committee declared, was being neglected in the factories, and the explanation of political problems had been limited merely to very general speeches made only on the occasions when major political campaigns such as elections were in progress.[29]

Local agitators were instructed, therefore, to concentrate on the major acts of the party and government; the abolition of rationing, the improvement in the supply of consumers' goods through cooperatives, and the readjustment in wage scales. Soviet foreign policy, the Italo-Abyssinian War, events in Spain's Civil War, were all to be given more attention. Developments in social life, especially the changes in the educational system and in the laws governing abortion, marriage, and divorce, were made the subjects of agitation campaigns. In its turn, the new Soviet Constitution, adopted in 1936, was made the center of a campaign of political agitation which surpassed in intensity anything the U.S.S.R. had seen before.[30] The extent of this shift in emphasis back to political questions was highlighted in the new set of model rules adopted in 1938 to guide the agit-collectives. Statements of the kind prevalent in the early years of the Plans, such as "to agitate is to organize," were notable in their absence from these new rules. Instead, agitators were told: "To agitate is not to administrate, but rather, to persuade."[31]

Along with the broadening of agitation beyond the narrow problems of getting out production, the party sought to extend the coverage of its agitation.[32] Thus, in his address to the plenary session of the Central Committee in 1937, called to discuss preparations for the new "free" elections, Zhdanov urged the party to give particular attention to collective farmers, employees, members of the intelligentsia, housewives, students, and the non-Russian nationality groups, all of whom had been insufficiently covered by the agitation previously concentrated at the factory level.[33] The agitation conducted among employees, housewives, and students, who were not directly connected with the production tasks of shop and farm, was primarily political rather than being simply geared in with the organizational needs of industry and agriculture. It thus gave further impetus to the trend toward a return to educational instead of merely practical agitation.

The party also found it necessary to make changes in the forms utilized in agitation and to adjust the tone of its appeals. It recognized that the type of agitation it had directed toward the new factory hands fresh from the countryside might not be equally effective in inducing a skilled worker to rationalize his production process and become a Stakhanovite. And entirely new methods and approaches were needed to handle such problems as inculcating patriotism and loyalty to the regime, or a "socialist" attitude toward women and the family.

Consequently, local agitators were told that they were needed not only to mobilize the population, but to reëducate them and to reform their attitudes as well. Agitators were instructed to make their material more interesting, and to make wider use of literary materials, political tracts, and newspapers. They were advised to give more attention to the individual, and to give personal attention to workers who lagged behind the others. In addition to daily agitation in the shop, local party organizations were ordered to hold periodically a special *politden'*, or political day, which would include a question period during which the questions of workers could be answered by the officials of the party, the trade unions, and the plant management.[34] It is most interesting, finally, to note that agitators were advised, in discussing their "professional" duties, to avoid the use of such "vulgar and banal" expressions as the following: "to train" (as a dog), "to pump up," "to set (like a bone) the mind," "to drive in" (as a nail),[35] and so on.

These shifts in agitation policy after 1935 by no means meant that agitation no longer was concentrated primarily at the factory-shop level, or that the problems of increasing production were no longer the central focus of attention. On the contrary, the instructions of the Central Committee to local agitators advised them to concentrate their explanatory work on clarifying the meaning of the Stakhanovite movement, on disseminating the experiences of the best Stakhanovite workers, and on drawing more workers into the movement.[36] And in the model rules for agitators adopted in 1938, this work on the Stakhanovite movement, along with that of mobilizing the workers for fulfillment of the Plan, was placed second only to the agitators' general responsibility to explain to the masses the policies of the party and government.[37]

But although the close connection between agitation and economic tasks persisted, the emphasis was much less strident. The element of storm was gone. Production problems no longer virtually engulfed all the other aspects of agitation. For the moment the balance between the practical economic ends of agitation and the more general political and educational goals had been restored.

But the balance developed after 1934 between political discussions and agitation directly related to increasing production was a delicate one. Maintenance of this balance depended on the condition that the party should feel sufficiently secure in the progress of industrial and agricultural production to permit diverting a significant portion of the average agitator's time to the discussion of political subjects. The whole history of the party's agitation policy indicated that, if the pressure on production became severe, political agitation would be sacrificed to agitation which was directly geared in with the needs of industry and agriculture. The unmistakable approach of war in the late thirties created just such a pressure on production, and its effect was once again to shift the balance between political and production agitation.

As the threat of war increased, the party intensified its efforts to bend every phase of the nation's activities to support of the program of military preparedness. The country was soon experiencing a new crisis in production, and the atmosphere associated with such crises in the past soon was apparent. A review of the contribution being made by agitation led to the conclusion that it was inadequate. The *Agitator's Guidebook* declared that the emphasis on political agitation in the preceding years had resulted in a weakening of production agitation. There were too many agitators, the *Guidebook* complained, who "stood aside from economic tasks." Agitators were criticized for approaching their duties as if agitation were merely an "educational task," instead of approaching it as an instrument for mobilizing people. The duty of all party organizations and all agitators, declared the *Guidebook,* was to unite "mass political with mass economic work," in order to press for the resolution of the outstanding economic problems and for the fulfillment of the Plan.[38]

This meant that the agitator had to be vigorous in carrying the fight to people who shirked, to the "floaters" and the "do-nothingers" in the plant. It also meant, the agitators were told, that the effectiveness of their agitation could not be judged simply on the basis of figures about the number of group sessions held and the size of the attendance. Instead, the agitators were to ask themselves whether their efforts mobilized the workers in the resolution of the specific tasks before them. The basic question, said the *Guidebook* in 1939, was: "Does the work of the brigade, shift, or department improve? There is the aspect that the Party organizations are concerned about."[39]

This kind of criticism, of course, came very close to the type that had arisen under similar pressure to get out more production in the early days of the First Plan. But the return was far from complete, for the party had learned at least some lessons from its earlier experience. The factory-wide mass meetings and the mass exhortation of the early thirties had too clearly revealed their inadequacy. The policy of centering agitation at the level of the particular shop and work brigade remained firmly entrenched, and indeed the party went even further by bringing agitation down to the level of the individual worker where necessary. And although political agitation was once again pushed somewhat into the background, it was far from being ignored. The Eighteenth Congress (1939) had stressed the need for a vigorous campaign to educate the people in the "spirit of communism." The agitators were warned that this did not constitute an invitation to hold general lectures on communism, but it did mean that they should seek to develop in the workers a "socialist attitude" toward labor. And, the party cautioned, the agitator could not expect that after one or two sessions the average worker or collective farmer would become "fully conscious" and understand the party's policy. The agitator was told that he had to realize that he was dealing with living people, who were held back by a "heavy burden" of past tradition and old habits. For these reasons, the agitators were advised, they could not throw up their hands in disappointment on the first failure, but were obliged painstakingly, firmly, and vigorously to carry on their work for the party line.[40] To this extent, at least, it would appear that the party had learned some of the lessons of giving fuller account in its plans to the human factor, and to the state of men's minds.*

Despite the significant changes in the party's agitation policy, traced above, personal oral agitation has manifested certain important and consistent lines of development during the years of Soviet rule. At present, personal oral agitation is systematically carried on in virtually every plant in the Soviet Union, more or less as a regular part of the daily work routine. This agitation is based on a stable and integrated organizational structure, which reaches from the Department of Propaganda and Agitation in Moscow down to the primary organization's agit-collective in some local factory or collective farm. The party has enrolled a great corps of nonprofessional agitators drawn from the local workers and intelligentsia, loyal to the party, and trained and experienced in agitation. This corps of agitators makes it possible for the party to place its emphasis on group and even individual agitation, and to vary its approach to take account of differences in the composition, location, and duties of the audiences to which it directs its message.†

Thus, the party has striven during its thirty years of rule to weld its agitation activities into an ever more effective instrument for mobilizing the workers of the Soviet Union and, along with them, the rest of the population. The availability of that instrument must be recognized as a central element in accounting for the capabilities the Soviet regime demonstrated during the recent war with Germany. The story of the party's wartime efforts at mobilizing

---

*A complete history of the Communist Party in the Soviet Union could be written around the theme of learning to take account of the human factor in planning. There have been many times when the party, as in the instance cited above, appeared to have learned its lesson. But again and again, under the pressure of immediate needs, the party has resorted to forced measures and to effecting change by wholesale decree. This is that "Bolshevik conceit" of which Lenin spoke as early as 1921.

†The factory-wide gathering or mass meeting is still utilized, however, to supplement individual and group agitation. These meetings, which may be attended by several thousand persons, are called to hear the reading of important government or party decisions, to "discuss" factory-wide problems, or to present the answers to those questions which the shop agitators report as common throughout the factory work groups. Kremneva, *Experience of Political Agitation*, pp. 41-45.

the Soviet population requires a special study in itself and cannot be presented here. But it is important to recognize that almost as soon as the Soviet Union entered the postwar period, the basic tensions which inhere in Soviet agitation policy once again became noticeable.

The party's agitation work in the postwar period has been governed by two major decisions of the Central Committee. The first of these, adopted in March 1946, set forth the agitation and propaganda tasks of the party organizations in connection with the launching of the Fourth Five Year Plan. This decision followed the well-established pattern of emphasis on agitation as a crucial force in affecting the mobilization of the population for the fulfillment of the Plan. It instructed the local organizations to explain the importance of the Plan to the workers, to foster socialist competition, to struggle for high productivity and low costs in the production of goods, and so on.[41]

But little more than a year had elapsed before the party found it necessary to adopt a second decision to deal with the inadequacies which it felt were present in the agitation work under the Fourth Plan. The Central Committee discovered what it described as an "intolerable" situation. Mass political work was described as being in a state of neglect resulting from the fact that many of the local organizations deprecated the importance of political agitation and conducted it only as an adjunct to the agitation sessions on technical production problems. It found that the most ·important aspects of the internal and foreign policies of the party and government were receiving little attention, and were being only superficially clarified for the workers and the peasants. In addition, most of the other characteristic difficulties of Soviet agitation policy, treated in earlier chapters of this study, revealed themselves as still being very much in evidence. Thus, the Central Committee found that local party officials dodged their responsibility personally to conduct agitation and instruct the agitators, that agitators were selected mechanically, without due consideration of their qualifications, and were improperly trained and guided after their selection, and so on.[42]

This brief sketch should suffice to indicate that the Soviet Union continues to experience real difficulty in its effort to utilize the same agitation system both to effect general political education and to conduct practical, concrete agitation for higher production. For in such a balance there is always the strong possibility that production agitation, which serves short-run ends and can produce immediate and visible results, will replace political education, which is oriented to long-run goals and which produces relatively intangible results. Since the need to improve production has always been pressing, and since the party has tended to evaluate the efficiency of its local officials in terms of the production record of their areas, the subordination of political education to production agitation has been a consistent phenomenon in the Soviet Union.

It may be anticipated, furthermore, that so long as this pressure for higher production continues to be a feature of Soviet society, and it is likely that it will be for some time, the tension in Soviet agitation policy between the needs of production and of political education will continue to manifest itself.

8

ORAL AGITATION
AND THE SOVIET SYSTEM

To SUMMARIZE THE ROLE PLAYED IN SOVIET SOCIETY BY the complex of relations that has been called personal oral agitation, three elements must be taken into account: the functions that agitation fulfills for the party, the needs it meets for its audiences, and the ends it serves for the Bolshevik agitator.

The leaders of the Communist Party determine basic social, political, and economic policy for Soviet society as a whole. But they must have some system for carrying that policy to the people, winning some degree of popular support for it, and, finally, mobilizing the population for its execution. The Bolshevik agitator makes his contribution to effective party leadership primarily at the level of bringing party policy to the people and seeking to enlist their support. But he plays an important part in bringing the leaders information that they must have as a basis for determining policy, and he has a central role in securing execution of policy.

1. The first and most obvious contribution of the agitator to effective party leadership is to increase and improve the coverage of the media of communication. The size and national diversity of the Soviet population, and the extent of the nation's territory, pose a major problem in mass communication. The difficulty is rendered more acute by paper shortages, by transportation bottlenecks, and by the inadequacy in the Soviet Union of the supreme mass medium—the radio.[1] Oral agitation, therefore, acts as a constant major supplement to the more formal media of communication. The inestimable value of that supplement was amply demonstrated during the recent

war, especially in besieged cities like Leningrad, where the local officials were able to keep in almost continuous contact with the population through the network of agitators at times when the newspaper and radio were unable to function.[2]

But beyond supplementing the other media, oral agitation lends an element of certainty to mass communication that is otherwise lacking. For even when available, the newspaper may not be read or the radio listened to, and when they are, the reading and listening may be selective, so that the party cannot be certain that its most important message is getting across. This is, of course, in many respects the same problem faced by the advertiser who utilizes the news value of the paper or the attraction of the radio to carry his advertising message.

The presence of the Bolshevik agitator gives the party additional assurance that its message will get across. His audience is visible and can be measured without complicated research devices and testing techniques. And that audience does not have to be attracted or mobilized to act—as in opening and reading the paper or turning on the radio—since the agitator comes to the audience and not the other way around. This, in turn, makes it possible to concentrate on just those elements the party wishes to emphasize at any given point without dilution of the material. Finally, since one of the major duties of the local agitator is to read aloud from the daily newspaper, he provides what is in a sense a certain "guaranteed read" circulation figure for the daily press.

This description represents, of course, the potentialities of personal agitation rather than its actual performance in the U.S.S.R. Soviet journals give no evidence to indicate the use of coercion, either direct or indirect, to get workers to attend agitation sessions. On the contrary, there are many reports indicating that frequently attendance may run as low as 10 per cent, in other places may average as low as 25 to 30 per cent, and frequently cannot be gotten above 50 per cent without extra effort.[3] In order to improve attendance, both the party organizations and individual agitators have introduced extra attractions into agitation, ranging from such simple devices as making the announcement of agitation sessions more inviting and interesting, to introducing group discussions of recent films and books which have special political interest. There is the possibility, therefore, that the audience may give attention to these "trimmings" to an extent that weakens the impact of the main agitation message. Furthermore, those who stay away from agitation sessions may be informally sanctioned through the withholding of theater tickets and other favors which local authorities, particularly the trade unions, dispense. Finally, those who persistently and willfully avoid agitation sessions may subject themselves to suspicion of political opposition and consequent investigation by the secret police. Clearly, in so far as the agitation audience is in any significant measure such an unwilling audience, the effectiveness of oral agitation must be in equal measure less effective.

2. The group agitation of the oral agitator provides a setting in which the party's agitation is most likely to be effective. Like all agitation and propaganda, that of the party is designed to affect attitudes and through attitudes to affect actions. Contemporary research in the field of attitude formation and change indicates that very frequently the effectiveness of formal methods such as films, articles, and lectures is less than had been anticipated.[4] Related research investigations have established the fact that a group setting, and particularly group discussion, are highly effective instruments for changing attitudes.[5] To a large extent the work of the Bolshevik agitator, since it includes regular contact in a group setting and provides an opportunity for group discussion, creates a situation which should be conducive to effective attitude formation.* This is especially important in the Soviet Union, where the party has been attempting to introduce great numbers of new values on a large scale in a very short space of time. Thus, personal oral agitation may be regarded as having served under conditions of rapid social change in the Soviet Union as a functional equivalent, at whatever low degree of intensity, for the family and the school, which in more stable societies have chief responsibility for communicating and inculcating the basic social values and symbols.

---

*The more personal the medium, the more effective it is in converting opinions. This means . . . that personal conversation is more effective than a radio speech, and that a radio speech is more effective than a newspaper account of it." Bernard Berelson, in Schramm (ed.), *Communications in Modern Society*, p. 172.

3. The Bolshevik agitator provides an important personal link between the party and the people. The party takes unto itself virtually sole and absolute responsibility for the formulation of policy, and in so far as its decisions frequently impose additional burdens on the population, the party runs a constant risk of creating a severe gulf between itself and the masses. Since the press and the radio are essentially formal and impersonal, they can bridge this gap only to a very limited extent. In part, the party seeks to minimize antagonism by demanding of all its members that they stand as examples and models in effort and sacrifice.* But it is the Bolshevik agitator who provides the really personal link between the party and masses. It is not some distant and impersonal force which the average worker sees as transmitting impersonal orders and making impersonal demands. On the contrary, it is a fellow worker or a foreman whom he knows and sees regularly who transmits these orders, who explains the demands, and who places the force of his own personal standing in support of the party or government decision.

And unlike a newspaper or radio, to which no response is possible and with which one cannot carry on a discussion or directly demand further explanation and clarification, the Bolshevik agitator is a person with whom each of these activities is possible. The Bolshevik agitator makes possible not simply the transmission but the explanation of party decisions, and through him the party is able to carry on not simply one-way communication but a form of two-way communication.

4. Furthermore, since the agitator is a real person, visible and tangible, he serves as a convenient target against which his listeners may direct aggression, hostility, and discontent. This is not equally possible with an impersonal object like a newspaper or radio. The Bolshevik agitator must be seen, therefore, as serving the party as an immediate target for the people's reactions to party policy. He is an instrument which serves to siphon off energies that might otherwise build up within the population to explosive proportions, or that

*The Rules of the party state as one of the four major obligations of the member that he "set an example in the observance of labor and state discipline." *Eighteenth Congress,* p. 678.

might be directed at more distant and, from the leaders' point of view, less desirable targets, such as the party leadership itself.

5. Personal oral agitation makes possible a high degree of differentiation in the content of agitation and facilitates concentration on pressing problems of a local nature. The mass media are relatively inflexible—a newspaper designed to reach several hundred thousand readers or a radio program with an even larger audience can only imperfectly take account of the tremendous differences in the membership of its audience.* The local agitator can adapt his work to the precise composition of his audience, and, unlike the newspaper or radio man, he knows the mood of his audience in advance. If he is skillful, his own experience will tell him what in his agitation can be effective, when, and why. He can adjust the form and content of his agitation almost instantaneously to take account of changed conditions.

The party, as already indicated, has oriented its agitation work very largely to the solution of production problems. But production problems vary widely from group to group, and the formal media are not able to take account of these variations. The local agitator is able to adjust his agitation to these concrete demands. Furthermore, he and the party have available a constant test of the effectiveness of that agitation in the form of production records, figures on the reduction of waste, lower rates of labor turnover,† and so on, and hence there is a continuous opportunity to make agitation conform to the fluctuations in these indexes.

6. One other important aspect of the flexibility of local oral agitation is its adaptability to work with individuals. The formal media

---

*The Soviet press and particularly the Soviet radio have been specifically designed and structured so that they give the greatest possible flexibility in taking account of such local differences. See Chapter 10 and Chapter 16.

†Agitation and propaganda officials in the Soviet Union frequently appear to attribute the success or failure of production to the effectiveness or lack of effectiveness of agitation to a degree which overlooks or excludes other very relevant influences. Thus, when the Novaya Ivanovskaya Manufaktura plant fulfilled its plan in advance and improved the quality of its product, the *Agitator's Guidebook* queried: "In what lies the secret of these noteworthy victories of the Party and non-Party Bolsheviks at the N.I.M. plant? It consists first of all in that the Party and Komsomol were able correctly to place their forces and to organize skillfully the Party-mass work and Bolshevik agitation in the shops." No. 3 (1940), p. 16.

of communication are essentially mass media. But there is always a significant number, if not percentage, of the people who stand outside the main stream of influence of the mass media or who present problems beyond the scope of those instruments. It is at this level that the personal agitator may be most effective, and it is for this reason that the party has stressed the development and extension of what it calls "individual" agitation.

7. Finally, the local agitator serves the party as a constant source of information on the attitudes and state of mind of the population. For obvious political reasons, mass public-opinion testing by modern sampling techniques has not been developed in the U.S.S.R., and the corps of agitators is consequently expected to serve the party as a kind of substitute for an apparatus of scientific public-opinion testing.* Thus, the agitator is told:

> Along with this [his agitation] the agitator should remember that he is the instrument through which the Party organizations come to know thoroughly the attitudes of the workers, the sources of negative views characteristic of particular groups of workers; they must be able to warn their Party organizations of gaps, disorders, inadequacies, and perversions of which we still have many in the plant, in the practical struggle for the plan, for workers' supply and workers' living conditions.[6]

Each agitator is expected to keep a careful account of the questions asked by the workers and the problems in which they show special interest. These are reported to and discussed by the agit-collective; they are then collected and collated by the director of the agit-collective and passed on by him to the local party committee, and thence on up the various levels of the party hierarchy. Thus, the local Bolshevik agitator makes his contribution to seeing that "from top to bottom and from bottom to top" there must be an uninterrupted flow of information on the state of mind of the masses.[7] At the same time, however, one must recognize the very real limitation on the effectiveness of this method of assessing public opinion which

---

*A similar role is played by the nonprofessional corps of worker and peasant correspondents (rabsel'kor). See Chapter 14. The general significance for effective party leadership of some form of testing public opinion has already been discussed. See Chapter 2.

lies in the position of the agitator vis-à-vis the party. For in so far as there is considerable unrest in his group and he reports this unrest accurately, he tends thereby to throw some doubt on his effectiveness as an agitator. The system leaves itself open, therefore, to serious padding in the reporting by the local agitator.

So much for the functions which personal oral agitation serves for the party. Attention must now be turned to the ways in which group agitation and the Bolshevik agitator affect the local work group.

1. Oral agitation serves as a convenient source of information about current local and national events for the members of the work group. For this reason, the workers' interest in the agitator's activities should not be underestimated. Many of the workers do not have the initiative (and some are unable) to read the daily newspaper, and access to radios is limited. At the same time, there is every evidence that the workers in the Soviet Union have at least as lively an interest in current events as do workers elsewhere. The agitator, reading aloud from the newspaper, presenting a news digest, or giving a report about Soviet foreign policy, acts as a convenient and effortless source of news for his group.

In addition, the agitator serves as a source for information of more immediate interest to the workers. At various times Soviet workers have found themselves overwhelmed by the welter of regulations surrounding their work, the complicated pay schedules, the elaborate rules of labor discipline, and other involved matters likely to bewilder the ordinary man, especially since these regulations have changed so frequently and sometimes so radically. In addition to its trade-union representatives, the small working group may turn to its group agitator for the explanation and clarification of these matters. It is his duty as an agitator to provide answers to such questions, and because he can, through the agit-collective, bring questions to the party committee for clarification, he is a valuable man to the members of his group.

2. Thus, the agitator provides the people with a direct line of communication with the party and the local governing authorities. In many ways his position between the party secretary and the group

of workers is the equivalent for the Soviet one-party system of the role played by the block captain who stands between the local residents and the ward boss in the American two-party system. Regarding him as the immediate representative of the party, the workers can, and apparently do, bring him personal problems arising out of their contacts with the bureaucracy; and they expect him to aid in a solution of such difficulties through the utilization of his knowledge of the administrative apparatus and his contacts in the party.

The agitator operates, furthermore, as an instrument through which the workers in his group can register complaints and impress their desires on the party committee for whatever they may be worth. Again, there is a clear link here with the Soviet one-party system, for the agitator who serves the local people as a line of contact with the party acts in part as a substitute for a system of free competitive elections. Soviet citizens can't "throw the rascals out" in the manner of the two-party system, but they can apply pressure through the instrument of the group agitator. The group agitator may, in addition, himself become the immediate target for the release of aggression against the party or the state of affairs in general, and he thus makes a certain catharsis possible for the group members in an otherwise severely circumscribed arena of targets for political aggression.*

3. The work of the group agitator serves as a focus for group activities, and in this respect local agitation performs a real social function for the workers of the shop or farm work brigade. This is one of the unintended consequences of the party's agitation program, but there are no indications that party officials, in so far as they recognize this fact, are at all opposed to it. Indeed, it often gears in to strengthen the effect of the agitation, as indicated by the remarks of that worker who said that as a result of the agitator's efforts he came to feel that the work brigade was like a family of which he was a member and toward which he had responsibilities.[8] Thus, the program of oral agitation provides an opportunity for the members of the work group to participate in a regular and focused social-

---

*An even more important partial substitute for competitive elections in the Soviet system is the practice of *samokritika* or self-criticism. It also plays a central role in the release of aggression. See Chapter 14.

group situation. Furthermore, in as much as the agitator is responsible for spreading the socialist competition movement, he may become a force in developing a team spirit within his group.

4. At the same time, it must be recognized that the attitude of the workers toward oral agitation can hardly be completely without ambivalence. In the person of the group agitator the party has placed in the midst of the work group one of its special representatives. It is largely in his person and through his activities that the workers experience the pressure that the party is so frequently applying for more production and for greater effort. These aspects of the agitator's work have frequently aroused the antagonism of the workers, and, as has been seen, this has posed one of the most difficult problems for the group agitator. And in so far as the workers come to associate oral agitation with the imposition of new burdens and the presentation of new demands, then a situation is created in which large numbers of workers will avoid these sessions as omens of ill tidings. Moreover, there will be greatly reduced chances that the party will be able to get its more positive messages across in a context which, on the whole, the workers view negatively.

Finally, consideration must be given to the ends agitation serves for the group agitator himself. What is there in the position that keeps the agitator on the job and enables the party to maintain this great force of nonprofessional and unpaid workers in its service?

1. The availability of agitators is primarily determined by the fact that agitation is a party duty to which members may be assigned. This statement, of course, merely raises a second question about why people join or remain members of the party, but answering that question is not a responsibility of this study.

2. A very real factor in the motivation of agitators, which it would be a mistake to minimize, is the conviction of many that the policies they are expounding are correct and the work they are performing is significant and meaningful. People who are unfamiliar with or unable to grasp the fervor of the convinced Bolshevik, which has certain basic common elements with the fervor of the religious zealot or the passionate adherent to any social movement, will be unable to credit this factor. It is a most powerful force, nevertheless,

as almost no end of evidence will testify. The confirmed Bolshevik, the vigorous believer in the correctness of the party's policy and its general line, forms the backbone of the agitator cadres.* Party officials are of course quick to recognize the value of such persons as agitators, and have made clear their preference for agitators who are people of "political conviction." The following example is an expression of that attitude.

The basic foundation of agitation is the force of personal conviction. If the orator comes forward . . . without firm conviction in the justice of the slogans for which he is agitating, the audience will have no faith in him and will not follow him. Without internal conviction there is no agitation. If you believe in the correctness of the Party slogans for which you agitate, then it will not be particularly difficult to make others believe, and the necessary words will come to you, clear, simple, from the heart. If you do not believe in them, then no manner of beautiful phrases will conceal from the masses the falsity of your speech.[9]

3. It is not necessary to be a political zealot, however, since the role of agitator has many potentialities for personal gratification and emotional reward which act as a stimulus to keep the agitator at his duties. In the first place, all personality types who enjoy the role of teacher have an opportunity as group agitators to fulfill their interests and drives in that direction, for the local agitator to a large extent plays the part of adult educator. Agitation also provides an outlet for those inclined toward the role of town crier, and for those who have a penchant for the oratorical or for dramatic reading. In the second place, it provides a route within the group by which the individual can come to enjoy a considerable degree of social and personal prestige. For the group agitator is something of a local figure; he has a special status-bearing role; and his participation in the agit-collective puts him in the "center" of things, gives him advance knowledge of important goings-on, and allows him personal contact with the local powers. These elements of status and personal

---

*At certain times, as for example during the recent war, the ordinary fervent Soviet patriot served almost as well; and indeed, during the early years of the war, the Soviet patriot rather than the convinced Bolshevik was somewhat preferred as an agitator. A return to the emphasis on the "tempered" or "hardened" Bolshevik appeared before the end of the war and has been predominant in the postwar period.

satisfaction which inhere in the role of group agitator probably play an especially large part in attracting to and keeping in agitation those agitators who are not party members.

4. Despite these potential attractions, it must not be forgotten that under Soviet conditions the agitator's role is extremely demanding and often very difficult. The facts of constant surveillance by the party, which is unceasing in its demands, and of negativism and even hostility on the part of the population, which has so long been hardpressed, face the agitator with a situation which demands to the full that Bolshevik "tempering" or "hardening" of which the party so often speaks. Not all men, not even all party men, can for long periods and in hard times meet the test which this situation poses for them. The result is that many agitators seek to escape their responsibility or perform their tasks in a way which the party judges inadequate, no matter how much the style of performance may ease the agitator's personal burden; and such defections from the ranks, along with a low level of actual performance, must act as a constant limit on the effectiveness of the party's agitation efforts.

PART 3

THE SOVIET PRESS

9

THE SOVIET CONCEPTION OF THE PRESS

VEN THE BRIEFEST CONTACT WITH THE SOVIET PRESS suffices to convince one that he is dealing with a phenomenon that is unique among the major press networks of the world. This impression is, if anything, strengthened when one goes beyond the printed page to Soviet discussions of the role of the newspaper in that society.[1]

Virtually every Soviet discussion of the role of the press begins by declaring that in the hands of the Communist Party and the Soviet government the press is a powerful instrument for the organization, education, and communist upbringing of the masses. The basic slogan provided by Lenin and quoted without fail in all Soviet discussions of the press states: "A newspaper is not only a collective propagandist and collective agitator; it is also a collective organizer."[2] In these discussions there is rarely any mention of how news and news events should be treated, even though that is probably the single most important subject of discussion for the average journalist in the United States or England. It is a striking fact that of the two basic collections of official decisions governing the activities of the press, one does not contain a single reference in its alphabetical index under the various Russian words for news; the second has but four such entries, and of these only two refer to general news.[3]

The Soviet press, of course, is in no sense a business venture, a means of investing capital for profit. Neither is it conceived of as an instrument for expressing the opinions of individual publishers, or as a means of reflecting or mirroring public opinion. The press in the Soviet Union is viewed as a major social force that must be harnessed and adapted to facilitate attainment of the society's defined goals.* And since it is the Communist Party that determines the goals of Soviet society, it is the party that controls the press. The Soviet press is expected to operate on the basis of the principle of *partiinost'*, or militant loyalty to the party. In this sense Stalin has spoken of the press as "a transmission belt between the masses and the Party." Stalin has also stated: "The press is the prime instrument through which the Party speaks daily, hourly, with the working class in its own indispensable language. No other means such as this for weaving spiritual ties between Party and class, no other tool so flexible, is to be found in nature."[4] This conception of the press as being primarily an instrument in the party's effort to eliminate the remnants of capitalism in the consciousness of the people, and to transform them into active builders of communist society, has had its impact on every aspect of the Soviet press.

In the first place, the basic communist position has a marked influence on the Bolshevik conception of press freedom. As a political and social theory, Bolshevism rejects the notion of absolute freedom in society. As Lenin phrased it, "to live in a society and to be free from this society is impossible." Consequently, the Bolsheviks maintain that assertions about the freedom of the press under capitalism are hypocrisy or worse, on the grounds that in a society based on money there can be no freedom from money. The Soviet press would be *free,* declared Lenin, in that it would be free of capital, careerism, and bourgeois anarchistic individualism. Nevertheless, it was to make no claim to *independence,* he affirmed, but would be quite openly tied to the proletariat. Thus, in one of those characteristic Bolshevik turns of phrase, he stated that "the independence of the Bolshevik press rests in the closest dependence on the working class."[5]

Yet despite this rejection of the notion of absolute freedom in society, the Soviet Constitution does declare that "the citizens of the U.S.S.R. are granted by law . . . freedom of the press . . . [and]

---

*It is worth noting, in this connection, that in 1947 *Pravda's* editorial offices were divided into the following units: Party Life, Propaganda, Agriculture, Economics, Foreign Affairs, Letters to the Editor, Information, Press Bureau, Local Newspapers, Military Science and Technology, Literature and Art, and Criticism and Bibliography, *Large Soviet Encyclopedia,* Supplement, p. 1640.

these civil rights are ensured by placing at the disposal of the working people and their organizations printing presses, stocks of paper . . . and other material requisites."[6] It would be a serious failure of understanding, and a major block to grasping what goes on in the Soviet Union, to assume that this constitutional provision is merely sham. For in Soviet thought freedom and responsibility are not merely associated, they are inseparably linked. Responsibility is the hub of a wheel of which the freedoms are simply spokes. Thus, the article in the Constitution which introduces the freedoms granted Soviet citizens begins by stating quite specifically that these freedoms are granted only "in conformity with the interests of the working people, and in order to strengthen the socialist system."[7] And since it is the party which determines what is in conformity with the interests of the people and what strengthens the socialist system, then it is the party which determines when one is free to exercise one's rights and when not.

Thus, if we are able to see the concept of press freedom as bipolar, involving both freedom and responsibility, we are placed in a position to distinguish the significant difference in the Soviet approach to press freedom and that of Western democracy. In the United States and England it is the freedom of expression, the right itself in the abstract, that is valued; and generally no positive considerations may limit its exercise, only negative considerations such as irresponsibility so great as to limit other freedoms or to limit the exercise by others of the same freedom. In the Soviet Union, on the other hand, the *results* of exercising freedom are in the forefront of attention, and preoccupation with the freedom itself is secondary. It is for this reason that discussions between Soviet and Anglo-American representatives characteristically reach absolutely no agreement on specific proposals, although both sides assert that there should be freedom of the press. The American is usually talking about freedom of *expression,* the *right* to say or not say certain things, a right which he claims exists in the United States and not in the Soviet Union. The Soviet representative is usually talking about *access* to the *means* of expression, not the right to say things at all, and this access he maintains is denied to most in the United States and exists for most in the Soviet Union.[8]

It is not our purpose to argue the merits of this case. It is essential, however, for the reader to recognize that when press freedom is seen as a bipolar concept, it is the pole of responsibility that comes first in Soviet thought, and that exercising the right or the freedom is subordinate to the goals such exercise advances. Hence, it is declared to be the responsibility of the press in the Soviet Union to see that elections are a success for the party, that the labor productivity of the people is high, and so on. If in serving these ends the press also provides an opportunity for people to enjoy freedom of the press, well and good; but this consideration of freedom is secondary in the Soviet Union to the responsibilities of the press, and may be and is sacrificed if need be. In the United States the emphasis is placed on freedom rather than on responsibility. Freedom of expression is the absolute value, at least for those who have the means to express themselves; if in so doing they advance the common weal or otherwise act to advance certain social goals and fulfill responsibilities to the society, that too is well and good. But this consideration of the common good is secondary to the freedom of expression and may, if need be, be sacrificed to that freedom.*

A second major aspect of the Bolshevik conception of the press to which attention must be given here is its rejection of the notion of objectivity in newspaper work. This position has its roots in Bolshevik philosophy, and to a lesser extent in all Marxist thought. The emphasis on objectivity is regarded as a device used by bourgeois philosophers and sociologists to establish the supposed stability of capitalist society. The notion of materialism is placed in opposition to this type of objectivity, and it is asserted that a correct approach to objective reality can be made only through dialectical materialism. Thus, Lenin is quoted as having pointed out that a man who sought to be completely "objective" in explaining any set of facts, such as the social composition of some country, always ran the risk of acting as an apologist for the facts he was explaining. In contrast to this

---

*More recently there has been a tendency in American thought to give increasing emphasis to the responsibility of the press, which was highlighted by the fact that the Commission on Freedom of the Press chose for its report the title *A Free and Responsible Press* (Chicago, 1947). There is no evidence of a comparable tendency on the part of Soviet officials to give greater emphasis to freedom of expression.

"objectivist," Lenin suggested, a materialist seeking to explain the same set of facts would concentrate on pointing up the element of class conflict in the social composition of the country with which he dealt, and would therefore emerge with a different picture. In other words, Lenin maintained, the Marxist's approach to reality, or materialism as opposed to "bourgeois objectivism," must include the element of *partiinost'*; and it must evaluate historical events from the point of view of the revolutionary proletariat.[9]

Against this background it is clear why all persons in the Soviet Union who are responsible for the conduct of the media of communication are warned against "objectivity," and why the central authorities have frequently criticized newspaper editors, writers, radio officials, and others for such manifestations. This kind of objectivity is flatly rejected, and only that approach is accepted which advances the cause of the Revolution and the interests of the party and working class which it claims to represent. This attitude permeates the instructions given to Soviet editors, and it determines the selection and the treatment of everything that goes ino Soviet newspapers.

A third aspect of the Soviet approach to the press to which attention must be given is its impact on the conception of what is news and how it should be treated. The conception of what is news is everywhere clearly dependent on the social system. In the United States, news is largely synonymous with events, incidents, and related "timely" happenings or people. The event may be trivial or important, but it is the event which is the focus of interest, and this is expressed in the popular phrase, "If a dog bites a man, that's not news; but if a man bites a dog, that is news." In the Soviet Union, on the other hand, not events but social processes are treated as news and regarded as being newsworthy. The major, and in a sense virtually the only, news item in the Soviet Union is the process called socialist construction, that is, the general effort to build up Soviet society.*

*The following list of chapters from a book about a newspaper regarded by the party as a model Soviet paper tells its own story about the basic orientation of the Soviet press: (1) The Path of the Newspaper; (2) Toward a Deep Study of the History of Bolshevism; (3) Questions of Party Life; (4) The Newspaper is the Organizer

Events are regarded as being news only in so far as they can meaningfully be related to that process. Thus, the Soviet press in the mid-thirties could for months devote the major part of its total space to discussions of the Stakhanovite movement, because of the importance which rationalizing production was held to have for increasing labor productivity. Or, to take an example from the field of ideology, it is literally beyond conception that a newspaper like the *New York Times* would devote almost half of its column space for a period of a week to a national conference of biologists which had met to formulate a basic "ideological" policy for the "scientific" work of American biologists and to affirm the essentially American character of the environmental as against the hereditary approach to genetics.* Yet this is precisely what *Pravda* did during one week of August 1948 in relation to a conference of Soviet biologists.

Along with this emphasis on social processes rather than events goes a virtually complete exemption for the Soviet journalist from any anxiety about getting news into his paper while it is still fresh news.† It is standard practice for a Soviet editor to hold a major news item for several days or even weeks if need be, until his newspaper's pages have been cleared of the material which is at the moment current business, for example, an especially lengthy party or government decision. And when that task is completed, the "news items" that would otherwise have been published several days before are printed quite without ceremony in the same position of prominence that they would have received while still "fresh" news. It is this basic approach to news that enables the editors of what is regarded as a model newspaper to make a detailed plan of the contents and layout one month in advance, and to have 50 per cent of

of Socialist Competition; (5) The Stalinist Brotherhood of Peoples; (6) The Work of the Editors with Letters from the Worker and Peasant Correspondents; (7) Literature and Art in the Pages of the Newspaper; (8) Organizing the Work on the Material. *Opyt Gazety "Zarya Vostoka"* (The Experience of the Newspaper "Dawn of the East"; Moscow, 1940).

*Of course, such a conference is itself beyond the realm of possibility in the United States as it is at present constituted.

†The Soviet editor is far from being free from anxiety, however, and in fact finds himself in a most unenviable position. He is particularly exposed to the dangers of ideological "deviations." See Chapter 12.

each current issue set in type and made up several days before the issue date.[10]*

This is possible, of course, because the editors do not have to wait for a social process to happen; it is going on all the time, and the particular point at which they pick up the thread of events is secondary. This is also possible because those functions of Soviet papers which do not involve dealing with news at all, bulk so large in the mandate of the Soviet press. For the press is expected to serve as propagandist, agitator, and organizer. And this means that a large amount of space must be devoted to articles about Marxism for the party membership, to instructions for local party and government officials on how better to organize production, and to material designed to exhort the workers to greater effort. The Soviet newspaper, in short, is not concerned so much with the transmission of news as it is with the conduct of propaganda and agitation, or with the transmission of information, ideas, and appeals.

Finally, it must be recognized that the meaning of human interest in the news, which continues to play a significant role in Soviet journalism, is not the same as its meaning in the United States. In America the chief figures in the news are persons, the individuals of national importance in politics, economics, the movies, radio, and so on. On the other hand, the chief figures in the Soviet press are impersonal. It is the Revolution, the party, the coming elections, or a new plan which plays the major role in the Soviet press. These social processes and not persons make the news in the Soviet Union.

This is not to say that persons do not figure in the news. On the contrary, letters from groups of voters to Stalin, and congratulatory messages from Stalin to groups of Soviet citizens, repeatedly and regularly consume large portions of the two- and four-page Soviet papers. But in so far as men figure in the news, they figure as social symbols and not as personalities. Thus, it is not the man Stalin, but the head of the party, and not the man Kalinin, but the President of the Supreme Soviet, who have been featured in the

---

*Any American newspaper which is made up largely of advertisements, as most of them are, naturally does about the same thing. It must be recognized, therefore, that Soviet newspapers carry little advertising, and their two or four pages are almost entirely filled with solid newsprint.

Soviet press. Beyond such symbols of the nation one finds very little in the Soviet press about the men who make Soviet history. And even in the case of those who are mentioned, it is practically impossible to discover anything from the press about their personal affairs.

In addition, it must be recognized that the very conception of who is a notable is different in the Soviet Union. The private lives of the nation's leaders are their private lives and no more. There is no "society" whose comings and goings can be chronicled, and a movie star is important because of her art, perhaps even her politics, but not her sex life. The notables, therefore, become those figures who are significant to the national effort, and they are treated as groups rather than individuals. Thus, the notables with whom the Soviet press concerns itself are the outstanding workers, the model teachers, the "mother heroines," and similar national heroes. And even where a man may lend his name to a mass movement, as did the coal miner Stakhanov, the man remains a figure in the news only until the social movement which is to bear his name is well launched. Then, in something approaching a geometric ratio, as the significance of the movement increases, so does the significance of the man as a subject of news decrease.

10

THE STRUCTURE
OF A PLANNED PRESS

THE BASIC STRUCTURAL FEATURE OF THE SOVIET PRESS IS that it is, along with all other aspects of Soviet life, developed according to a definite plan. The First Five Year Plan launched in 1928 included a precise program for the growth of the press during the following five years,[1] and each of the subsequent Plans has included a similar program for the press.

Establishing the press on the basis of a plan is made possible, of course, by the absence of private enterprise and the concentration of power and authority in the hands of the Communist Party. This press planning, however, itself makes possible the closest integration of the ends the party pursues in mobilizing public opinion and the means it has at its command to achieve those ends. For the party is thus able to concentrate its newspaper resources on that area which is of crucial significance at any given time, whether it be industry, agriculture, the armed forces, or the general political arena that presents the special problem. And in the long run it can design each segment of the press to reach a particular audience with a particular message.

In addition, planning has enabled the party to adjust its press apparatus to changes in the size and qualitative composition of the population, in particular to the increase in literacy, but equally to shifts in the occupational and geographic distribution of the population. And when deficiencies in the plan allow duplication to arise, correction is possible simply on the basis of administrative decision. Thus, in March of 1939, several dozen central and regional newspapers were reorganized, some joined to form larger papers, others simply eliminated. Among those eliminated was *Krestyan-skaya Gazeta* (The Peasant Gazette), whose circulation of almost three hundred thousand made it one of the largest papers in the Soviet Union.[2]

THE GROWTH OF THE PRESS

The central importance which the party has attached to the press as an essential instrument for its leadership and control is probably best reflected in the great increase in the number of newspapers and in their circulation during the years of the Soviet regime. According to Stalin, "The press should grow not by the day, but by the hour, for it is the sharpest and most powerful weapon of our Party."[3] Table 1 indicates the extent of this growth since 1913.

TABLE 1

EXPANSION OF THE SOVIET NEWSPAPER NETWORK: 1913-1949[a]

Year	1913	1928	1939	1949
Number of newspapers	859	1,197	8,769	7,200
Circulation at a single printing (in millions)	2.7	9.4	38.0	31.0

[a]*Figures on the Press*, p. 14. The data for 1949 are from *Pravda*, May 5, 1949, p. 1.

It is to be noted that between the last prewar Tsarist year and the last complete peacetime Soviet listing, there was a tenfold increase in the number of papers published and a fourteenfold increase in circulation. This rate of growth was much more rapid than the rate at which the level of literacy rose; and it therefore reflects not only the growth of literacy, but also the party's insistence on a broad newspaper network through which it could carry its line to the people. It is worthy of note, furthermore, that by far the greatest and most rapid gains were made in the years since 1928, an advance made both possible and necessary by the industrialization and collectivization programs under the Five Year Plans. In the five-year period from 1934 to 1939 alone, the yearly circulation of all Soviet newspapers rose by 45 per cent.

The recent war considerably reduced both the number and cir-, culation of Soviet newspapers—directly through the destruction of plant and personnel, and indirectly through its adverse effect on the paper supply. Special emphasis was placed on the restoration of the press network as the German occupied areas were retaken,[4] however, and by 1947 there were about seven thousand newspapers in operation, with a circulation of about thirty million copies per issue.[5] As the 1949 data indicate, recovery since that time has been slow. Apparently the initial recovery was largely achieved by reconstructing damaged facilities, but once that was accomplished further advance depended on new construction. At the present rate of development, it does not appear that the prewar network will have been exceeded by the end of the Fourth Five Year Plan in December 1950. Since the party frequently introduced marked changes in the total number of papers published in order to meet special situations,* however, the number of newspapers published is not the best test of recovery; the crucial test of the recovery must be the size of the total newspaper circulation.

These data on the gross increase in size of the press network must be supplemented by information about the relative rate of increase in the Russian as compared to the non-Russian language press. Table 2 clearly reveals the tremendous transformation in the language structure of the press affected by the party. On its 1913 base, the Russian-language press had increased about seven times by 1947, while the non-Russian press increased twenty-three times. In 1913 there were almost nine times as many Russian newspapers as non-Russian, but by 1947 there were less than three Russian newspapers for each one in another Soviet language. In the same period, the number of languages in which Soviet newspapers were printed rose from twenty-four to almost eighty. These basic trends

*In 1934, for example, several thousand newspapers were created in the political departments of the Machine-Tractor Stations. This raised the total number of newspapers to 10,668, the highest in Soviet history. But this number was sharply reduced in the succeeding years, when these papers were reorganized by combining several in each area and converting them to district newspapers. A similar but less sharp decrease came in 1937. Throughout these changes in the total number of papers, however, the circulation of the press continued to grow at a relatively even rate of development. For details, see *Cultural Construction*, p. 218.

were well established long before the war—in the Russian Republic in 1939 newspapers were published in fifty-one languages; in the Ukrainian and Georgian Republics, in eight; and in other union-republics, in four or more languages.

TABLE 2

NEWSPAPERS OF THE U.S.S.R.: By LANGUAGE, 1913-1947[a]

Language	1913	1928	1939	1947
Russian	775	861	6,475	5,204
Others	84	336	2,294	1,959
Totals	859	1,197	8,769	7,163

[a]Adapted from *Figures on the Press,* p. 14; *The Soviet Press,* p. 112.

It must be recognized, however, that the 2,294 non-Russian newspapers published in 1939 accounted for only about one fourth (9,376,000 copies) of the total circulation, although the non-Russian peoples represented more than 42 per cent of the total population. Furthermore, 74 per cent of all newspapers were printed in Russian, even though the Russian people constituted only 58 per cent of the population. Thus, despite the growth of the native-language press, a disproportionate segment of the total is in Russian. This is in part a reflection of the greater literacy among the Russians, and their widespread distribution throughout the nation. It is also a product, however, of the dominance of Russian culture and influence in the Soviet Union. Russian, although not the official language of the U.S.S.R., is the *lingua franca* of the land, and a great deal of the governmental, technical, and scientific business is conducted predominantly in Russian.

The great shift which took place in the language composition of the press after the Revolution deserves special attention. In the first place, the growth of the non-Russian press must be recognized as an application of the Soviet nationality policy, and the present regime should in this respect be given credit for a notable achievement. Whereas Tsarist policy discouraged the development of native cultures and the use of native languages as media of public communication, the Soviet system has made it possible for virtually every minor nationality group to have its native language press.

At the same time, however, we should not overlook this development's significance as an aid for the party in leading and controlling its vast domain. The present regime's stability is to a large extent dependent upon the support, or benevolent neutrality, of the diverse non-Russian peoples, among whom nationalist and separatist tendencies have frequently run very high. To a significant degree, the Soviet nationality policy serves to keep those separatist tendencies at a minimum and to provide a nondisruptive outlet for local national pride. Its native language press may serve as a symbol of group status for the members of any one of the national minorities. There is another respect, however, in which the nationality press is of equal or greater importance. In contrast to Tsarist policy, the Soviet regime has devoted a very considerable share of its energies to developing economically the national minority areas; and to a great extent the success of the Plans has depended upon the industrial and agricultural development of those territories. This has faced the party with the task of mobilizing the native populations much as it mobilized the industrial workers and peasants in the center of Russia, and often against greater odds. And the party recognized that to effect such a mobilization a well-developed press apparatus was essential.

THE LEVELS OF THE PRESS

The basic principle on which the distribution of the Soviet press is based is a high degree of specialization. In its over-all structure the press has been carefully designed so that each of its parts reaches specific audiences and serves a definite function. The whole apparatus has been built to give it maximum effectiveness as an instrument of the party for mobilizing public opinion and executing the national economic, social, and political plans.

It must be noticed, first, that the breakdown of the Soviet press into its component parts very closely follows the territorial-administrative structure of the Soviet government and the Communist Party, as indicated by Table 3. This table clearly reveals the horizontal structure of the Soviet press. At each level of the territorial-administrative hierarchy there is an appropriate press apparatus to serve the government, party, and public organizations. At the apex of the Soviet press pyramid stands the "central" (all-union) press, consisting of twenty-five newspapers with seven and a half million in circulation. In the middle are the 462 republican, territorial, and regional papers of the "provincial" press, with over ten million copies at a single printing. At the base of the pyramid are the district, city, factory, and farm papers of the "local" press sector, with a combined circulation of over thirteen million copies. Below this, as a kind of

TABLE 3

TERRITORIAL DISTRIBUTION OF THE SOVIET PRESS: 1947[a]

Press level	Type of newspaper	Number published	Circulation: single printing (in thousands)
Central	All-union	25	7,513
Provincial Sector	Union-republican	126	4,316
	Territorial and regional	336	5,948
Local Sector	District and city	4,333	8,620
	"Lower" (factory and farm)[b]	2,343	4,710
	Totals	7,163	31,107

[a]Adapted from *The Soviet Press*, p. 107; for comparable figures for 1939, see *Figures on the Press*, p. 17.

[b]Includes only papers produced by typographic means.

foundation for the entire structure, come several hundred thousand wall newspapers found in every shop, office, and farm. Thus, as we move down this structure from top to bottom, the number of papers increases rapidly, and the average circulation of each paper decreases equally rapidly, ranging from an average of three hundred thousand at the all-union level, through the district and city newspapers which average about two thousand copies per issue, down to the wall newspapers which are handwritten or typed in but a single copy for the shop or farm bulletin board.

Of equal importance with the horizontal division of the Soviet press, however, is its vertical structure. The horizontal levels of the press hierarchy are carefully subdivided along functional lines into separate groups of newspapers such as those of the party, governmental, trade-union, agricultural, and industrial press. Some of these are general newspapers. *Pravda* and *Izvestiya,* for example, are directed to all citizens throughout the Soviet Union. Newspapers like *Pravda Ukrainy* (Ukrainian Truth) and *Turkmenskaya Iskra* (Turkmen Spark) are directed to all citizens of their respective republics. There are similar general newspapers at the city level, like *Vechernaya Moskva* (Evening Moscow), and the same is true down to the level of the urban or rural district.

There are others, however, that are directed to special audiences, primarily on the basis of occupation, but also on the basis of age and sex. In many cases these specialized newspapers form major vertical structures of considerable importance, which have the same horizontal subdivisions as the press apparatus as a whole. In other instances the pattern may be adapted to special conditions: for example, the military press, beyond the all-union *Krasnaya Zvezda* (Red Star), is broken down by military districts, armies, divisions, and so on; and the press of important industrial commissariats is usually broken down into trust, combine, and then particular plant newspapers.

These specialized newspapers can by no means be regarded as a minor segment of the Soviet press, for they represent a very large part of all newspapers printed and of the total circulation. The agricultural press, for example, numbered 3,991 newspapers in January 1939, or almost half of all newspapers then printed in the nation; and they accounted for well over ten million copies at each printing, or almost a fourth of the total circulation. At the top of this agricultural network there were twenty-five all-union, republican, and regional papers with a combined circulation of over two million, including such major newspapers as *Sotsialisticheskoe Zemledelie* (Socialist Agriculture); below these came over three thousand agricultural district papers; and at the base there were almost seven hundred newspapers of Machine-Tractor Stations and State Farms.[6]

Another interesting group of specialized papers is that for young people and children, of which there were 150 in 1939, with a circulation of three million. At the head of this structure stood the central Young Communist League organs, *Komsomolskaya Pravda,* with a circulation of six hundred thousand, and the children's newspaper *Pionerskaya Pravda,* with 850,000 copies at a single printing. Beyond this, every republic, territory, and region had its own newspaper for the children and youths.[7]

These examples should help to point up the fact that the Soviet press is specialized not only in its horizontal but also in its vertical structure. The Soviet mass press apparatus is not a simple, undifferentiated system of "large" and "small" newspapers. It represents a complicated but well-integrated structure, in which each newspaper is precisely patterned according to the territory it serves and the audience to which it is directed. This should be kept clearly in mind as we proceed to an examination of the press at each of its administrative levels.

The central or all-union press, as the term indicates, is intended for nationwide consumption. Emanating from Moscow and printed in Russian,* each of the newspapers in this group reaches the widest audience of any newspaper of its type in the country. Of the forty-three central papers published in 1939, twenty-six had a circulation over fifty thousand and eleven over two hundred thousand per issue. Reduced to twenty-five papers in 1947, this group still constitutes the hard core of the Soviet press, accounting in 1947 for about one fourth of the total circulation at a single printing and almost one third of the yearly press output.†

The all-union newspapers reflect the functional division of the Soviet press better than any other group. The first place is held by the party press, headed by the official organ of the Central Committee, *Pravda,* which currently has a circulation of about 2,500,000.[8] *Komsomolskaya Pravda* and *Pionerskaya Pravda* are published at the plant of the parent *Pravda.* Together, these three chief organs of the party accounted for one tenth of the total newspaper circulation of the nation, and for more than a third of the output of the central sector in 1939.

*The *Vedomosti Verkhovnogo Soveta* (Bulletin of the Supreme Soviet) is published simultaneously in the sixteen languages of the constituent republics.

†The difference in the two percentages results from the fact that the highest proportion of dailies is to be found in the central-press group, thus raising its total circulation on a yearly as compared to a single-issue basis of computation.

The all-union government press, next in line, is headed by *Izvestiya,* official organ of the Supreme Soviet, with a circulation of 800,000 copies in 1947.* Behind *Izvestiya* stands a long line of government newspapers, attached to the different ministries, of varying size and importance. These range through the better known, such as *Red Star* (500,000) † and *Red Fleet,* the military newspapers, down to organs of the lesser industrial ministries such as *Rechnoi Transport* (River Transport), organ of the Ministry of Inland Water Transport.

Trud (Labor; 144,900), official organ of the Central Committee of the All-Union Trade Union Council, and one of the most important newspapers in the country, is the foremost representative of the third element in the central press sector—namely, the press of the so-called public organizations. The central committees of particular trade unions frequently share their newspapers with the corresponding government agency; *Uchitel'skaya Gazeta* ('Teachers' Gazette; 250,000), for example, is published jointly by the teachers' union and the Ministry of Education of the Russian Republic. Beyond the labor press, there are several other newspapers of some importance among the publications of public organizations such as the physical culturists' *Krasny Sport* (Red Sport; 50,300). One of the most interesting of these publications, that of the Atheists' Society, *Bezbozhnik* (The Godless; 70,000), was suspended in 1941.

The newspapers of the all-union sector are all official in the fullest sense of the term. They all emanate from the seat of power, and they speak with authority in their particular area of competence. They are directed not only into the hands of individuals but very largely toward a group audience, to the reading rooms and bulletin boards of trade-union halls, collective farms, party units, factories,

---

*The Soviet Press, p. 107. This represents a sharp drop, since before the war (1939) *Izvestiya's* circulation was 1,600,000, second only to *Pravda* (*Cultural Construction,* p. 222). This fact, in the face of the postwar rise in circulation of *Pravda* and its subunits, *Komsomolskaya Pravda* and *Pionerskaya Pravda,* is valid testimony, if it be needed, of the continued predominance of the party over the government in the Soviet Union.

†Unless otherwise indicated, the circulation of a single issue given, where available, in the succeeding pages is for the year 1939.

offices, and apartment houses.* Each in its sphere, the newspapers
of the all-union press carry the word of the central authorities down
the line, and their word is law. They provide the chief source of
material for all newspapers of similar type on local levels,† and
in every case they set the pattern on which newspapers of the corresponding type on lower levels model themselves.

In the middle of the Soviet press pyramid stand the 462 republican, territorial, and regional newspapers of the provincial press.
Although Soviet statistics observe the amenities by separately listing
the segments of this group, in administrative practice‡ they are
treated as a unit and are referred to by such general terms as the
"regional press." Their average circulation per issue, about 22,000
in 1947, is markedly smaller than that of the central press. This
average includes such "giants" as *Radyans'ka Ukraina.* (Soviet
Ukraine), the chief Ukrainian language newspaper printed in 400,-
000 copies (1947), and *Leningradskaya Pravda* with 275,000 copies
(1947),[9] so that the median point must fall far below 20,000 copies.
Of these middle papers in 1939, about two in five were dailies; and
dailies plus papers issued every other day accounted for about four
out of five of the newspapers in this group.[10]

These middle sector or provincial newspapers serve essentially
the same functions for their republics or regions that the central
papers serve for the nation at large. They are permitted to discuss
almost as wide a range of problems as the central papers, and to
deal with many of them "in depth" to a degree forbidden newspapers lower down in the hierarchy. In addition to seeing that the
decisions of the government and party are carried out throughout

*The reading room of every collective farm, for example, is expected to receive
one or two copies of the central press, although actual deliveries are far from regular.
Party Life, no. 22 (November 1947), pp. 37-38; *Culture and Life,* no. 27 (September
30, 1947).

†The daily *Pravda* leader, or editorial, is wired or radioed in full to all other newspapers in the Soviet Union each day by the telegraphic agency Tass.

‡Despite the precise constitutional distinctions between republics and regions, for
many administrative purposes the party and government treat them as equal units.
In point of fact, several of the regions equal or exceed the smaller republics in territory and population.

their area, they have important economic and political responsibilities. They are expected to provide a thorough analysis and clarification of such problems as plant and factory economy, planning, technological processes, financing, costs and quality of goods, the rationalization of labor, and so on. They are also supposed to deal with problems of party propaganda, aiding the regional cadres to raise their ideological-theoretical level. They must deal not only with the history of the party in their area, but must provide material on general history, political economy, and international policy, for the guidance and education of party and Soviet officials.[11]

The position of the provincial newspaper, serving as a step between the all-union and the strictly local newspapers, is an exposed and vulnerable one. For at the same time that it is charged with the responsibility for problems of real scope, it is expected to be very concrete and to deal specifically with the special administrative and economic problems of its area. This has meant that regularly, and more or less alternately, the party leadership has criticized these newspapers for being either "superficial" in their treatment of economic and other broad questions, or for neglecting the particular economic and political problems of their areas in favor of questions properly belonging in the hands of the central press.[12]

The position of editors of the local press is somewhat less ambiguous, although they are no less closely supervised and are frequently brought under critical review by the authorities. The party does credit the local press with having superior ability to know the precise composition of its audience and the character of the area it serves, to get at the special problems and to deal concretely with them. For this reason, it is particularly deemed "a powerful weapon of communist upbringing of the masses, and of socialist construction."[13] Although their tasks are much alike, there are actually three distinct divisions of the local press: the district and city, the "lower" or factory and farm, and wall newspapers.

The most important segment of the local press is composed of the district (or county) and city newspapers, each of which must be "a mass political organ and have a clearly expressed production character."[14] The average circulation of the 4,333 newspapers in this group in 1947 was under 2,000.* In 1939 about one in six was a daily, and about the same proportion was published six times a month or less.[15] Almost all of the district newspapers are regarded as component parts of the vertical structure of the national agricultural press, and more than two thirds were actually issued in rural localities in 1939.[16] The city newspapers were only 143 in number in that year, but they accounted for almost a fifth of the combined district and city circulation.[17]†

The district press is defined in party decisions as having special capabilities to teach and to educate the masses politically, and "to organize them in the resolution of the tasks standing before the district." An important decision of the Central Committee in 1940, reaffirmed in 1946, declared that "the basic task of the district press is the ideo-political upbringing of the workers on the basis of daily propaganda about the current policy and decisions of the Party and government—propaganda resting on concrete, immediate, and easily grasped facts from local affairs, from the life of the district, collective farm, or enterprise."[18] Problems of theory, party history, and complicated economic questions are considered as beyond the ken of the district newspapers. They are expected to concentrate on the concrete and practical economic, political, and cultural problems of their district, such as improving local sanitation, increasing agricultural yield, introducing "Bolshevik order" in plants and factories, and inculcating in their readers a conscientious attitude toward labor and socialist property.[19]

The so-called "lower press" is the last link in the chain of printed newspapers. This group was reduced by more than half as a result of the war.[20]‡ The great majority come out once a week or less

*In relation to the prewar situation, this represents an increase in total number of district papers of 720, or almost 20 per cent, and a decrease in average circulation of about 1,000 copies, or one third. Both figures are explained by the fact that, in the effort to meet the postwar crisis in the press, many smaller "lower" (factory, farm) papers were raised directly or through consolidation to the level of district newspapers.

†The city newspapers referred to here are not those of major cities like Moscow or Stalingrad, which are regional (republic or *oblast*) capitals, and whose papers are therefore listed with the middle-press sector. Urban papers of the district and city press are generally located in smaller cities not capitals for larger areas.

‡This decrease was in large part due to the postwar emergency measure of combining several smaller newspapers to fill the gap in the district press.

often, and their average circulation per issue in 1947 was about 2,000. A large number of these lower newspapers are located at Machine-Tractor Stations and at State Farms.[21] Some are issued at important construction sites. In 1939, for example, the *Udarnik Metrostroya* (Subway Shockworker) was published for the construction workers on the Moscow subway in 5,500 copies. The great bulk of them, however, are published at major industrial establishments and in government offices with large staffs. There are some dailies in this group, and some papers with a respectable circulation even in 1947, such as the *Avtozavodets* (Autoplant Worker) of the Gorkov auto plant with 12,000, and the *Stalinets* of the Moscow auto factory with 7,000.[22]

The duties of the lower press are simple, direct, and precisely defined. Their central task is to assist in securing maximum quantity and quality production at the particular plant, enterprise, or farm at which they are located, and the smooth and prompt execution of government, party, and trade-union decisions applicable to their production unit. Their responsibilities include: mass explanatory work to convey to the workers important government-party decisions, particularly as they affect the given plant; efforts to improve the material and cultural conditions of the local workers; clarification of problems of intra-party life and work at a given plant; and most important, the exchange and dissemination of the experience and techniques of the most skilled and successful workers.[23]

Beyond these printed lower newspapers there are "hundreds of thousands" of typewritten and handwritten "wall newspapers," in factories and shops, on collective farms, in schools, Red Army units, offices, and housing developments. These wall or bulletin-board "newspapers" are not haphazard or uncontrolled phenomena, but are considered a definite part of the total press apparatus. They are the organs of the local party and trade-union organizations and have regular editors, editorial boards, and correspondents. The party keeps a careful account of their number* and operations, and has

*Just before the war, for example, Chernigov Region had 39 district and 3,000 wall newspapers; the Krasnodarsk Territory had 78 newspapers in the district and city category, and 10,000 wall papers. *Bolshevik Press,* 1940: no. 15, p. 33; no. 16, p. 45.

from time to time issued regulations defining their functions and responsibilities.[24] Their tasks are much like those of the lower press papers, except that they have a narrower scope; they concentrate on really immediate production problems, give hints on improving production, criticize lagging brigades and workers and praise the outstanding, and give local notices of all kinds.

There is a strong temptation for an outside observer of the Soviet Union to pass over a phenomenon like a bulletin-board or wall newspaper as a matter of no significance. To do so would actually involve a serious oversight. The wall newspaper, like the Bolshevik agitator, represents one of the striking examples of the Communist Party's vigor in utilizing meager local resources to extend the coverage of the more formal media of mass communication, to increase their penetration, and to enhance their effectiveness. Like the agitator, the wall newspaper has the particular advantages for mass communication of flexibility and adaptability. It can be adjusted to local conditions and local needs, and has considerable capacity for response to the reactions of its readers. And it is an activity that can be, and is, conducted entirely by volunteer workers, making its cost negligible at the same time that it permits widespread popular participation.

The total number and circulation of Soviet newspapers is not large in relation to the size of the population. This is largely compensated for, however, by careful planning of the distribution of available press resources and by utilization of wall newspapers. The party has precisely designed each newspaper to serve a given area, to reach a specific segment of the population, and to fulfill concretely defined functions. In this way the press can serve as an effective instrument in the party's hands for mobilizing the Soviet population. It is this organization of the press which makes a reality of Stalin's slogan that the press must be "a transmission belt between the Party and the masses."

11

THE FUNCTIONS AND
CONTENT OF THE PRESS

THE NEWSPAPERS OF ANY COUNTRY DISPLAY CERTAIN characteristics that mark them as special products of the social milieu in which they originate. Despite their particular national characteristics, however, the newspapers of the United States, England, and France have more than enough in common to be properly classified as belonging to the same species. The assigned functions and the content of the Soviet press, on the other hand, are so distinct that they clearly stamp the average Soviet newspaper as definitely belonging to a different species.*

An adequate grasp of the distinctive qualities of the Soviet press may be obtained only by reading extensive extracts from Soviet newspapers, and such material is not readily accessible to the average person outside the Soviet Union.[1] Unfortunately, limitations of space and time do not permit an extended discussion to be undertaken here of those characteristics that give the Soviet press its unique stamp, such as problems of format, style, and language. As a substitute for a general discussion of these matters, however, it may perhaps suffice to present in some detail the contents of a single issue of a major Soviet newspaper. The issue of *Pravda* for January 7, 1948, has therefore been selected, more or less at random. This procedure, it should be noted, is not entirely without justification. *Pravda,* the organ of the Central Committee of the party, is

---

*The number of varieties that make up this species has recently been greatly increased by the general tendency of the newspapers in the Soviet satellite states to model themselves after the Soviet press.

the most important and the largest newspaper in the Soviet Union, with a circulation currently well over two million copies. Its distribution is nationwide, since the matrices are flown each day from Moscow to cities like Leningrad and Kiev for local printings, so that a copy of this central newspaper may reach every collective farm and trade-union reading room in the country. Yet *Pravda,* far from being unrepresentative, will reveal in microcosm the distinctive features of the Soviet press. For it should be remembered that *Pravda* is expected to serve as a model for the rest of the Soviet press, that the regional and republican press in particular are supposed to follow the pattern thus set, and that these local newspapers actually reprint each day a considerable amount of material taken from the columns of *Pravda.*

On January 7, 1948, there was no major "news event" to report,* and there was, therefore, no banner headline on the masthead next to the title *Pravda,* the slogan "Proletariat of All Countries, Unite!" and the reproduction of the medal for the Order of Lenin, which the newspaper has displayed each day since its receipt of that award. To the right of the masthead there was simply the usual list of contents of the four pages of print which *Pravda* boasted on that day.†

On the first page of this issue the two left-hand columns were, as usual, occupied by the daily leader, a combination editorial, news story, and instruction feature. On this day, the leader heading was "Forward to the Elections of the Local Soviets of the Union Republics." The lead story began by eulogizing the "friendly brotherhood" of the Soviet peoples and by praising the nationalities for their display of unity and patriotism, which was held up as a symbol of the postwar economic and political progress of the country. The elections, it continued, were an example of Soviet democracy,

---

*Such a major event may be nothing more than the Council of Ministers' announcement of the Third State Loan to finance the postwar Plan, which on May 4, 1948, merited banner headlines and accounted for about two thirds of the space and material in the paper that day.

†Just before the recent war *Pravda* usually ran to six or eight pages. The editor of *Pravda* has expressed the hope of having a paper as thick as the *New York Times,* but the Soviet paper situation is so poor that it is difficult to visualize this event in even the distant future.

and every vote for the party slate of candidates was a vote for Stalin. The leader then addressed itself to its real business, the instruction of local party organizations on the manner in which they were to run the elections. In particular, it called attention to inadequacies in the pre-election work. In Kirgizia, for example, the election agitators in one city did not speak the native tongue of the majority of the voters, who were Uzbeks. In Tadzhikistan and in Turkmenistan, *Pravda* continued, the superior party organizations did not properly supervise the management of the election campaign by the local party groups; and so on. The leader concluded by insisting on the elimination of these deficiencies, and called for raising the quality of political agitation to the level demanded by the importance of the elections.

In addition to this leader, there were eleven items on the first page, all of them reporting varying degrees of success in fulfilling the then current quarterly plan in production, and promising greater efforts in the future. Of these eleven items there were four, most prominently displayed, that were in the form of letters to Stalin from local engineers, workers, and farmers of different plants and collective farms.

On the second page, three of the six columns were occupied by an article on "Monetary Reform and the Advantages of the Soviet Monetary System," in which the main burden of the argument was that capitalist countries were going ever further along the road of inflation, crises, and hardships for the masses, while the Soviet ruble had been adjusted to insure ever higher real wages for the population. About a column of space on this second page was given over to the regular department on party life, in this instance devoted to criticism of the Penza City Party Committee for neglecting the problems of industry in its area. Another column of space, under the title, "To Equal the Leaders in Repair Work," was devoted to a story from *Pravda's* correspondent in the Novosibirsk Region, in which he described the work of an outstanding Machine-Tractor Station in repairing agricultural machinery and urged other Tractor Stations to do likewise. The remaining column of space was occupied by five brief items. One of these announced the signing in Moscow of a Soviet-Norwegian trade protocol, and a second reported on the approaching election of delegates to the forthcoming party conferences to be held in Soviet military units. The remaining items dealt with the series of films being shown by the Moscow Movie House on the culture and art of the "new democracies," the celebration of the 130th anniversary of a hospital in Ryazan, and the recent publication of a series of eighteen brochures on agricultural problems printed in Kursk to assist the collective farmers of that region.

The third and fourth pages were devoted to foreign affairs, and about half the space went to the activities of communist parties abroad in Hungary, Italy, Yugoslavia, and England. Since the Soviet press treatment of foreign news is better known to American readers than the treatment of domestic news, these items need not be described any further. The standard pattern prevailed: sympathy and praise for the friends of the Soviet Union, and hostility toward and criticism of groups outside the Soviet orbit for their reactionary tendencies.

Certainly, this very brief review of the contents of a single issue of *Pravda* cannot be taken as adequately representing the contents of the Soviet press as a whole. Even this hasty sketch, however, serves to highlight many of the salient features of Soviet newspapers. It is clear that the Soviet press is predominantly an instrument for communication going from the party and government to the people and the public organization of the nation. The newspaper is a device through which the party and government transmit decrees and decisions, in which they present, explain, and justify their policies. Throughout all the material, domestic and foreign, there runs a constant theme of exhortation for greater effort and sacrifice and for firmer support of the authorities. The emphasis is primarily practical and businesslike. Through the press instructions are issued to local organizations, and their work is subjected to criticism. The press is a kind of house organ of the party and government units at all levels. It is a clearing house for the exchange of advice and information, and no problem relating to the improvement of production is too small to deserve a column of discussion. These and related functions of the Soviet press, with which we will deal in detail below, are embedded in the traditions of this press and have their origins in the very conception of the newspaper's role developed by Lenin.

THE ORIGINS OF THE PRESS

It is significant that the origin of the Soviet press is officially dated not from the beginning of the Revolution, but from the time of the appearance of the first issue of *Pravda* on May 5, 1912.* And, in fact, the roots of the Soviet press go back to 1900, the year in which the first issue of *Iskra* (The Spark) appeared.† The original *Pravda* was repeatedly closed down by the courts and the Tsarist police, and at times operated as an illegal, underground newspaper. Both papers were almost entirely devoted to discussing political questions, to revolutionary strategy and tactics, to propagandizing Marxist principles, and to agitation against the Tsarist regime. It is essential to an understanding of the contemporary functions and content of the Soviet press to recognize the elements of continuity between these prerevolutionary newspapers and those published in the Soviet Union today.

The key to an understanding of the role of the Soviet press is to be found in the remark made by Lenin, quoted earlier, that a newspaper must be a collective propagandist, agitator, and organizer. He compared it to a scaffolding, surrounding a building under construction, which marked out the contours of the structure, facilitated communication among the builders, enhanced the effective assignment of tasks, and made possible a clear view of the results achieved by the common, organized efforts of the builders.[2]

Lenin presented this famous dictum in the *Iskra* period, and he was thinking primarily of the relation of the press to the building of a revolutionary party. The practical conception of a newspaper's role which he presented was, however, carried forward by Lenin into the period following the Bolshevik seizure of power. In the earliest days of the Soviet regime, Lenin declared that it was a

*May 5 is celebrated throughout the U.S.S.R. as Soviet Press Day.

†*Iskra* was the organ of the Russian Social Democratic Labor Party, and Lenin was a central figure in its organization and a major contributor. Some of his most important early articles appeared in its pages. It ceased publication in 1905, but long before that the Bolsheviks had lost control and it was regarded as a Menshevik organ.

fundamental necessity "to transform the press from an organ which primarily reports the political news of the day into a serious organ for the economic education of the mass of the population." He felt, after the Revolution, that too much space was being given to personalities, to the country's political leaders, and to elaborate expositions of political measures and plans.[3] Lenin offered the Soviet newspapers the slogan of "less politics and more economics," and he made it clear that when he spoke of economics he did not mean theoretical arguments, learned reviews, and high-brow plans, which he labeled "twaddle." Instead, he demanded that more attention be paid to the workaday aspects of factory, village, and military life. The principal task of the press in the period of transition from capitalism to communism, Lenin asserted, was to train the masses for the tasks of building the new society, and this meant that the newspapers must give first place to labor problems and to their immediate practical resolution.[4]

Lenin's plans for the Soviet press were given formal sanction in a series of decisions and instructions of the party's Central Committee directed to the newspapers. In April 1921, the editors of local newspapers were advised that their basic task consisted in uniting the masses of workers and peasants around the construction of a new economic and political life.[5] The editors were given detailed instructions on the problems they were to stress, even to the number of lines to be devoted to each subject, and at the head of the list stood problems of agricultural and industrial construction. Even at that early date, the present-day pattern of the Soviet press was stamped upon the newspapers. Compare, for example, the contents of the issue of *Pravda* described above with the following instructions from the Central Committee on the make-up of regional newspapers in 1922: there was to be a leader of 80 to 120 lines of a "concrete" character, containing information and facts on some issue of local political and economic life; the second major article was to be an exclusively "practical" or "technical" discussion about problems of local construction; the remaining space was to be distributed as follows—life of the nation, 120 to 150 lines; foreign affairs, 80 to 100; agricultural, 100 to 150; and so on.[6]   Table 4 indicates clearly that the pattern is distinct and continuous to the present day.

TABLE **4**

THE FOCUS OF INTEREST IN PRAVDA AND IZVESTIYA[a]
Distribution of space by subject, 1947-1948[b]
(Column inches in percentages)

SUBJECT	PRAVDA		IZVESTIYA	
DOMESTIC NEWS				
Agriculture	17.5		16.0	
Industry	13.6		12.5	
State Administration	11.3		15.7	
Communist Party Affairs	7.2		4.8	
Arts	3.5		4.0	
Military News	1.5		1.6	
Science, Education	1.7		2.3	
Sports	.6		.6	
Soviet Far East	.5		.8	
Public Welfare	.3		.5	
Total Domestic News		57.7		58.8
FOREIGN NEWS				
Western Europe	13.3		11.2	
Soviet Europe	6.9		6.8	
World Affairs	3.9		4.4	
United States	3.4		2.4	
Far East	2.3		2.7	
Middle East and Africa	1.5		1.3	
Latin America and Canada	.6		.4	
Southeast Asia	.6		.7	
Total Foreign News		39.8		38.4
MISCELLANY	2.5		2.8	
Total Miscellany		2.5		2.8
TOTALS	100%	100%	100%	100%
	132,865 column inches		109,111 column inches	

[a]This table is based on data given in the biweekly *Soviet Press Translations*, Far Eastern and Russian Institute, University of Washington.

[b]The period covered in *Pravda* was August 1947 through August 1948; the month of June 1947 was not surveyed, leaving a total of twelve months. The period covered in *Izvestiya* was August 1947 through September 1948, with January and June 1948 not included.

It is clear that in every aspect of its work, the Soviet press is expected to make some contribution to the effective rule of the nation by the Communist Party and to the attainment of those goals which the party has set for the nation and its component parts. But such an over-all statement cannot take account of the various specific ways in which the press plays its role in Soviet society. One can, however, subsume under the three broad categories provided by Lenin—agitation, propaganda, and organization—all of the relevant activities of the Soviet press.

THE PRESS AS AGITATOR

In a sense all the material that appears in the Soviet press comes under the heading of Bolshevik agitation, that is, it involves spreading a single simple idea among a great number of people. In practice, however, it is both necessary and possible to distinguish between the different types of agitational material to be found in Soviet newspapers. Each type is of a distinctive character and is designed to fulfill a particular task.

Information and News. News events, at least as that term is used by Western journalists, play a relatively minor part in Soviet newspapers. But the papers do contain a large amount of straightforward informational material. Social and economic developments proceed at a rapid and ever changing tempo in the Soviet Union, and the daily actions of the party and government apparatus directly affect almost every aspect of the average citizen's life. One of the major functions of the Soviet press, therefore, from the largest to the smallest newspaper, is to transmit to the population the party's and government's basic decrees and decisions, along with authoritative comment and interpretation.[7] There is hardly an issue of any major Soviet newspaper that does not contain the text of some important party or government decision, or that does not feature some important announcement like the inauguration of a new state loan or the beginning of the spring sowing on the farms.

Such informational material occupies a considerable portion of the total space in the Soviet press. It is, in fact, one of the special characteristics of Soviet newspapers that three fourths or more of an issue of even a national newspaper like *Izvestiya* may often be devoted to the publication of such laws and announcements. Almost an entire issue, for example, will be devoted to listing, column after column, the names of persons who have won particular awards or orders such as the title "Hero of Socialist Labor." Since such awards are usually made on an occupational basis, that is, to teachers at one time and to collective farmers at another, and since the number of occupations is considerable, these announcements account for a sizable portion of the total space in the Soviet press.

Government decisions, announcements of campaigns and awards, and similar items are usually presented in the most straightforward manner; that is, the official text as adopted by the party, the government, or the trade unions is simply reproduced in its entirety.

It is standard practice, of course, to accompany such material with a front-page leader and other articles commenting on the government or party decision. It would be possible in the Soviet Union, as in other countries, to publish such material in special official government releases rather than in the daily press. The *Bulletin of the Supreme Soviet* and to some degree *Izvestiya* serve as such official gazettes. But it would hardly suit the purposes of the party or the government to restrict the publication of decisions to these sources. For it is their intention that such materials shall come to the direct attention of the population, and the most certain way of insuring the fact that the people will see these materials is to fill the daily news with them. The average reader has the alternative of not reading his newspaper on that day, but if he does read he will be learning in detail what the latest action or decision of the authorities holds in store for him. And this is, of course, precisely the intention of the authorities.

Political Agitation. The party does not, to be sure, limit itself to publishing the texts of important decisions and announcements. It seeks directly to influence the formation of political attitudes; and this requires not the mere presentation of party decisions, but the explanation and justification of party policy. The party has set for the press no less a task than changing the very consciousness of the Soviet citizen. In an editorial on Soviet Press Day in 1947, for example, *Pravda* declared: "The press is the most powerful means for the communist upbringing of the masses, for strengthening their socialist consciousness, speeding up the forward movement of Soviet society, and increasing the sources of its power and glory." The press is expected to inculcate in the people a feeling of national pride and to develop "an unwavering, courageous spirit and unyielding faith in our great endeavor."[8]

This is clearly no small task. It is not approached as a special problem in and of itself, however, but rather enters directly or indirectly into the treatment of any ordinary item of Soviet news. Whether it be a report on forthcoming elections, the celebration of any one of the numerous Soviet revolutionary anniversaries, the announcement of some loan or campaign, the completion of a road in Central Asia, or any other item which constitutes major news for the Soviet press, it must make its contribution to political agitation.[9] Consequently, any one of these items, no matter how diverse in subject matter or origin, will ordinarily be treated according to a standard pattern, a pattern that is well illustrated by the *Pravda* leader on local elections described above. There is always the eulogy and glorification of the Soviet system and its products, the criticism of the inadequacies which still exist despite the great success so far achieved, and finally, the crucial exhortation for still greater effort and firmer support of the regime.

The political agitation in the press bears some responsibility for popular education. In the early years of the Soviet regime it was stated that one of the three chief tasks of the press was "to spread knowledge among the masses of workers and peasants, and to raise their cultural and political level."[10] A considerable amount of newspaper space was indeed devoted to straightforward adult education in the first Soviet decade, but with the fuller development of regular formal education, decreasing emphasis was placed on such material. On the whole, "political education" in the Soviet press currently means the explanation and justification of party policy past and present.

The press does, of course, continue to publish a large number of items about cultural developments, and the literary and art criticism it conducts is extensive and important. The treatment of a figure like Pushkin affords an excellent example of the pattern of the Soviet press in this sphere. On the occasion of the 100th anniversary of Pushkin's death in 1937, the Soviet press was for many days literally filled with materials on Pushkin and his work. The equivalent in the United States would be for the *New York Times* to devote most of its front page and over half of the rest of its columns to the anniversary of Walt Whitman's death, and to do so for several days in succession.

Such spreads, and they are not infrequent in the Soviet press, testify to the serious interest of Soviet newspapers in cultural matters and the cultural education of the reading public. The picture is not complete, however, unless it is pointed out that apart from their service to cultural education such spreads have a very specific political goal. In the case of Pushkin, for example, every effort was made to make him appear to be a radical and a poet of the people. The magic name of Pushkin was drawn on to emphasize the continuity between all that was great in the old Russia and all that the Soviets had developed. The reverence for Pushkin was held up as an example of the high cultural level of the U.S.S.R., and much was made of the claim that more copies of his works had been published in the average year under the Soviet regime than had been published altogether under Tsarist rule. Thus, the ever present dual purpose is served. For whatever the subject, and however independently worthy the object of the newspaper's effort, the material used must always be treated so that it will make a special contribution to the over-all goal of strengthening the Soviet system and its base of popular support.

Agitation for Production. Lenin's demand that the Soviet press concentrate on practical economic problems, and in the first instance on the workaday problems of the farm and factory, has already been noted. An emphasis on the day-to-day problems of economic life has indeed been one of the most characteristic and striking features of the Soviet press, and since the inauguration of the First Five Year Plan in 1928 this has tended to overshadow all other phases of newspaper work. Agitation for higher production in the Soviet press, like political agitation, is not represented by a single type of newspaper story, but involves a complex of materials and approaches.

In meeting this responsibility the press is expected to explain and justify to the men and women in field and factory the economic measures adopted by the party and government, to bring to public attention and to glorify the economic achievements of the country, and to exhort the population to ever greater effort. The press is defined as a central driving force in initiating and carrying through those mass campaigns—for higher productivity, less waste, and fulfillment of the plan in record time—on which the success of the industrial and agricultural programs are so dependent. Thus, *Pravda* instructed the nation's editors on Press Day in 1947: "The task of the Bolshevik Press is to pick up and publicize everything . . . which increases the patriotic initiative of the masses and facilitates stepping up the pace at which the national economy is built and developed."[11]

Although such items have their place even in the principal national newspapers like *Pravda,* as has already been pointed out, they represent the single most important aspect of the local newspaper's work. For it is at this level that the most direct and personal appeal for improved production can be made, and in the case of the factory wall newspaper, the praise or criticism can be narrowed to a given work brigade or even individual. It is at this level of the factory press that the general campaign is reduced to its most concrete terms, and the factory wall newspaper has long been instructed to "shun general political reviews and articles," and to concentrate its energies on serving as "an instrument for affecting the masses and for influencing their activities."[12]

Through its agitation for higher production the press is expected to make a signal contribution to the resolution of the difficulties, such as low productivity of labor and poor labor discipline, that have plagued the party's economic efforts from the beginning of the Soviet regime. And frequently the party has had no recourse to a solution of these problems except by psychological means, because it is unable to provide the goods, the housing, and the other things that might of themselves result in higher labor productivity and better discipline.* One approach has been based on the adoption of various restrictive or punitive administrative measures. Of much greater importance in effecting an increase in labor productivity,† however, have been the campaigns or "movements" for the exertion of extra effort by the workers and for the rationalization of the work process. Exhortation among the masses for increased production and better labor discipline, therefore, became a central task of the press. What this has meant, in effect, is that in large measures the Soviet press, at the national as well as the local levels, has been transformed into a kind of master "trade" journal.

The press's responsibility for agitation on production involves gathering and disseminating information about the experience and techniques of the most successful factories and farms, and about the methods of outstanding workers and farmers.[13] In the words of *Pravda,* "The general dissemination of the experience of the foremost, making their achievements available to the masses of workingmen and workingwomen and thus effecting a general advance, is the first duty of the Bolshevik press."[14]

The first manifestation of what was later to become a standard pattern came in the early days of the Revolution when large groups of workers, called *subbotniki,*‡ contributed their "day off" to the state and unloaded freight cars or performed other services without pay. These first sporadic efforts were later formalized and systematized, especially as the introduction of the Five Year Plans placed heavier and heavier demands on the country. The *udarnik* or shock worker, who increased his production by exerting extra effort, the *otlichnik* or exemplary worker, and finally the *Stakhano-*

---

*This inability to provide goods, housing, and other necessities cannot, of course, be assumed to result solely from lack of the means to produce them. The emphasis of the Five Year Plans has been predominantly, at times overwhelmingly, on industrialization and heavy industry rather than on the production of consumers' goods. In very large part the scarcity of necessary goods and services for civilian consumption is a result of that emphasis.

†This is not meant to belittle the extent to which coercive administrative measures have been utilized in Soviet industry. Such measures have meaning primarily in the realm of labor discipline. They have not figured particularly in the efforts to raise labor productivity.

‡From the Russian *subbota,* for Saturday.

vite, who increased production by rationalizing his work process, were all in turn major figures in these efforts to increase labor productivity. In addition, there were and still are various other campaigns of all sorts, the best known being the socialist competition, or emulation, between individuals and groups of workers. Some of these movements and campaigns were purely local in origin.[15] The party has always been quick, however, to seize on those it deemed most useful in order to make them national in scope. And it has been one of the major responsibilities of the press to foster and spread these campaigns and to carry them through to a successful conclusion. The most striking example of this activity was provided at the time the Stakhanovite movement was introduced in 1935, when for months on end the Soviet press concentrated, to the virtual exclusion of all other material, on explaining, encouraging and spreading the movement.

It continues to be true today that not a single issue of any Soviet newspaper is complete unless it includes some material agitating for higher production, reporting on the successes made in repairing tractors, as our *Pravda* issue did, giving a detailed description of how some worker in a cotton mill manages to tend twice the average number of machines, or reporting the progress of the competition between two different shops in some local factory. In this way, the press fulfills its mandate to make available to the masses of the rank and file the experiences and the methods of the outstanding workers and farmers.

THE PRESS AS PROPAGANDIST

Communist propaganda, we have noted, is defined as the means by which the party membership is "armed" with the knowledge of Marxist-Leninist theory. Since the work of Marxist training for party members is considered of the utmost importance, and since the press is regarded as the "chief, decisive weapon in the propaganda of Marxism-Leninism,"[16] the party has not hesitated to set aside a significant portion of the space of all newspapers for this specific purpose. Since the early twenties every newspaper has been expected to maintain a special department on "Party Life," and one of its main functions is to see to the ideological education of the party rank and file.[17]

The utilization of the press for propaganda purposes was given fresh impetus in 1938, when the Central Committee called for liquidation of what it termed the tendency to undervalue the significance of the press as the most important instrument of Marxist-Leninist training. The editors of *Pravda, Red Star,* and the *Komsomolskaya Pravda,* as well as the editors of republican and regional newspapers, were ordered systematically to incorporate in the pages of their newspapers articles, "consultations," and "lectures" on theoretical questions of Marxism-Leninism written by the best available propagandists. In the staffs of the central, republican, and regional newspapers special departments of propaganda were to be established, to be headed by newspaper workers adequately prepared theoretically and able to encourage the participation of qualified propagandists in writing the material. The columns run by this department were also to serve as a medium through which propagandists could discuss their problems and exchange experiences, and in which the best propagandists could make available to the others advice and information on how to conduct propaganda work.[18]

Ever since, the press has continued to play a major role in the work of communist propaganda.[19] Most newspapers regularly devote several columns to this activity. If one thinks in terms of a newspaper with as many as forty-eight pages, such as the *New York Times,* there appears to be nothing striking in such an allocation of space. When one recognizes, however, that *Pravda* at present generally runs to only four pages, and that some of the lesser local newspapers boast of only two pages, then granting so much space to so specialized a subject appears in a different light. This situation is given increased significance when it is recognized that the propaganda material carried by the newspapers is not expected to appeal to the entire reading audience of the papers concerned, but is directed specifically toward that segment of the readers which constitutes the party membership and non-party intelligentsia.

An understanding of this practice is possible only if one takes account of the operation of the Bolshevik leadership principle. It is essential to the party's direction of the nation that its personnel, those in positions of leadership in the government, trade-union, and related structures, have sufficient theoretical training to enable them intelligently to grasp and to carry out party policy. But because of the shifts in that policy, which are so frequent and rapid in the Soviet Union, the initial Marxist indoctrination of the personnel does not suffice. To keep the old cadres abreast of the party line, and effectively to incorporate into the structure those people newly advanced to positions of responsibility, the party must have a regular and direct channel of communication from the center to the numerous "actives" working in all the spheres that make up the nation and the society. Such a channel of communication is provided by the daily press, and the party does not hesitate to adapt this mass medium to reach a very restricted audience.

Thus, even the general newspaper becomes, in significant measure, an instruction and information sheet for the so-called party and Soviet "active." Through its "Party Life" columns and other propaganda features, the newspaper is expected to contribute to "broadening their ideological-theoretical, cultural-political horizon." Concretely, this means that the newspaper must provide these people not only with material on the history and principles of the party, but must also facilitate their study of general history, political economy, international politics, and practical economics.[20]

Since Soviet authorities have shown little interest in developing systematic, statistical analyses of the reading habits of their newspaper audiences, it is not possible to say whether or not these materials directed toward the party and Soviet cadres are also read by the average reader. The evidence at hand suggests that a large proportion of the ordinary readers finds this material rather deep. But there are no signs that the party feels this to be a matter of serious concern. When the importance of the audience justifies it, the Soviet authorities are always ready to sacrifice scope or coverage to the need for more effective communication in areas where it is most required.

THE PRESS AS ORGANIZER

In addition to serving as a kind of trade journal by making available to a wide audience the experiences and techniques of the best workers and farmers, Soviet newspapers function as the equivalent of house organs for the government and party. In this sense the press is regarded as a collective organizer, and it does in fact represent an important adjunct to the more usual methods of organizing the operations of the administrative hierarchy.*

From their inception, the newspaper departments devoted to party life have been expected to serve the various party committees as a channel of communication for the transmission and explanation of party directives. It is to a large extent through the newspaper that the higher party organizations instruct and guide the lower units. At the same time, the newspapers lower down in the scale are expected to report in detail the activities of the party organizations at the same level, so that the higher units can supervise the activities of the lower units and verify the extent to which the orders given have been executed. It is also the duty of any local newspaper to serve as an instrument by which the central committee in any area can unify and integrate the activities of its own departments and divisions.[21]

The press is expected to play a similar role in facilitating the resolution of the organizational problems of the government, particularly in the realm of economic life. This applies both to newspapers which are national in scope and to purely local papers. Many of the state ministries are publishers of important newspapers, and although these are more specialized than the average newspaper, many of them have large audiences. For example, *Sotsialisticheskoe Zemledelie* (Socialist Agriculture), published by the Ministry of Agriculture, is directed to the whole of the rural population, which accounts for the majority of the people. Through these newspapers the various government agencies issue orders and instructions to the local units subordinate to their authority and supervise the fulfillment of those directives.[22]

*The conception of the press as an organizer used here is a narrow one. The press is also an organizer in the sense that it plays a central part in initiating and fostering mass campaigns such as the socialist-emulation movement or the drives to reduce waste in factories. But in practice, as was noted in Chapter 7, this type of organizational activity has been largely merged with what had formerly been straightforward political agitation. This latter aspect of the press's function as an organizer was the one stressed by Stalin in his widely quoted *Pravda* article of May 1923, "Pechat' kak kollektivnyi organizator" (The Press as a Collective Organizer). Stalin, *Sochineniya,* V, 281-285.

The less specialized local newspaper has no less responsibility in this regard. District newspapers, for example, are supposed to concentrate on and be thoroughly familiar with the economic problems of the district. The editors are expected to hold regular conferences with specialists and responsible officials in economic, government, and cultural life, to discuss practical questions of socialist construction with them, and to make the results of these gatherings available to all through the pages of the newspaper. A similar responsibility is assigned to regional and republican newspapers. The editor is expected to secure in the pages of his paper a concrete approach toward each and every collective farm served by his paper, to offer criticism and suggestions, and to insure that the decisions of the party and government are carried out. For the benefit of the industrial managers and technicians of the area it serves, the regional newspaper is supposed to discuss and clarify questions about the internal workings of the plant, problems of planning, technological processes, the rationalization of production, and matters of plant financing and production costs.[23]

These technical discussions in the newspapers are not, of course, at the same level as those appearing in special journals devoted to the different professions and industries. They are frequently sufficiently technical, however, to be beyond the interest of the average newspaper reader. Consequently, the newspaper in serving as an organizer, in much the same way as when it serves as propagandist, more or less excludes a large part of its audience from the reading of a significant portion of the total printed matter. If you are dealing with an omnibus newspaper of the kind common in the United States, this poses no particular problem; if there is enough newsprint there can be as many financial pages as are needed, even if these pages are directed to a far more limited audience than that of the news pages. But in the Soviet newspaper of from two to six pages, every inch of space comes at a high price. The fact that there is no hesitation about devoting a considerable amount of space to discussing economic subjects of such restricted interest is another striking illustration of the fact that the party is willing to sacrifice the scope of its coverage in favor of securing the greatest certainty of effective communication in crucial areas.

12

EDITORS AND WRITERS OF THE SOVIET PRESS

SELECTION AND TRAINING OF EDITORS

SINCE THE PRESS IS REGARDED AS AN INSTRUMENT OF THE party for making effective its leadership of the country, the newspaper editor becomes the representative of the party and is consequently appointed by it. The party Rules provide that the editors of the party press organ at each level of the territorial hierarchy shall be appointed by the corresponding party committee. Thus, the Central Committee directly appoints the editors of the all-union papers as *Pravda,* and the primary party organization appoints the editor of the factory or farm wall newspaper. Appointments of editors for republican and regional party newspapers require the confirmation of the Central Committee, while the appointment of editors for papers lower down in the scale must be confirmed by the republican and regional party committees.[1] This party control of the appointment and confirmation of editors is not limited to newspapers and journals which are official organs of the party. The appointment, removal, and promotion of the editors of all newspapers, governmental, trade union, and so forth, must in practice be approved by the responsible party organization on the same administrative level. The editor of a regional trade-union newspaper, for example, while appointed by the officials of the regional trade-union organization, must have approval of the regional party organization and be confirmed by the Central Committee.[2]

The editor of any Soviet newspaper, by virtue of his position as editor, is at the same time a responsible official of the organization which publishes the paper. In the case of party organs, furthermore, the editor will be a member of the executive committee of the party unit which publishes the paper.* This principle was accepted in practice before 1930 and was made a formal rule by the decision of the March 1937 plenum of the Central Committee.[3] In this way, the party insures the most direct and flexible line of communication between itself and the Soviet press, and facilitates utilization of the press as an instrument of party policy.

The definition of the Soviet press as a collective propagandist and agitator largely determines the qualifications and training demanded of newspaper personnel. The Central Committee has declared that all Soviet editors must have "a fundamental Bolshevik firmness and organizational capacity, the ability aggressively and at the required pace to organize the masses in the resolution of the basic tasks of socialist construction." [4] In brief, political training and ideological reliability are the prime characteristics that qualify a man for a position as editor of a Soviet newspaper.

A certain degree of technical competence is, of course, absolutely indispensable for a newspaper editor, and in recent decades the progressive professionalization of newspaper work has been apparent in the Soviet Union. Throughout this development, however, the predominance of political considerations in the training and retraining of editors has persisted. In the first decade of its rule, the party had to depend for its supply of editors on its limited available resources. Reliable party members who qualified by education and background were drafted as newspaper editors. Their training was acquired either on the job, in special short courses, or in the newly created communist institutes for journalists.[5]

The great expansion of the press apparatus which accompanied the Five Year Plans faced the party with an acute shortage of journalists. To fill this gap, the party drafted students of the higher schools in Moscow and other centers, and drew particularly on the students of the various communist academies as part-time journalists. At the same time, it established a unified system for training press cadres.

*The editor of *Pravda,* for example, is a member of the Central Committee of the party.

Editors for central, republic, and regional newspapers were to be trained by pursuing courses in Marxism in the editorial department of the Institute of Literature and Languages of the central Communist Academy. The less important editors of these papers, and the chief editors for large district and city newspapers, were to be trained by the branches of the Communist Institute of Journalists. Editorial personnel for smaller district and for factory and farm newspapers were to be trained by the press department of local communist academies (komvuzi).[6]

In an effort to systematize the training of journalists and to improve their professional qualifications, the development of regular schools of journalism was encouraged throughout the thirties. By 1937 there were seven universities and fifteen other higher schools for training journalists, with a student body of about four thousand; and in the last prewar year four hundred professional newspaper workers were graduated from them.[7] These schools currently offer a five-year course at the college or university level, are regarded as fully accredited higher schools, and are under the supervision of the Ministry of Higher Education.[8]

A major part in the development and retraining of newspapermen, however, continues to be played by the party organizations and by major newspapers. The Central Committee and local party organizations periodically call in the editors of papers at all levels of the press hierarchy for special courses and for political indoctrination.[9] A central role in this retraining process is played by the most important papers in each of the vertical subdivisions of the Soviet press. In 1943, for example, the regional newspaper *Moscow Bolshevik* established in its own editorial offices a two-month course for retraining district editors; while a specialized central newspaper like *Pionerskaya Pravda* will give courses for editors in its own sphere of competence, that is, for the editors of children's newspapers at the republic and regional level.[10]

In both the regular schooling and in the special retraining of Soviet journalists, the question of political indoctrination continues to be first in importance. For example, the special course given by *Pionerskaya Pravda* for the editors of children's newspapers dealt not only with their practical problems, but in the first instance concerned itself with political questions, theoretical problems, and the study of selected themes from the party *History*.[11] The pattern established in 1938 of training and retraining editors in the same courses in Marxism-Leninism utilized to train propagandists[12] has persisted through the war years down to the present time.[13] It is most revealing, in this connection, to examine the list of part-time courses offered to members of the Central House of Journalists in Moscow, which is the equivalent of the National Press Club in Washington. In 1940 the House of Journalists offered the more than two thousand newspapermen and publishing house editors in its membership a choice of nine different courses. They ranged from such subjects as the foundations of Marxism-Leninism, and dialectical materialism, to Russian language and literature; but subjects having to do with the treatment of news were noteworthy by their absence from the list.[11]

The prime emphasis given to the Soviet journalist's political preparation is, of course, completely logical if viewed in terms of Bolshevik theory about the role and functions of the press. A newspaper which is conceived of primarily as an instrument of political policy, as a collective agitator and propagandist, requires an editor who is above all else politically trained and ideologically indoctrinated. Through its policy on the selection of editors, the party has resolved what would otherwise be a most difficult if not insuperable problem of censorship. The party's security in the political reliability of Soviet editors is the guarantee of its security in the political reliability of the newspapers themselves.

THE ROLE OF THE NONPROFESSIONAL JOURNALIST

One of the most striking features of the Soviet press apparatus is the small size of the regular professional staff on even the more important newspapers. For example, a major newspaper like *Zarya Vostoka* (Dawn of the East), chief Russian newspaper in the Georgian Republic and one of the most important newspapers in the Soviet Caucasus, had in its home office in 1940 a full-time professional editorial staff of only twenty-five persons, exclusive of secretaries and technical personnel. This included all editors, assistant editors, heads of departments, reporters, copy writers, and so forth.[15] The staffs of outside full-time correspondents are equally small, and party regulations prescribe that the largest republican and regional newspapers, those regarded as being in the first category, may have no more than ten or twelve correspondents, while the smaller republican and regional papers, those in the fourth and fifth categories, may have no more than four or five correspondents.[16]

The small staffs of Soviet newspapers are not to be explained as a product of the shortage of press personnel. On the contrary, the party has repeatedly protested that the staffs of newspapers were "swollen" and "bloated," and has in recent years issued a series of instructions calling for sharp reductions in their size.[17] Newspapers in which the material written by non-staff members constitutes only 15 per cent of the total space are severely castigated, and even papers in which 25 per cent of all the material is written by non-staff writers are criticized.[18] It is apparently assumed that in a model newspaper at least half the contents will come from the pens of nonprofessional journalists.[19] Newspapers which do not follow this pattern are regarded as violating the traditions of the Bolshevik press, and in 1940 the party ordered an end to the practice of paying honorariums to staff members for their articles, in an effort to reduce the amount of staff-written material appearing in the nation's newspapers.[20] The party has ruled, furthermore, that the first task of all editors and correspondents is to encourage and to draw into active participation in the writing of their newspapers the maximum number of nonprofessional journalists. Editors are obliged to maintain systematic contacts with these non-staff writers, to supply them with aid and materials, to call them together for conferences, to discuss editorial plans and activities with them, to invite them to make periodic critical reviews of the editor's conduct of his newspaper.[21]

What is the significance of this extraordinary emphasis on the participation of nonprofessional journalists in the writing of Soviet newspapers? Here again the explanation is to be found in the special role assigned to the press in the Soviet Union. The press has been given a series of practical and highly specialized functions which have no direct connection with the reporting of "news," but which do involve detailed participation in local economic affairs. The local newspaper must be both a technical guide and a forum for the exchange of experience about the economic life of the territory it serves.

The party feels that it is clearly impossible for ordinary staff news-papermen to discuss such problems effectively, or to avoid being inaccurate or superficial. Effective writing on such problems, it holds, can be done only by the specialist actually participating in the eco-nomic activities involved. For this reason, the local newspaper is instructed to call upon its noneditorial "active" to secure the collab-oration as newspaper writers of plant managers, engineers, techni-cians, teachers, doctors, agronomists, Stakhanovites, and other out-standing workers. It is only by drawing upon such specialists rather than on the services of professional newspapermen, the party insists, that newspapers can be lively and interesting and, above all, effi-ciently serve as instruments for advancing the party's policies in all phases of economic life.[22]

To take another example, it has been noted that the press serves the party organizations by discussing all aspects of their work. Here again the party feels that the effective use of the press in assisting the local party organizations and membership depends on the utilization of nonprofessional journalists. Only the party leaders themselves, the propagandists and agitators, it is maintained, can adequately write on such subjects. Consequently, it is again the task of the editors to secure the collaboration of party officials and party workers in writ-ing those sections of the newspaper that deal with party affairs.[23] In *Dawn of the East*, which is regarded as a model newspaper, about 65 per cent of the material in the columns devoted to party life was regularly written by party officials and other nonprofessional journalists.*

Thus, the special functions which the party has assigned the Soviet press have had a profound impact on the composition of the newspaper staffs, and have greatly determined the fact that a large part of the average Soviet newspaper is written not by professional journalists, but by party, government, and economic specialists writ-ing for the newspaper at irregular intervals in those areas in which

---

*In addition to the specialists and other members of the intelligentsia, and the party officials and workers, a major role in the so-called noneditorial "active" is played by the *rabsel'kory,* or worker and peasant correspondents. Because of their im-portance as an adjunct to the press in its task of public criticism, the discussion of the activities of the *rabsel'kory* has been included in Chapter 14.

they have special competence. This fact, of course, in turn determines the quality and the content of the newspapers. Both factors, however, are a result of the initial commitment made by the party when it decided on the role the press was to play in Soviet society.

PROBLEMS OF SOVIET EDITORS

The lot of the average Soviet editor, like that of Gilbert and Sullivan's policeman, is not always a happy one. It should be clear from the preceding discussion that the functions assigned the Soviet press place the most varied and difficult demands upon the editor. He must not only be a capable newspaperman, but also must be a specialist in ideology, a technical expert, an organizer and teacher, and an adroit politician. He is subject to a constant dual pressure, coming simultaneously from the authorities above and from those on his own territorial level. He is subject to constant supervision and can never tell when he may become the object of scathing criticism from the central authorities, either in the form of a critical review in one of the major newspapers or in a decision of the Central Committee and its Press Department.

Although this situation prevails in varying degrees at all levels of the Soviet press, it is probably most acute for those editors whose newspapers appear at the regional level and to a lesser extent for district newspaper editors. The editors of the major all-union papers are close enough to the center of power to be able to keep abreast of events and trim their sails with shifts in the political winds.* The editors of wall and minor local newspapers, on the other hand, have such specific and limited goals and are so intimately connected with the local party organizations that individual editors, if not the group as a whole, are able to navigate with some assurance of calm. The scope of the newspaper headed by the regional editor, however, is much more extensive than that of the purely local paper, and at the same time the editor is separated by considerable distances from the source of instructions and directives in Moscow. He appears to be, in consequence, the most frequent subject of the withering criticism of

*The central press's editors are by no means exempt from critical attack. See the criticism of *Pravda, Izvestiya, Komsomolskaya Pravda,* and other central papers for their handling of news about local events in *Culture and Life,* no. 9, March 30, 1947.

the central authorities.[24] Two problems which illustrate the difficulties faced by these editors warrant brief comment.

The basic problem which editors of Soviet middle-rank newspapers face, a problem which in a sense is inclusive of all the others, is that of correctly interpreting the instructions which come to them from above. Although the decisions issued by the Central Committee are detailed and extensive, they can hardly be directly applied by editors in all the different parts of the country without local interpretation. It is this basic fact which frequently causes the editor to find himself falling between two stools. The problem becomes particularly acute when the editor has to deal with questions having ideological significance. During the recent war, for example, a major aspect of the campaign to capitalize on popular patriotic sentiment revolved around the revival of interest in the national heroes of the peoples making up the Soviet Union. In keeping with this policy, historians of the Tatar Republic were invited to contribute articles on the subject for the Tatar press. In these articles major emphasis was placed by the writers on Idegei, who had been one of the leaders of the Golden Horde. The editors of the Tatar newspapers, and the Tatar party organization, were undoubtedly much surprised to find a severe criticism of their action directed at them by the Central Committee, charging them with ideological deficiencies. It appears that although Idegei was indeed a genuine Tatar hero, some of his famous exploits had to do with pillaging expeditions against the Russians of his day. Making him a hero, therefore, was regarded as violating the principle of the "brotherhood of Soviet peoples," and this principle clearly took precedence since there were presumably many other Tatar heroes who might have been revived.[25]

Another problem facing the regional editor is that of striking a correct balance between material originating in and written about the area served by his paper and material reprinted from the central press and the Tass wire service. The regional newspaper, unlike the lower papers, is expected to serve not only the specifically local economic and political needs of its area, but is also supposed to supply material on events of national and international significance. Since the editor can feel complete security in the acceptability of articles reprinted from such newspapers as *Pravda* or *Izvestiya*, or taken from the Tass wire services, many editors have apparently taken refuge from their problems by filling their pages with such material. One newspaper cited by a party press official, for instance, was reported to have had 42 per cent of its material taken from the Tass wires.[26] Such avoidance of his responsibilities is not permitted the editor, however, and the party has frequently castigated regional editors for mechanically reprinting material from the central press, both on the grounds that this made their newspapers trite, and that it reflected carelessness and lack of initiative which frequently led to the neglect of matters of local importance.[27] So the regional editor must strive to preserve a precarious balance. For if he neglects to carry material of national import, he is regarded as derelict in his duty; yet if he carries too much, he is held guilty of neglecting his responsibilities to his locality. And when he uses articles about national and international events, if he simply reprints material from the central press and the wire services, he is termed thoughtless or unoriginal; but if he writes original stories on such subjects, he runs the risk of committing some ideological heresy. The golden mean is not easily found.

13

CENSORSHIP AND
SUPERVISION OF THE PRESS

THE LIMITS OF CENSORSHIP

IT IS NOT A CHARACTERISTIC OF THE BOLSHEVIKS TO TRUST to luck; they are, in fact, inclined toward over-administration. The Soviet press, it is clear, has a series of important and precisely defined functions to perform. But in order to make the press a more refined instrument for the fulfillment of its responsibilities, the Soviet leaders have found it necessary to develop the press into an elaborate, diversified, and highly specialized apparatus including a large number of units widely dispersed. In so far as the party insists on close supervision of this vast apparatus, and it must if it wishes to be sure that the press achieves its defined ends, it is faced by an imposing administrative problem.

Experience with control of the press in other countries immediately suggests, of course, that censorship is the key to the problem. In point of fact, however, censorship, at least as traditionally conceived, plays a relatively minor role in the supervision and control of the Soviet press. To secure an adequate appreciation of the interrelations between the Soviet press and the social system within which it operates, it will be necessary to go far beyond the narrow conception represented by the term censorship.

The Soviet Union does indeed have a government consorship agency, which is known as *Glavlit*, a short form for its full title of Chief Administration for Literary Affairs and Publishing.* *Glavlit*,

Glavnoe Upravlenie po Delam Literatury i Izdatel'stv.

in the absence of any government agency directly responsible for propaganda, is attached to the Ministry of Education of the Russian Republic. Its authority was defined by a decree of the Council of People's Commissars in June 1931, and the powers then granted appear to be formally in effect at this time without major change.[1]

Glavlit was established, the decree indicates, in order to effect political-ideological, military, and economic security or control over press materials, manuscripts, photographs, and similar materials intended for publication and distribution.* It has the power to prohibit the publication and distribution of materials which agitate against the Soviet regime and the dictatorship of the proletariat, which disclose state secrets, arouse nationalistic or religious fanaticism, or are of a pornographic nature. *Glavlit* discharges its responsibilities by both preliminary, or prepublication, and post-publication censorship, the latter designed to verify that the text as printed is the same as the original text as approved.

Despite the rather sweeping powers that the decree appears to bestow on *Glavlit*, the statute contains two limitations which have been of the greatest importance for the development of censorship in the Soviet Union. In the first place, the materials to be published by the Unified State Publishing House (*Ogiz*), which accounts for the bulk of Soviet book publishing, are not given their prepublication censorship by ordinary deputies of *Glavlit*. Instead, the regular editors of the subsidiary publishing houses which make up *Ogiz* are regarded as the legal representatives of the censorship agency, and they may appoint members of their staffs to carry on the censorship operations.† In the second place, the publications of the Central Committee of the Communist Party‡ and those of all republic, territorial, regional, and district committees of the party, as well as the

---

*Glavlit also censors lectures, exhibits, and some aspects of radiobroadcasting.

†These appointments of assistant editors for political control must be approved by *Glavlit*.

‡The Communist Party has its own special publishing house, *Politizdat*, for book publication. The *Pravda* press alone publishes not only the three central party newspapers, but also twenty party journals which accounted for 44 per cent of the total number of magazine copies issued during the year 1939, even though there were 1,572 other journals published in the nation. *Figures on the Press*, p. 25; *Bolshevik Press*, no. 14 (1940), pp. 59-61.

government newspaper *Izvestiya,* and publications of the former Communist Academy* and the Academy of Sciences are exempt from political-ideological examination by *Glavlit.*

These two provisions actually remove from the immediate political control of the legal censorship agency the greater and most important part of all printed material in the Soviet Union. This is particularly true of the newspaper field, which is our prime interest here, since the majority of all newspapers are the instruments of party organizations at some level of the territorial hierarchy and account for the greater part of the newspaper circulation of the nation. The further exclusion of the government organ *Izvestiya* makes the exemtion almost absolute.

Under the impact of these two provisions, *Glavlit* has never held a position of more than secondary political importance. In the newspaper and magazine field, and to a lesser extent in book publishing, the official censorship agency has been reduced very largely to the position of a mere technical agency. Its prepublication censorship is largely limited to seeing that the material examined does not reveal any military or economic state secrets. It exercises this function for party newspapers as well, even though it has no political responsibilities in regard to this group. Its post-publication censorship is even more clearly a routine, technical matter, designed to verify that the material as printed coincides with the manuscript as sent to the printer. The *Glavlit* number which is affixed to all Soviet publications testifies to this secondary or post-publication censorship.

The relative unimportance of the official censorship agency in the Soviet Union† is of special interest, because this fact helps to emphasize the need for examining a general function like censorship in relation to the total social system in which it operates. In the first place, censorship, in the form which it takes in most other countries, assumes a given relation between two distinct bodies: a government agency which exercises the censorship, and a body of newspapers

---

*This exemption has, in all probability, been extended to the Academy of Social Sciences, successor to the Communist Academy.

†I am speaking here only of internal press censorship. Censorship does, of course, play a major part in controlling the content of dispatches sent abroad by foreign correspondents.

which are not part of the government apparatus but are independent organs of opinion for either private owners or political parties. This distinction breaks down in the Soviet Union, where there is only one political party which is more or less synonymous with the government, and where there is no private ownership of the press. Since the press is primarily a party press, and since the distinction between the government and the party is more a matter of form than of substance, the logical center for control of the content of the press would be within the party itself.

Second, censorship is normally an instrument of prevention; it is designed to keep out of the press material which the censoring government finds detrimental or hostile to its interests. This situation arises, again, where the press apparatus is outside the government. Editors may then seek to print forbidden material because they have no way of knowing the government's desires, because they are motivated by political reasons (including adherence to some normative concept of freedom of the press), or simply because the material is news and good copy. In the Soviet Union, however, the press is essentially part of the government apparatus. The editors are in all cases indirectly part of the government through their position on the executive bodies of their respective party organizations all the way from the Central Committee to the party committee of some local factory; and considerations of "selling" the paper through its news value are virtually nonexistent. Furthermore, the chief problem that arises in the supervision of the Soviet press is not keeping material out, but putting into the newspapers that material which will most efficiently insure the fulfillment by the papers of the specific functions they are designed to meet. This is a problem of censorship in only a limited sense, and it requires a type of control that is quite distinct from it.

Third, censorship is a slow and costly task, and if it were to be performed on the scale required in the U.S.S.R., involving thousands of newspapers spread over thousands of miles of territory, the administrative problem would be overwhelming. By no means the least of these difficulties would be that of finding a sufficient number of people who would be qualified to exercise the censorship function on such a vast scale.

It is clear that the term censorship, at least as traditionally conceived, is of only very limited applicability in describing the mechanisms for controlling the content of the press that are required in the U.S.S.R. In the Soviet Union the problem is one of internal supervision rather than external control. As for the administrative aspect of this supervision, it does not differ in kind from the surveillance exercised over subordinate units in any hierarchical organization. It must be kept in mind that the Soviet press is a carefully ranked, thoroughly unified system of newspapers. Within this system different vertical and horizontal segments have distinct assigned functions to perform. Once this principle is recognized, it follows that there must be some method for verifying the degree and quality of conformity by lower units to the orders of those at the top of the hierarchy, and also for testing the extent to which each newspaper fulfills the functions assigned to it.

The control aspect of press regulation poses a separate, if not unique, problem, which has its roots in the fact that the press serves the party as an organ for the theoretical orientation of its membership and for the general ideological indoctrination of the mass public. Ideological matters are, of course, notoriously subject to varying interpretation; and the greater the distance from the ideological center, the greater the potentialities for variation. It has been pointed out that the body of doctrine known as "Marxism-Leninism-Stalinism" is a kind of orthodoxy in which the heresies are "deviations" from the party line, and that they are met with the same intensity that generally greets heresies in every orthodoxy. Consequently, a most important feature of the party's direction of the press is the critical examination of its ideological content; and initially the party takes other measures to insure that this examination will find a minimum of deviation.

PARTY SUPERVISION OF THE PRESS

The party effects its direction of the press primarily by three means: the selection and training of editorial personnel; the issuance of broad directives governing the content and operations of all newspapers or particular groups of papers; and the utilization of a formal supervisory machinery.

A detailed description has already been given of the special efforts exerted by the party to secure a staff of newspaper editors who are unquestionably loyal to the party, and whose level of political indoctrination is high enough to insure that they can accurately interpret and carry through the current party line in all of their editorial activities. It is very largely this corps of men, selected and trained by the party, that makes possible the absence of a more formal system of press censorship. As one Soviet commentator put it, "The success of the Bolshevik press is decided by the cadres of editors."[2]

The newspaper editors, no matter how carefully selected or well trained, nevertheless require constant direction from the party. This is in part necessary because all men are fallible and there are always errors and inadequacies that require correction. But beyond this, such direction has been necessary to adapt the entire press apparatus to changed conditions and responsibilities. Important changes in the structure and content of the newspapers must be made regularly to keep them in line with the party's definition of its immediate goals and tasks. Every new major effort of the party and government, such as the programs of industrialization and the collectivization of agriculture, and all lesser campaigns of any magnitude have been the stimulus for extensive instructions from the party to the nation's newspapers.

The collection of the party's major directives about the press through 1940, under the title *Party Decisions on the Press,* runs to over 220 pages. The party decisions included in this collection range from the most general definitions of the functions of the Soviet press, through instructions governing particular segments of the newspaper hierarchy such as the factory press, down to detailed criticism of a single district newspaper.* The major divisions of the volume's subject index serve not only as evidence of the scope of the party's regulations, but also as an excellent outline of the structure, content, and problems of the Soviet press. There are

---

*When criticism of a particular local newspaper appears under the signature of the Central Committee, it is generally meant and is treated as an example for the rest of the press at the same level to follow. Regular day-to-day criticism of local papers is handled differently, as shall be seen below.

sections on the major territorial and functional levels of the press, on press personnel, and on such special subjects as workers' and peasants' correspondents, self-criticism, and the handling of letters from readers.

The party has not merely laid down both the general and specific lines of policy it wishes newspapers to follow, but has from time to time issued the most detailed regulations, prescribing how many departments of given kinds certain groups of newspapers should have, how many lines should each day be devoted to the various sorts of news, what the cost of newspapers should be, how and in what quantities they should be delivered,[3] and so on through virtually any phase of newspaper work that might be mentioned. It has been largely through these decisions that the top leaders of the party have made known to the rank and file of its editors how they were expected to adjust and adapt their work to meet the changing demands the party set before them.

But the party's success, like that of any hierarchy, depends in the last analysis on its ability to insure that the instructions issued at the center are faithfully carried out on the periphery. Editors may be inefficient or misinformed, and directives cannot cover all the situations that arise from day to day. Daily, systematic surveillance of the functioning of the press requires a formal supervisory machinery, and the party has found it necessary to supplement the other measures it takes by creating a special apparatus to guarantee that the instructions it issues will be effectively carried out at all levels of the Soviet press.

Since the press is divided into distinct horizontal and vertical segments, the supervisory system has been shaped according to the same structural pattern. In practice, the apparatus for press control constitutes a unified and integrated system, but in order to simplify the problem of description it will be necessary to treat its two major phases separately, dealing first with the centralized and then with the local phases of control.

The Central Committee's Department of Propaganda and Agitation has several subdivisions in the hands of which general supervisory responsibility for all phases of newspaper publishing in the Soviet Union is concentrated. The Central Press Sector controls the all-union press; the Republican, Territorial, and Regional Press Sector, newspapers on the corresponding administrative levels; and the Local Press Sector, the district, city, and lower press.* Thus, the central sector has charge of the twenty-five central newspapers, while the local sector controls the work of the more than four thousand factory and farm newspapers.

In the latter case, of course, every issue of each local newspaper is not regularly read. The basic pattern of operation appears to be that each sector periodically subjects some individual newspaper or a sample of the newspapers under its control to careful scrutiny. This examination then forms the basis, where such action is indicated, for criticism of offending papers or groups of papers and for the issuance of general or specific directives. The criticism may be sent directly to the papers concerned, it may form the basis of a "press review" article in some central party organ,[4] or, when the matter is deemed of sufficient importance, a regular decision under the signature of the Central Committee may be issued. Some indication of the scope of this supervisory activity of the press sectors is given by the report that they employ more than four hundred persons to carry on the continuous work of scanning the nation's press in order to keep the central authorities informed about the degree of compliance the nation's newspapers manifest with the directives of the party.[5]

The decentralized supervision of the press is more limited in scope, but at the same time is more intensive. Each republican, regional, and district or city committee of the party has a press section within its own department of propaganda and agitation. These press sections have a dual responsibility: they are expected to guide the work of the newspapers published at their own level, and to control and supervise the activities of the papers published by the lower territorial organizations. For instance, the press section of a regional party committee expects to receive regular reports from the editors of the regional newspaper or papers. It is supposed to confirm the plans of the editorial board and will usually instruct

*The list of sectors given here may not be complete. It represents simply those sectors which have been identified through the description of their activities in such sources as *Culture and Life.*

the editors regarding the contents of each issue of the newspaper, in order to make it a more effective instrument for resolving the problems facing the region. At the same time, the press section of this regional party organization will survey and criticize the work of the district, city, and lower newspapers in that region, provide them with stories, and make specific suggestions about material which should be carried by these smaller papers. The press section may also call conferences of these lesser editors for purposes of discussion and instruction.[6]

Regional newspapers are, of course, subject to the same sort of supervision from the press section of the republican party organization and from the Central Press Sector. In addition, the officials of the various ministries are responsible for direction of the activities of their newspaper organs. This supervision is exercised, however, under the general control of the party apparatus.[7] Thus, from the smallest factory newspaper to *Pravda,* there is a continuous and interlocking system of guidance and control of Soviet newspapers exercised by the various party press departments.

Apart from the regular administrative machinery described here, the task of controlling the press is facilitated by the direct participation of Soviet newspapers and journals in the work of criticism and supervision. There was, until the beginning of the recent war, a special party journal, *The Bolshevik Press,* which very largely concerned itself with the critical review and discussion of the work of the press, particularly at the middle and lower levels. Since the war this activity of press review has been vigorously carried forward by *Culture and Life,* the organ of the Department of Propaganda and Agitation. Most of the other organs of the Central Committee, and especially *Pravda,* conduct this activity by regularly publishing a special press review column. In keeping with the functional division of responsibility in the Soviet press hierarchy, each of the major central newspapers performs this review function for its specialized press segment. Thus, the army paper *Red Star* undertakes the review and criticism of divisional and other army newspapers, and the central trade-union organ *Trud* (Labor) does the same for all trade-union newspapers. In turn, the major newspapers in each republic review and criticize all the papers of the same type issued in the republic. The regional newspaper does the same for the district and other papers in the region. This pattern is carried on down the line, each newspaper supervising the activities of those lower than it in the territorial hierarchy, until the last handwritten wall newspaper is reached for comment and criticism.

14

PUBLIC CONTROL, SELF-CRITICISM, AND THE PRESS

UP TO THIS POINT THIS DISCUSSION OF THE FUNCTIONS of the Soviet press has been based on Lenin's popular formula about the press as collective propagandist, agitator, and organizer. This particular formula, however, omits a fourth function to which Lenin assigned the utmost significance. That fourth function is the responsibility of the press to serve as an instrument of mass or public "control," and as a medium for official and popular criticism of the course of development of Soviet society and its component parts. These supervisory and critical activities of the Soviet press are among the most important aspects of its total social role, and no picture of that role is complete or analysis adequate which does not take account of this aspect of the Soviet press's activity.

SOCIAL CONTROL AND SELF-CRITICISM

The Soviet system has from its inception in 1917 been mobile and dynamic, undergoing a process of very rapid social change. The basic fact that must be kept in mind relative to the social transformation experienced in the Soviet Union in the last three decades is that the changes effected have been carried out according to a definite plan, conceived by a small group of men in accordance with certain ideological and practical considerations, executed by specialized, designated agencies, and backed by the full power of a massive state apparatus.* This fact of planned change has largely determined

---

*To say that social change is carried out according to plan in the Soviet Union is by no means to assert that the change may not and cannot move in directions both unintended and unanticipated by the social planners.

the development of distinctive forms of social control in the Soviet Union. Carrying out a plan involves the establishment of a hierarchical apparatus to which orders and instructions are issued, and whose execution of those orders must be tested and checked. The demands created by this situation are reflected in Soviet usage of the term "control," which is defined in the official *Political Dictionary* as "the verification of the execution of adopted decisions or the fulfillment of duties charged to a given organization, establishment, or official."[1]

This emphasis on verification of the execution of orders and instructions, coupled with the fact that the planners' responsibility extended to every phase of national life, rendered inadequate the common formal instruments of control such as a body of laws and the associated enforcement officers, court machinery, and legal sanctions. The scope of the plan was so great that the entire nation was transformed into one huge administrative hierarchy. Hence the law, which on the whole specifies only those acts that are forbidden, had to be supplemented by administrative decisions specifying the behavior that was required. And when such administrative orders are issued, securing their fulfillment falls not to courts but to special supervisory bodies. Thus it was necessary from the early years of the regime for both the party and the government to create special bodies, or control commissions,* to insure that the tremendous numbers of complex regulations and orders issued were indeed carried out.

Even the extension of the instruments of formal control through the creation of such special control commissions did not suffice, however, in the face of the complexity of the tasks which fell to this party seeking to regulate every minute detail of the nation's life. In the first place, no matter how competent they might be, these control commissions could not possibly hope to encompass in their supervisory efforts all of the manifold activities for which they bore some responsibility. In the second place, to attempt complete

---

*These control bodies have assumed various forms and titles during the course of Soviet history. At the present time, the party unit performing this function is known as the Party Control Commission, and the governmental unit is called the Ministry of State Control. See Towster, *Political Power,* pp. 172-175.

coverage of the execution of all orders by a single centralized agency would involve a tremendous staff which could be maintained only at great cost. The party found it necessary, therefore, to supplement these formal commissions with informal procedures of control over the execution of administrative decisions.

Such informal agencies of social control are, of course, to be found in all societies. It is a distinguishing characteristic of the Soviet Union, however, that these activities are not left to chance or the operation of spontaneous social forces. Instead, the party has designated particular individuals and institutions which are held responsible for conducting the informal work of supervision and control. It is this fact which accounts for the special social role of the Soviet *aktiv* or activist, a person in Soviet society who, in addition to his regular duties and responsibilities, takes it upon himself to see to it that the decisions of the party and government are carried out in all spheres with which he has any connection. Although this activism is by no means limited to the party, the average party member and the primary party organization are its foremost examples, and they are bound by the party Rules to carry on this supervisory or control work.

One of the most important instruments of informal control developed in the Soviet Union is known as *samokritika,* which is translated as self- or auto-criticism. Soviet *samokritika* is related to the phenomenon of public criticism found in many other countries, but it differs sufficiently in many important respects to constitute a distinctive manifestation of the Soviet way of life. In the Soviet Union this public criticism has been formalized and elaborated into a major social institution.

The Soviet institution of self-criticism has its roots in the early development of the Communist Party. Marx is reported to have maintained that the proletarian revolution differed from every other revolution in that, among other things, it criticized itself, and in criticizing itself strengthened itself. Lenin, in laying down the fundamental principles for building a revolutionary workers' party, took it as axiomatic that freedom for strong self-criticism within the party would be a virtually inviolable rule.[2]

When the party came to power, Lenin insisted on a continuance of this rule and its extension to other areas of Soviet life. Stalin adopted a similar position. He declared that self-criticism should be neither temporary nor fleeting, "nor is it something suited only to a party seeking power or threatening to one in power."[3] Finally, the Bolshevik tradition of self-criticism received additional impetus at about the time that the First Five Year Plan went into effect. In a circular addressed to all members of the party and to all workers on June 23, 1928, the Central Committee declared that the tasks of the reconstruction period could not be resolved without the boldest and most decisive rallying of the masses for participation in the process of checking and controlling the entire Soviet apparatus. The party, therefore, called upon the masses to undertake "sharp self-criticism" of all "elements of corruption," including those in the ranks of the party.[4] Since that time *samokritika* has continued to play a major role in Soviet society.

The definition of *samokritika* now current in the Soviet Union speaks of it as "exposing the deficiencies and errors in the work of particular persons, organizations, and institutions on the basis of a free, businesslike discussion by the toilers of all the problems of economic-political life . . . [and] developing the ability to see, to uncover, to acknowledge one's mistakes and to learn from them."[5] Two forms of self-criticism are recognized. Criticism conducted by the party and by other supervisory organizations is termed criticism "from above." "Criticism from below" is the term applied to criticism which emanates from ordinary citizens, both when it relates to the functioning of the state apparatus and when the workers "criticize themselves" in shop production conferences. Both forms are credited with particular importance as instruments for improving the work of the party apparatus,[6] for educating the masses and teaching them to rule,[7] for controlling the bureaucracy.

Its utilization as a means to control the bureaucracy is probably the most important aspect of self-criticism, and it is certainly the area in which the theory of what Bolshevik *samokritika* is supposed to accomplish comes closest to being realized in practice. Most readers are probably familiar with the remark that unless socialism succeeds in destroying bureaucracy, bureaucracy will destroy socialism. And indeed, one of the most persistent problems that has faced the

Soviet leaders has been the excessive bureaucratization of the governmental apparatus. Since the party has great need of this bureaucratic structure to accomplish its ends, however, it cannot realistically seek to eliminate it. The only recourse left to the party has been to seek to contain and control it. And in this effort self-criticism has been an invaluable tool. In this endeavor criticism from both above and below are utilized. That coming from above takes the form of the usual orders, instruments, and decisions from higher party and government quarters designed to check on the extent to which the lower echelons are carrying out the set policy. But this administrative control from above is supplemented by inviting and encouraging the rank-and-file party member and the average worker to participate in the process of supervision, to report to the authorities, and to criticize publicly all manifestations of behavior defined as a perversion of the party line, a corrupt or criminal act, or a plain example of bureaucratism and red tape.[8]

It must be recognized, of course, that Soviet self-criticism is in practice not precisely the thing one might anticipate on the basis of the preceding description of its assigned function. Bolshevik self-criticism operates within carefully defined limits which considerably restrict the scope of its impact as a democratic force in Soviet society. This applies to more than those obvious potentialities for abuse which reside in any widespread campaign of self-criticism and which Stalin referred to as the "vulgarization" of self-criticism.* The restrictions the party places on self-criticism go far beyond insisting that it not be used to probe into the private lives of officials for sensation mongering.

In the first place, criticism inside the party must remain within the limits of the principles set down by the party program. This means that no criticism is permitted which would give aid or comfort to those defined as enemies of the party. Furthermore, it means that no criticism is permitted which destroys the basic

---

*Among the examples of the vulgarization of self-criticism which Stalin noted were lurid outcries about the excesses in the private lives of individuals, turning self-criticism into a sport by exaggerated caricaturing and seeking after sensation, and "badgering" local officials and economic managers for minor, unintentional errors. *Party Decisions on the Press*, pp. 12-18.

"unity" of the party. In brief, once a policy or line has been set by the party, it is no longer subject to criticism, although the execution of that policy by particular *lower* officials may be criticized. Taken together, these restrictions act to limit severely the scope and content of inner-party criticism. In practice, the bulk of the criticism within the party has emanated from the central authorities, and criticism on the lower levels does not deal with issues, but is restricted to minor matters of form.*

In the second place, criticism outside the party, or mass criticism, must also remain within carefully defined limits. In the words of Stalin, the party "does not need just any kind of criticism." He cautioned that it was necessary to distinguish between "harmful" self-criticism, the variety which destroyed faith in the party and which was used by "enemies" of the Soviet system, and true Bolshevik self-criticism. For example, Stalin noted, self-criticism by the masses on the subject of labor discipline was acceptable only if it strengthened discipline, supported the factory leaders, and increased their authority.[9] It was not to be directed against party policy but only against those "corrupt elements" in the party's ranks who departed from the line, and against *kulaks* (rich peasants), "wreckers," and other defined enemies.[10]

THE OPERATION OF SAMOKRITIKA

Among the formal media of communication the party has assigned the foremost responsibility for *samokritika* to the press. In the early years of the new regime Lenin, in setting forth the goals of the press under Soviet conditions, held that the press should be the chief instrument for exposing the inadequacies of the nation's economic and political progress.[11] This position has been periodically reaffirmed in the basic party decisions on the press. The press is thus expected to serve as a major force in social control, as public guardian and party watchdog, exposing delinquencies

---

*Leninist theory insisted that whatever the state of affairs in the country as a whole, *within* the party democracy was to prevail. The later history of the party testifies to the difficulty of maintaining democratic forms within a party operating in a society in which democracy is severely circumscribed by that party itself.

on the part of functionaries and institutions and pointing out mistakes in the work of party and Soviet organizations. It is supposed to be unrelenting in its exposure and merciless in its criticism of persons guilty of squandering or wasting the public wealth, and of those who are lax in their duties and responsibilities. And all this is supposed to be done, according to the standard formula for Bolshevik self-criticism, "without respect of person, from top to bottom, and from bottom to top."[12]

The press is, of course, ideally suited to the transmission of criticism from the top to the bottom. The Soviet press serves this function, as has been seen, by devoting a large proportion of its total space to printing critical decisions issued by the party and the government. This activity is also carried out through editorials and articles in the press. And because of the close connection between the editors of newspapers and the corresponding party organizations operating at the same level, these editorials and articles have the same force as the instructions which come directly from the party organizations.[13]

As the defined guardian of the "public" interest, the Soviet press's critical functions are related to the activities of the press in the United States and elsewhere. It is certainly part of the tradition of the press in the West to keep a watchful eye on the activities of the government and public institutions and officials, and to expose what is regarded as malfeasance in office, bribery and corruption, departures from democratic practices, and so on. Newspapers in the West also have a tradition of campaigning for programs and causes which are supposed to advance the common weal.[14] But to say that the activities of the Russian and Western press are in this respect related is by no means to say that they are the same.

In the first place, when a Western newspaper carries on a crusade as a guardian of the public interest, what is defined as the public interest is determined by the editors of the given newspaper; and this question is, in turn, largely settled for the editors by the publisher and owners of the paper. In the Soviet Union the publishers of newspapers are always public organizations, and most of the papers are published by the party and the government. In this sense, the campaigns in the Soviet press always deal with issues that are officially rather than privately defined as being in the public interest.

This is not to say that the definition given by the party of what is in the public interest is of necessity closer to the "real" interest of the public than is the definition given by a private publisher. ("Real" interest is taken to mean here what the public itself, by a democratic vote based on adequate knowledge of all the facts, would decide upon.) Political parties wielding power as governments have, to be sure, been known to act primarily in their own interests even though speaking in the name of the public. And even in the case of a party like the Communist Party, which apparently sincerely acts in what it believes to be the public interest, the decisions taken may be very different from those the public itself might decide upon. It is indeed on the basis of the assumption that the masses cannot themselves correctly act in their own interests that the conception of the "revolutionary vanguard" primarily rests. It cannot be stated conclusively that there is less chance for decisions to be based on caprice simply because such a party is making the decisions. In fact, when such a party wields absolute power, as it does in the U.S.S.R., the absence of checks and balances increases the chances that decisions will be based on considerations other than the public interest as defined by the public itself.

In the second place, although crusading public criticism is a common activity in the Western press, it is by no means an indispensable function of that press. The publishers of a Western newspaper may or may not crusade and conduct public criticism as they see fit, and frequently the repercussions of such criticism, particularly the fear of alienating segments of the newspaper buying public, have led newspapermen to leave well enough alone. On the other hand, crusading and public criticism are strictly defined as indispensable functions and responsibilities of the Soviet press, and the party has made such activity a basic condition of the continued tenure of any editor.[15]

This fact leads to other significant differences. Newspaper crusades in the West tend to be irregular and sporadic. They depend for their appearance not on any force internal to the newspaper, but must wait for the appearance of a crusading publisher and editor. In contrast, the Soviet press conducts this activity as a regular daily function. The range of interest, furthermore, differs significantly. The slogan of self-criticism in the Soviet press does not include freedom to criticize the basic socio-economic system which is in force. The Anglo-American tradition does. But despite this fundamental difference, the Soviet press does in practice include comparatively more material about local economic affairs, particularly those which concern the execution of set policy—as in the management of a local factory. On the whole, in the American press, one draws a relative blank if he is interested in what goes on in industry, and especially in our large and powerful banks and corporations. Lenin sought to make this a special point of emphasis, and he declared that the Soviet press would be distinguished from the "capitalist" press in that it would deal in detail with every phase of economic life.[16] It has indeed been remarked that in the United States one criticizes the President but little else, whereas in the Soviet Union one never criticizes Stalin or his policy but does criticize virtually everything else. This generalization is certainly too broad, but it represents an element of reality.

Finally, the impact of criticism from the top in the Soviet press is generally much greater than that in the Western press. For it is not an individual who speaks, who may have no authority other than the popular indignation he can personally arouse. When the Soviet press criticizes an official or an organization, it speaks for the highest authority in the land, the Communist Party.

This criticism "from above" conducted by the press is important to the party and government as a means of controlling the execution of policy by officials and administrators at all levels of the governing apparatus. It also has significance for the over-all state of public opinion, because it gives some indication to the people that they are not left completely without protection from on high against the massive bureaucratic machine. But on the whole, this criticism from above leaves the average citizen untouched, and only indirectly enters into his daily life. It is through criticism "from below," emanating from the average citizen and the rank-and-file party member, that ordinary people are able to participate meaningfully in the work of Bolshevik *samokritika*. This criticism from below provides one of the most vital links between the top party leaders and the mass of the Soviet people. It gives the people a channel of communication with the party, a means for expressing grievances and complaints and addressing appeals to the distant foci of power in Moscow and elsewhere. And it provides the party with an opportunity to check on the effectiveness of the bureaucratic machinery without relying on that machinery itself.* As such it constitutes one of the most important elements of strength in the Soviet social and political system. Yet the two major channels through which this self-criticism flows, namely, reports of special worker and peasant correspondents and letters to newspapers from their readers, have been almost completely neglected in non-Soviet literature on the U.S.S.R.

Rabsel'kor: The Worker and Peasant Correspondent.† In a series of special decisions and in its general instructions to the press, the party has affirmed its belief that the crucial test of a newspaper's success is the extent of its ties with the masses. It has further declared that the most effective tie is found in the letters from readers to newspaper editors, and the efficiency of editors has at times been judged by the number of letters they were able to encourage their readers to write.[17]

In keeping with Lenin's dictum that Soviet newspapers must secure close ties with their mass public, the editors of those papers, from the earliest years of the regime, have had the responsibility of maintaining a broad network of nonprofessional correspondents. Stalin gave additional force to Lenin's enjoinder on this score, and in an article in *Pravda* in May 1923 he pointed out that such a net

---

*Clearly, if the party had to rely solely on some agency within the bureaucratic structure for reports on the operation of that structure, there would be many important defects in the bureaucracy's activities that it would be likely to conceal from the party leaders.

†The adjectival forms of the words for worker (*rabochii*) and for village or rural (*sel'skii*), along with the word for correspondent (*korrespondent*), are contracted and combined to form the composite words *rabkor*—worker correspondent; *sel'kor*—peasant correspondent; *rabsel'kor*—both worker or peasant correspondent; and finally, *rabsel'korskoe dvizhenie*—meaning the worker and peasant correspondents' movements.

of correspondents was essential "in order that the Party might spin threads, through the newspaper, reaching out to all of the workers' and peasants' districts."[18]

The movement of worker and peasant correspondents is based on this conception of mass participation in the work of Soviet newspapers. This movement is regarded in the U.S.S.R. as having great socio-political significance, because it opens up a channel of communication between the masses of workers and peasants and the party leaders through the medium of the press. As such it is defined as a "conductor" along which the party diffuses its influence among the masses, and at the same time is enabled to determine the temper of the masses.[19] The movement is also regarded as a school for training journalists for the Soviet press.[20]* Finally, the worker and peasant correspondents are supposed to serve as the eyes and ears of the party press in every area of the nation's life.[21] It is this latter aspect of their work which integrates the worker and peasant correspondents with the institution of self-criticism from below.

Strictly speaking, any Soviet citizen who writes some item for a wall newspaper or a regular paper is regarded as a worker or peasant correspondent. It is said of the rabsel'kor that he "is not called and he is not elected, [but] he voluntarily takes upon himself the social responsibility of informing the press about the inadequacies and the attainments of his shop, production in general, and the work and life of the workers and employees."[22] It is not to be expected, however, that the Communist Party would leave any activity it regarded as so important purely to chance or to simple voluntarism. Actually, the worker and peasant correspondents play a well-defined role, and their movement is built upon a substantial organizational foundation.

Although the process of recruiting rabsel'kory is based on voluntarism, it is nevertheless selective. The core of the worker and peasant correspondent movement is made up of party and Young Communist League members, and those who are close enough

---

*This was a significant aspect of the movement until the middle thirties. The development of regular professional schools of journalism sharply reduced the importance of the rabsel'kor movement as a means of training journalists.

to the party to be called "party sympathizers" or "non-party Bolsheviks."[23] In serving as a *rabsel'kor,* the average party member may both fulfill his obligation "daily to strengthen his connections with the masses" and exercise his right "to participate in free and businesslike discussion of practical questions of Party policy in Party meetings or in the Party press."[24] The *rabsel'kor* movement is spoken of directly as "an active carrier of the general line of the Party," and it must be recognized as one of the many "popular" or mass adjuncts to the party apparatus.[25]

The party began formally to organize the *rabsel'kor* movement in the early years of the new regime, and by 1923 the first All-Union Conference of Worker and Peasant Correspondents was held in Moscow. By 1925 there were more than 150,000 people in the movement, and by the fourth national conference in 1928 there were about five hundred thousand members represented.[26] The movement's growth kept pace with the expansion of the Soviet press network, and in 1939 there were over two million worker and peasant correspondents.[27] To choose but one example of local experience, in 1940 the *Taganrogskaya Pravda,* serving a city of 188,000 and the surrounding countryside, had seven thousand registered *rabsel'kory;* in the same year some district or county newspapers had from three hundred to five hundred such correspondents.[28] The precise number active throughout the nation at the present time is not known, but it is probably close to the 1939 figure.*

The over-all supervision of the *rabsel'kor* movement rests with the central Department of Propaganda and Agitation. The special magazine designed to guide the activities of these correspondents, *Worker and Peasant Correspondent,* which began publication in 1924 and appeared until the war, was an official organ of the

---

*Maintaining the lists of active *rabsel'kory* poses many problems similar to those presented by the task of keeping accurate records about the number of agitators. Many of the *rabsel'kory* carried on the lists apparently seldom do any actual work. The problem of supervising the *rabsel'kory* is intensified because they are widely scattered. One editor reports, for example, that of the four hundred *rabsel'kory* listed with his paper, no more than twenty-five to forty attend the trimonthly conferences held by the paper. The number of "active" *rabsel'kory* is apparently on the average half or less of the total number registered. *Worker and Peasant Correspondent,* no. 2 (January 1940), pp. 12-16; no. 4 (February 1940), p. 24.

Central Committee of the party and was run off by the same presses that turned out *Pravda*.[29] But the organization of local *rabsel'kory* is the joint responsibility of the newspaper they serve and the local party organizations. Major regional and city newspapers, which have large numbers of worker and peasant correspondents, maintain a fairly elaborate organization for them, including special "circles" of correspondents at major plants or in heavily populated residential districts. Some of the larger newspapers have a special room or *kabinet rabkora* at the newspaper office, supplied with books and instructional materials and serving as a center for lectures, conferences, and consultations conducted for the correspondents by the members of the newspaper's staff. But all newspapers, large and small, are expected to have good records on their net of correspondents, and to call them together periodically for instruction on their special tasks.[30] Frequently, those correspondents whose regular occupation puts them in a strategic position, and those who are the heads of the local "circles" of *rabsel'kory,* are enrolled for special training and instruction in the same courses which are from time to time organized by regional and district newspapers to train and retrain the editors of wall newspapers. Such courses were held on a nationwide basis in 1940, and of the 110,000 participants, about 32,000 were worker and peasant correspondents.[31]

The worker and peasant correspondents, whom Stalin referred to as the "commanders of proletarian public opinion,"[32] have a wide range of duties. Their general responsibility is defined as aiding in directing the "inexhaustible forces" of Soviet public opinion toward support of the party and government in the task of socialist construction. This includes helping the party organize the masses for higher production, better labor discipline, the development of the socialist emulation movements, and so on. They are expected to pass on to the press, and thus make the common property of all, reports about the achievements made in their place of work in setting higher production records, obtaining better labor discipline, increasing the rationalization of labor, and otherwise improving production. The prime responsibility of the *rabsel'kory,* however, is "to take a deep look into all the important phases of socialist construction" in order to expose the inadequacies in the work of the largest trusts and the smallest shop brigades, to fight the deficiencies in the government apparatus, to uncover bureaucratic manifestations, opportunism, and deviations from the party line both to the left and the right.[33]

Letters to the Editors of the Soviet Press. The communications which the editors receive from their net of nonprofessional correspondents are supplemented by letters from the average Soviet citizen who wishes to register a complaint, express a grievance or opinion, make a suggestion, or ask a question. For example, the leader of a Pioneer unit* writes that he has been obliged to move his youth group to new quarters twice on orders of the local housing authority, and he wishes to know whether such action is justified after all the efforts expended in setting up the old quarters. A group of citizens in Kharkov send a joint letter complaining that the public baths operate only infrequently and work inadequately when they do at all, and these citizens charge the directors of the local government with neglecting their duty and call on them to set the baths to rights. Or the editor of a local newspaper writes to *Pravda* and asks its opinion in a controversy the editor has been having with the secretary of the local party organization about what types of criticism it is proper for the editor to carry in his paper.[34]

The majority of the letters involve such complaints and calls for action, and they may be concerned with virtually any aspect of local Soviet life. One cannot, of course, find any letters printed which attack the Soviet system, the policies of the party, or its highest leaders. Beyond this, however, and despite the fact that most of the letters concern purely local matters like the baths or the trolley system, there is hardly any phase of local or national life which may not become the object of a critical letter. Obviously, no individual in the Soviet Union who had any grasp of the system under which he lives would write a letter, or at least a signed letter, in which he attacked the top leaders or the Soviet system. But if they are properly couched, letters may be written asking for clarification of

*The Pioneer movement is a communist organization for youth, which includes boys and girls from the ages of 10 to 16, and which operates under the supervision of the Komsomol or Young Communist League.

basic points of Marxist doctrine, and individuals and organizations standing as high as a Republic Ministry may be criticized in a letter for failing to carry out established policy.[35] Such letters are, to be sure, less frequent, and must be approached by the writers with greater caution. There is some evidence to indicate, furthermore, that on matters of really major importance, or in cases affecting responsible officials, the party organization on the corresponding level will request or designate some member to write the necessary critical "letter from a reader."[36]

Statistics are not available on the precise number of letters received by the newspapers of the Soviet Union, although the party has indicated that even the smallest papers, with a circulation of less than one thousand copies, should daily receive them in tens and the larger newspapers by the hundreds.[37] Certainly actual performance does not always reach these levels.[38] The most impressive record, of course, is achieved by the central newspapers which reach a national audience. For example, in 1935 and 1936 *Pravda* received an average of more than 120,000 letters per year. In the next two years the inflow of letters almost doubled, the average annual receipt approaching 210,000, and in the first two months of 1939 letters arrived at the *Pravda* office at the rate of 22,000 per month.[39] The record of the intermediary sectors of the press is less impressive. If we take a Ukrainian language newspaper published in Kharkov as representative, it would appear that the average republican and regional newspaper received less than twenty thousand letters in the course of a year. For district newspapers, which in 1939 had an average circulation of under three thousand copies, something between three thousand and seven thousand letters per year was regarded as a commendable performance in 1940.[40]

It may be said that the *rabsel'kor* makes a contribution to this flow of letters because that is part of his social role as an "activist" in Soviet society. And it may be that to some extent other people continue to write these letters because they are aware that Stalin and the Central Committee have invited the masses to participate fully in the work of self-criticism and supervision of the bureaucracy. But it is equally likely that the best explanation of the flow

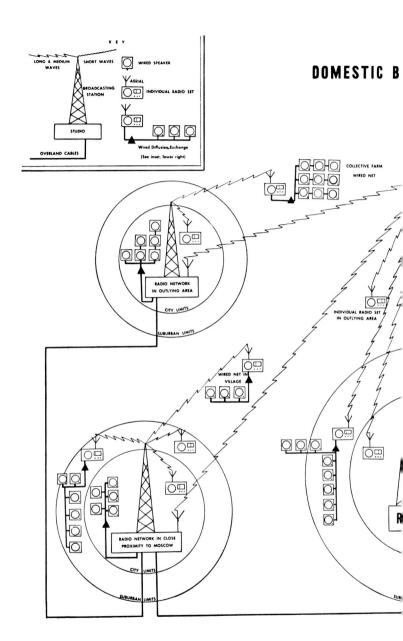

DOMESTIC B

KEY

LONG & MEDIUM WAVES   SHORT WAVES

BROADCASTING STATION

STUDIO

OVERLAND CABLES

WIRED SPEAKER

AERIAL

INDIVIDUAL RADIO SET

Wired Diffusion Exchange
(See inset, lower right)

COLLECTIVE FARM
WIRED NET

RADIO NETWORK
IN OUTLYING AREA

CITY LIMITS

SUBURBAN LIMITS

INDIVIDUAL RADIO SET
IN OUTLYING AREA

WIRED NET IN
VILLAGE

RADIO NETWORK IN CLOSE
PROXIMITY TO MOSCOW

CITY LIMITS

SUBURBAN LIMITS

R

SUB

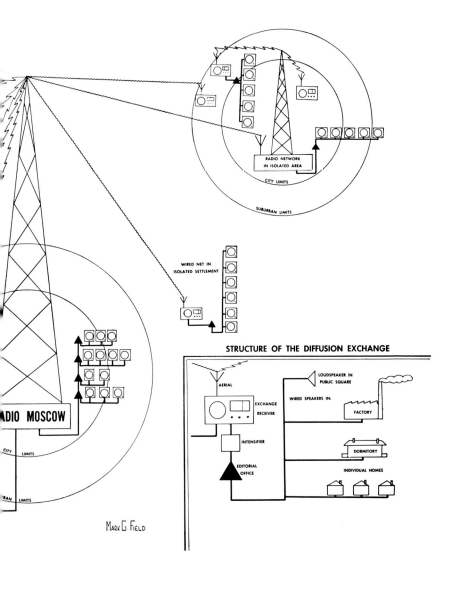

RADIO NETWORK
IN ISOLATED AREA

CITY LIMITS

SUBURBAN LIMITS

WIRED NET IN
ISOLATED SETTLEMENT

RADIO MOSCOW

CITY LIMITS

BAN LIMITS

Mark G Field

STRUCTURE OF THE DIFFUSION EXCHANGE

AERIAL

EXCHANGE
RECEIVER

INTENSIFIER

EDITORIAL
OFFICE

LOUDSPEAKER IN
PUBLIC SQUARE

WIRED SPEAKERS IN:

FACTORY

DORMITORY

INDIVIDUAL HOMES

of letters lies in the fact that the average citizen or party member recognizes that these letters are his most direct channel of communication with the party leaders. More than most other recourses available to the Soviet citizen, such letters frequently get action. For almost all Soviet newspapers regularly print at the bottom of their "Letters to the Editor" columns brief items reporting the action taken on complaints raised in previously published (and unpublished) letters. And these reports frequently mention the reprimanding, the dismissal, and at times the indictment of officials and others whose activities were brought to the fore in the letters.[41] Since the Soviet citizen thus has an opportunity to release his aggression against frustrating inadequacies in his civic institutions, and at the same time has some hope of securing ameliorative action, he continues to write letters to the press.

A more or less standard procedure has been developed for handling the letters received in the offices of Soviet newspapers. This procedure is a product of specific instructions from the party and the exchange of experience among editors through the pages of their trade journals.[42] Since there is available a fairly complete description of the treatment of these letters in the offices of a representative republican newspaper, it will be convenient to describe the operations of that particular paper. The paper in question is *Dawn of the East*,[43] published in Russian in Tbilisi as one of the organs of the Communist Party of the Georgian Republic, and serving as the chief Russian newspaper of that republic of about three and a half million people and surrounding areas in the Transcaucasia.*

Like all other newspapers in the Soviet Union, *Dawn of the East* has a special department to handle letters to the editor,[44] and in this paper, as in many others, it is one of the largest departments. The letter department of *Dawn of the East* has eight members on

---

*Two thirds of the people in the Georgian Republic are Georgians, and the official language is Georgian. Naturally, the Republic Party Organization also publishes a Georgian newspaper. The appearance of a major Russian-language newspaper in this area, however, is not unusual, both because there are many Russians in the region served by the paper, and because Russian is widely used, particularly among the officials and professional people. The newspaper *Dawn of the East* is regarded as a model republican paper by the Central Committee of the party.

the staff: a director and assistant director, four rewrite men or "literary collaborators" who are usually newspapermen in training, and two secretaries.

When a letter, from either a *rabsel'kor* or some other reader, arrives in the department, it is read through by one of the staff members, who then fills out a master index card for the newspaper's files. This card gives a brief synopsis of the content of the letter and notes necessary background data such as the date, the name and position of the sender, to whom the letter was addressed, and why it was written. Following this, the letter and the file card are passed along to the department director or his assistant, who checks the information and determines to whom the letter should be forwarded for further action. A note is also supposed to be sent to the letter writer informing him of the receipt of his communication, reporting the disposition of the letter, and suggesting any further action which the letter writer should take.[45]

The director of the letter department may forward a letter either to one of the news editors of the paper or to an agency outside the newspaper. Only those letters which are regarded as most important or interesting are forwarded to the editors. They survey the letters sent to them by the letter department, and make a final selection of those which will be used in the newspaper. These letters may enter the paper in a variety of forms. They may be printed outright, either in the original or condensed; or extracts from several letters on the same subject may be run under a single heading. Frequently the content of several letters will be used as the basis for a critical article written by a staff member, or a letter may be printed along with critical comments on the subject by the editors. In many newspapers, of course, little more is done with the letters than to allow them to pile up and collect dust.[46]

There are apparently no fixed rules for the placement of this material, but some fairly standard practices exist. Letters of special interest and importance may be placed on the front page. Usually, however, the letters appear on an inside page and are grouped in one or two columns under such headings as "Letters to the Editor," "From Our Readers," or "Signals," the latter referring to warning signs about deficiencies in the operation of the party-government apparatus contained in the letters. These columns generally appear in close proximity to critical articles written by the editors or regular correspondents, reviews of the local press, and similar materials.

There is considerable variation among newspapers in the number of letters that they publish. The general-circulation national newspapers such as *Pravda* and *Izvestiya* generally carry only one or two letters in any issue, and these appear only in occasional issues. This is in part because of the large amounts of official and semi-official information and releases that they contain. But *Pravda* and *Izvestiya* are also limited in this respect because their circulation is so completely nationwide, whereas most critical letters deal with specific local issues. In contrast, a paper like *Evening Moscow,* which among Soviet newspapers is probably the outstanding example of a "popular" paper, may carry five or more letters in one issue and will have some letters almost every day. A similar contrast may be drawn between a newspaper like *Labor,* which is the national organ of the All-Union Trade Union Council and is addressed to all union officials and members in the Soviet Union, and a paper like *Gudok* (Whistle), which is addressed to the more restricted audience of railway workers and which carries a significantly larger number of critical letters.

Frequently letters are published along with a response from some official promising corrective action, or with a note from the editors calling for such action. If there has been no response or satisfactory action taken after the publication of a letter on a given subject, the editors will generally run another letter on the subject and a stiffer editorial note calling for satisfaction. In addition, the press runs regular items which sum up the action obtained as a result of the earlier printing of various letters.[47] All of this activity is defined as necessary "to show the workers the power of the Bolshevik press."[48]

It is obvious that only a small portion of the letters can be printed, however, and it is necessary to follow the movements of the remainder. The majority of the letters are supposed to be forwarded to the responsible government officials and public agencies like the trade unions for their advice, information, or action.[49] Obviously, this invites a situation in which the agencies receiving those letters will simply file and forget them. Consequently, the newspaper is expected to maintain a regular check on the action taken on the letters forwarded. It requests the agencies to report back the action on any letter, and in case the answer is unsatisfactory, the newspaper can back up its demand by a stinging critical article which is more likely to bring a response. The newspapers that are conscientious in this matter conduct periodic checks or "raids" to verify the extent to which letters are given proper attention by the agencies to which they are directed, and publish regular reviews of the results of these checks.* In cases that warrant it, the newspaper may take direct action. For example, the editors of *Dawn of the East* report that after having received letters about the inefficient organization of bread baking in Western Georgia, they notified the Chairman of the Council of Commissars of the Georgian Republic, who then ordered the Commissariat of Trade to send a special investigating commission. The story was fully covered in all of its stages in *Dawn of the East*. In another instance of direct intervention, the newspaper had received a letter from a Red Army man stating that the local finance officials were about to confiscate his household belongings for non-payment of taxes. The editors phoned the local procurator (equivalent to a district attorney) and asked him to intercede in the case.[50]

In this way the newspaper seeks not only to be a center to which the grievances of the citizenry against the bureaucratic apparatus are directed, but also tries to keep a watchful eye for the party on all the activities of the local government and public organizations. The letter department of *Dawn of the East,* following a pattern reported by other papers,[51] sought to facilitate this task by carefully charting the inflow of letters. The territory it served was divided into districts, and each of the major government, party, and public organizations was broken down into component parts on a large chart. Then, as letters came in, they were recorded in the

---

*The *rabsel'kory* play the major role in such "raids." The newspaper office provides them with details about specific complaints, including the date on which the letter was forwarded to some agency and the action requested. The local officials are then "confronted" and asked why some action on such and such a letter was not taken. The results of these raids are written up in critical press articles and also form the basis for conferences between local officials and the local newspaper editors. For examples, see *Worker and Peasant Correspondent,* no. 15 (August 1940), p. 62; *Culture and Life,* no. 7, March 11, 1947.

proper box, and thus the editors had available a frequency chart showing the districts and the agencies or parts of agencies about which they had the greatest number of complaints. Whenever the frequency got too high in any box on the chart, the editors started to investigate or notified the responsible authorities.*

In addition to dealing directly with various agencies concerning the subjects mentioned in letters, the newspapers are expected to maintain close ties with the Soviet justice authorities. The party has made it a major responsibility of the Soviet newspaper to watch not only for minor bureaucratic manifestations, but to search as well for corruption, bribery, misappropriation of funds, and other serious violations of either the law or party discipline and the party line. Many of the letters received by the newspaper refer to alleged illegal acts of this kind. The party and government have therefore issued detailed instructions to guide the collaboration of the justice authorities and the newspapers. In 1929, for example, the Commissariat of Justice provided that each region should have a three-man commission, including the local procurator and the local newspaper editor, to work out procedures for coöperation in this matter. And the party has instructed its Control Commission that it must investigate all criminal actions revealed in the press.[52] In practice, the director of any letter department on a Soviet newspaper sends a copy of all letters that might require their action to the appropriate justice or control agencies in the government and the party.[53] This includes, of course, letters which the editors feel are written by people who are "hostile" to the regime.

Just as publication of a letter together with the response of some official, or his report of action taken, completes the cycle for those letters used directly in the newspaper, so the cycle is supposed to be completed for those letters sent to outside agencies for action. This is done by informing the letter writer of the action that has been taken on his letter. The response may come from the newspaper, or directly from the responsible agency.[54]

*This should not be taken to mean that the newspapers receive or show interest in only critical letters. Both the worker correspondent and the average reader are urged to report the successes and achievements of their work or residential group to the press. These letters are as much featured in Soviet newspapers as those of a critical nature. Such materials, however, are treated more like straight news items.

What has been described here is, of course, simply a model of what standard procedure is supposed to be in the handling of letters written to Soviet newspapers. It is clear that the reality is frequently far from the stated ideal. The massive demands made by such a procedure are in themselves sufficient notice that this plan can operate with only very limited effectiveness, and our knowledge of past Soviet difficulties with less ambitious schemes having much higher priority lends support to this assumption. If additional evidence is needed, one can always turn to the long series of decisions issued by the party castigating newspapers at all levels for their failure to give proper attention and treatment to the letters they receive from their readers.[55]

There are, in addition, important limitations on the effectiveness of this procedure which arise before letters reach the newspaper office. The most important limitation, of course, is that the citizen who writes a letter automatically exposes himself to potential political scrutiny in a society in which political misunderstanding can have serious consequences. In addition, the exposure of officials or fellow workers through a letter to the press runs counter to many of the standards of in-group solidarity. Stalin has noted, for example, that a serious defect in the operation of *samokritika* within the party lies in the fact that some party officials hesitate to engage in criticism because they anticipate that this might make enemies, or because they hope that someday when they make a similar error themselves the person whom they did not criticize at an earlier time will return the compliment.[56]* A letter of criticism also exposes the writer to retaliatory action, especially in cases where he may be criticizing a superior or any person in a position to make his accuser uncomfortable. The worker and peasant correspondent, for example, served as a kind of "finger-man" during the collectivization, exposing ku-

---

*Conversations with Soviet displaced persons indicate that frequently an individual assigned by the local party unit to write a critical letter would draft that letter only after private consultation with the person being criticized. In this way, he could satisfy the demand of the party without alienating friends and associates. For cases of controversy, drawn from the Soviet press, concerning such delicate problems as who may criticize whom and when, see *Worker and Peasant Correspondent*, no. 10 (May 1940), p. 54; *Pravda*, November 28, 1947; *Culture and Life*, no. 6, August 20, 1946.

laks and peasants who hid their grain or cattle. In these and other situations they have been attacked, on occasion even murdered, and otherwise made the subject of retaliation. It became necessary for the justice authorities, therefore, to take special measures for the protection of the "rights" of the *rabsel'kory*.[57]

But even as an imperfectly operating system, the Soviet pattern of handling letters to the newspapers remains an impressive indication of the efforts made by the party to encourage mass participation in the work of social control, albeit within the narrow limits set by the party itself. A grasp of this phenomenon is essential to an understanding of the operations of the Soviet social system and is indispensable for an accurate assessment of the strength of the regime.

SELF-CRITICISM AND THE SOVIET SYSTEM

The major manifest functions of press *samokritika* are readily discernible. In the first place, self-criticism in the press is expected to serve as an instrument for controlling the activities of the party and government bureaucracy. It is assumed that this criticism will supplement and make more efficient the efforts at supervising this bureaucracy exerted by more formal instruments such as the party and government control commissions. In this sense self-criticism is regarded as being functional for the Soviet system as a whole, since it presumably facilitates the society's efforts to achieve its stated goals. The party at least also looks upon the criticism as being "good" for the bureaucracy, in that it is expected to enable the bureaucrats to fulfill their responsibilities more effectively.

In the second place, the extensive participation of the masses in self-criticism is regarded as a means of training them eventually to take over the task of ruling the country. Actually, however, this "taking over" by the masses seems to lie somewhere in the very distant future, and there are few signs that the Soviet regime is moving energetically in that direction. In this light, mass participation in self-criticism may be viewed as a functional substitute for the very condition toward which it was supposed to lead.

It should be noted that at one stage in the development of his thinking, Lenin made the assumption that the progress of capitalist society had so simplified certain operations of the state that they could easily be performed by every literate person.[58] This was summed up in his popular slogan that under socialism every housewife could help run the government, and it took concrete form in the early years of the regime in the extensive development of workers' management in the plant and efforts at rotation of workers between the workbench and the office desk. Even within Lenin's lifetime, however, experience demonstrated that this theory was not workable,[59] and the extent of the shift in the official party position can be clearly traced in the changes over the years in Stalin's attitude toward the role of the technical intelligentsia in Soviet society.[60] But even though direct mass participation in government and economic administration was not feasible, the ideal of such participation continued to be an important element of Bolshevik ideology. And mass participation in criticism of the execution of policy by officials has enabled the party in some measure to approximate this ideal. In short, even though every housewife cannot take a direct part in actively managing the country, she can at least participate in criticizing the manner in which individual officials and organizations execute the policy established by the party and government. This is not necessarily to say, of course, that this substitution, which seems to satisfy the interests of the party leaders, is equally satisfying to the masses. It is certainly a most limited form of self-rule.

A third major function of press self-criticism is to serve as a channel of communication between the party and the people. It is a principle of Bolshevik tactics, as we have noted, that the party must be careful not to run too far ahead of mass thinking or lag too far behind. Yet the Soviet Union has not developed any system for public-opinion polling such as those elaborated in the United States, and there would be serious obstacles to establishing such a system in the U.S.S.R. Through the medium of critical letters to the press, however, the party is able to obtain a rough, if not completely accurate, picture of the state of popular thinking. At the same time, the people are provided a channel of direct contact with the party for registering complaints which might otherwise be screened out or repressed if they had to pass through the bureaucracy against which they are primarily directed.

Attention must also be called to those aspects of the operation of self-criticism in the press that may be regarded as latent functions. First consideration should be given to the way in which self-criticism acts as a device for releasing tension and channeling aggression in Soviet society. Participation in any social system is associated with the generation of tension in individuals and with the development of some aggressive tendencies. Although there is some doubt whether or not all societies tend to generate equal or different amounts of tension and aggression, it is perfectly clear that they differ widely in the means they make available, and in a sense encourage, for the release of such tension and aggression. In some societies the predominant pattern is for the individual to suppress such feelings and tendencies, in others to express them against specific individuals or groups within the same social system, and in still others to direct aggression outwards toward persons or institutions outside the given society.[61]* These different modes of expression frequently have a significant impact on the effective functioning of the society as a whole. In some cases the mode of expression for aggression may hinder the effective functioning of the social system and be disruptive to the total social fabric. In other cases, and these are obviously more common, the mode of expressing aggression may be geared in to support the existing social system and to facilitate its smooth functioning.

Self-criticism in the Soviet press is an interesting example of the latter method for the release of tension and the direction of aggressive tendencies. Even if one assumes that the amount of tension generated by life in the Soviet Union is significantly less than that generated by life in the United States, and as yet there is no valid information to this effect, it certainly cannot safely be maintained that there is no hostility generated or aggression expressed. There remains, therefore, the question of what form this expression, whatever its extent, actually takes. Viewed in this context, it is clear that the institution of self-criticism provides a channel for the expression of popular feelings that is not only relatively harmless to the existing

---

*There are also significant differences in the mode of expressing or handling aggression between different social groups within the same society. No effort is made here to distinguish these class and other differences as they are manifested in the Soviet Union.

social system but is actually designed and operated to support it.

The aggressive tendencies produced by the frustrations of daily life in the Soviet Union, especially those resulting from the gap between expectations and reality in the consumption of goods and the provision of comforts, could be expressed in the form of hostility toward the regime and toward the party leadership.* Whatever value judgment one might make of such expressed hostility, it must be recognized that this would be disruptive to the basic pattern of Soviet life as it now exists, and that in particular it would hinder the effective leadership of the party.

By placing the symbol of the bureaucrat as a screen between itself and the masses, however, the party is able to deflect much of this aggression against an object other than itself. And it is able to do so without the necessity of undertaking to suppress or discourage all popular criticism, for it is well known that open criticism of the leaders or the Soviet regime is most harshly treated. On the contrary, the party places itself in the role of champion of popular criticism, as the group that encourages it and holds the objects of criticism accountable for their deeds.[62] At the same time, popular *samokritika* serves more than simply this negative function of harmlessly draining off hostile energies which might otherwise be directed against the party leadership. It serves a positive function as well, in that it contributes to controlling the bureaucracy and helps the party in keeping that bureaucracy on the line dictated by the nation's formal leadership.†

A second major latent function that self-criticism performs is to serve in the Soviet regime as a substitute, however inadequate, for a system of free elections. The Soviet Constitution provides for universal, equal, and direct suffrage based on the secret ballot. In practice, however, this system does not operate in anything like the fashion of elections in the United States or England. The electors are

---

*That such hostility against the regime, expressed both covertly and where possible overtly, does actually exist in major proportions is not at all questioned here. There is an important problem, however, regarding the degree to which it is thus directly expressed, as compared to the degree to which it is otherwise drained off.

†The effects thus achieved are not always precisely those that were intended or desired. This problem is discussed below as an element of dysfunction in the operation of the system of self-criticism.

presented with but a single slate of candidates, known as the "Party and non-Party bloc." The voter may vote for or against these candidates, but he has no real opportunity to vote for alternate candidates who might stand for a different position. Furthermore, this initial bloc of candidates is chosen primarily by the local party organizations.* And when deputies to the legislative bodies have been elected, the average citizen has but slight ability to affect their actions. The Constitution does provide that the deputies shall report back to their electors, but the majority of the deputies are party members and are bound by party discipline to give their first allegiance to the orders of the party. It is worth mentioning in this connection that even if the Soviet citizen had more effective control over his elected officials, it would not mean any profound change in his life patterns, since the bulk of his daily actions are governed not by legislative decision but by administrative action.[63]

This exceedingly brief sketch is meant simply to indicate the very limited ability of the average Soviet citizen to affect the actions of his government. The two- or multiple-party system and the freer elections in Western democracies provide the citizen with the opportunity to vote a change of officials and in some cases a change in the basic form of government. He can, in short, always act according to the popular slogan, "throw the rascals out." As Lincoln Steffens and a number of other political scientists have pointed out so well, this may result simply in another group of "rascals" coming into office. But whatever its limitations, the threat of being turned out of office acts as a positive influence on the conduct of public officials and provides the electorate with an opportunity for a periodic political catharsis.

The structure of the Soviet political system is such that it does not provide for or permit a periodic opportunity to "throw the rascals out" by means of voting another party into public office. But the

---

*Public organizations, like trade unions, also have the right to nominate candidates. The Communist Party is the only legal party in the Soviet Union, however, and it alone has the right to form caucuses within these public organizations. In practice, the party leaders do consult with these organizations before selecting the bloc of candidates, and before their final nomination the names of the candidates may be placed before public groups for discussion and criticism. Unpopular candidates may be withdrawn, but in the end only those acceptable to the party may run.

Soviet system of self-criticism does act as a functional substitute for a system of free elections in that it provides a roughly equivalent restraining influence on administrative officials, and it provides the citizenry with the satisfaction of at least feeling that it exercises some public control over those officials. This applies, of course, specifically to administrative officials, or the bureaucracy, alone. It does not apply to the top party leaders.

This discussion has concentrated on the ways in which press self-criticism may be viewed as functional in the framework of the Soviet social system. But there are also several aspects of the operation of self-criticism that must be seen as dysfunctional for the Soviet system. In the first place, the institution of self-criticism has great potentialities for getting out of hand, and this must be regarded as particularly threatening by the leaders of a society such as the Soviet Union where so much emphasis is placed on careful control from above of every aspect of the nation's activities. When self-criticism is encouraged, there is always the possibility that it may be turned against the regime, that it may become "destructive" rather than "constructive." It was, among other things, such manifestations that Stalin noted when he spoke against the "vulgarization" of the slogan of self-criticism, and stressed that not any kind of self-criticism but only that sort which strengthened the party's rule was acceptable.[64] These restrictions which Stalin placed on self-criticism, and which were described in Soviet sources as a "sharpening" of the slogan, clearly indicate the potentialities of this institution for operating in a manner that would make it, at least in terms of the party's interest, dysfunctional rather than functional.

A second respect in which self-criticism appears as dysfunctional has to do with its potentialities for having a boomerang effect on Soviet public opinion. For it would appear likely that in so far as the Soviet citizenry is encouraged to criticize its public officials and administrators, that citizenry also develops certain expectations about the results to be obtained from this criticism. Frequently, however, the deficiences of which the Soviet citizen may complain are not the fault of any administrative failure, but are imposed by the Soviet system itself.

For example, a worker may write to the press and ask why more and better quality shoes are not available; and the letter writer may go so far as to say that he has seen a party and government decision calling for the production of a certain quantity of shoes of given quality. The newspaper may follow up this letter with a criticism of the local directors of shoe production and distribution for bureaucratic tendencies and failure to meet the party's demands. But however efficient the local shoe industry officials might be, they would be helpless, or very nearly so, in their ability to affect the basic shoe supply. For the insufficient numbers of shoes and their low quality are essentially the end product of a long chain of events going back to questions of the availability of leather, adequate plant and shoe production facilities, the supply of skilled labor, and so on. And these matters are in turn settled at the higher levels of national planning, over which the local shoe officials have no control. In the last analysis, the worker probably does not get his shoes, no matter how many critical letters he may write, for that would require a central decision to devote more of Soviet production to consumer and less to machine-goods industries. It may be assumed, therefore, that this consistent failure to get results in such matters would tend to undermine faith in the effectiveness of public criticism. Thus, as an additional frustration, it might add to the alienation of the citizen from the Soviet regime. In this way self-criticism may boomerang, producing just the opposite effect on public opinion from the effect intended by the party.

One additional aspect of the institution of self-criticism that deserves mention here is its inadequacy as a means of testing public opinion. This is not, strictly speaking, an element of dysfunction, but it is certainly a serious limitation. The most obvious difficulty presented by the use of letters as an index of public thought and sentiment is the problem of sampling. Not everyone writes letters, whereas some people write a great many. And there is a strong probability that the element of selectivity in the letter writers may give a consistent bias in the picture of public opinion thus obtained. To some extent this may be compensated for by the activities of the *rabsel'-kory,* who are selected both because they are opinion leaders and because it is assumed they are sensitive reporters of public opinion.

But here again the Soviet system has important internal limitations. As party members and local opinion leaders, the *rabsel'kory* may seek to give the best possible interpretation of the state of public opinion in their area, since this reflects favorably on their activities as party members and opinion leaders. Similarly, newspapers may seek to soft-pedal certain critical items, since the newspaper also has a major responsibility for the state of public opinion in the area it serves. Too much criticism of certain types makes the editors appear in an undesirable light, as men unable effectively to mold and control public opinion among their newspaper readers. It may well be, in fact, that what the higher party authorities have labeled "negligence" in the handling of letters by newspaper offices was actually a conscious or unconscious effort to suppress and keep from the view of the party leaders critical materials that might be interpreted as demonstrating the inadequacy of the newspaper's efforts to shape public opinion. And as a result, the institution of *samokritika*, designed to clear the channels of communication from bottom to top, might actually contribute to clogging those very channels.

PART 4

DOMESTIC BROADCASTING IN THE U.S.S.R.

15

THE ADMINISTRATION OF RADIOBROADCASTING

THE RADIO IS WIDELY REGARDED AS THE SUPREME MEDIUM of mass communication. In the Soviet Union radio does not enjoy the overwhelming importance attached to it in the United States, but this is primarily a product of the technical deficiencies that have held back the development of Soviet radiobroadcasting. The radio is, however, recognized as one of the most important means of communication, and as such it manifests the same basic patterns that are characteristic of personal oral agitation and the press in the Soviet Union.

One of the most striking features of the radio apparatus in the U.S.S.R. is that its entire physical structure differs markedly from the radio system familiar in the United States. This has been determined in large part by restrictions imposed by Soviet geography and demography, and by limitations on the resources available for developing radiobroadcasting. It has also been determined, however, by the party's conception of its role in Soviet society as teacher, guide, and leader of the masses. The party has therefore designed the Soviet radio apparatus to give it maximum effectiveness as an instrument for mobilizing the population in much the same way it has developed its press apparatus.

Beyond its physical structure, the entire pattern of radio operations has also been determined by the party's needs. The Soviet radio is not regarded as being chiefly a source of amusement or a means of recreation for the population.[1] Rather, it is defined as an instrument of popular education, a tool for the "communist upbringing" of the masses. The Soviet radio is conceived of as being primarily a channel of communication between the party and the masses, as another one of those "driving belts" by which the party seeks to mobilize the population for the attainment of the nation's goals.[2]

This conception of the functions of radio in turn determines the content of radiobroadcasting, the establishment of program policies, the approach to testing the reactions of the radio audiences, and so on.

THE ALL-UNION RADIO COMMITTEE

The first major broadcast in the Soviet Union was sent out on September 17, 1922, by a 12-kilowatt station alleged to have been the most powerful in the world at the time. Thus the Soviet Union claims to have entered the radio race during the first lap, about two months ahead of England and three months ahead of France, according to the estimates of the Vice-Minister of Communications.[3]

In October 1924 the Council of People's Commissars established a "Joint-Stock Company for Radio-Broadcasting," known as *Radioperedacha* (Radio Transmissions), whose stock was held jointly by the trade unions and public education authorities. During the same month, on October 12, 1924, the Sokolnicheskaya radio station, operated by the cultural section of the Moscow Trade Union Council, went on the air, and this marked the beginning of systematic radiobroadcasting in the Soviet Union. The first radio-diffusion exchange went into operation at Moscow in 1925 with a net of fifty wired speakers.[4]*

In July 1928 *Radioperedacha* was dissolved and the control of radiobroadcasting transferred to the Commissariat of Posts and Telegraphs, already in charge of radiotelegraphy.[5] The development of broadcasting and reception under these auspices was apparently not satisfactory, however, and, with the aim of achieving centralized control of radio work, an All-Union Committee for Radiobroadcasting and Radiofication under the Council of People's Commissars of the U.S.S.R. was established by a decree of January 31, 1933. Nine

---

*The radio-diffusion network, which forms the basis of radio reception in the U.S.S.R., is fully described in Chapter 16.

months elapsed before the Council of Commissars, in a regulation dated November 27, 1933,[6] defined the authority and powers of the Radio Committee and charged it with "the organization, planning, and operational direction of all radiobroadcasting in the U.S.S.R., including radio diffusion by lower radiobroadcasting exchanges in district centers, Machine-Tractor Stations, and so forth."

According to the original regulation, the All-Union Radio Committee, designated by the letters VRK in Russian, was to have a chairman, vice-chairmen, and members of the committee. The law provided that the work of the Radio Committee should be carried on by administrations, sectors, and other administrative units to be developed by the committee. A detailed description of the current structure of the Radio Committee is unfortunately not available, the latest fairly complete table of organization being that for 1936.[7] Later references to particular parts of the organization, however, indicate that the structure of the committee is today substantially the same. The All-Union Radio Committee appears to be divided into the following chief units:

The Administration of Central Broadcasting plans, organizes, and executes the programs broadcast by stations directly under the operational control of the Radio Committee. These programs, which issue primarily from Moscow, are designated as central or all-union broadcasts, that is, they are intended for nationwide consumption. The administration is apparently also responsible for sending out programs beamed to certain outlying regions of the country, in particular the far North and the Soviet Far East, and for those programs intended primarily for consumption within the Russian Republic (RSFSR), the largest and most populous of the sixteen constituent republics.

The Administration of Central Broadcasting appears to be functionally divided into sectors, also referred to as editorial offices, of which the following have been identified:[8] the Propaganda and Agitation Sector, the Late News Sector, the Editorial Office of Defense, the Sector of Literary-Dramatic Broadcasts, and the Sector of Children's Broadcasts. The activity of these sections is further spread among subordinate administrative units according to subject matter; the Literary-Dramatic Sector, for example, includes a Literary Department which in turn has subdivisions such as that for Soviet literature.[9]

The Administration of Musical Broadcasting has been identified,[10] but relatively little information concerning its structure is available. In former years musical broadcasting was controlled by a sector, and its elevation to the status of an administration reflects the continued importance of music in the composition of Soviet radio programs.

The Administration of Local Broadcasting does not itself conduct any broadcasts, but is limited to the supervision of broadcasting done by local radio committees and by the directors of diffusion exchanges. Its chief task is to secure the fulfillment of the directives of the All-Union Committee by organizations operating on lower levels. It also has been reported to train radio performers and assign them to local radio committees, and to organize the formation of all-union and zonal networks. The administration is believed to be divided primarily on a territorial basis, and to include editorial offices for literature, music, education, and other subjects, which assist local committees with their programming.

The International Bureau appears to be the same as an office frequently referred to as the Foreign Broadcasting Sector, which is responsible for broadcasts directed outside the Soviet Union.

The Administration of Radiofication is primarily a technical agency and carries the responsibilities in this sphere with which the Radio Committee is charged by law.[11] These responsibilities include consulting with the Ministry of Communications and other interested government agencies, and advising them concerning plans for "mass radiofication," that is, the construction of receiving networks and broadcasting stations, the assignment of wave lengths, and the distribution of sending and receiving equipment. The Radio Committee is also expected to coöperate with scientific and technical research organizations, the Ministry of Communications, and other agencies in organizing national radio conferences, and in representing the U.S.S.R. in international radiobroadcasting negotiations.

The Planning, Financial, and Accounting Sector handles administrative matters within the Radio Committee. The committee is obliged, as are all Soviet organizations, to prepare detailed annual and quarterly plans for all of its operations. The All-Union Radio Committee is also charged with arranging the financing of radio-broadcasting and with collecting the fees that must be paid by subscribers for the services of diffusion exchanges and by owners of regular radio sets. These fees, which are in part turned over to the Ministry of Communications,* provide the committee with a sizable budget. It is intended that the committee be self-sustaining in time, with an excess in earnings which can be turned over to the government, but as late as 1941 the committee was still receiving a considerable allotment from the state budget; in that year the sum was 3,686,000 rubles.[12]

In addition to these major units, the Radio Committee has in the past included a State Publishing House for Affairs of Radio, a Recording Plant, and a Technical Supplies Section.

It may be noted, finally, that despite the rather sweeping terms of the first article of the regulation defining the committee's scope, other sections provide for considerable participation by other interested departments and organizations. This has resulted in the initial self-defeat of the declared goal of centralized control of radio work. The division of authority has been a regular source of complaint both by the administrative and political directors of broadcasting and by the authorities in charge of the technical aspects of radio.[13]

The All-Union Radio Committee also serves as the Radio Committee for the Russian Republic (RSFSR), which includes more than half the population and an even larger proportion of the territory of the entire Soviet Union. Each of the remaining fifteen constituent union-republics has its own radio committee, as do the autonomous republics, the territories, most of the regions, and a number of the larger cities of the nation. The council of ministers of each union-republic appoints its own radio committee in con-

---

*Only the actual broadcasting studios are controlled by the Radio Committee; all sending equipment, including the long-distance lines, is administered by the Ministry of Communications. The conditions under which the Radio Committee uses the stations, equipment, and lines, as well as the costs to be paid for such use, are settled by agreement between the Committee and the Ministry of Communications. See Goron, *Radiobroadcasting,* p. 4.

sultation with the All-Union Committee. These union-republic radio committees, in turn, confirm appointments made by the respective local government bodies to the radio committees for autonomous republics, territories, and regions. Thus a high degree of centralized control is assured. This control is fixed by law, since the local radio committees are defined as being the "local organs" of the All-Union Committee, and their chairmen as "representatives" or "authorized agents" of the VRK.[14] At the present time the All-Union Committee has under its general direction 163 local radio committees in republics, territories, and regions, and up to two thousand editorial boards (*redaktsii*) operating the more important diffusion exchanges in district centers, at major industrial installations, and elsewhere.[15]

The local radio committees have two chief responsibilities: rebroadcasting to their locality, on their own frequency, programs emanating from the central apparatus; and planning and executing their own broadcasts. The organization of these local committees varies with their size, the importance of their broadcasting facilities, and the relative amount of original broadcasting that they do. These committees usually have administrative subdivisions for social-political, artistic, children's, and adult education programs, as well as for local news and relayed broadcasts. The majority of these local committees exercise control over the work of the "lower" broadcasting net, that is, the radio-diffusion exchanges, and therefore usually include a department of lower broadcasting.

The All-Union Radio Committee is authorized to plan and organize the training, through regular courses and other means, of directors and rank-and-file personnel for service in the broadcasting field.[16] Relatively little information is available, however, concerning the qualifications and training of personnel making up the various local radio committees and editorial boards. In the first years of the Radio Committee's operations, the bulk of the workers in radio-broadcasting appear to have been new to the field, being drawn from the administrative ranks of the party, the trade unions, and government organizations. In 1936 the Radio Committee maintained an "Institute for the Improvement of Qualifications" through which the responsible directors of all diffusion exchanges were expected to pass during the course of the year.[17] Early in 1937 the committee also initiated a special series of radio programs, "Instructions for Radio Exchanges," whose task was to aid workers in the radio-diffusion exchanges with their daily problems.[18] In addition, before the war, the committee published a special periodical, *Bulletin on Methods,* to guide local radio committees. It would appear from the available literature that considerable, if not wholly satisfactory, progress in building up a corps of trained radio workers had been made by the beginning of the recent war, but it is probable that along with most other specialized personnel this group suffered severe war losses. A. A. Puzin, Chairman of the All-Union Committee, has cited the need to develop adequate cadres of trained radio workers as one of the more pressing postwar problems of the committee.

One qualification and characteristic that workers in the field of Soviet radiobroadcasting appear to have in common to a high degree is Communist Party membership. For example, of the sixty delegates who attended the All-Union Conference on Problems of Political Broadcasting in December 1934, 95 per cent were members of the party or the Young Communist League;[19] and· of the twenty-five members of the Radio Committee of the Donets Region in 1936, all but one were members of the party or Komsomol.[20] The party has in fact been especially insistent on precautions in the composition of the cadre of radio workers as a result of the alleged use of the local radio by nationalists, "anti-state," and even "counterrevolutionary" elements.[21] The microphone, consequently, must be placed only in "trustworthy Bolshevik hands,"[22] and every party organization is obliged to see to it that cadres of radio workers consist of "people who are of the utmost reliability and unconditionally devoted to the affairs of communism."[23]

THE PARTY AND THE RADIO COMMITTEE

This review of the organization of the Radio Committee and its legally defined authority cannot be considered adequate without some indication of the place occupied by the committee in the more general political structure of the Soviet Union. The Radio Committee operates directly under the supervision of the Council of Ministers, which determines its general policy and to which it is accountable. Although it does not bear the name, the committee has approximately the status of a ministry and shares its form of organization with the Committee on Physical Culture and Sports and similar administrative agencies created to meet problems of a special nature.[24]

Although no mention is made of the Communist Party in the regulation establishing the Radio Committee, it is probably of even greater importance to understand the committee's relation to the party than to the Council of Ministers. The party exercises control and supervision over the Radio Committee through the same three chief means it utilizes to guide all government agencies.

In the first place, the party issues decisions criticizing the work of the VRK and directing its future course of activity. It is not intended to review here the important party instructions directed to the Radio Committee, except to indicate that they have been of a fundamental nature including detailed criticism of all phases of the work of the committee, setting forth at length the expectations of the party in regard to the work of the radio agency. One of the latest of these decisions, issued by the Central Committee early in 1947, called upon the VRK to improve the quality of its broadcasting, particularly in the sphere of political, musical, and literary-dramatic broadcasts.[25]

In the second place, the party places trusted officials in positions of control and responsibility in the Radio Committee.[26] Its first chairman, Platon Mikhailovich Kerzhentsev, was an "old Bolshevik" with party membership dating from 1904 and a history of over thirty years of service to the party. This record included participation in the Revolution of 1905; exile; underground and *émigré* work before the 1917 Revolution; and a host of party and government positions following it, among them several ambassadorships, the editorship of the main state publishing house, and a vice-presidency in the Communist Academy. He was the author of several books on Leninism and the editor of numerous journals.[27] The present chairman, A. A. Puzin, was formerly Director of the Department of Agitation in the Communist Party's Administration of Propaganda and Agitation, and his predecessor, D. A. Polikarpov, was one of the vice-directors of that administration.

And third, the party maintains a large number of party members among the rank-and-file employees of the organization. Some indication has already been given of the concentration of party membership among the workers in the field of radiobroadcasting. These members are bound by party discipline to see that the Radio Committee carries out the directives of the party and government, and are expected to report to their cells any deviation from the official line. Thus, virtually absolute supervision and control of the operation of the Radio Committee by the party is established.

Just as the All-Union Radio Committee is controlled by the Central Committee of the Communist Party and its Department of Propaganda and Agitation, so the local radio committees are supervised by the local party organizations.[28] In radio-diffusion exchanges which are located at industrial establishments, the "editors" of the exchanges are also supervised in their work by the local trade-union committees. *Glavlit,* chief censorship agency of the Soviet Union also exercises some degree of control over the work of the Radio Committee.[29] Lest this control appear too omnipresent, it should be noted that both the party's Central Committee and the Trade Union Council have on many occasions stated that their local units give inadequate attention to both the work and needs of radio authorities, and have complained that in some areas the radio is not properly "valued" by local authorities and its operation inadequately controlled or even ignored.[30]

16

BROADCASTING AND RADIO RECEPTION IN THE U.S.S.R.

THE BROADCASTING NETWORK

THE PRESENT BOUNDARIES OF THE U.S.S.R. ENCOMPASS about 8.5 million square miles, or more than one sixth of the earth's total land surface. Adequately to service this area with broadcast radio programs is no small task. The problem is rendered much more difficult by the great diversity of language groups inhabiting the Soviet Union, where more than eighty major languages and up to 140 different language groups are recognized. Frequently three, six, or more languages will be in common use in a relatively small area in the Caucasus or Soviet Central Asia. For example, in the Dagestan Autonomous Republic, which has a population under one million, fourteen languages are used in broadcasting.[1]

Although a related problem is faced by broadcasters in certain metropolitan centers of the United States, the difficulty is largely alleviated by the overwhelming predominance of English. In the U.S.S.R. the nationality policy of the government encourages the use and development of local tongues. Although Russian is the *lingua franca* in the Soviet Union, it is the native tongue of no more than 60 per cent of the population. And in each of the union-republics, there is an official native language—Ukrainian in the Ukrainian Republic, Georgian in Soviet Georgia, and so on.

Soviet industry has not found itself fully capable of coping with the demands and difficulties of the "radiofication" of the U.S.S.R. In the United States the flowering of radio stations during the late twenties and early thirties was aided by a great flow of capital in a period when radio appeared as one of the few expanding opportunities for investment.[2] The productive capacity and technical skill of American industry found itself fully master of all the demands for equipment and operating technique that the radio industry created. Soviet radio authorities were not able to draw upon adequate resources in any of these respects. The construction of radio stations had to compete with demands for capital investment in heavy industry, in relation to which radiobroadcasting received only a relatively low priority. In addition, the slow development of broadcasting stations resulted from the concentration on building radiotelegraphy transmitters, a program rendered urgent by the combination of a vastly expanding economy and the political necessity of rapid telegraphic communication across the great spaces of the U.S.S.R. By 1938, according to Soviet estimates, the U.S.S.R. was first in the world in absolute number of radio telegrams transmitted, and by 1941 first in Europe in the total of the power of its stations.[3]

The transmitting apparatus of the Soviet radiobroadcasting system, however, has consistently lagged behind the demands made upon it. Thus, Rose Ziglin, Director of the International Bureau of the Radio Committee, observed in 1935[4] that the existing "transmission base is by far insufficient to accommodate the receiving network." A decade later A. A. Puzin, the President of the Committee, commented as follows:

> The further development of Soviet radiobroadcasting and the improvement of its quality is closely tied in with the broadening and strengthening of its material-technical base. The material-technical base of the radio sending and receiving nets significantly lags behind the expansion of radiobroadcasting requirements.[5]

Soviet broadcasting began, as has been noted, in 1922 with one station of 12 kilowatts in Moscow. In the six years intervening before the inauguration of the First Five Year Plan in 1928, development was rather slow, and at the beginning of the Plan there were about twenty stations in operation.[6] In December 1932, on the eve of the Second Plan, there were fifty-seven stations in operation,[7] and this number was increased to seventy-seven (eleven below the goal) by the end of the Plan in 1937.[8] In the early part of 1940, two years after the commencement of the Third Plan, it was announced that there were ninety broadcasting stations in operation.*

The impact of the war on the Soviet transmitting apparatus was very severe, however, and the Germans are reported by K. Sergeichuk, Minister of Communications, to have destroyed twenty-nine powerful stations with a combined strength of 2,200 kilowatts, and a large number of smaller stations.[9] This would indicate that the Germans destroyed close to half the transmitting stations in operation at the beginning of the war. Reconstruction in the wake of the German retreat was very rapid, however, spurred on by recognition of the radio network's great importance for reëstablishing Soviet political control over the liberated areas. Thus, at the beginning of the Fourth Five Year Plan in 1946, the number and power of radio stations in operation was reported to exceed the prewar level, and new stations were under construction in Moscow, Leningrad, Riga, Lvov, Minsk, and several other cities.[10]

In mid-1947 there were more than one hundred stations in operation in the U.S.S.R.,[11] and of these about seventy appear to be long- and medium-wave stations. Several are located at or near Moscow, which is the core of the entire radio network of the U.S.S.R. Of the remaining stations, some are used only to rebroadcast central programs, and the remainder serve as local stations as well. This combined network is on the air for a total of 520 hours daily,† sending out programs in seventy Soviet and thirty foreign languages.[12] The present Five Year Plan calls for the construction of twenty-eight new radiobroadcasting stations by 1951,[13] which will bring the Soviet transmitting net to approximately 125 stations.

*The rate of growth and the capabilities of the sending network should not be judged by the number of stations alone. Thus, between 1930 and 1935, the number of stations increased by only four, but their total power rose from 395 to 1,503 kilowatts, including the 500-kilowatt station Komintern in Moscow. The U.S.S.R. rates high in the scale of nations according to power of stations, especially in terms of the ratio of power to the total number of stations.

†Soviet sources frequently refer to a total of between 1,500 and 1,750 hours of broadcasting, but this total includes the programs originating in the diffusion exchanges, some 2,000 of which are authorized to transmit up to one hour per day of programs originating in the exchange. *Izvestiya*, May 7, 1945; *Large Soviet Encyclopedia*, Supplement, p. 1659.

The available Soviet transmitters operate at three distinct "levels" of broadcasting. Central broadcasting is done by the cluster of Moscow stations, which plays a role in the Soviet radio system similar to that of London in the British broadcasting system or the major New York stations in the American networks. The operations of these stations constitute the first functional level of Soviet broadcasting, designated as central broadcasting. The central stations account for about one hundred hours of the 520 hour daily total of Soviet broadcasting,[14] and it has been estimated that Moscow alone puts more than a half million words on the air each day.[15] Radio programs emanate from Moscow during all but two of the twenty-four hours each day. Moscow offers three major programs, in part overlapping, which are directed toward the entire Soviet listening public, in all the various geographic and national subdivisions, either directly or by means of network hookups. Such programs are referred to as all-union programs. In addition, the central broadcasting apparatus sends out a variety of special broadcasts for outlying areas, for the local press, and for other selected audiences.

Beyond the central apparatus there is a network of stations that is said to provide every republic and region* with its own broadcasting facilities.[16] The work of these stations constitutes the second functional level of Soviet broadcasting and is designated as local broadcasting. In 1947 the stations in the capitals of the sixteen union-republics daily broadcast for a total of 120 hours, and those of the other local radio committees for 300 hours.[17] Some of these local stations are gathered into zonal networks, but every local station is also part of the national network, receiving programs from the central apparatus either by aerial wave or over the intercity telephone lines for rebroadcast on its own wave length.

The larger regional stations, such as that of Leningrad, and the major stations in the national republics, such as Kiev and Kharkov in the Ukraine, Minsk in Belorussia, and those in Georgia, Azerbaidzhan, and the Central Asian Republics, have extensive and varied programs of local origin, in addition to those relayed from the central apparatus. The current distribution of broadcast time

*Sparsely populated and economically unimportant regions frequently share a radio station with other regions.

on these stations is not known, but in the period from 1931 to 1934 programs relayed from Moscow or larger regional stations made up as a national average about 20 per cent of their total broadcast time.[18] In the case of any single station, the percentage of nonrelayed broadcasting is largely determined by the language composition of the area, since the central broadcasts are predominantly in Russian. The Ukranian Radio Committee, for example, has generally done about 80 per cent of its broadcasting in Ukrainian, the remainder in Russian, Yiddish, and other languages.

The third operational level of the Soviet radio is described as lower broadcasting, and the term refers to the activities of the network of radio-diffusion exchanges. Although the chief function of these exchanges is to transmit over a system of wires leading to the subscribers' speakers the programs sent out by central and local stations, they are also authorized to originate a small number of programs of their own. In 1944 more than two thousand exchanges in district or county centers and an unspecified number of urban diffusion exchanges had their own programs, which totaled from a half to one and a half hours each day.[19] These programs are not strictly speaking radiobroadcasts, as shall be seen, since they never go on the air but move entirely over wired nets.

RADIO RECEPTION IN THE U.S.S.R.

The term radiobroadcasting has been used here to describe the operation of the radio apparatus in the Soviet Union. In so far as that term represents the transmission and reception of radio signals by means of electric waves without the use of a connecting wire, it does not accurately describe radio as it functions in the U.S.S.R. In regard to transmission, the Soviet radio system fits the definition so far as central and local broadcasting is concerned. The third or lower level of broadcasting, however, is not a system of aerial broadcasting; it is a system of wired diffusion of radio programs. Viewed from the other side of the coin, or more appropriately, from the other end of the wire, the use of wired nets for the *diffusion* of radio programs automatically means the use of wires for their *reception*. In regard to reception, therefore, the Soviet radio, on the whole, does not fit the usual definition of radiobroadcasting.

The radio listener in the Soviet Union may hear programs on an ordinary radio set capable of receiving aerial waves directly and transforming those impulses into sound through the medium of tube and speaker. Only a relatively minor role is played in the Soviet Union by such direct reception of radio programs, however, and early in 1947 only 18 per cent of all radio-receiving equipment in the U.S.S.R. consisted of regular radio sets.[20] The vast majority of listeners hear their programs over wired speakers located in their homes, in communal dwellings and dormitories, and in public gathering places such as club rooms, reading rooms, recreation halls, and so forth. Finally, the listener may hear programs over the public-address system, generally tied in to the same wire net as the other speakers, which reach him in public squares and in his factory shop, meeting rooms, or lunchroom.[21]

The Radio-Diffusion Exchange. In May 1947 there were more than six million wired radio speakers in the Soviet Union.[22] They are gathered into nets, each of which is called a radio-diffusion (relay) exchange.* These nets of wired speakers constitute the core of the Soviet radio-receiving system, and the Soviet radio authorities are committed to their development, extension, and improvement.[23] This method of wired reception is one of the characteristic features of Soviet broadcasting that distinguishes it from other large systems, since it is possible to transmit programs from Moscow to the homes of listeners several thousand miles distant without the programs ever going on the air. A full understanding of radiobroadcasting in the U.S.S.R. is not to be had without some grasp of the structure and operation of the radio-diffusion exchange.

The equivalent of the radio station in the system of wired reception is the diffusion exchange. The exchange has a powerful aerial receiver that picks up the broadcasts from the central or local radio stations. The broadcasts picked up by the receiver as well as those brought in directly over the intercity telephone lines, as in an ordinary radio hookup, are intensified and strengthened. They are then sent over a system of wires, radiating in all directions from the exchange, to the home of the subscriber. There the subscriber's

Radiotranslyatsionnii uzel.

wired radio speaker transforms the electrical signal into the usual radio sounds.

The exchange's receiver, which is the core of the system, may range from complicated, specially constructed, multiple-tube receiving sets capable of picking up short, medium, and long waves at considerable distances, to ordinary battery-type receivers such as are frequently used on farms. The intensifying equipment ranges from those with a power of only a few watts capable of serving only a handful of speakers,* through the 50-watt intensifier for club and factory exchanges, the 100-watt intensifier which services several hundred subscribers, and the 500-watt unit which supplies current sufficient to operate several thousand speakers of the most common type, an electromagnetic unit known as the *Rekord*.[24]

Besides this run of the mine equipment, special exchanges have been built in the larger cities of the U.S.S.R., generally consisting of a high-powered central station and a network of weaker substations. The most powerful unit of this type in the country, under construction in Kiev, will have a power of 50 kilowatts.[25] The largest wired net is that in Moscow, where there are more than one million wired speakers.[26] At the present time the more powerful substations in such exchanges serve 40,000 to 45,000 subscribers, and it is planned to construct some capable of serving 80,000 to 85,000.[27] Special equipment is also produced for rural areas lacking electrical current; the latest of this type of exchange has a wind-driven motor putting out current sufficient to serve 400 or 500 speakers of the *Rekord* type.[28]

In 1940 the president of VRK placed the number of these exchanges at eleven thousand.[29] Further expansion of the exchange system was severely curtailed by the advent of the war, and one third of the nation's total receiving network was destroyed in the territories occupied by the Germans.[30] By the end of 1944, fifteen hundred exchanges had been rebuilt or restored, and seven thousand were again in operation.[31] Reconstruction thereafter was rapid. Special attention was given to rural areas, and of the first 1,085 exchanges built up and reconstructed after the beginning of the

---

*It is probable that these minor exchanges are not included in the total of 11,000 exchanges noted below.

Fourth Five Year Plan, 1,056 were in district centers.[32] At the start of the Fourth Plan, the number of exchanges operating was reported to exceed the prewar total. During 1947, 2,250 new exchanges were to have been constructed.[33]

The radio-diffusion exchange, as has been seen, is primarily a technical apparatus that enables a minimum of actual radio equipment (tubes, condensers, aerials, and so forth) to serve a maximum number of radio listeners. The chief function of the exchange is essentially passive—it simply carries over its net to the wired speakers of subscribers those programs broadcast by central and local stations which are picked up by the exchange's radio-receiving apparatus or which come to it over the long-distance lines. This fact largely determines the duties of the personnel, referred to as "editors," who manage the exchange's affairs. Their chief function is to select from the available central and local broadcasts the programs best suited to the exchange's audience of subscribers, to schedule these programs throughout the operating day, and to inform the subscribers of what the net will carry each day. Beyond this they are responsible for maintaining contact with their subscribers—assessing their needs, satisfying those which they are able or authorized to meet, and informing higher authorities of their findings. The officials of the exchange are apparently also charged with the collection of fees that subscribers to the net must pay, part of these fees being retained in the exchange and the remainder passed on to higher echelons.[34]

The task of managing a radio-diffusion exchange, one may conclude, is primarily technical and routine. Of about eleven thousand exchanges operating, only three thousand have "editorial boards"[35] analogous to the local radio committee in charge of republican and regional broadcasting stations. These boards are found primarily at exchanges authorized to originate their own broadcasts, such as the major rural exchanges located in county centers. These editorial boards, as well as the directors of all other exchanges, are subject to the authority and follow the regulations of the All-Union Radio Committee in all matters of program policy. The Radio Committee, however, does not own the exchanges and apparently does not undertake their actual operation or management.

The chief agency engaged in the business of operational management of radio-diffusion exchanges is the Ministry of Communications of the U.S.S.R. In 1940 it was reported to operate more than a third of all exchanges,[36] and in May 1947 it apparently accounted for an even larger percentage, since it then included 5,700 exchanges—1,700 more than its prewar net.[37] The exchanges of the ministry service the great bulk of all wired speakers, probably in excess of 80 per cent of all such equipment.[38] Its exchanges are located not only in large urban centers, but also in smaller cities and in district centers and rural localities.

A large number of exchanges is managed by the All-Union Central Committee of Trade Unions; they are located at important factories and plants and in workers' settlements, and function under the direction of local trade-union committees. These exchanges generally service speakers in the homes of the plant's workers, in the workers' dormitories, reading rooms, and meeting places. They frequently also serve the surrounding community and the public-address system of the plant or enterprise. The Fifteenth Plenary Session of the Trade Union Congress called for an increase of one million in the number of receivers in the trade unions' exchanges by the end of the Fourth Plan in December 1950.[39]

Other important exchanges are run by the Ministry of Agriculture and the Ministry of State Farms, both serving the rural localities, in particular the collective and State Farms and Machine-Tractor Stations. Other nets are operated by municipal authorities and similar local organizations of a public nature.

The role of networks of speakers, connected by wires to a central receiving apparatus, as the chief means of radio reception in the Soviet Union differs so markedly from the system of aerial radio-receiving sets with which we are familiar in America and England that it is difficult to describe analogous situations. We are, however, far from being totally without comparable experience. In a general way, the radio-diffusion exchange is very much like an automatic telephone exchange whose wires go out to the homes of subscribers and to public phone booths, except that radio programs substitute for telephone messages, all subscribers receive the same message, and only one-way communication is possible.

More directly in the field of radio, the Soviet system is actually applied on a smaller scale in some American hotels and hospitals, where each room is equipped with a speaker connected by wires with a central receiving apparatus. The occupant of the room has simply to switch on his speaker and the program picked up by the central receiver is piped into the room. This system, when magnified to serve a large number of speakers distributed over a large area, is essentially what the Soviet radio-diffusion exchange represents. The chief difference is that in most cases the wired speakers operating in the United States provide the listener with a choice of three or four stations, whereas the bulk of those in the U.S.S.R. are capable of carrying only one program. The hotel occupant, therefore, has five choices (any one of four programs or not listening), but the average Soviet owner of a speaker has but two (one program or not listening).

This predominance of wired speakers over aerial radio-receiving sets for the reception of radio programs is the product of a complex of technical, economic, and political considerations. Probably the chief determinant has been the shortage of broadcasting stations and regular radio sets. Soviet authorities have, however, set out in considerable detail their view of the relative advantages and disadvantages of the two systems.[40]

These authorities[41] claim four major advantages for the system of wired speakers as compared to regular radio receivers. They maintain that the wired system is more economical[42] and assert that it provides the subscriber to the wired net with better reception than he could obtain with an individual set.

A third advantage claimed for the wired net is its ability to carry programs that originate at the exchange, which makes possible utilization of the radio for mass communication of a purely local nature. This ability to broadcast without actually going "on the air" proved itself invaluable during the war, since the local radio could continue to function and maintain contact between the authorities and the population without the risk of having enemy aviators make use of the signals to guide them to their objective. The siege of

Leningrad provides an outstanding example of such use of the wired net. Under siege conditions the Leningrad wired net operated around the clock. During hours when no regular programs were on, and throughout the night, the Leningraders kept their speakers tuned in. The slow beat of a metronome kept the wire alive. Whenever it was necessary to make an important announcement, the beat of the metronome was rapidly increased. Thus, at all times, the officials were able to maintain direct contact with the people, to transmit orders, warn of danger, or make special announcements.[43]

Finally, the wired net is praised for its adaptability to propaganda control. Since the subscriber to the services of the exchange can tune in only the programs carried by his net, it is possible to control absolutely the listening of the radio audience, completely excluding the possibility of intrusion by enemy radio propaganda. This again proved itself of considerable advantage during the war, almost entirely nullifying the effect of German propaganda broadcasts to the unoccupied parts of the U.S.S.R. It is, of course, also of considerable advantage to the regime in time of peace, since it largely guarantees that the Soviet population will hear only the voice of Moscow, rather than that of America or the BBC.

These advantages of the system of broadcast reception through the wired net of the radio-diffusion exchange cannot, of course, be taken as conclusively establishing the greater desirability of that system over one of aerial radio-receiving sets. They are presented here simply to indicate the line of reasoning adopted by Soviet radio leaders to justify their methods, and they must be understood in that context. If, for example, Soviet authorities were able to divert a large portion of the nation's resources to the development of the radio industry, it might be possible to produce regular radio sets whose cost would be considerably less in relation to the wired speakers. Similarly, the problem of radio interference might be eliminated by technical improvements. The Soviet radio industry has, however, been consistently unable to meet the demands for a large output of high-quality receivers, and in this sense the utilization of the wired nets has been as much a matter of graceful acceptance of the inevitable as it has been a matter of choice.

As for the ability to control listening, that clearly has less relevance in countries where listening to propaganda from abroad or from clandestine stations is not considered a problem or a threat. If enemy troops capture the net, furthermore, they are then able to prevent radio listening to the broadcasts of the home government. The advantages of being able to do local broadcasting to a special audience over the wired net are considerable, it is true, but this has at times been almost as much a political liability for Soviet authorities as it has been an instrument of positive value.*

Soviet radio officials do not make so one-sided a case for the system of wired reception that they deny its chief deficiency. On the contrary, they are very conscious that the most serious shortcoming of the wired system lies in the fact that the listener is limited in his choice of radio program, and must in fact listen to the program that is coming over the net at the moment he tunes in. His position is contrasted with that of the listener who has a regular radio set and may choose his own program by tuning one station or another, limited only by the availability of nearby stations.[44]

This difficulty may be overcome to some extent by constructing radio diffusion nets capable of simultaneously carrying two or more programs on the same wire. Such is indeed the eventual goal of Soviet radio authorities, and as early as 1936 Soviet engineers set their sights for five programs on city wires and at least two on the wires of rural exchanges.[45] This improvement, however, involves costs and technical difficulties of such magnitude that its universal introduction cannot be expected for some time. At present the effort to enrich the listening of wire net subscribers is largely limited to painstaking care concerning program quality, and a broadening of the base of broadcast programs from which the exchange can choose the material it relays to its subscribers. This plan is being accomplished by increasing the number of local broadcasting stations and by placing the central broadcasting system on a two-program basis similar to that recently introduced by the BBC.

Size and Growth of the Receiving Network. The term "receiving network" is used in the Soviet Union primarily to refer to the

*See section on local programming below.

two chief types of radio-listening equipment—the wired speakers in the nets of the radio-diffusion exchanges, and regular radio sets.

The quantitative and qualitative development of the receiving network, no less than that of the transmitting apparatus, has not matched the expectations of the party and government radio authorities or the demands of the actual and potential listening public.[46] The reasons adduced for this failure are generally the same as in the case of the transmitting system: technical inadequacy; the pressure of demands for materials and skilled workers by higher priority segments of the national economy; and, from time to time, charges of bureaucratic deficiencies, lack of local initiative, and "sabotage." An important factor not to be overlooked, however, was the diversion of a very large part of the production of radio equipment of all types to the Red Army to keep pace with its expansion and mechanization.

A comparison of the receiving network of the U.S.S.R. and of other countries is more revealing than data on the gross size of the Soviet apparatus. Soviet radio officials have been extremely conscious of the resulting contrast. Thus, a survey of Soviet and other radio systems as of January 1935 noted the great gap between the 2.3 million sets (wired speakers and regular sets) in the U.S.S.R., the 25.5 million sets in North America, and the 23.5 million sets in Western Europe, all despite the greater population of the U.S.S.R. The same survey called attention to the fact that there were then only 13 to 14 receivers per 1,000 of population or 1 for every 75 persons in the U.S.S.R., as compared to 160 receivers per 1,000 of population, or 1 for every 6 persons in North America.[47] Again in 1940 it was noted that the U.S.S.R. boasted only about 24 to 27 receivers per 1,000 of population, although "technically advanced capitalist countries" possessed from 120 to 200 receivers per 1,000 of population.[48] If the planned production quotas set by the Fourth Five Year Plan are achieved, the U.S.S.R. will have approximately 15 million receivers by the end of the Plan in 1950. Assuming a population of 200 million at that time, the Soviet Union would still have only about 75 receivers per 1,000 of population. It is clear that in regard to apparatus for radio reception the Soviet Union is a poor country.

An even less encouraging picture is presented by the radio-receiving network in the rural areas and some of the nationality areas of the Soviet Union. In 1935 there were 50 receivers per 1,000 of population in the urban areas, but only about 4 receivers per 1,000 of population in the villages and on the farms;[49] and by 1941 there were still only 8 receivers per 1,000 population in the rural areas as against 67 in the urban districts.[50] Although the rural areas of the country account for about 65 per cent of the population, they contain only about 20 per cent of the nation's radio-receiving equipment.[51] Furthermore, even this figure does not present an adequate picture of radiofication in the rural areas, since the term "rural areas" includes the district centers (usually a large village or small town), which have a significant portion of the nonurban radio receivers. Consequently, as late as May 1947 it was reported that the majority of collective farms did not have any receiving apparatus, thus depriving large numbers of collective farmers of the opportunity to listen to the radio in any form.[52]

Similarly, in many border regions and national areas the receiving network has been consistently underdeveloped,[53] and as late as 1940 in five constituent union-republics—the Azerbaidzhan, Turkmen, Georgian, Uzbek, and Tadzhik Soviet Socialist Republics containing over 16 million people—the average number of receivers was a mere 3 per 1,000 of population.[54] The rural regions and the national areas were given high priority in the radiofication plans of the Fourth Five Year Plan, but they are once again apparently falling far behind the developments in the urban centers of the Soviet Union. For example, the city of Leningrad had reached its 1950 planned goal for the installation of radio equipment by the third quarter of 1947, and other cities like Moscow and Voronezh overfulfilled their plans for 1947. At the same time, however, the rural areas as a whole and many of the national republics, both those formerly occupied by the Germans, like the Ukraine, and those never occupied, like the Turkmen Republic, consistently failed to meet their planned quotas by large margins.[55]

The wired speakers: The so-called *radiotochki* or radio-listening points on the net of the diffusion exchange consist primarily of a transformer, a loudspeaker, and a switch and volume control—the whole of which may or may not be in a radio cabinet. The loudspeaker, which is the heart of the apparatus, is in most cases an electromagnetic type, but during the war piezoelectric speakers were developed and are now coming into use.

TABLE 5

EXPANSION OF THE SOVIET RADIO-DIFFUSION NETWORK

Year[a]	Number of speakers in the radio-diffusion exchanges	Year[a]	Number of speakers in the radio-diffusion exchanges
1929	22,000[b]	1945	5,000,000[e]
1933	1,360,000[b]	1946	5,700,000[f]
1937	2,946,000[e]	1947	6,500,000[f]
1940	4,934,000[e]	1948	7,300,000[g]
1941	5,500,000[d]	1951	10,000,000[h]

[a] All data are for January 1 except the 1941 figure, which is for June.

[b] Adapted from data in *Socialist Construction in the U.S.S.R.*, 1936.

[e] Goron, *Radiobroadcasting*, p. 14, does not specify the month, but other evidence indicates reference was to the first of the year.

[d] *Izvestiya*, December 16, 1944, stated the number to be in excess of 5.5 million.

[e] Fortushenko, *Fifty Years of Radio*, p. 77.

[f] An estimate based on statements in *Izvestiya*, May 7, 1946, and May 7, 1947, and in *Pravda*, May 7 and 8, 1947.

[g] An estimate based on data given in *Radio*, 1948: no. 1, pp. 1-2; no. 3, p. 2; no. 6, pp. 1-4.

[h] An estimate based on the plan to increase the net of wired speakers by 75 per cent during the Fourth Plan.

Table 5 presents the increase in the number of wired speakers since the beginning of the Five Year Plans, and projects it forward to the end of the Fourth Five Year Plan in December 1950. This table presents a picture of the slow and sometimes halting progress in the increase of wired speakers. Nevertheless, these speakers in 1947 constituted more than 80 per cent of all equipment capable of bringing radio programs to the home, dormitory, reading room, or recreation hall of the Soviet worker or farmer.[56] They form the core of the entire receiving network, and, as has been indicated, the Soviet government is committed to the extension and further development of the system.

On the eve of the war there were more than 5.5 million wired speakers. Production was sharply curtailed during the war, however, and a "significant number" of speakers were destroyed in the German occupied areas of the U.S.S.R. A special decree of the Council of Commissars on August 19, 1944, took steps to secure the production of equipment necessary for the restoration of the exchanges and called for the installation of one million speakers during the following year.[57] More than seven hundred thousand were rebuilt or restored by the end of 1944,[58] and, with the addition of new production, the number of speakers in operation had been brought to about five million by January 1945.[59] During 1945 reconstruction and new construction accounted for approximately another seven hundred thousand speakers,[60] and by the beginning of the Fourth Five Year Plan in 1946 the number of speakers was reported to exceed the prewar level.[61] With the advent of the Fourth Plan, restoration was almost completed and the installation of speakers placed primarily on a new production basis, and in 1946 more than five hundred thousand speakers were added to the wires of exchanges operated by the Ministry of Communications alone.[62] This should have brought the total number of speakers in the country to considerably more than six million. It was planned to build 945,000 new speakers during 1947.[63] The over-all plan was not fulfilled, but the Ministry of Communications, the chief agency in the field responsible for over two thirds of the installations, did overfulfill its plan. It is likely, therefore, that there were well over seven million wired speakers in the U.S.S.R. by the beginning of 1948. The plan for 1948 called for the installation of nine hundred thousand new wired speakers.[64]

The problems faced by Soviet radio authorities in increasing the number of wired speakers are by no means minor, and besides the problems of producing speakers they are already faced by acute shortages of line and other equipment.[65] The Fourth Five Year plan has set the goal of an increase of 75 per cent over the prewar level in number of speakers by the end of the plan in 1950,[66] which is considerably less ambitious than the goal of an increase by 2.3 times set for the Third Five Year Plan.[67] This lesser goal may in part be due to the speed-up in the production of regular radio sets. In any event, if the planned quotas are met, the Soviet Union will have about ten million wired speakers in 1950, about eight million of them in the radio-diffusion exchanges operated by the Ministry of Communications.[68]

It is not known what proportion of the new speakers will go to rural areas, although it has been announced that special importance will be attached to radiofication in district centers and rural localities.[69] Of more than four million wired receivers operating in 1939, about 750,000 were in rural areas in diffusion exchanges operated by the Ministry of Communications, the Ministry of Agriculture, and the Ministry of State Farms.[70] Of the 600,000 speakers that were to be added to the net of the Ministry of Communications in 1947, 150,000 were to be installed in rural localities. Most of these were placed in district centers, however, and the people on the farms had to rely primarily on exchanges installed by the Ministries of Agriculture and State Farms. It should be noted, in this connection, that the plans for the installation of wired speakers by those agencies were not met in 1947. The Ministry of Agriculture met its quota only to the extent of 19 per cent, and the Ministry of State Farms completed only 22 per cent of its plan.[71]

The chief producers of the wired speakers are the recently established Ministry of the Communications Equipment Industry and the Ministry of the Electrical Equipment Industry of the U.S.S.R., but some production is undertaken in plants of the Ministry of Communications, the Ministry of Local Industry of the Russian Republic, and other ministries of local industry.[72]

Regular radio sets: Probably the least successful effort of Soviet authorities to build up the receiving net has been in the sphere of ordinary radio-receiving sets. On January 1, 1936, the whole of the U.S.S.R. possessed 650,000 such sets; of these 270,000 were crystal receivers, and about 200,000 were considered outmoded types in need of replacement.[73] According to plan, 500,000 receivers were to be built and delivered in 1936, 125,000 for the collective farms,[74] but this plan was never fulfilled. So many sets were in fact idle for lack of current or repairs that at the end of the year a publication of the Radio Committee was able to claim only 500,000 sets as being "ready" to broadcast Stalin's address before the Supreme Soviet on November 25, 1936.[75]

The Third Five Year Plan begun in 1938 was expected to bring the number of aerial receivers to a level where they would constitute 25 to 30 per cent of all receiving apparatus,[76] but this goal was apparently not reached, since late in 1940 there were reported to be only 760,000 regular receivers[77] compared to more than five million wired speakers.[78] Shortly after the war began, all regular radio and television sets were called in by the government for the duration. Such a collection presented no great inspection difficulty since, as with the BBC, all sets must be registered and a fee paid for their possession and operation. Some journalists and government officials whose work sanctioned possession of such equipment during wartime were allowed to retain their sets. In any event, all sets apparently were returned to their owners at the end of hostilities.*

Data on the number of regular radio sets now operating are very scanty. In May 1947 it was announced that such sets constituted 18 per cent of all receiving equipment,[79] which would put the number of regular radio sets at about 1,300,000. The building of radio sets has apparently been given special priority during the current Fourth Five Year plan; a total of three million sets are supposed to be built over the five-year period, with a progressive increase in output. The plan for 1946 was not met, however, and so far as is known the goal of 400,000 regular sets planned for 1947 also was not reached. The plan for 1948 called for the production of 548,000 sets, but production was behind schedule in mid-year. In the light of these facts, one may conclude that the 925,000 goal set for 1950 and the over-all goal of three million sets for the Fourth Five Year Plan are not likely to be reached.[80]

The responsibility for producing radio sets is spread among a variety of authorities. Chief producer is the Ministry of the

---

*It should be noted, however, that before the war all foreigners, citizens, and organizations could legally use long- or short-wave receivers to listen to whatever programs they chose. This privilege is apparently once again available to Soviet citizens who have sets capable of foreign reception, at least as far as the formal law is concerned. In practice, people who listen to foreign broadcasts may be exposing themselves politically. Soviet efforts to jam the Voice of America and the BBC, have, of course, also been made.

Communications Equipment Industry of the U.S.S.R., but the Ministry of Communications, various national ministries of local industry, coöperatives, and amateurs in the schools and in the Radio Friends Society also engage in the production of receivers. By April 1946 Soviet radio plants had reached their prewar level of production, and during 1947 the Ministry of the Electrical Goods Industry was producing ten types of radio sets, including a radiola and an automobile set.[81]

The low output of the Soviet radio industry in the face of the overwhelming demand for sets has led increasingly to emphasis on easily produced, simple, and cheap receivers.[82] Recently both A. A. Puzin,[83] President of the Radio Committee, and K. Sergeichuk,[84] Minister of Communications, have reiterated the necessity for concentration on simple sets of two or three tubes with a low production cost, low selling price, and ease of operation and maintenance so that sets may become available to wider strata of the population.

In the villages and on collective farms, where electric current for the operation of a wired net is generally not available, aerial radio sets are especially important, particularly as group or collective listening points. At the present time a special receiver utilizing battery current and known as *Rodina* (Motherland) is put out for the village. In 1946 no more than 90,000 of these were produced, however, and ony 116,000 (more than one quarter of all aerial radio set production) were planned for 1947.[85] That this is hopelessly inadequate in relation to the need is well recognized by Soviet radio authorities, and it has led to a most interesting development—the demand for large-scale construction of the almost forgotten crystal receiving sets. This demand was simultaneously sounded by the Minister of Communications[86] and the President of the Radio Committee. The latter, in an article written for *Pravda* on Radio Day, declared:

The crystal set has undeservedly been completely forgotten. It is a seriously mistaken point of view to regard the crystal set, as many do, as outmoded, having significance only for the early development of radio technique. To meet the needs of the rural population, 20 to 25 million radio receivers are needed. To provide this number by means of radio-diffusion exchanges or to build tube radio sets would not be a mere matter of a decade. It is clear that the village cannot wait upon such a tempo. Organizing the output of crystal receivers will enable us to reduce by several times the period required for the mass radiofication of the village.[87]

Mr. Puzin went on to declare that contemporary techniques make possible the production of crystal sets of high quality. They are, he asserted, very simple and can be produced in large numbers at low cost. They are to be built not only in plants of the Ministry of the Electrical Goods industry, but by local industry, producers' coöperatives, radio amateurs, and students in their school shops. The Young Communist League has been charged with responsibility for mobilizing people in local campaigns for building crystal sets. Thus, the provision of the rural areas of the country with radio receivers is to be placed in good part on the principle of self-help. This method of production with local resources, which places a minimum strain on the higher priority projects, is, of course, not unique to the field of radio but has been widely applied in the U.S.S.R. during its period of forced economic development. Since the output of crystal receivers is apparently included in the planned figure of three million new aerial sets by 1950, that figure appears as a much more modest goal. And even with these simple sets the Soviet radio industry has not adequately met the demand; in 1948 it was reported that the sets were still not in mass production for lack of the necessary earphones.[88]

17

PROGRAM POLICY AND
THE CONTENT OF
SOVIET BROADCASTS

THE SOVIET RADIO IS DISTINCT NOT ONLY IN ITS PHYSICAL structure, but also in another respect which will be of greater interest to communications research workers, sociologists, and political scientists—namely, in the goals set and the functions prescribed by the party and government. The following tasks are regularly set before the responsible directors of Soviet radiobroadcasting:[1] (1) to disseminate political information and to increase the "political knowledge" and "political awareness" of the broad masses of the population; (2) to secure the cultural education of the masses, to increase their acquaintance with and understanding of the great works of music, literature, and drama; (3) to rally the population in support of the policies of the party and government, and to mobilize the working masses for the fulfillment of the political and particularly the economic tasks faced by the nation; (4) to assist the education authorities in raising the general education level of the population, especially in the realms of hygiene and sanitation, basic science, and techniques of production; (5) to provide the population with a positive and constructive means of relaxation.

In their scope the goals set for the Soviet radio are clearly more sweeping than the regularly stated aims of the ordinary run of commercial broadcasting, although commercial broadcasting may in effect serve some of the same ends. The BBC, municipally operated stations such as WNYC, or quasi-commercial stations such as

WHCU in Ithaca, New York, are more directly devoted to broadcasting based on some of these principles, but even here the profound differences in political orientation make comparison difficult. In both the theory and practice of programming on the Soviet radio, these goals are so intimately intertwined that it is frequently impossible to state which goal is being served, except to note that in all respects the broadcast material serves to support the Soviet system and the current party line.

CENTRAL AND LOCAL BROADCASTING

Detailed analyses by subject of the 1,750 hours of daily broadcasts[2] currently sent out by Soviet transmitters or originating in the diffusion exchanges are unfortunately not available. The last complete reports are more than a decade old and therefore can be regarded as merely indicative of the general distribution of radio time. More detailed information is available, however, on the composition of the programs of the Moscow or central stations, which at present send out a total of more than 90 broadcast hours daily. In 1946 the central broadcasting apparatus in Moscow began to issue two major programs simultaneously, in an innovation not unlike that adopted by the BBC. A third program was added in 1947. These three main programs form the core of central broadcasting, accounting for well over a third of the more than 90 hours of broadcasting done each day by the central stations. During 1947, before the addition of the third program, the two then issued were on the air for 30 hours and 30 minutes of broadcasting on week days, and for 37 hours on "rest days." This time was distributed as follows: music, 60 per cent; political broadcasts, 19.4 per cent; literary programs, 8.6 per cent; children's programs, 7.9 per cent; and others, 4.1 per cent.[3]

The first, or regular, program is broadcast from 6:00 A.M. until midnight, although during this period there may be a total of an hour or more when no broadcasts go out. It is intended for general consumption, and its time is distributed as follows: seven hours of serious music and music appreciation; three hours of lighter music (folksongs, operettas, and popular music); two and a half hours of news and commentaries distributed over about eleven periods per day; two and a half hours of children's programs; one and a half hours of literary readings and dramatic materials; and about one hour of miscellaneous material.

The second program has an eight-hour spread from 5:00 P.M. to 1:00 A.M., is directed to a more restricted audience, and might be regarded as highbrow. Six of the eight hours of broadcast time are devoted to serious music, the remainder to literary readings, newscasts, and other material. Opera from the Bolshoi Theater or from other major theaters is carried about three times a week by this program, and during the intermission short literary pieces are read, or there are lectures and commentaries on the life and work of composers and authors.

These two programs are accessible to all who have regular radio sets that are capable of picking up the frequency. The programs are chiefly intended, however, for retransmission by local radio stations and for diffusion by the wired relay exchanges, which supplement the material they pick up from the central stations with their own broadcasts. In addition to the material made available by these two major programs, the individual listener and local stations and exchanges may select their material from the special broadcasts sent out from Moscow for peasants, youth, women, Red Army and Red Fleet men, and other groups, or the special broadcasts beamed to the Far East, Siberia, and Central Asia.

Cultural broadcasts: Radio in the Soviet Union is viewed as "one of the most powerful weapons of the cultural revolution" and as "a great source of cultural growth,"[4] whose "force, activities, and capabilities . . . as a means of cultural education of the mass . . . it is difficult to overvalue."[5] From its earliest days, the radio has been expected to make a major contribution to "the transformation of the Soviet Union into a country of complete literacy and high culture," and this has been held to be the basic aim behind all activities of the Radio Committee. In view of this responsibility, all central broadcasts must be planned with the purpose of "lifting the cultural standard of the toiling masses to a higher plane," and spreading knowledge of and interest in music, literature, art, and science.[6]

"Artistic" broadcasting, that is, musical, literary, and dramatic broadcasts, have consistently occupied more than half of all radio time in the Soviet Union. This area of broadcasting is not, however, without its potential political implications, and these have hardly been ignored in Soviet broadcasting. This is, of course, in keeping with the general rejection in Soviet ideology of the principle of art for art's sake, and an expression of the belief that "a play, a picture, and a song are also propaganda and agitation, although expressed in artistic forms."[7] Radio workers received clear instructions in this matter early in the career of the Radio Committee. Witness the opening words of Platon Kerzhentsev, then Committee Chairman, to the All-Union Conference on Political Radiobroadcasting in December 1934:

All of our work in radiobroadcasting must be politically purposeful. A great part of our broadcasting is occupied with music and literature, and we feel that even in these spheres there should be strong support of the political line, that it is necessary there [as well] to exclude an un-Partylike . . . and simplistic view toward the elements of Marxism.[8]

These remarks are by no means to be interpreted as indicating that the musical programs of the Soviet radio are largely limited to the *International,* and its literary fare to readings from *Das Kapital.* The quality of Soviet musical and literary broadcasting is consistently high, and the nature of its support of the party line, while unmistakable in general, is in particular instances rather difficult to perceive.

Music is the chief ingredient of Soviet broadcasting. It currently accounts for more than half of all broadcast time for all stations in the Soviet Union, thus continuing a practice which has been in force for over a decade.[9] To judge by the program content, the musical directors of the Soviet radio take rather literally their instructions to raise the cultural level of the broad masses and to familiarize the radio listener with classical music and the work of foreign composers.[10] Precise indexes of the attitude of the Soviet audience to its musical fare are not available, but the Radio Committee seems to have set its goal at producing a nation of lovers of good music. As V. Stepanov, Vice-Chairman of the Committee, described the situation, musical broadcasts are "not merely a form of entertainment but are also of great artistic-educational significance."[11]

In any event, serious music predominates, and on the two regular programs of central broadcasting it stands in the ratio of about four to one in relation to popular music, although this ratio is considerably lower on some local stations. Russian composers are presented most frequently, and of these Tchaikovsky is probably the most popular, followed by Rimski-Korsakov and Moussorgsky. Although this is perhaps quite natural, it also has a political overtone, since Soviet policy in the art realm stresses the creativeness of the native talent of the past as well as the present. During the war, of course, patriotic music was particularly featured.[12] Non-Russian composers are by no means excluded, however, and Beethoven is highly esteemed, probably ranking next to Tchaikovsky. Several other German composers are frequently heard, as well as the musical giants of other countries. Relatively little eighteenth-century music is played, although Mozart is regularly represented.

It should not be concluded from this sketch, however, that the strong medicine of fine music is indiscriminately poured into the ears of the Soviet listeners because it is "good for them." Account is taken of national tastes and the audience's level of preparation. Symphonic music, which generally has a wider appeal, is much more common than chamber music, which is a standard but not a major item. In this category piano solos, say a Rachmaninoff program, or vocalists with piano accompaniment, are the chief element, trios and string quartets being infrequent. Modern music appears to be as difficult for the general Soviet audience to understand as it is elsewhere, but the Soviet composers such as Shostakovich, Khachaturian, Prokofiev, and Bely are often played, and the works of other moderns are sometimes heard.

Popular or light music, of which there are about four hours daily on the two chief central programs, does not refer to jazz, although it is played, or to the Russian equivalent. The chief ingredient in light music programs is choral singing, usually of folk songs or of contemporary songs such as those of the Red Army. These programs also include a significant number of selections from operettas and music of a similar genre. Ensembles of popular instruments, such as the balalaika and domra, are also a central element in the broadcasts of popular music. The central apparatus also regularly carries for nationwide transmission programs of the music of particular nationality groups. Apart from its musical value, this again serves quasi-political ends by stressing "native creativity" and the "friendly brotherhood of the peoples of the U.S.S.R."

The responsibilities of the Radio Committee in the sphere of music are only partly fulfilled by planning and putting on the air a steady flow of good music. The other half of its responsibility lies in the direct musical education of the people. For well over a decade the Soviet radio has presented cycles of musical programs on special themes to "present to the listener the opportunity of going through a complete course of musical education over the radio."[13] The central broadcasting apparatus organized its first cycle of directly educational musical programs in 1936, designating it "Musical-Cultural Minimum." As the title indicates, the cycle was designed to give listeners basic and elementary knowledge necessary for an understanding of musical works.[14] Under the general rubric of "propaganda of classical music," a variety of programs of this type is presented each year. During 1944 a "great cycle" on Tchaikovsky was produced, and, in coöperation with the Bolshoi Theater, an operatic cycle. In 1945 a series known as the "Radio Musical University," designed to give listeners wider knowledge of musical art, presented a series of "conferences" on the "Russian Classics," "West European Music," "Contemporary Soviet Musical Artistry," "Popular Music," and other subjects, with appropriate illustrations.[15] Soviet composers are regularly brought to the microphone to discuss and play their latest works, and these programs are organized into cycles under such titles as "Composers at the Microphone," which appeared in 1944, and "Developments in Soviet Music," which ran in 1946.

The opera, important symphonic concerts, and other major live-talent programs are generally carried during the evening hours, but fifteen- and thirty-minute musical broadcasts are presented throughout the day on a flexible schedule filling most of the time between other broadcasts. Whether they utilize live talent or records, musical programs are generally announced as "concerts," and the central apparatus carries more than thirty each day. All the musical resources of the national capital are at the disposal of the Radio Committee for its central broadcasts, as well as the best musical talent of other major cities and national republics. The Radio Committee also has musical resources of its own, including a symphony orchestra, a choir, and an ensemble.

In 1935 literary and dramatic programs were reported to rank second in total number of broadcasts.[16] Although detailed recent data are not available, an examination of Soviet broadcast schedules indicates that these programs still rank high. There are, however, no soap operas on the Soviet radio—nothing in fact that could in any sense be considered comparable. Like the musical broadcasts, the dominant tone in Soviet literary-dramatic broadcasting is serious. It is based, on the whole, on the best in literature and the theater, and is characterized by an educational "uplift" quality in keeping with the radio's task of raising the cultural level of the population.

From its earliest days, a standard feature of Soviet radiobroadcasting has been the literary program, that is, the reading of selections, or in series an entire work, of prose or poetry from contemporary writing and the world's classics. Russian classics and contemporary literature predominate, of course, but a wide selection of writers from other countries is represented. For example, in reviewing his twenty years of radio reading, O. Abdulov made special mention of Mark Twain, Maupassant, O. Henry, and Anatole France as good radio reading material, held Dickens' *Pickwick Papers* to be most successful of all, and reported that he had read from *The Good Soldier Schweik* more than 120 times over the twenty-year period.[17] The choice of reading matter, of course, shifts with the political winds, and during the war the chief emphasis was on patriotic broadcasts, with *War and Peace* leading the field.[18]

These literary readings are not a haphazard phenomenon and are not used primarily as fillers for dead space. Neither are they placed in the category of "quality" broadcasts toward which an occasional gesture is made. The reading sessions are a regular part of the broadcast day and are one of the standard ingredients of the programs directed to special audiences such as collective farmers, where the readings tend to be about rural life, or Red Army men, where the reading usually is on military themes. In the field of Russian literature alone there is a repertory of three hundred standard reading programs, an average of almost one a day, representing numerous authors and several centuries. It is maintained, in fact, that there is no ordinarily well-known work of Soviet literature that has not been presented, at least in part, over the Soviet radio. In the first ten months of 1944, these programs included the work of 260 authors (115 poets and 145 prose writers), of whom about one hundred, including Alexei N. Tolstoi, N. Tikhonov, and Illya Ehrenburg, appeared in person to read their own work.[19] These personal appearances, similar to those of composers, are arranged in coöperation with the Union of Writers and represent the continuation of an early tradition of the Soviet radio, since the most famous Soviet poet, Vladimir Mayakovsky, frequently appeared on the radio to read his new poetry. There are, in addition, supplementary lectures on Russian and other writers, and educational programs on literature like those on music.

Responsibility for originating these literary programs for the central apparatus lies with the Literary Division of the Literary-Dramatic Sector of the Radio Committee. The literary readings emanating from the central studios are supplemented by literary programs originating on the local level. In such broadcasts the stress is on the work of writers from the area served by the local station, and on works dealing with the locality. Criticism of the joint literary activity of local radio committees and local offices of the Union of Soviet Writers is frequent and sharp. *The Literary Gazette* has charged that writers submit for radio presentation only those materials which newspaper and magazine editors have turned down, "and as a result the radio listeners frequently are forced to listen to absolute potboilers." It has also expressed dissatisfaction with the fact that on local literary programs frequently no more than one fourth of the material read is local literature, the remainder duplicating the central broadcasts.[20]

Those whose familiarity with radio readings does not extend

beyond hearing Sunday comic strips on the air may be hard pressed to understand the persistence of radio readings as one of the major Soviet broadcast categories. Initially these readings may have been part of the effort to meet two difficult conditions facing the party and government during the formative period of the Soviet radio. At that time almost half the entire population of the Soviet Union was illiterate (in 1926 the figure stood at 49 per cent), while books for those who could read were exceedingly scarce in a period of rapidly growing interest in literature. It was inevitable, accepting the radio's responsibility for popular cultural development, that the medium of radio should have been used to bridge the gap and to minimize the impact of both the high rate of illiteracy and the book shortage. There is every indication, furthermore, that far from reducing the desire and need for books, the tradition of radio reading has contributed in significant measure to the ever growing demand for books in the Soviet Union.

Since the formative period of the Soviet radio, however, the literacy rate has risen rapidly, standing at 81 per cent by the time of the 1939 census, and the output of the Soviet publishing industry has increased markedly; yet radio readings continue to be a major element of Soviet broadcasting. This is not to be explained as simply a holdover from earlier times. Well-handled radio renditions of fine literature have a quality of their own that requires no further justification. A well-executed radio reading provides some approximation to the pleasures of reading aloud in the family circle, and such group experiences are assiduously sought out and fostered in the Soviet Union.

Nor is this procedure without its practical aim despite the increase of literacy and the greater availability of books. For the majority of contemporary Soviet literary works have to varying degrees a pointed political orientation, and their dissemination to the wide radio audience thus serves the political ends of the party and government.

The bulk of the dramatic broadcasts on the Soviet radio are simply transmissions direct from the actual performances in the major theaters in the capital, supplemented by readings at the microphone of scenes from the classics and contemporary plays. The latter activity is carried on primarily by the same actors who perform in the theaters, and so far as is known the Soviet radio does not have a group of actors devoting their time primarily to radio performances. In the first ten months of 1944, for example, the central studios put about 150 "radio spectacles" on the air,[21] including scenes from fifty shows in the current repertory of Moscow theaters.[22] Soviet dramatic broadcasts are apparently regarded more as a supplement to the theater than as a distinct form of radio drama. Radio dramatics are viewed mainly as a way of popularizing the best presentations of the capital theaters.[23]

The development of radio drama, an innovation appearing only in recent years, has been given increased attention by the Radio Committee, and this may be expected to change the balance in dramatic programming. Emphasis is being placed on the preparation of radio dramas, based generally on literary materials, but specially written for radio and taking full account of the characteristic specifications and capabilities of radio presentation. It is reported that the radio directors are acquiring experience in this field and that they are encouraging the development of creative writing especially for radio.[24] This development is not without precedent in Soviet dramatic broadcasting, since the beginning of such broadcasting is said to date from 1929 with the presentation of a dramatization of a chapter from the well-known humorous work, *The Golden Calf,* by Ilf and Petrov.[25]

Political broadcasting: Soviet propaganda and agitation broadcasts are under the supervision of the Sector of Propaganda and Agitation of the Radio Committee.[26] News programs are closely geared in with the general propaganda line, but are under the control of a separate Sector on Latest News. These two program areas will be treated as a unit. Together they account for about one fourth of the total broadcast time of the Soviet radio apparatus.

The Soviet radio, as "a mass agitator and propagandist"[27] and "a powerful weapon of political propaganda and education,"[28] meets its responsibility for political education by familiarizing the population with important party and government decisions, and by transmitting the official explanations and "clarifications" of established policy. All political broadcasts "must rally the broadest masses of workers and collective farmers under the banner of the Party."[29]

The nature of this responsibility of the Soviet radio in securing the political indoctrination of the masses cannot fully be appreciated apart from the very phrasing of the instructions given radio workers:

> Possessing an audience of millions and penetrating to the most far-flung and "deaf" corners of our immense country, the Soviet radio must carry to the widest masses the teachings of Marx-Lenin-Stalin, must raise the cultural-political level of the workers, must daily inform the workers of the success of socialist construction, must spread the truth about the class struggle taking place throughout the world.[30]

> The Soviet radio is not only a rapid and reliable means of communication, but also a powerful means of political development of the workers. It carries to the masses the inspired word of Bolshevik truth, aids the people in its struggle for the full victory of Communism in our country, summons them to heroic deeds in the name of the furthest strengthening of the power, of the economic and cultural prosperity, of the U.S.S.R.[31]

In addition to its general political assignment of securing the Bolshevik upbringing of the masses, the radio has a very specific role to play in mobilizing the population in the fulfillment of the political and particularly the economic tasks set it. Thus, in connection with the celebration of Radio Day in 1946, the Chairman of the Radio Committee stressed that since the country was entering upon a new Five Year Plan for the development of the national economy there stood "new responsible tasks before the workers in radio." The most important of these he described as the broad clarification of the significance of the new plan and the "mobilization of the workers in the fulfillment and overfulfillment of the tasks of the Stalin Five Year Plan."[32]

The general tenor of political broadcasting in the Soviet Union was more or less permanently set at an all-union conference on questions of political broadcasting in December 1934. In his opening remarks Platon Kerzhentsev, then Chairman of the Committee, set forth five major inadequacies of Soviet political broadcasting as it existed at that time,[33] and his comments were further elaborated by Tamarkin, then Director of the Sector of Political Broadcasting.[34] Together these two addresses provide a clear picture of the qualities for which Soviet political broadcasting strives.

The great inadequacy of political broadcasting, according to Kerzhentsev, was the absence of enough "pointed Bolshevik material." A great part of the political information given suffered from a lack of political sharpness and from being too "objective" and "quiet." The radio, Comrade Tamarkin stressed, is "a powerful weapon in the hands of the Party" and must operate accordingly:

> Political information . . . must mobilize the masses for the fulfillment of the tasks of socialist construction . . . In order . . . to become a genuine loudspeaker for the Party addressing the millions of workers, political information [on the radio] must be outstanding in its loyalty to the Party's interests . . . and activity. We reject all indifferent, "objective" information.[35]

The second inadequacy found by the committee president was a certain timidity in the use of the radio for the criticism of officials and citizens who were lax in their public duties, political and economic.* Radio editors, he noted, refrained from naming the culprits by name, which he found "an extraordinarily polite form." Criticism, he insisted, must be pointed, taking its example from *Pravda*. "We reject all hallelujahs in our work," echoed Tamarkin, "and all complacency; political information must show up disorder and mobilize the masses to fight with inadequacies."[36]

The third cardinal sin which Mr. Kerzhentsev noted was the academic quality of much of the political broadcasting, which he alleged frequently ignored the most important news. There is no point, seconded Tamarkin, in merely announcing that a particular collective farm brigade previously working poorly has as a result of socialist competition come to the front line with its production record—unless you tell precisely *how* the improvement was obtained. Such information "has meaning only in the event that it can teach some radio listener, if it can tell of concrete measures

---

*What is referred to here, of course, is the participation of the radio in the work of public self-criticism or *samokritika*. See Chapter 14.

for securing success in work." In short, concluded Tamarkin, it is necessary to avoid dull, empty, and uninteresting material:

> We stand for live and active information, for an original and full-blooded form of presenting material . . . But at the same time we renounce the broadcast of material whose only purpose is to divert the radio listener without consideration of the significance of the content of the given fact. Such things we regard as unhealthy trickery.[37]

By way of example, the speaker told of the Rostov radio station which seemed unable to find time to broadcast certain "glorious revolutionary news" from Spain, but seemed to have no trouble in finding a spot for some "twaddle" about a man living somewhere in Africa who had reached the age of 146 years.

The other sins noted were narrow localism and provincialism. The Leningrad Committee, for instance, broadcast only news of city life on its city program and only news of agricultural life on its collective-farm program. This, it was declared, "is based on the incorrect, anti-Party view that the worker is not interested in the collective farmer and vice versa. The Party cannot allow such separation of the city from the village."[38] Finally, attention was called to the "nationalist errors" made by some local committees, particularly in the Ukraine, Central Asia, and Belorussia, and to the frequent imposition on the listening audience of all varieties of personal potboilers and tediously long political addresses.

While the above-mentioned goals and deficiencies of political broadcasting apply to news programs as well as other political or propaganda-agitation broadcasts, a characteristic of Soviet newscasts that deserves special attention is the effort to tie in all news items, even "so-called trivia," with larger questions. For example, various minor notices about some interesting manifestation in the zoological gardens or about the opening of a new theater "must be tied in with the general problem of improvement in the life of the workers."[39]

The basic unit of political broadcasting by the central apparatus is referred to as an "article," and is generally a short talk, about ten minutes in duration, read from script. These articles may be written especially for radio, but are equally likely to be adaptations or condensations of newspaper or journal articles. Their form is fairly constant, and even in content they represent a kind of annual cycle. Thus, for several days before the anniversary of the adoption of the Constitution of the U.S.S.R. there will be articles on the virtues of Soviet democracy, and there are similar series before all important anniversaries and government campaigns. Standard subjects for these articles are the correctness of the policies and leadership of the party, the success of the Soviet nationality policy, and the high standard of social insurance in the U.S.S.R. There are regular talks on foreign policy. Finally, the lead article or editorial from *Pravda,* and less frequently from *Izvestiya,* is regularly read over the radio, as well as other items from the central press.

The talks that form part of the programs for special audiences are usually of less general nature and call upon the group to fulfill some specific task. On a program for the Red Army the article might be a message urging all men to be constantly alert against spies and saboteurs; in a program for collective farmers it might stress the importance of an early harvesting of the crops. This type of exhortation is most important in the work of local and lower broadcasting units, which are able to concentrate on the specific economic tasks facing their audience.

On the whole, the tone of these political broadcasts, which account for the bulk of the spoken words that go out over the air in the U.S.S.R., is calm and unhurried. Great emphasis is placed on clear diction, slow presentation, and directness if not simplicity of language calculated to reach the average or even the least advanced segment of the radio audience. Sentences tend to be short and vocabulary limited and simple. The announcers who read the political "articles" and present the news items appear to be well trained, are competent and experienced, and generally have radio know-how. They frequently work in pairs as mixed teams, and the man and woman alternate in announcing, presenting news items, or reading parts of long articles and announcements.

It is apparent that in its political broadcasts the Soviet radio appears more as an adjunct to the press than as an independent medium. In part this has resulted from the extensive use of wireless telegraphy as a means of mass dissemination of information and party and government decisions in the early years of the Revolution. Lenin referred to radio as a newspaper without limits of space or time.[40] Ever since, most Soviet discussions have tended to compare or link it to the press. The dependence of the radio on the press for political material is not merely accidental or traditional, however, but is the product of the political conditions under which the Soviet radio operates. Nothing may be broadcast, of course, that is not fully in keeping with the party line and that does not have full approval of the party's central Department of Propaganda and Agitation. And the party has decided to place its chief propaganda emphasis, as has been noted, on the written rather than the spoken word; perhaps taking cognizance of the Russian proverb that the spoken word is like a bird in a cage—once it's out of the mouth it is gone forever.

The party puts the greatest part of its propaganda energies into material for the press, and apparently propaganda officials find no reason to duplicate that effort for the radio, since this would involve not only new demands in the preparation of material, but the endless problems of censorship and checking on the political acceptability and "correctness" of the new material. Most radio propaganda material is, therefore, simply drawn from approved and correct sources, that is, the newspapers and journals, and reworked in a form acceptable for radio presentation.[41]

Radio personnel have on many occasions been vigorously reminded that they are after all in radio and are not running a newspaper, but under the circumstances their plight can be readily appreciated. Some radio devices, such as bringing the microphone into the shop or office, as well as radio conferences and discussions, provide a certain amount of variety in the field of political broadcasting, but on the whole the radio editors are limited in applying their ingenuity to adapting for the radio material that is essentially intended for the printed page. It can no longer be charged, as the Soviet humor magazine *Crocodile* did at one time, that it is only proper for Soviet citizens to see the news first in the morning paper and hear it next in the evening over the radio, since, as everyone knows, light reaches the eyes sooner than sound reaches the ears.[42]

But Soviet political broadcasting has by no means tested the full potentialities of the radio as an instrument for the indoctrination and mobilization of the population.

Children's Programs: Broadcasts for children, under the guidance of the Sector on Children's Broadcasts, are sent out by the central apparatus to the extent of a half dozen or more each day. The tasks of these programs were recently defined by the Chairman of the Radio Committee as follows: "They assist the school and the family in raising the children, organizing their leisure, encouraging their interest in science, and developing their love of the motherland."[43] These have been substantially the goals of Soviet children's broadcasts from their inception. The radio does not seek actually to instruct children or carry out any of the school's pedagogic functions, but to "supplement in an artistic and interesting way the knowledge which children acquire in school or kindergarten." This end is sought through an effort to "develop their inventive interest, arouse their creative fancy, give them, without tiring them, a certain amount of historic and literary knowledge, and foster the appreciation of music."[44]

Children's programs are carefully graded according to age, and there are special programs for preschool and kindergarten children, the Octoberists of the first two years of school, the Pioneers from ten to fourteen, and so on. The programs are much like good children's programs everywhere, drawing heavily on folk tales and adventure stories, on the imagination and impressibility of youth, and on their desire for interesting information. There are no scare programs or hair-raisers for children; special attention is paid to purity of language, and the general tone is very positive and "proper."

Although the Moscow Children's Theater is heavily relied upon, more truly original programming of the type especially adapted to radio seems to be done in the sphere of children's broadcasts than in any other area, probably because political encumbrances are at a minimum. Recent features which attracted some attention were the "Captain's Club" program and the "Radio Magazine." The Captain's Club was a once-a-month series designed to give children greater acquaintance with the geography of foreign lands. The club's "members" were leading characters of popular children's books, such as Robinson Crusoe and Gulliver, and at one stage Baron Munchausen appeared in an effort to crash the club. Each program of the Radio Magazine was devoted to a different phase of serious music, the main purpose being to popularize, and develop a taste for good music among the children.[45]

Advertising: Although announcements of local events such as film showings, theater performances, lectures, and dances have always had a place in Soviet broadcasting, commercial advertisements as such were forbidden in 1935.[46] It must be recognized that despite the almost complete socialization of the means of production and distribution, many Soviet economic organizations have felt the need of some medium for bringing their products and services to the attention of the public. Organizations as large as the Ministry of the Food Industry and as small as the local shoe-repair coöperative have advertised their old and new products or services in the newspapers as a means of increasing sales and thus improving their economic position. Advertisements for certain types of skilled labor have been most common.

In recognition of this need, and as an important means of gaining revenue, the Soviet radio began broadcasting commercial advertisements at the end of May 1947.[47] These retain the shape of the earlier announcements of local events, and the program format is probably the least objectionable for the presentation of commercials. All of the commercials are grouped in a single program of eight or ten minutes' duration, broadcast three times a day, and the announcements are read alternately by male and female announcers without interruption. The commercial programs represent a type of shoppers' service, or a form of radio "red book" in the absence of other advertising media resulting from the paper shortage.

Comedy and recreation: In the early days of Soviet broadcasting an article in a Soviet encyclopedia noted rather noncommittally that "abroad radio broadcasting is regarded as an amusement and in part as education."[48] Although the article did not pass judgment on this view of radio as an amusement, there can be no doubt that it does not coincide with that of Soviet radio authorities. The word amusement is not applied to the radio by Soviet officials—the furthest that they will go in that direction is to refer to it as "a form of entertainment,"[49] and this is very quickly followed by reservations to indicate that it is really much more. The Soviet radio, it appears, is much too important a medium of mass communication, too central a link between party and populace, too viable an instrument of education, to be classed with circuses, humorous magazines, and the comic theater as amusements.* The Soviet radio may carry programs which amuse, in the form of readings of humorous prose or verse, but the Soviet radio does not have comic programs or radio comics in anything like the sense of American comic programs. The Soviet radio does not seek to amuse. Its task in this regard has been carefully defined: it provides the workers of the nation with "a pleasant, sensible recreation,"[50] above all "providing them with cultural relaxation."[51]

PROGRAMMING ON THE DIFFUSION EXCHANGE

The program activities of the local, that is, republican and regional, radio stations are largely a replica of those of the central apparatus, and in the case of local stations that use the Russian language, the bulk of their broadcasts are actually relays of central material. The programming of the diffusion exchange, however, merits more extended treatment.

Owing to its unique physical structure, the diffusion exchange is peculiarly adapted to a vigorous and experimental program policy which can be completely adjusted to local needs. For the same structural reasons, however, namely, that they are numerous and that their programs do not go on the air, the exchanges present a difficult monitoring problem. Along with their experimental possibilities, therefore, they run the risk of consistently putting out inferior programs, and, what is an even more serious offense in the Soviet Union, they may be used for "private," non-party, po-

---

*And in the Soviet Union these amusements, of course, also have political purposes to fulfill. The Soviet circus, for example, is a most striking example of the political adaptation of a popular form of amusement.

litical purposes. A conflict between experiment and local initiative, on the one hand, and central control, on the other, was experienced during the early development of exchange broadcasting in the Soviet Union. The conflict was resolved in favor of control.

Throughout the early thirties, when supervision was somewhat decentralized and weak, the exchange editors had a relatively high degree of freedom in developing their own broadcasts. Finding what it considered to be a serious subversion of the purposes of the diffusion exchange, the All-Union Radio Committee, within two years of its establishment, issued a special decision on February 3, 1935, completely reconstructing the system for control of exchange broadcasting.[52] The committee noted that some exchanges had completely ceased to retransmit central and local broadcasts, and instead diffused only their own broadcasts. Many of these programs, the committee held, were of the primitive potboiler variety. Others were experiments which for one reason or another (the reasons were not given in any detail) were unacceptable, such as radio "traveling shows," radio circuses, the walking radio, and the radio newspapers. Finally, some were regarded as politically illiterate or even "harmful," and cases were cited of alleged nationalist diversions and of antistate speeches made under the guise of scientific lectures. For example, it was noted with horror, if not a little suspicion, that one exchange while carrying Molotov's address to the Seventh Congress of Soviets had its own recorded music playing in the background and even made an announcement in the midst of the speech.

Consequently, in 1935 and 1936 the right of exchanges to present their own broadcasts was limited to a specified number of major exchanges so certified by the republican and regional radio committees; all other exchanges were forbidden to originate broadcasts and were completely restricted to the exclusive diffusion of programs sent out by the central and local stations. Authorized exchanges were granted the right to send out their own programs for a total of as little as one half hour or at most two hours during the broadcast day. In originating programs they were instructed to restrict themselves to three areas: (1) political information and a review of the local press; (2) production problems, which meant primarily practical talks by administrative and leading workers on improving production or agricultural yield; and (3) musical programs, which, however, were not to be put on by professionals hired by the exchange but were to represent the work of local musical clubs and amateurs. Permission was also given to present announcements, to answer listeners' questions, and to broadcast the more important local meetings and gatherings. All other forms of exchange broadcasting were forbidden, and, although a few of the major exchanges were excepted, special control measures were taken to supervise their activities.

The regulations then adopted by the All-Union Committee are still largely in effect. Only certain authorized exchanges may originate their own programs (it appears that less than a third of all exchanges are so authorized), and their maximum allotment for such material is one hour daily.[53] Their chief task is rigorously defined as the high-quality diffusion of the central and local broadcasts, some of which, such as the setting-up exercises and news roundups, they are obliged to carry at specified times. The programs that the exchange originates must strive to assist the local party and the trade-union organizations in the economic tasks facing the plant or locality. In a plant of the Trekhgornaya Manufaktura Combine, for example, the exchange broadcasts include news about the "production advance" of the plant as a whole and the progress of particular shops, brigades, and Stakhanovite workers; reports on the meetings of party, Komsomol, and trade-union committees; agronomy talks to aid the local gardeners; announcements of new books, films, and dances; a "technical library" on the air; talks by leading workers about their methods; and similar material of an educational and "agit-prop" nature.[54] At the group-listening points in the plant or on the collective farm, the local agitators are expected to be on the premises at the time of these "home" programs (and during the transmission of the central news and political broadcasts) to answer questions, to organize summaries of the material transmitted, and to stress the immediate tasks and responsibilities of the group in the production or political campaign discussed on the broadcast.[55]

18

THE RADIO AUDIENCE IN THE U.S.S.R.

T HE SIZE OF THE AUDIENCE REACHED BY THE RADIO SETS and wired receivers of the U.S.S.R. is not precisely known. Even with an accurate index of the average number of listeners reached by each receiving point, which unfortunately is not available, it would be necessary to exercise considerable caution in making an estimate from the mere size of the receiving net. Owing to lack of repairs and replacement parts, a considerable number of receivers are regularly inoperative. In one exchange in 1943 more than five hundred of a total of 940 receivers were inactive throughout the year.[1] Although this undoubtedly reflected wartime conditions, less severe but striking deficiencies are apparently not unusual in less troubled times.[2] Account must be taken, furthermore, of the general inactivity of the system as a whole. In one district of the Kirov Region in 1946, for example, the district radio was off the air for half the year, and there were many similar instances in other areas. On January 1, 1948, more than 350 diffusion exchanges were not operating.[3] It was reported in 1940 that on the average the nation's diffusion exchanges were silent during 3.7 per cent of the time that they were scheduled to be operating, owing to lack of current or mechanical failures.[4]

There are, however, some indexes on which an estimate may be ventured. At the end of 1934, with 64 stations broadcasting and 2.5 million units in the receiving network, a Soviet official estimated the number of listeners as over ten million.[5] Another official placed the total at 13 to 15 million.[6] This audience was made possible by the extensive use of group listening based on the installation of sets in clubs, reading rooms, and other public places. Early in 1936 it was reported that in the city of Gorkov, with 1,200 receivers, one hundred of them in the "houses of culture," dormitories, and stores, there were not less than four to five thousand radio listeners.[7] Since 1936, however, group listening has been constantly stressed by the radio authorities, and every major diffusion exchange has been expected to establish a large collective listening point known as a "radio auditorium." By 1940 there were six thousand such auditoriums.[8] A Soviet source estimated the radio audience for early 1947 at 25 to 30 million.[9] Since there were approximately 7.5 million receivers (all types) in existence at the time, a ratio of four listeners per receiver seems reasonable. With approximately ten million sets of all types operating on January 1, 1949, the Soviet radio audience at that time was probably close to forty million. At the time of important announcements and addresses by major government officials, of course, the audience might be expected to be significantly larger, both because greater interest might attract listeners to group-listening points and because of the ability of local propaganda officials to mobilize the population for radio listening.

Adequate data on the geographical distribution and social composition of the radio audience are lacking, but the main outlines of this distribution may be derived from available material.

The majority of collective farms, as has been noted, in 1947 had no radio apparatus of any kind, neither regular sets nor wired speakers. It must be remembered, furthermore, that the term "farm" does not mean one family; on the average, collective farms include about 75 to 100 peasant households. Thus, a large part of the rural population is outside the reach of radio in the Soviet Union, except for the peasants' visits to district centers which are better equipped. Similarly, for the national minorities of the country the number of radio receivers is very low.

The radio audience is largely restricted, therefore, to those living in district centers in the rural regions, in the better developed minority areas, and particularly to the urban population.

Even within these limits the radio is not uniformly available to all elements of the population. The possession of a regular radio set is limited by the scarcity of such sets, by the availability of electric current to operate them, and by the costs of these sets, which in the past have been high enough to put them beyond the reach of the average worker. It is probable, therefore, that such sets are largely in the hands of officials, members of the intelligentsia, and more skilled workers, some of whom may have acquired them as rewards for their high production records. The remainder are used as collective or group-listening points in dormitories, clubrooms, and so on, and on collective farms where wired receivers are not available. The costs of the crystal sets, when they reach mass production, will be low enough to put them within the reach of anyone who can obtain one.

In the case of the wired speakers, the costs are much less a factor, and accessibility to radio-diffusion exchanges is the chief determinant. The major urban centers are well provided with such equipment, and at most large industrial plants the trade unions have established exchanges which serve the workers' dormitories and the surrounding workers' settlements or apartment houses. Those people who live in parts of the city which have exchanges, or who work at major industrial establishments, have an opportunity to have wired receivers installed. The rest must wait upon the future development of the radio-receiving network.

THE RADIO AUDIENCE AND LISTENING POLICY

In discussing the Soviet audience, it is not possible to produce anything like the beautiful array of charts, tables, and graphs that is available on the listening habits of the American radio audience. The Soviet pattern must be derived from the structure of the radio apparatus and from other secondary sources.

In the early part of 1949 there were about ten million wired speakers and regular radio sets in the Soviet Union. If it is assumed that there are about forty million households in the nation, this would yield a ratio of one radio for each of four families. As a result, an outstanding feature of radio listening in the U.S.S.R. is group listening or, as it is called in Soviet terminology, collective listening. Those who have sets at home, or those who live in workers' dormitories having radio equipment, may hear the radio at their place of residence. Those not so fortunate who want to hear the radio have to go out—to the home of a friend who has a set or to some gathering place such as the reading room of a plant, housing community, or collective farm, the recreation hall of the trade union, or to one of the six thousand collective listening auditoriums maintained by the diffusion exchanges. They may also hear radio programs at their place of work, piped in over the public-address system, and in some cases carried out to farm brigades by portable sets.

The nature of the Soviet receiving apparatus has an effect not only on the time and place of radio listening, but on the choice of program as well. When you visit your neighbor, courtesy requires that you listen to his choice of program. When listening is done in public places, the choice of program becomes a joint decision, or is the responsibility of the director of the reading hut or recreation hall. This applies, furthermore, only to the regular radio sets. Most radio listening depends on wired receivers, and except for the limited number of exchanges that carry more than one program, the listeners are restricted to the program that the editor of the exchange chooses to put on the wire at the time.

The structure of the audience and the predominance of group listening has also had its effect on the program policies of Soviet radio directors. Soviet broadcasting policy has been consistently dominated by the principle of orienting and directing programs to carefully defined segments of the population, and apparently no really serious competition has been offered by the opposed principle of the maximum audience at any given time. This is one of the few luxuries that can be afforded by noncommercial radio which is free of the advertiser's need for maximum audience coverage for any given unit of cost.*

*Soviet radio authorities, like all radio men, do not escape the problem of the evening hours when the entire family gathers around the one radio set. See Goron, *Radiobroadcasting,* p. 14.

As early as 1930 it was asserted that "Soviet radiobroadcasting is oriented toward specific elements of the audience of toilers . . . taking into consideration their interests and stage of development."[10] The chief groups toward which programs are directed are industrial workers, collective farmers and agricultural workers, employees, women, youth (in particular members of the Young Communist League), children, Red Army men, members of the Red Fleet, and various nationality groups. Women, it might be noted, are treated as just another group, albeit important, among many others in the radio audience. They do not enjoy the overwhelming importance granted them by American program directors by virtue of their position as the chief force in setting the consumption pattern of the American family.

The dominance of the principle of group-oriented programs is not merely a device in keeping with the pattern of radio listening. It is closely related to the functions that the Soviet radio is expected to serve. From the point of view of the audience, the radio is supposed to satisfy certain predefined "needs" for political information, for cultural education, for relaxation; from the point of view of the party and government, it is expected to secure political support of the regime, to mobilize the population for the fulfillment of its economic tasks, and so on. But such "needs" of the listeners and the expectations of the party and government vary from social group to social group. They are not the same for the workers, the peasants, the intelligentsia, the housewives, or the Red Army. Under the circumstances, the Soviet radio must of necessity be based on the principle of group-oriented programs if it is effectively to serve the purposes for which it was built and is operated.

The technical base of Soviet radiobroadcasting both facilitates and hampers the operation of this principle of group-oriented programming. In so far as the radio-relay exchanges, which are the foundation of the receiving network, have a homogeneous audience, as in the exchanges which serve collective farms or industrial enterprises, the wired speaker lends itself admirably to this type of programming. The directors of the exchange may then choose for transmission those programs which are best suited to the needs of the particular audience. And since the subscriber is able to tune in only the programs that the exchange is sending out, he will hear, if he listens at all, a program designed to reach him rather than a program designed for another audience and therefore presumably less effective.

A system of wired diffusion, however, is not so well suited to group programming in exchanges that serve a heterogeneous audience, such as those in urban centers and in some rural localities where industrial plants and local farms may be served by the same net. In such cases, the fact that the majority of the exchanges are capable of transmitting but one program at a time makes it difficult to carry programs for one part of their audience without cutting off another part with different needs and interests. The solution here lies in constructing new exchanges and reconstructing old ones so that the exchange is capable of simultaneously transmitting more than one program over its wires, thus giving the subscriber an opportunity to choose his program according to his needs and interests. This system, apart from presenting its own technical difficulties, is also dependent upon an increase in the number of transmitters simultaneously sending out programs in any given area, a requirement not to be met easily by Soviet industry at this time.

AUDIENCE RESPONSE AND TESTING

Very little is known concerning the response of the Soviet radio audience to the fare offered to it by the Radio Committee and local stations. There is apparently no systematic technical testing of audience reaction to radio programs, although that testing would not involve serious obstacles comparable to those facing any inquiry into political attitudes in the Soviet Union. The general absence of such testing may be attributed to several influences. Chief among these is the conception of the radio's function not as primarily a source of entertainment but as an instrument of government policy and as a means for the general cultural and political education of the population. Under the circumstances, it is not too surprising that greater efforts are not made to test audience response, for the party and the radio authorities assume that as specialists they are better equipped than the listening audience to judge what types of programs will achieve these ends. It should be noted, furthermore, that extensive audience testing is a complicated and expensive operation, which the radio officials, if they were so inclined, would have difficulty in justifying to the Soviet budgetary authorities.

It would be unduly glib to assert that after all the Soviet population has no choice but to listen to the radio programs offered it, and that therefore the radio authorities need show no concern for or interest in the reactions of their listeners. There is evidence that they do. Respect for the radio listener is reflected in the generally high quality, the scope, and the content of Soviet radio programs. Moreover, Soviet officials have always stressed the responsibilities of the radio workers to the radio audience. Even in the sphere of political broadcasting, where one might expect the least compromise, the director of political broadcasting complained in 1934 of excessively long and dry speeches and declared that many programs "stuffed with figures and indigestible material only clutter up the air."[11]*

The radio authorities are not unaware that the vast majority of listeners are served by relay exchanges and thus cannot choose their own programs. There are standing instructions that special attention be given to the work of the exchanges, in particular to their programming policy and their contact with the subscribers.[12] The general tenor of the instructions given to radio officials by the party in regard to the audience's needs is fairly well reflected in this statement from a *Pravda* editorial written on the twentieth anniversary of Soviet radiobroadcasting:

Our radio serves the widest mass of the toilers and therefore it is faced with especially high demands. The workers in radiobroadcasting are responsible before the tens of millions of listeners. Complacency in this important sphere of our mass political-educational work would be full of the most serious consequences. Workers in radiobroadcasting of the central and local stations must work like demons, sparing no pains, to carry out honorably the work entrusted to them. They must unceasingly show concern about their listeners, improve the quality of radiobroadcasting, diversify the programs broadcast, secure the high ideo-direction of all that they put out.[13]

*This should not be taken to exclude the fact that the speaker may have had in mind the diminishing effectiveness of long political speeches.

Although the actual extent of the efforts to test audience response is limited and does not appear to include careful sampling and polling techniques, the amount of this activity in the sphere of radio appears to be greater than that in the field of the press and the films. This is most likely a result of the fact that the bulk of radio time is devoted to nonpolitical work, that is, music and literary-dramatic broadcasts, and a greater leeway for audience choice is therefore feasible.

The chief means of judging the response of the radio audience is, as in the case of the newspaper readers, the encouragement of extensive letter writing by radio listeners. As early as 1934 it was reported that a single central station received from 25,000 to 30,000 letters each month.[14] In 1937 it was asserted that the Radio Committee received "hundreds" of letters each day.[15] During the war, undoubtedly encouraged by the frequent reading on the air of letters from and to the front, the committee was apparently receiving almost fifty thousand letters each month.[16] It would appear that these letters, or a representative sample of them, are carefully read and studied. It has been stated that "these letters and the conference of radio listeners serve as the material from which the All-Union Radio Committee and the local commissions derive the information necessary for the improvement, the correction, and the direction of broadcasting in a manner which will more fully satisfy the interests and the requirements of the broad mass of radio listeners."[17]

The conference of radio listeners referred to above is a special feature of the radio-relay system of transmission. The exchange does indeed offer unique opportunities for close contact between those in charge of broadcasting and the listening public. The name and location of each subscriber is known to the local directors, and frequently in the smaller exchanges real personal contact between radio worker and listener is possible through conferences held in the group-listening room, the trade-union hall, or in a similar public place. These conferences are supposed to provide the listeners with an opportunity for complaint or praise, and to give the exchange's workers a chance to learn the listeners' views and to defend their own performance.[18]

Other practices used from time to time to test audience response at the local level are visits to the homes of subscribers by employees of the exchange, and the use of "brigades" of radio workers who visit clubs, collective farms, and other points of group listening to question radio listeners on their tastes and their reactions to the quality of local broadcasting. Such information as is gathered appears primarily to concern the reaction of subscribers to the choice of programs by the editors of the local exchange from among the central and local station offerings, rather than their response to the content of individual programs. The latter type of information is presumably also gathered, however, and then is supposed to be passed up the administrative hierarchy by the directors of the exchange to the point at which the program actually originates.

There have been only occasional references to the use of questionnaires by Soviet radio officials. The directors of youth programs have sent schedules of future broadcasts to listeners for their comments.[19] In one diffusion exchange a listener's conference was followed up by the distribution of one thousand questionnaires which sought to find out which programs listeners wished the exchange to carry;[20] and another exchange distributed one hundred questionnaires for a similar purpose.[21] Copies of such questionnaires are not available, and in general the procedure does not seem to have been encouraged.[22] Greater stress is placed on conferences and meetings of listeners and on the development of "listeners' councils" or panels for constant contact between the audience and the exchange's workers.[23]

Little is known about the extent and type of program pretesting used by the Soviet radio authorities. It has been reported that children's programs are presented before a sample audience of children, who are questioned on the merits of each scene, and, it is said, their suggestions are often followed.[24]

THE SOVIET RADIO AND THE SOVIET SYSTEM

The interest in the Soviet radio is not limited to the fact that it is "Soviet," or that its operations differ from the dominant radio pattern in the West. This survey of domestic broadcasting in the U.S.S.R. has sought to emphasize the close relationship between the structure and functioning of the Soviet radio apparatus and the complex of social, political, and economic conditions under which it operates.

To understand the program policy of the Soviet radio, for example, it is essential that account be taken of the Communist Party's conception of its relationship to the masses and the media of communication. For in the light of that social role of the party in the Soviet Union, the program policy of the Soviet radio appears as a meaningful extension of the Bolshevik theory of leadership and the broader ideological framework from which that theory is derived.

Thus, serious music and literature predominate on the Soviet radio to a much greater extent than might be.expected if program policy were decided by popular choice. This emphasis is determined by the party and is viewed as the fulfillment of its assumed responsibility for the cultural education of the people. The high proportion of "agit-prop" material and its pervasiveness are regarded as necessary and proper concomitants of the party's self-defined role as directing vanguard and general staff. It follows, finally, that in this relationship between the party and the masses the function of public-opinion testing is sharply circumscribed. The party not only determines the goals of broadcasting, but is assumed to be best qualified to select the means of attaining these goals. The party cannot be indifferent to public opinion about the radio. This is not because it seeks to follow that opinion, but primarily because it feels the need to check and regulate its own pace. This is a highly political rather than a statistical conception of public opinion, and the judgment about the state of opinion is arrived at by means other than the public-opinion poll.

The interrelation of the Soviet system and the Soviet radio is no less marked in respect to the physical structure of Soviet broadcasting. Unable to provide enough radio stations to cover its vast domain, and lacking sufficient regular radio sets for its great population, the Soviet government turned to the use of wired diffusion and to group listening. This choice was not simply accidental; the alternative chosen dovetailed with the political and social pattern of Soviet life. From the point of view of the party and government, it was functional in the extreme.

First, group listening means group contact and group experience, which has been generally fostered by the Soviet regime in its efforts to reshape the *Geist* of the population. Second, group listening lends itself admirably to agitation work.[25] It brings the agitator's audience to him of its own volition, and it gives him the unique opportunity of combining his personal appeal with the authority of the impersonal radio. In addition, wired diffusion eliminates the possibility that his audience may have been subjected to radio counterpropaganda. Third, the diffusion system facilitates the task of the agitator (and the educator) by making known to him the precise composition of the audience with which he is working. Fourth, by making possible direct contact between the local radio official and the listening audience, the diffusion network provides a well-defined channel for popular criticism and thus aids the party and government with the ever present problem of controlling the administrative bureaucracy. At the same time, by channeling public dissatisfaction toward immediate targets at the local level, that is, diffusion-exchange officials, the party and government are able to siphon off in a relatively harmless form criticism that might otherwise be aimed at higher and more important targets.

It is clear that the radio apparatus is fairly well designed to meet the needs of the party and government. This does not mean, of course, that in its structure and functioning the Soviet radio does not generate some stress and strain that may in the last analysis prove dysfunctional from the point of view of the ruling power. This is probably the case in at least three respects which may be regarded as potential generators of tension throughout all areas of Soviet life— the scarcity of consumers' goods, the pervasiveness of agitation and propaganda activities, and the extensiveness of political controls.

It is not unlikely that, despite the possible gratifications of group listening, large numbers of the Soviet people feel dissatisfied at being so frequently obliged to listen in public rather than in the comfort or seclusion of their homes. In addition, the fact that they are limited to a single program can hardly escape the notice of those who have wired speakers instead of radio sets. Thus, the situation in radio contributes to the general adverse impact of the scarcity of consumers' goods and the deficiencies of those that are available.

It may be assumed, furthermore, that the public's attitude toward the radio as a means of relaxation is probably affected both by the high propaganda content of a considerable part of the broadcasting and by the frequent linkage of group listening and group agitation, and that consequently some avoidance of the radio might result. A related ambivalence toward the radio has, of course, been noted among some segments of the population in other countries subjected to intensive commercial exploitation of the air waves.

Finally, it may be noted that while the ability of the diffusion's subscribers directly to criticize the officials of the exchange may effect some change in the choice of program diffused, it can create only very limited change in the content of programs. The local directors are rigidly guided by regulations from above; and the officials at the top, as has been seen, are bound by political principle and by force rather than by an interest in presenting primarily the type of program that the audience might want. Thus, the freedom to criticize the diffusion exchange's directors may in the last analysis have a boomerang effect, thereby increasing frustration and resentment against the total system.

In the absence of adequate data, however, this enumeration of possible areas of dysfunction in the operation of the Soviet radio must be regarded simply as suggesting a line of investigation rather than as presenting established conclusions. In evaluating them, however, it must be remembered that the Soviet radio functions in a milieu in which scarcity, extensive propaganda activities, and rigid controls and decision from above form the dominant and apparently widely accepted pattern in most spheres of social and political life. It should also be kept in mind that radio listeners in the United States and elsewhere are regularly subjected to intensive commercial advertising which many of them might choose not to hear; still, most of them continue to listen to the radio. Furthermore, many Americans may well have the feeling that they are powerless to affect significantly the choice of program content; yet this has not resulted, up to this point, in serious economic or political consequences for the radio industry as a whole, or for the total social-economic system in which it operates.

If this background is kept in mind, there is some basis for making a prediction about the future development of the Soviet radio. It has already been indicated that in the immediate future the physical expansion of radio facilities will continue slowly. Several five-year plans will be required before the volume of radio-receiving equipment approaches that currently existing in the United States and the more advanced areas of Western Europe. We may expect a significant redressing of the disproportion in the distribution of radio equipment between city and country and a noticeable shift in favor of the proportion of regular radio sets as against wired receivers, although wired receivers will continue to predominate. Considerable progress may also be anticipated in placing the wired net on a multiple-program basis. Despite an increase in the availability of receivers, however, it is likely that group listening will continue to be encouraged because of its adaptability to agitation work.

So far as program policy is concerned, it appears certain that so long as the forced pace of Soviet economic development continues and, particularly, so long as international relations remain unsettled, the basic relationship of the ruling party to the population will remain the same. Consequently, it may be anticipated that for the foreseeable future the basic pattern of Soviet radio program policy will remain in substantially its present form.

PART 5

THE FILM IN SOVIET SOCIETY

19

THE SOVIET FILM INDUSTRY

DEVELOPMENT OF THE SOVIET CINEMA

THE FILM, IN CONTRAST TO THE RADIO, IS WIDELY RECOGnized as a distinct art form. Yet, of all the arts, the film is most clearly also a means of mass communication. This characteristic was early recognized by Lenin when he said, in 1907, that "when the masses take possession of the film and it comes into the hands of true supporters of socialist culture, it will become one of the most powerful means of educating the masses."[1] Indeed, the entire history of the film's development in the Soviet Union may be viewed as a struggle to place that instrument firmly and securely in the hands of the Bolsheviks, the "true supporters of socialist culture." In that struggle there have been two major campaigns which in part overlapped. The first, in which the goal was control over the administrative machinery and the physical means for producing and distributing films, ended in a decisive victory for the Bolsheviks before the end of the New Economic Policy. In the second campaign, the goal is the complete ideological and artistic subordination of the film to the needs and interests of the party. The outcome of the issue in this second campaign is by no means in doubt, but there are still at this late date sporadic flare-ups and minor skirmishes which indicate that the battle has not yet been fought to a completely successful conclusion for the Bolsheviks.

Although no motion-picture cameras, raw film, or projectors were produced, the cinema was not unknown in Tsarist Russia. Indeed, the country had a well-developed moving-picture industry. In 1917 some twenty-five producers were making more than five hundred films each year. Those films were shown in 1,045 cinema houses, more than 60 per cent of whose offerings were Russian productions.[2]

The Soviet government took only a few tentative steps toward control over motion pictures in the period immediately following the seizure of power. "Workers' control" over the film industry was rapidly instituted; and special governmental Film Committees were established in Moscow and Petrograd * in March 1918, with authority to exercise economic and ideological control over the film enterprises, which remained predominantly in private hands. The difficult physical conditions created by the Revolution, however, severely restricted the production and screening of films. Many of the major film producers, along with their staffs and equipment, joined the emigration. Those who remained vigorously resisted state control, and films considered hostile to the regime continued to be produced and to be shown.[3]

To meet this situation, the government undertook the nationalization of the film industry on August 27, 1919.[4] But the difficulties that the government was facing were intensified rather than eased by this decision. The nationalization decree met strong resistance from the film industry, which reacted by further emigration, closing studios and theaters, and hiding equipment and films.[5] The situation was rendered still more acute by the Civil War and foreign intervention. Many of the available resources were destroyed, and the making and showing of films were hindered by the absence of sufficient electric current and the means to heat studios and cinemas. Eventually, the production of new films was brought to a virtual standstill when the supply of raw film stocks imported from abroad was cut off.[6]

By 1920-1921 less than half of the thousand cinema theaters re-

*These Film Committees were the first of a series of government organizations of increasing power and complexity developed to keep pace with the extension of state control over the film and the growth of the industry. They were succeeded by the All-Russian Photo-Film Department under the Commissariat of Education at the time of the nationalization of the film industry in 1919. This was followed in 1922 by the Central State Film Enterprise (Goskino) and in 1925 by the Soviet Film Trust (Sovkino), both under the Commissariat of Education; the Chief Administration for the Photo-Film Industry, directly under the Council of People's Commissars, in 1933; the All-Union Committee on Affairs of Cinematography in 1938; and finally, the Commissariat of Cinematography in 1946.

mained open. Of the original 143 cinemas in Moscow,[7] only ten were functioning regularly; and, because of lack of equipment, current, and films, there were many weeks when not a single theater in the city was able to put a picture on the screen.[8] The number of full-length films produced fell to about a dozen.[9] Most of the available film stock was used for newsreels and agitation films with such titles as *Hammer and Sickle* and *Speculators*.[10]

With the introduction of the New Economic Policy in 1921, the film industry gradually began to revive. In addition to the production facilities remaining in the hands of the government and coöperative film-producing societies which it sponsored, privately financed studios were permitted to operate. A large part of the distributing apparatus with many of the theaters returned to private hands. This created a more normal situation for the person wishing to see a moving picture, but it intensified the control difficulties faced by the government. The vast majority of the films being shown were either made before the Revolution or imported from the West. Many of the new films being produced in the Soviet Union were made by people who were far from being strong supporters of the new regime. As a result, the Soviet screen was filled with material considered antagonistic to the regime, or at best regarded as politically indifferent.[11] As the Twelfth Party Congress phrased it in 1923, the film "has in fact been transformed into an instrument for bourgeois influence and for corruption of the toiling masses."[12]

To counteract the effects of free enterprise, the government moved decisively in the direction of censorship over the production and screening of films. It ruled that all films be numbered and registered, and provided that only films so registered might be shown. It stipulated, in addition, that each cinema program maintain a specified balance between entertainment films, selected to eliminate those regarded as counterrevolutionary, and propaganda films about internal and foreign events.[13] The government film agency was given a monopoly over the rental of films, in order to provide it with real power to exclude from the screen those pictures regarded as harmful.[14] To facilitate the selection of acceptable films, a special Chief Committee for Repertories was also established in the Commissariat of Education.[15] Similar measures were shortly thereafter introduced

within the government structure of the other Soviet republics between 1923 and 1925.[16]

These control measures rapidly stabilized the distribution and
screening work of the film industry and gave the Bolsheviks secure
knowledge that foreign and prerevolutionary films considered hostile
to the regime would no longer appear on Soviet screens. But they
did not achieve the more positive goal of bringing to the screen films
that would further the program of the party and the government.
Even among the propaganda films made in government studios there
were many that were felt to have an effect opposite to that desired
by the regime.[17] To meet the situation, propaganda films were in
1922 placed under review by qualified Marxists so that such instances
of inverted effect would be reduced.[18] But the decisive fact was that
as late as the end of 1923 only 13 per cent of the films shown in the
Soviet Union were domestically produced.[19] It became clear that the
only solution lay in establishing Soviet film-producing organizations
and staffing them with reliable personnel. To this end a series of
joint-stock companies and coöperative producing societies were organized, among them the ARK, or Association for Revolutionary
Cinematography (1924), which adopted the slogan: "The film is a
most powerful weapon in the struggle for communist culture." [20]

The films produced by these organizations were far from successful. [21] In his address to the Thirteenth Party Congress in 1924, Stalin
was obliged to declare: "Things do not stand well in the matter of
the film. The film is a great means of mass agitation. The task is to
take this affair into your hands."[22] As a result of the Congress' action on this call, a special organization composed of representatives
of the party's agitation and propaganda department, the Commissariat of Education, the trade unions, and the film associations was
established in each republic to supervise the content of the films produced.[23] Finally, the party set up its own special commission under
the Propaganda and Agitation Department to coördinate and effect
this control.[24]

In the mid-twenties, as the technical deficiencies of the early
period were progressively overcome, the party shifted the center of
its attention more to questions of the content, themes, and artistic and
ideological quality of Soviet films.[25] Under control of the new film

trust *Sovkino,* the Soviet cinema industry entered a period which in Soviet sources is defined as the "flowering of the silent film," [26] and which film critics abroad have termed "the most vital period of innovation which the film industry of any nation has yet experienced."[27] This was the period in which the great film masters of the Soviet Union—Sergei M. Eisenstein (*The Battleship Potemkin, October, Old and New*), Alesander Dovzhenko (*Earth*), Vsevolod Pudovkin (*Mother, The End of St. Petersburg, Storm Over Asia*), and others— produced that striking series of silent films so well known to all people interested in the history of the cinema.

Despite these notable successes, however, the party was not fully satisfied with the personnel in the film industry or with the quality of their products. In March 1928 the Department of Propaganda and Agitation convened the First All-Union Party Conference on the Film. The Conference's resolutions were full of references to the "remnants of bourgeois influence" and to the pernicious tendencies toward "naturalism" and "formalism" among the directors.[28] Behind these imposing charges, however, it was apparent that the party felt that there was too much art and not enough direct propaganda and agitation in the films. The Conference made this perfectly clear when it declared that "the basic criterion for evaluating the art qualities of a film is the requirement that it be presented in a form which can be understood by the millions." No concessions were to be made to "narrow-minded, petty-bourgeois taste," but instead the film was to be filled with material intimately familiar to the worker and peasant audience.[29]

The Conference on the Film was followed in January 1929 by a decision of the Central Committee which took concrete measures to implement the conference's resolutions. The Central Committee asserted that "the task of the Party is to strengthen the supervision of the work of the film organizations by every means, and to secure the ideological firmness of film productions, decisively struggling against manifestations of the accommodations of the Soviet film to the ideology of nonproletarian elements." To accomplish this end, the Central Committee ordered its own organizations, those of the Komsomol, and the trade unions, to take a more active part in supervising film production. It particularly urged that tried and trusted cadres of new workers be sent into the film industry by those organizations, and it specifically ordered that "proletarian scenario writers" be sent into the industry in order to strengthen the basic cadres and insure party control.[30]

The Central Committee's decision to permeate the staffs of the movie industry with individuals of proletarian origin was part of a general movement to increase the proportion of people of working-class background in all responsible positions, which followed as a consequence of the Shakhtinsky industrial sabotage trials.[31]* The decision came, furthermore, in the very early stages of the First Plan, when the effort to bend all resources in support of the program of new construction led to a movement for the "proletarianization" of literature. This was the period in which the Russian Association of Proletarian Writers (RAPP) was the virtual dictator over literary production in the Soviet Union, and it had its film counterpart in the Association of Revolutionary Cinematography Workers. The prime duty of the writer was to report on the achievements of the Plan, and many workers and peasants without artistic training or skill were mobilized in "literary shock brigades" to accomplish this purpose.[32] In the realm of the film, as in the realm of literature, they produced little of lasting value or importance, and the entire system succeeded in silencing many of the best talents. On the whole, the effect of the RAPP period on film quality was deleterious, to say the least, and this is acknowledged by Soviet authorities.[33] The Central Committee finally brought an end to this situation in a sweeping decision in 1932, which liquidated the RAPP and its film counterparts.[34] But it was almost 1934 before the Soviet cinema recovered from the impact of this attempt at "proletarianization."

With the end of the RAPP era and the succeeding period of readjustment that accompanied the transition to the sound film, the Soviet cinema industry entered another period of relative stability and high-quality production. The predominant official principle in

---

*The Shakhtinsky trials involved charges of industrial sabotage purported to have been perpetrated by engineers who were trained in prerevolutionary times. The experience of the trials formed one of the bases for the major effort soon launched by the regime to give rapid technical training to trusted workers in order to develop a technical intelligentsia of proletarian origin.

cinematic as well as in literary production was the slogan of "socialist realism." This is not the place to enter into a full discussion of that elusive expression except to point out that the qualification "socialist" before the word realism gives the latter a very distinct meaning. Indeed, this socialist realism has only the slightest connection with realism in literature and art as the term is understood in most other parts of the world. For socialist realism in art does not so much seek to depict the actual as it does to present the ideal, or, as the Soviet phraseology describes it, the present in the process of becoming the ideal. This is most strikingly illustrated in the search for a new "positive hero," which has been one of the main elements of the effort to apply the principle of socialist realism in Soviet art. For this "positive hero" is not a creature whose flesh-and-blood counterpart can be found in the real world, but is rather a composite of all the qualities that the ideal Soviet man should have.

By way of encouragement along their new road, the leaders of the film industry were sent special greetings by Stalin and the Central Committee on the fifteenth anniversary of the Soviet film in 1935, and were decorated by the government in a ceremony that Stalin attended.[35] But along with this encouragement the film workers were administered the usual warnings indicating that the film must continue to serve the interests of the party. The Central Committee warned the workers in cinematography "not to rest on their achievements,"[36] and Stalin reminded them that "the Soviet state expects new successes from you—new films . . . which mobilize the workers and peasants for the fulfillment of new tasks and remind them of both the advances and the difficulties of socialist construction."[37]

Under these auspices in the prewar period, the Soviet directors produced a series of successful films well known in the West, such as the Vassiliev brothers' *Chapayev*, Vladimir Petrov's *Peter I*, and S. M. Eisenstein's *Alexander Nevsky*. Despite these achievements, however, the film makers continued to be subject to almost continuous criticism for the ideological deficiencies of their work. The film *Zakon Zhizn'* (The Law of Life), for example, was withdrawn under sharp attack from *Pravda* [38] after it had gone through all the stages of film censorship and had been publicly shown.

Although it imposed extremely difficult physical conditions on the film industry, the recent war gave it momentary respite from political attack. The definition of its tasks was simple and direct. It was to fan the hatred of the people for the German invaders, to stimulate their patriotic feelings, and to rally them for greater efforts at the front and in the rear. Under wartime conditions of high emotion and patriotic fervor, this mission was easily accomplished, and the task was facilitated by the general relaxation of the party's ideological controls over art in the early war years.[39] But in 1944, when the party became more certain of victory, it began once again to give attention to the ideological adequacy of film productions, and it ordered the establishment of a special Art Council within the government's Cinematography Committee to examine all film productions with a view to insuring their artistic and ideological orthodoxy.

With the end of the war the Soviet Union entered a period of tremendous upheaval in intellectual life and in the realm of art, in which the major outbreak was Andrei Zhdanov's notorious attack on the magazines *Leningrad* and *Zvezda* and the writers Michael Zoschenko and Anna Akhmatova. In a very short space of time the party carried out a huge campaign of ideological criticism of all intellectual endeavor in the Soviet Union, directed not only at people in the field of literature, but in the theater, music, architecture, history, and so on.

The Soviet cinema did not escape, and both the film producers and the film critics came under repeated attack in the press.[40] In 1947 the Council of Ministers decided to reorganize the Art Council of the Ministry of Cinematography and to staff it with political specialists and film personnel of the proper ideological firmness.[41] But it appears that even these measures did not suffice to put an end to the production of films considered ideologically and artistically inadequate. A year later, in June 1948, the Council of Ministers, simultaneously with its confirmation of the plan for the production of artistic films for 1948, noted that because of ideological and artistic deficiencies many of the films being produced did not "answer the high requirements of the Soviet audience."[42] Thus, more than twenty-five years after Stalin had advised the delegates to the Thirteenth Party Congress to take the film into their own hands, the party still found it necessary to conduct a continuous and relentless campaign to secure the production of films which it considered ideologically acceptable and to prevent the making of films which it regarded as ideologically harmful.

THE STRUCTURE OF THE FILM INDUSTRY

The effectiveness of the party's efforts to transform the film into an instrument for mobilizing the population depends in the last analysis on its ability to translate its directives into motion pictures thrown on the screen before Soviet audiences. This of course requires an elaborate and extensive administrative and technical apparatus, and the Soviet film industry is in fact one of the largest in the world. Under the prewar Third Plan the Soviet government was to invest 821 million rubles in the film industry, and under the Fourth Plan it intended to invest 500 million rubles in the restoration and extension of the industry.[43] In the prewar years the industry employed over 100,000 persons in all of its various branches for administration, film production, and local screening.[44] This number had been reduced to 88,000 in 1946 as a result of wartime restrictions, but it was planned to have the industry employ 178,000 people by the end of the Fourth Plan late in 1950.[45] To teach the most important personnel, the Ministry of Cinematography maintains an All-Union Institute of Cinematography, which in the course of the Fourth Plan was to train about four hundred directors, actors, cameramen, scenarists, and artists.

The administration of the Soviet film industry is effected through the Ministry of Cinematography of the U.S.S.R. established in 1946. Since the Ministry is of the union-republican type,* there are corresponding ministries of cinematography in the constituent union-republics, through which the federal Ministry maintains its control of local film facilities. The federal Ministry directly operates only cer-

*The Soviet Constitution provides that the federal government shall have two types of ministries. The All-Union Ministry directly manages a branch of the national economy throughout the Soviet Union. Union-Republican Ministries directly administer only specific aspects of some branch of the national life and effect their control over other aspects by acting through corresponding ministries within the framework of the governments of the constituent republics. See Towster, *Political Power,* pp. 280-282.

tain specific aspects of the film industry requiring centralized control, such as the major film studios, the rental and importation of films, and the production of technical equipment.

The organizational structure of the Ministry is apparently very close to that of the former Committee on Cinematography, which was charged with responsibility for directing all aspects of cinema work, including the production of films and their rental, and the "kinofication* of the country.[46] To fulfill its mandate the Ministry is divided into a large number of administrative subunits (the earlier Committee had twenty-two), the most important of which are the administrations for producing art films, for scientific and technical films, and for newsreels and documentaries.

The Technical Base. The technical base of the Soviet film industry has in each of its parts gone through roughly the same cycle of development. There was a precipitous drop in productivity during the years of the Revolution and Civil War, followed by steady recovery and growth up to the prerevolutionary level during the period of the New Economic Policy. A rapid advance was then accomplished during the early years of the Five Year Plans, but throughout the prewar years the progress made was attended by constant technical difficulties and was characterized by achievements well below the planned level. Finally, there was a catastrophic decline under the impact of the German invasion. Recovery in the postwar period has been considerable, but the pace has been slow and uneven and in many respects the film industry will not have advanced very far beyond the prewar level by the end of the Fourth Plan in 1950.

The film studies that the Soviets inherited from the Tsarist regime were concentrated in Moscow and at a secondary base in St. Petersburg and were particularly exposed to deprivation and loss during the years of the Revolution and Civil War.[47] As the studio base was restored, however, the number of full-length films of all types that it was able to produce rose from twelve in the business

*The term *kinofikatsiya* (kinofication) is used to describe the process of providing the country with cinemas, projectors, screens, and related equipment required for the showing of films.

year 1922-1923 to forty-one in 1923-1924, and reached seventy in the following year.[48] By 1930 the prerevolutionary level of production had been well exceeded, with a total production of 820 films,[49] of which about 120 were full length, the remainder being documentaries, newsreels, and other shorts.[50] This increase was made possible by the quite considerable expansion of the Moscow and Leningrad studios, and by the construction of new studios in several of the constituent republics. Because of the difficulties posed by the introduction of sound, however, the number of full-length films added to the permanent film fund in 1938 was only eighty-three, fifty-nine of which were equipped with sound.[51] Just before the war there were about a dozen art-film studios operating in the U.S.S.R. and they produced an average of from thirty-five to forty art films of feature length each year[52] in addition to the feature-length films produced by other types of studios.

The war severely curtailed the output of films, and the progress under the Fourth Plan has not been impressive. According to the Plan, the film industry was to be producing between eighty and one hundred art films of feature length each year, by the end of 1950.[53] This level of production was to be achieved by rebuilding the Moscow Film Studio (*Mosfilm*) and its subordinate Black Sea Base as the core of the studio network with a capacity of forty feature films per year.[54] Rebuilding and construction were also to go forward in other areas of the Soviet Union.*

By 1946 there were fourteen art-film studios, more than the prewar level, but only twelve of the twenty-one films scheduled were completed.[55] The record for 1947 was even less impressive, with only six feature films completed by October, out of a total of nineteen scheduled for the entire year.[56] At the same time it was reported that the studios in Baku, Alma-Atinsk, Tashkent, and other areas were not working at all, and that the large studios in Kiev and Tbilisi were each making but a single film during 1947. Many of the films scheduled for release during the year had not yet reached the

---

*Beyond the Moscow Studios the most important studios producing art films are the Children's Studio (*Soyuzdetfilm*) in Moscow, the Leningrad Studios (*Lenfilm*), and those in Kiev. There are, in addition, Soviet studios in almost all of the national republics.

stage of having a completed scenario.[57] In the meantime, the period required to produce a feature film rose from eleven and a half months in 1940 to fifteen months in 1944, and had reached seventeen months by 1945.[58] The Minister of Cinematography was chastised for this performance by an editorial in the party newspaper *Culture and Life*, which declared that he was better at producing grandiose schemes on paper than he was at putting films on the screen.[59] The role played by difficulties with the ideological content of Soviet films in these production failures can easily be surmised.

The lowered productivity of Soviet studios in the postwar period has also been significantly affected by shortages of camera equipment and film. The Soviet regime did not succeed in establishing an independent base for producing raw film stock until the early thirties. Between 1930 and 1933 the government was able to reduce the importation of film from abroad from forty-six million to one million meters, and by 1940 only certain types of color and sound film were imported.[60] A comparable reduction in the imports of camera and recording apparatus was made possible by the development of a technical base for producing cameras in Soviet industry.[61]

But in both of these respects the Soviet film industry suffered its most drastic wartime losses. The production of cameras and related technical supplies for the film industry was concentrated to the extent of 80 per cent in factories at Leningrad and Odessa which were almost completely destroyed during the war.[62] The losses were less severe in the production of film stocks, and by 1946 output was expected to surpass the prewar level.[63] But the capacity of the plants for turning this film into copies of the completed motion pictures had actually decreased. Before the war the film copying plants of the Soviet Union were making 88 million meters of film copy annually, but in 1945 the figure barely surpassed 60 million meters. As a result, even the best Soviet films could be produced in no more than 500 to 600 copies, as compared to a prewar standard of 1,000.* By the end of 1950 it was planned to regain this level and to make possible the production of 1,200 copies of the most important films by increasing

---

*Actually, very few films were produced in over a thousand copies before the war. Between January 1, 1934, and December 1, 1939, only fifteen films reached that limit. *Cultural Construction*, p. 197.

the capacity of the copying plants to 140 million meters annually.[64] In June 1948, however, there were still reports from regions, each containing several million people, that they could secure only three or four copies of many of the most important films to serve the population of the entire region.[65] Consequently, the audiences in many parts of the Soviet Union are largely restricted to seeing older films drawn from the Soviet film fund.

TABLE 6

FILM PROJECTORS[a] IN THE SOVIET UNION: 1915-1951[b]

Year[c]	Number in cities	Number in rural areas	Total number of projectors
1915	1,279	133	1,412
1922	560	211	771
1925	1,141	331	1,472
1927	2,058	1,134	3,192
1929[d]	5,594	4,104	9,698
1932	9,624	17,514	27,138
1936	10,078	18,853	28,931
1939	12,117	18,802	30,919
1946	6,800[e]	8,400[f]	15,200[g]
1951	no data	no data	46,700[h]

[a]Exclusive of projectors for film of 16 millimeters or less.
[b]Based on a table given in *Cultural Construction*, p. 192.
[c]Data are for January 1, unless otherwise indicated.
[d]Based on data for October 1928.
[e]An estimate based on the figure given in footnote f below.
[f]In October 1946 the figure was reported to be 9,462 (*Culture and Life*, no. 11, October 10, 1946). Since 1,300 rural projectors were installed in the Russian Republic alone in 1946 (*Culture and Life*, no. 9, March 30, 1947), the total number of rural projectors at the beginning of 1946 was most likely more than a thousand less than the October total.
[g]I. Bolshakov, *Five Year Plan*, p. 19.
[h]The estimate is for the end of 1950 (Bolshakov, *Five Year Plan*, p. 19).

The showing of the completed films depends, of course, on the projection network, the growth of which is described in Table 6. Although the size of the projection network is currently considerably greater than that of the prerevolutionary period, it is relatively modest in respect to the size of the Soviet audience and the importance attributed to the film. The table, furthermore, gives an impression of comparatively even development over the years, hiding from view many of the serious difficulties encountered by the regime in its efforts to establish an adequate cinema base. The Second Plan, for example, anticipated that there would be seventy thousand projectors at the end of the Plan in 1937, but at that time there were actually only 28,574 projectors or only about two fifths of the number originally specified.[66] The fact that the over-all increase in the number of projectors during the Second Plan was only 3.9 per cent was in large part owing to an overly hasty decrease in the number of silent projectors, which was reduced by 36 per cent. That reduction was made in anticipation of an increase in the number of sound projectors, which was in fact not forthcoming. This deficiency was, as might be expected, attributed to the work of enemies of the state.[67]

The German invasion took a heavy toll of projection equipment in the Soviet Union, so that early in 1946 little more than half of the prewar net was again in operation. Under the Fourth Plan the prewar level was to be reached by January 1948, and a total of more than 46,700 units was to be attained by the end of the Plan.[68] Although this new goal is decidedly more modest than that set for the Third Plan, which anticipated that there would be well over sixty thousand projectors by the end of 1942,[69] reports of serious difficulties in the process of "kinofication" make it appear unlikely that the planned figure will be reached.[70]

Beyond the fact of its size, account must be taken of the quality of the projection network. Much of the equipment is old and outmoded, and this helps account for the frequent reports of projectors that do not function because of lack of repairs or parts.[71] More striking, however, is the high proportion of the total network still capable of projecting only silent films almost twenty years after the introduction of sound. As late as 1936 only 21 per cent of the projectors were equipped for sound. The Third Plan called for a sixfold increase in the number of sound projectors, and by the end of 1938 the proportion of sound equipment had been raised above 50 per cent.[72] But by the time the war began it was clear that the plan to base the projection network entirely on sound equipment would not have been met by the end of 1942. This aim was then carried over into the Fourth Plan, although the total number of sound projectors required to reach the new goal is much smaller.

These deficiencies in the size and quality of the projection network are to some extent compensated for, however, by the unique pattern in which the projectors are distributed. Table 7 places in

TABLE 7

DISTRIBUTION OF FILM-PROJECTION
EQUIPMENT[a] IN THE SOVIET UNION: 1939[b]

Type-location	In cities	In rural areas	Totals
Theaters	1,427	1,517	2,944
Clubs	6,265	3,921	10,186
Schools	1,198	245	1,443
Other stationary	2,277	—	2,277
Portable	950	13,119	14,069
Totals	12,117	18,802	30,919

[a]Exclusive of 6,678 projectors for film of 16 millimeters or less.
[b]Adapted from a table in *Cultural Construction*, p. 196.

a very different light the assertion frequently made by Soviet publicists before the war that the film-projection network of the U.S.S.R. was one and a half times as large as that in the United States. This claim was based on statistics that listed 28,600 projectors for the Soviet Union and 18,182 for the United States.[73] But the total for the U.S.S.R. included all of the projectors in the country (exclusive of 16-millimeter equipment), regardless of their location, whereas the figure given for the United States included only the number of film theaters. Actually, the true picture was quite the reverse of the Soviet claim, since, as Table 7 indicates, the Soviet Union in 1939 had under three thousand regular film theaters or less than one sixth of the American total.

Nevertheless, it cannot safely be assumed that the fact that less than 10 per cent of the film projectors in the U.S.S.R. were in regular theaters in 1939 represents as serious a deficiency as it might appear to be in Western eyes. Placing film projectors elsewhere than in regular theaters is, of course, in part an adaptation to the grave shortage of building facilities in the Soviet Union, where all space must do double or triple service. But at the same time, the location of about one third of all the projectors in workers' clubs and peasant reading huts insures that the average citizen will in the course of time see most of the Soviet films. And such exposure is naturally essential if the Soviet film is to achieve the propaganda purposes for which it is designed.

It is perhaps equally important, in this connection, to note the heavy emphasis placed on portable projectors in the Soviet Union. In 1939 almost half of all the equipment was of that type, and in the rural areas portable projectors accounted for more than 70 per cent of the total.[74] Despite the utilization of such equipment, however, the regime has met marked obstacles in its efforts to provide the rural areas with an adequate network of projectors. The Soviet government must certainly be given credit for having increased the number of projectors in the rural localities from 10 per cent of the total in 1915 to about 60 per cent in 1939,[75] thus bringing the proportion of equipment in the rural districts very close to the proportion of the total population found there. This fact, however, does not accurately indicate the availability of the motion picture for the average peasant, because of the wide dispersion of the rural population. There are, for example, some sixty thousand village Soviets in the country, and the Fourth Plan did not estimate that more than 30 per cent of these would have village cinemas by January 1951.[76]

The attempt to meet this situation by using portable projectors has simply posed new production difficulties, since such projectors require trucks for transportation and special generating units to compensate for the lack of electric current in many villages. It is a striking fact that of the 13,119 portable projectors in the rural areas in 1939, only 2,633 were mounted on trucks.[77] During the Fourth Plan, twenty-five thousand generating units and about nine thousand specially equipped trucks were to be built for this purpose,[78] but the results have apparently been very uneven. Of some ten thousand projectors produced in 1947, only three thousand could be sent to the rural areas because the others lacked trucks or generators or both.[79] Thus, for many members of the rural population, seeing a motion picture remains an infrequent and sporadic event. In the Altai Territory (1939 population, 2,500,000) in 1947, for example, there were only 34 sound and 40 silent film projectors to serve 4,483 collective farms, Machine-Tractor Stations, and State Farms. More than half the existing projectors in the territory were not in operation, furthermore, for lack of projection lamps and other equipment. Of 30 projectors sent by the Ministry of Cinematography after the war, only 10 came equipped with generating equipment, with the result that the majority remained idle after their arrival.[80] And in the Tula Region in 1947, there were no film showings throughout the entire year in more than half the village Soviets.[81] Such examples can be obtained in great numbers.

The picture presented by the national minorities of the Soviet Union is not much brighter. Thus, in 1939 the Tadzhik Republic had a total of 122 projectors to serve 1,485,000 people; the Armenian Republic had 153 projectors to serve 1,281,000 persons; and comparable situations existed in several of the other national republics.[82] Although on a national average more than 75 per cent of all county (district) centers were equipped with film apparatus, only 55 per cent of county seats in the Turkmen and Tadzhik Republics were so equipped.[83] It is not surprising, therefore, that a national area such as the Mordvinian Autonomous Republic reported that throughout 1947 there were no film showings in 516 out of republic's 602 village Soviets.[84]

The continued manifestation of such difficulties in the postwar period must be recognized as severely limiting the effectiveness of the Soviet cinema in achieving the agitation and propaganda goals that the party has set for it.

The Film Audience. In the last analysis the determining factor in assessing the adequacy of the film network is not its physical condition, but the size of the audience that it reaches. Fortunately, the size of the film audience is more easily computed than that of the radio, and there are sufficient figures available. Table 8 gives striking indication of the tremendous impact that the war had on the Soviet film industry. It had been estimated that by the end of the Third Plan in 1942 the Soviet film audience would be 2,900 millions per year,[85] but instead it stood at about a fifth of that figure in 1945. It must be noted that even with five years of recovery work under the Fourth Plan,

TABLE 8

THE SOVIET FILM AUDIENCE: 1928-1950

Year	Audience (in millions)	Year	Audience (in millions)
1928[a]	310	1939[a]	1,200
1934[a]	440	1945[c]	573
1938[b]	872	1950[d]	1,100

[a]*Twenty Years of Soviet Cinematography*, p. 14.
[b]*Cultural Construction*, p. 198.
[c]Bolshakov, *Five Year Plan*, p. 21.
[d]Estimated by the Minister of Cinematography in 1946 (Bolshakov, *Five Year Plan*, p. 21).

the annual audience for Soviet films is still not expected to reach the prewar level. There is probably no clearer evidence of the relatively slow speed at which the industry is to recover from its wartime losses.

Unfortunately, detailed information on individual patterns of film attendance in the U.S.S.R. is not available. Assuming a population of about 200 million in 1950, the estimated total audience for that year would yield an average of about five and a half film attendances per individual each year. Certainly that is not an impressive average, especially since the total film attendance on which it is based includes the audiences at schools and other institutions. Even if this estimate is adjusted to exclude all children under ten years of age, the national average number of film attendances for 1950 will be only about seven per person. The national average is, of course, negatively influenced by the lower frequency of film attendance in the rural population, which before the war represented almost two thirds of the people but accounted for only about one third of the annual film audience.[86] It is hoped that by January 1, 1951, there will be no less than two sound-film showings per month in each rural village.[87]

Of the total number of film attendances in the average prewar year, only about one half were at regular film theaters. The greater part of the other half was accounted for by the fixed and portable projectors at workers' clubs and peasant reading huts.[88] The fact that almost half of the total film audience sees its motion pictures in small groups at such institutions greatly facilitates the party's attempt to integrate the film with its other propaganda and agitation efforts. Frequently, film showings will be followed by the appearance of a local agitator who is supposed "to clarify" the film's content. As the party journals phrase it, "a good film full of ideological content is a powerful instrument in the hands of an experienced propagandist, agitator, lecturer, or speaker."[89] At the same time, of course, this may often lead those Soviet citizens who would rather not have agitation blended with their film pleasures to avoid such programs. In a rather revealing admission in *Culture and Life*, for example, it was reported that in many rural regions there was a significant falling off in film attendance whenever the main feature was a documentary film.[90] Audience resistance of that order, to be sure, must significantly affect the impact of the film as an instrument for mobilizing public opinion.

THE FUNCTIONS AND CONTENT OF THE SOVIET FILM

The Soviet conception of the proper functions and content of the film was made absolutely clear from the earliest days of the Revolution. According to Lenin, the film was to deal with science and production as well as comedy and drama, "and all this must be directed toward a single unitary goal—the struggle for the new life, for new customs, for a better future, for the blossoming of science and art."[91] To Lenin the newsreel was a "pictorial publicist," the educational film "a pictorial public lecture," and the feature of art film "artistic propaganda for our ideas in the form of an absorbing picture."[92] Stalin, in turn, conceived of the film as "a great and invaluable force . . . aiding the working class and its Party to educate the toilers in the spirit of socialism, to organize the masses . . . and to raise their cultural and political battle-fitness." [93] Similar formulations have been embedded in a long series of decisions by the higher organs of the Communist Party.[94]

Soviet leaders have been well aware, furthermore, that in the film they are dealing not simply with another medium of mass communication, but with an art form that has special abilities to effect the party's purposes. Various film conferences, the Central Committee, Lenin, and Stalin have all commented on the fact that as an art form the film has unique capabilities for exerting "spiritual influences," for affecting attitudes and changes in the very "consciousness" of men,[95] and indeed for "shaping all the manifestations of the human personality."[96]

Most of the prescriptions and proscriptions governing the making of films in the Soviet Union have been continuously in effect throughout the history of the regime. But the specific content of films—the historical periods emphasized and the heroes lauded—has changed significantly with changes in the internal development of Soviet society. During the twenties the task was defined as "mirroring in the film the problems posed by the great October Revolution." [97] In the major films of that period such as *Potemkin, October,* and *The End of St. Petersburg,* the camera focused primarily on mass movement, and the individual hero was submerged. With the introduction of the Five Year Plans the center of attention shifted to themes about "socialist construction," and the great building projects and the collectivization program became the predominant subjects of Soviet films. By the middle thirties, under the general impulse of the search for a positive hero, the individual came to figure more prominently in the Soviet cinema and in time replaced the group as the central character. Films like *Chapayev,* which told the story of a revolutionary guerrilla leader, and others about Stakhanovites in industry and on the farms filled the Soviet screen. Then, as the period of the Second World War approached, the historical epoch came to the fore, and films such as *Peter I* and *Alexander Nevsky* sought to impress upon the Soviet people a sense of the continuity of the present regime with the traditions of a powerful prerevolutionary Russia, to glorify great leaders, and to stimulate patriotic sentiment.

With the end of the war and the Soviet Union's entrance upon a period of reconstruction at home and of vigorous and expansive policy abroad, it was necessary to develop a new set of instructions to guide the work of the cinema industry under the Fourth Plan. The fundamental task of the industry, according to the Minister of Cinematography, was to produce "films which sing the passion of great construction and poeticize labor." This poeticizing, Mr. Bolshakov continued, should be based on concrete examples of Soviet "labor heroism," depicted so that it highlighted the moral and spiritual qualities of the Soviet people, their love of the motherland, and their devotion to the party. The central figure in these films must be the "new Soviet man" whose unique character, with its elements of love of labor, resourcefulness, spiritual strength and firmness, and limitless attachment to the ideals of communist society should be clearly delineated. And all of this must be directed, of course, to the single aim of the communist upbringing of the Soviet audience, meaning more specifically, to the rallying of that audience for new labor sacrifices in "the struggle for transforming the country into the most powerful and advanced" in the world.[98]

Beyond this central task the film has been assigned a long list of responsibilities in the postwar era, which continue trends established in the prewar years. The film, for example, is expected in the current period to demonstrate the unique character of Soviet life and Soviet democracy, and their superiority over the capitalist system. The special urgency of producing such films was made absolutely clear from the context in which the call was issued, since Mr. Bolshakov pointed out that millions of Soviet citizens were abroad during the war and had had an opportunity to observe the dire workings of decaying capitalism at first hand![99]

Among the other themes that the Soviet film was to stress during the Fourth Plan were: the leading role of the Communist Party, the nationality policy of the Soviet regime, the glorious wartime exploits of the Soviet armed forces, and the nation's achievements in science and technology. An interesting addition to the postwar list were the films about the Soviet family and its mother heroines, the bearers and educators of the new Soviet generation. Such films were expected to reveal the great care given to the problems of the family by the Soviet state.[100] The addition of this subject to the list of proposed films was, of course, a reflection of the changed attitude manifested toward the family in the recent decades of Soviet history, and it gives a clear indication of the manner in which the Soviet film is adapted to the altering conditions of Soviet society.

The definition of the film as an instrument for spreading communist ideology and mobilizing the masses in support of the party and government has affected every genre of film production. The news or "chronicle" and the documentary film are naturally particularly subject to the requirement that the cinema serve as a means of agitation and propaganda. The documentary film has from its earliest days been under obligation "to translate to the screen the truth about the new reality" of Soviet life and the process of socialist construction.[101] In keeping with that tradition, the newsreel and documentary films of the postwar period were expected to tell the Soviet audience "of the grandeur of the plans for construction in the new Five Year Plan, of the labor activities and advances of the Soviet people, of the foremost individuals in industry and technology, of all those who by their tenacious and self-sacrificing labor assist our Party and government in the fulfillment of the glorious tasks set by the new Stalin Five Year Plan." [102]

Children's films, no less than the newsreel and documentary, have been affected by the Soviet conception of the role of the cinema. They are regarded as a means for the communist upbringing of the young and for spreading the influence of Soviet pedagogical ideas. Films for the Soviet youth are expected to struggle for a "realistic" representation of the life of children under the new conditions of Soviet life as opposed to the purportedly false sentimentality of bourgeois youth films, which are accused of directing the consciousness of youth away from reality into an artificial dream world.[103] Thus, the children's films of the twenties are credited with having had "major significance for educating Soviet children in the spirit of collectivism, an active approach to life, and the communist materialist world-view."[104]

As one might well anticipate, the film comedy has not been extensively developed under Soviet auspices. The cinema is referred to as a means for facilitating popular "rest and recreation,"[105] although the word "expedient" is sometimes added to qualify the terms.[106] But the film is never officially described as a form of amusement. The Soviet Union did produce several politically acceptable film comedies in the twenties, regarded as part of "the struggle against the influence of bourgeois comedy." [107] The 1928 Party Conference on the Film warned, however, that such motion pictures must not be apolitical or be motivated solely by an interest in sheer amusement. It laid down the rule that even the amusing material in any film must "organize the thoughts and feelings of the audience in the required proletarian direction."[108]

The pattern thus established has persisted to the present day. In 1946, for example, the Minister of Cinematography declared that "the Soviet film comedy, as well as productions in any other genre, must be built on contemporary material, on the heroism of labor, and on our daily life." Mr. Bolshakov went on to admit that "it is unquestionably very difficult to produce comedies which are simultaneously both gay and sapient." Apparently many Soviet producers had met this problem by producing film comedies that were regarded as "frivolous and without ideas." This tendency is the line of least resistance, the Minister warned, and must be overcome.[109]

FILM CONTROL IN ACTION

No mater how specific the party makes its instructions on the content of Soviet films and the aims to be achieved, those instructions must be correctly interpreted by the producers and directors engaged in the business of putting out motion pictures. As has been seen, this task is not without its pitfalls even in the case of media like the press and the radio. The problem is greatly magnified in the film industry, where the party's instructions must be interpreted through an art form. The party must therefore maintain an elaborate supervisory organization to insure that the films produced in accord with its directives do indeed serve the purposes for which it intends them.

The measures utilized to effect ideological control over Soviet film production follow the well-established procedures for supervision over the other media of mass communications in the U.S.S.R. The party maintains a special sector for film affairs in its Department of Propaganda and Agitation as its chief instrument for controlling the Soviet cinema.[110] Corresponding units within the framework of the local party organizations are supposed to maintain this control over film activities in their areas of competence.[111] By issuing general and specific directives,[112] by calling conferences of film workers,[113] by a careful and continuous program of newspaper review and criticism, and by placing trusted party members in positions of responsibility wherever possible, the party seeks to insure the ideological correctness of the films produced. These measures are supplemented by various special devices. For example, the Ministry of Cinematography must each year submit for the approval of the Council of Ministers its annual plan for film production, and the Council generally takes this opportunity to express itself on the progress of the film industry and particularly the quality of its production efforts.[114] On occasion Stalin and other party leaders apparently speak directly to the film producers to transmit their reactions to some film or to give instructions about future work.[115] Finally, there is the Art Council of the Ministry of Cinematography, staffed with the most reliable personnel, which not only supervises the early stages in the preparation of each film, including the scenario and choice of the cast and director, but sits as a final court of judgment on each picture before it receives the stamp of approval for release to the public.[116]

Despite all these precautions, however, major films are regularly produced which are found politically and artistically unacceptable. In some of these cases the Central Committee will directly intervene to criticize and even to order the withdrawal of the film. A striking example of this direct intervention was provided by the Central Committee's decision on the film *A Great Life* (*Bol'shaya Zhizn'*) in September 1946.[117] *A Great Life*, in accord with party directives which urged that the film depict the efforts of the regime to rebuild the occupied areas, concerned itself with the reconstruction of the Donets Basin's coal mines and industry. This film went through all the stages of Soviet film control and censorship and had been approved for release with unqualifiedly high praise by the Art Council of the Ministry of Cinematography. Yet the Central Committee found the film to be "extremely weak artistically and ideologically, and politically perverted," and forbade its presentation on the screen.

In its four-page decision, the Central Committee found *A Great Life* lacking on more than a half dozen counts. Because it dealt with only one minor incident, the film was charged with having given an incorrect view of Soviet efforts to reëstablish the Donbass. Instead of concentrating on the efforts at reconstruction, the film erred by focusing its attention on "primitive" descriptions of personal experience and scenes from private life. On these grounds, the Central Committee declared that the film did not live up to its name. The Committee also asserted, in a most revealing comment, that the very title itself, *A Great Life,* sounded as if the realities of Soviet life were being mocked by the producers.

A Great Life, the indictment continued, made it appear that the miners' initiative was not given support by the government and was even opposed by it. Such a representation of the relations between government agencies and groups of workers was deemed false and erroneous, "for as it is well known, in our country any initiative on the part of the workers is met by wide support on the part of the government." The film was charged with presenting an equally false picture in its description of the local party secretary, by giving the impression that the party could conceivably expel from its ranks a member who supported the initiative of the workers. Even more, the film manifested "backwardness, lack of culture, and ignorance" by depicting the promotion to responsible positions of technically unqualified workers with backward views, when everyone knows that the Soviet regime places first importance on promoting only forward-looking and advanced people who know their work well. It gave, in the view of the Central Committee, a distorted and false view of the average Soviet citizen, showing him as backward, uncultured, narrow, and morally limited. The heroes engaged in idle chatter and heavy drinking, and had habits that clearly were "absolutely foreign to our [Soviet] society." And so this amazing document continues through point after point.

The Central Committee concluded its strictures on *A Great Life* by instructing the Ministry of Cinematography and its Art Council to extract the necessary lessons and draw the required conclusions from the party's decision, so that "henceforth all possibility of putting out such a film will be excluded." But a realistic assessment of the history of the film in the Soviet Union must lead to the conclusion that the Central Committee's expectations will not be fulfilled. For so long as the party continues to demand that the cinema follow patterns and serve ends such as it has set for the film during the Fourth Five Year Plan, then Soviet film producers are certain to continue putting out films, however unintentionally, that have errors and perversions similar to those found in *A Great Life*. This arises from the very nature of their medium as an interpretative art form. If political conditions comparable to those now existing continue in force and Soviet film producers are no longer periodically found guilty of creating ideologically deficient films, the necessary conclusion will be that the scenarists and directors have ceased to be artists and have become mere technicians.

PART **6**

CONCLUSION

20

A NOTE IN CONCLUSION

THE SOVIET REGIME HAS DEVELOPED ONE OF THE LARGEST and most complex systems of public communication in the world. The Communist Party has forged a parallel system of control which is more elaborate and thorough than any other still in existence in the postwar era. Both the system of communication and the control apparatus are oriented toward a single goal. They must serve as instruments through which the party and government mobilize the mind and will of the population; they must see to it that what ought to be done *is* done, what should be thought and felt *is* thought and felt. Mass communication in the Soviet Union is not based on the pursuit of profit; it does not aim to provide either a vehicle for the expression of individual opinion or an instrument for the amusement of its audience. These are defined as "private" goals, unacceptable as a basis for public communication. The media of communication in the Soviet Union must serve "social" goals set by the party, the state, the nation. But the specific definition of what is a social end is arrived at on an extraordinarily narrow basis.

The selection of the ends which the media of communication will serve is not made by the audience itself and is not justified on the grounds that it is the expressed decision of the electorate. The ends to which mass communication must be put are justified in terms of Marxist-Leninist theory. And that theory is interpreted by the only group with the right to interpret it in the Soviet Union —the Communist Party—as meaning that the media are to be used primarily to strengthen the party's leadership in its self-assigned role as leader, teacher, and guide of the Soviet people. There are other goals, it is true, and in terms of total space they occupy a large part of all Soviet communication. The Soviet media give a relatively large amount of space to educational and cultural material. But even these "nonpolitical" activities are far from truly being ends in themselves. They are justified to the extent to which they facilitate the prime task of more effective party rule of the nation. There is no such thing as art for art's sake in the Soviet Union.

But state control, however imposing, is not sufficient to explain the particular functioning of the media of communication in the Soviet Union, any more than private ownership and control are adequate to explain some of the peculiar characteristics of mass communication in the United States. One should not minimize the fact that either alternative of state or private ownership and control involves significant limitations and consequences. But this book has sought to demonstrate that control, private or public, or any other feature of the system of mass communication, cannot be considered apart from the general pattern of political and social life.

The basic criterion is not the fact of control, but the nature of the group that exercises it and the theory that guides the operation of the system of control. Soviet control of communications is not designed to facilitate or improve the free exchange of ideas among men. Indeed, the Soviet leaders clearly regard such a free flow of ideas as dangerous and as likely to impede the attainment of the party's goals. The Soviet state, furthermore, does not conceive of itself as a relatively impartial arbiter which seeks to maintain standards of conduct arrived at independently by the consuming public or the men who work directly in mass communication. Rather, the state establishes for the media specific, concrete, and practical goals, which are treated much like the production norms set for Soviet industry. The media are conceived of as tools or instruments for effecting the purposes of the party. Finally, Soviet control is absolute. There can be no competition for the message of the central authorities, not even from small meetings or, for that matter, from private conversations between individuals. All must be harnessed for attainment of the greater goal of party leadership.

It is true that there are public organizations like the trade unions which may publish newspapers, but the subordination of these newspapers to the purposes of the party has long been guaranteed by the subordination of the parent organization themselves. There exists no independent locus of power in the U.S.S.R. save the party, and all organizations public and private, as the Constitution provides, are merely its assistants in the task of ruling the Soviet Union.

The Soviet system of communication and its parallel control apparatus are very imposing indeed, but this alone does not form a sufficient basis for judging their effectiveness. Are the Soviet people convinced? Do they believe what they are told? Are they firm in their support of the regime? These questions are today asked in the capitals of most of the world, but the answers are extraordinarily hard to obtain. It is probable that even the men in the Kremlin, dependent as they are on crude methods of ascertaining the facts, are not sure of the precise answers. But whatever the exact distribution of favorable and unfavorable sentiment toward the regime in the Soviet population, there can be no doubt that the system of Soviet communication is far from completely successful and is far below the level of effectiveness that the Soviet leaders would like to see it attain.

There is, of course, indirect evidence for this conclusion in the presence in Western Europe of several hundred thousand individuals who chose the overwhelming hardships and uncertainties of life as displaced persons rather than return to the Soviet Union. It would certainly be overemphasizing the role of communications to charge this great defection solely or even predominantly to the failure of the regime's efforts at persuasion. It is not very meaningful to test the efficacy of propaganda in favor of the Soviet system against the fear of personal reprisal or the bitter memories of police terror directed against family and friends. But for what is probably the majority of the "nonreturners," less striking considerations more amenable to the influence of propaganda, such as the extremely low standard of living and the general lack of freedom, lay behind the decision to give up Soviet citizenship. The fact that for so many people these considerations were not outweighed by the elemental human desire to return to one's native land, home, and family, hardly lends support to any claim of omnipotence for Soviet propaganda and agitation. Indeed, that very propaganda and agitation may have contributed to this defection in large measure. For it had so misinformed Soviet citizens about economic and political conditions in the West that confrontation with the realities of life outside the U.S.S.R. shook the faith of many in the propaganda and even in the whole social system that it represented.

But since these "non-returners" may be unrepresentative of the total population—and certainly some were collaborators who had real cause to fear a return home—it is perhaps best to rely on evidence internal to the Soviet system. Such evidence, drawn from the field of communications itself, is not lacking. One of the most striking facts about Soviet mass communication is its repetitiveness. Anyone who has conscientiously read *Pravda* for any length of time can with surprising accuracy write models of the editorials which will appear in it on holidays, anniversaries such as press day, or on the occasion of the launching of public drives such as those for a new government loan, for the sowing or harvesting of the crops, and so on. Key words and sentences, indeed whole paragraphs, appear day in and day out in the same newspaper and simultaneously in other newspapers, in magazines, and on the radio. The message is simple enough in its essentials: work harder, trust the party, hate the defined enemies of the regime within and without, and believe in the future. But in all its simplicity the message must be repeated endlessly in a thousand contexts, and always in the distinctive tone of Soviet communications materials, by turns strident, demanding, and cajoling. This is not the communication of a government and of leaders who are sure of the response of their audience and who feel that they are speaking to a convinced and loyal population. It strongly suggests that the leaders have little faith in the extent to which the people have adopted the maxims put to them, or how far they can be expected, on the basis of their own experience, to continue believing in them without constant restatement.

It may be argued, of course, that such repetition is less a reflection of insecurity on the part of the leaders than it is an example of their ritualistic reiteration of sacred formulas—a kind of political litany. But if this be true, it argues no better for the quality of mass communication in the U.S.S.R. For so much liturgy displaces independent inquiring discussion and discourages the free flow of new ideas. As a matter of fact, this constant repetition of a few simple themes strongly suggests the vulnerability of Soviet communications to Lenin's charge, originally directed against the capitalist world, that the press tends in effect "to divert the attention of the popular masses from the really serious, deep, and fundamental problems of their daily life."[1]

An equally striking indication of the incomplete success of the party's attempt to convince the population through efforts at persuasion is the apparent inability of the regime to reduce the intensity of its controls over mass communication. Indeed, the control must be periodically tightened, even after more than thirty years of Soviet rule. The agitator, the press, the radio, the film are constantly criticized for their inadequate performances. If this criticism is necessary because the task of persuading the masses is so difficult, if not disheartening, that itself reflects the state of mind of the Soviet people. And certainly the present difficulties do not argue well for the success of the past efforts that have been made to shape popular thinking. On the other hand, this criticism may be necessary primarily because of the inadequate performance of Soviet intellectuals, including party members and sympathizers, who are entrusted with the task of mobilizing Soviet public opinion; but this again merely indicates that the regime has not been very successful in its efforts to win over that group and to inculcate in its members the ideas which the party seeks to have them bring to the people.

This is not to say that the Soviet system of mass communication, as a system, is essentially deficient. Despite certain major flaws, it is an impressive apparatus, carefully thought out, conscientiously administered, and vigorously utilized. The difficulty lies not in the system of communication but in the task which it is assigned. For in comparing the content of Soviet communication materials with the actual conditions of Soviet life, one is compelled to ask how long a population can be expected to continue exchanging today's sacrifices for tomorrow's promises. How can the media of communication convince the people of the all-pervasive solicitude of the government for their welfare in the face of the persistent shortages of consumers' goods and housing and the recurrent shortages of food? How can the party prove that it is the unyielding enemy of bureaucracy, when it appears always to be creating bureaucracy anew on every hand? How teach the population to despise the "false freedom" of the slaves of bourgeois society, when it can recognize that it has so little freedom itself? For every man convinced, there must be one lost to disillusionment; for every person who renews his faith, at least one who has just lost it. And after each successive loss of faith, the chances that any individual will recapture it decrease in something approaching a geometric ratio.

In such a situation one must wonder about the extent to which Soviet public-opinion specialists are really oriented toward teaching and convincing the population of the meaningfulness of the goals Lenin and Stalin set for the society. So long as internal conditions remain similar to those of recent decades, the Soviet publicist must run on a kind of treadmill on which heavy exertion is the price of maintaining a constant position. Each time there is an internal crisis, and they are periodic, the publicists must work extra hard to make up the lost ground. There is little time left for real educational efforts, for rational persuasion. And unfortunately one cannot safely attribute this deficiency solely to the unceasing pressure of events. For it is by no means certain that the present leaders are effectively oriented toward all of those specific social goals which Lenin visualized and which Stalin in his early writings ascribed to "that 'promised land' known as a socialist world." [2]

It was noted in the beginning of this book that there were two strains in Lenin's thinking. One of these, that closest to the Western liberal tradition—basically humanist, with its utopian faith in the essential goodness of man and his perfectibility through social progress, its promise of greater freedom and less oppression, and its belief in fundamentalist popular democracy—has been very largely submerged by the hard, revolutionary, elitist strain, with its emphasis on organization, its insistence on absolute discipline, its devotion to hierarchical authority, and its reliance on the use of force. Time has not significantly closed the gap between the early popular dream of what socialism would be and the realities of contemporary Soviet society under Bolshevik rule. Soviet society has changed profoundly in the last two decades, however much those changes may have inhered as potentialities in the original philosophy. This change has been reflected in, and has permeated, Soviet policy in the realm of mass communication. It has indeed been asserted that the contemporary Soviet publicist does not seek to convince but to pacify, not to arouse but to lull the Soviet people, not to instill new ideas but to inoculate against them.

The figure most apt for describing the state of Soviet public opinion is that of a forest fire.[3] On the broad peripheral front the blaze rages in full intensity. Here is found a thin line of convinced and confirmed Communists. But behind this line comes a much larger area, which has already been swept by the flames and which now boasts only glowing embers. This is the line of the half-believers, which includes some party members as well as the non-party supporters of the regime. And beyond that there lies a still broader sweep of the burned-over timber, in which here and there a spark still glows but which is predominantly cold, ashen, and gray. The work of mass persuasion is the wind which fans this blaze. But like the wind in the forest fire, it not only spreads the flames but hastens the burning, and behind the line of flames and embers it can only stir up little swirls and eddies of ash.

There are, of course, always unburned areas, and in time the new growth. The young generation does not depend for its inspiration solely on the system of mass communication, but is trained under more favorable conditions in the schools. Here the Soviet youth acquires its predisposition to believe, and since this *predisposition* is the single most important element in securing belief itself in the audience of any medium of mass communication, the products of the Soviet schools provide the Soviet agitator, newspaper, radio, and film with an ever-renewed and susceptible audience.

Nor can it safely be forgotten that whatever difficulties the party may experience in its efforts to mobilize Soviet public opinion, it has at its command a large and capable apparatus, which makes up whatever it may lack in means by its monopoly of communication. Even when it cannot effectively inculcate Soviet ideas, it can effectively keep out information and ideas that might operate to weaken the impact of the party's efforts. And when conditions are advantageous for the regime, as they were during the recent war, this machine can accomplish very formidable results.

As to the prognosis for the future, that naturally depends on the future course of events within the Soviet Union, and this is in large measure dependent on what takes place on the international scene. No matter how one might wish it, however, it cannot be safely predicted that a major improvement in the general economic welfare of the Soviet Union would itself automatically bring a significantly freer flow of communication either within the Soviet Union or between the Soviet population and the world outside. The Soviet leaders have given little indication that they intend or wish such a transformation.

21

ADDENDUM: 1950-1960-?

STALIN DIED IN MARCH 1953, PRECISELY THREE YEARS after the last of the preceding pages were written. His successors introduced a surprisingly large number of sweeping changes in Soviet society, most important of which was the virtual elimination of large-scale police terror. Easing of the terror, substantial efforts to improve the standard of living, encouraging initiative and responsibility in local administration, economic concessions to the peasant, and the opening of the country to foreign visitors all were interpreted by some observers as evidence of the mellowing of Communist dictatorship and as presaging the probable democratization of Soviet society. Other less sanguine observers note that while the terror is more limited and selective, in principle it is still there and gives no sign of yielding to effective constitutional guarantees of personal liberty. They point out that a rising standard of living follows from increasing wealth, but the *proportionate share* of consumption in the national budget remains fixed, and overwhelming priority continues to be held by heavy industry. They remind us that the Communist Party still monopolizes political and economic power, and is itself organized and operated on elitist principles with precious little intra-party democracy. To settle the argument they point to the Soviet armed intervention in the Hungarian revolution and the later wanton execution of Premier Nagy and General Maleter.

Whether the death of Stalin marked the beginning of the end or merely the end of the beginning, it seems to have made no great difference in the realm of mass communication. To revisit the Soviet press, radio, and cinema, to read again its propaganda or hear the speech of its agitator, is to renew acquaintance with thoroughly familiar terrain. The old features are all very much in evidence. Some are worn smooth, perhaps here and there a new stone has been turned up, but basically the structure remains unchanged, the landscape as unvarying, as dull and arid as ever.

Consider the leaders' conception of the functions of mass communication, the purposes which it is thought to serve and the goals which it must pursue. These seem to have changed not one whit since the death of Stalin. Speaking to the Twentieth Congress of the Communist Party in February 1956, Khrushchev characterized the cinema as "a powerful weapon of Communist education of the working people."[1] Later, speaking to a gathering of writers and artists in tones reminiscent of the slogans of Stalin, he declared: "The press is our chief ideological weapon. It is called upon to rout the enemies of the working class, the enemies of the toilers. Just as an army cannot fight without weapons, so the Party cannot successfully carry on its ideological work without such a sharp and militant weapon as the press."[2]

There is no talk here about the peaceful coexistence of ideologies to match the coexistence of economic systems. Indeed, in his address to the Twentieth Congress, Khrushchev branded this idea "a harmful mistake."[3] The chief Communist Party journal followed up with the warning: "There can be no conciliation in the field of ideology. On the contrary, under the conditions of peaceful coexistence of socialist and capitalist systems the ideological struggle between them will not slacken but be intensified."[4] Nor is there any talk here of initiative or independence in journalism and radio broadcasting, or of freedom for writers and film directors. In 1955 and 1956 there was a brief display of independence by the writers of Leningrad and Moscow, even though the heavy hand of the regime soon stopped their mouths. But personnel working in the field of Soviet mass communication did not muster even such a momentary expression of vigor and initiative.

Whatever dreams of independence the specialists in mass communication may have harbored, they were largely repressed by the time Khrushchev and his cohorts called them to the Great

Palace of the Kremlin on February 8, 1958, for a reception at which they were "honored" by repeated affirmations of their servile role and in which they responded by grovelling before the Soviet leaders. The writer N. S. Tikhonov, for example, distinguished himself by shouting, "Soviet literature is and has been the weapon of the Party, and Soviet writers are proud of this." Bulganin, then Chairman of the Council of Ministers, toasted the representatives of the film industry by telling them, "It is the duty of cinema workers [to produce] films that help to educate the masses in the spirit of the ideas of Communism. . ." In his turn Mikoyan, then Vice-Chairman of Ministers, spoke his piece about the theater workers, whom the Party leaders knew "to be united in their common desire to rally the people in the struggle for building Communism. . ." To this, People's Artist of the Soviet Union, M. I. Tsarev, replied for the entire theatrical profession: "We regard ourselves as faithful assistants of our Communist Party in the cause of the Communist education of the working people. . . We must view every artistic phenomenon from the standpoint of its ideological content, its party spirit, and its closeness to the people."[5]

Since the functions of the mass media remain the same, the necessity for their close control persists. As Khrushchev bluntly told the leading writers: "We cannot put the organs of the press in unreliable hands. They must be in the hands of the most faithful, most trustworthy, those politically most steadfast and devoted to our cause."[6] The Department of Propaganda and Agitation continues to be one of the dozen or so main departments operating directly under the Central Committee of the Party. Each republic, regional, city, and local district Party organization also retains its corresponding department or section for propaganda and agitation to direct the work of mass communication on the appropriate administrative level.[7] As in the past these organizations guide and control the work of mass communication in the most intimate detail, appointing editors, dismissing film directors, criticizing plays, starting newspapers, and even specifying the contents of particular newspaper issues or the size of the sheets on which certain papers are to be printed. Thus on October 16, 1956, the Central Committee of the national Communist Party found time among its numerous weighty deliberations to decree that on the appropriate anniversary the nation's newspapers and radio broadcasts should contain materials on the life and thought of G. V. Plekhanov, stressing that he was the first great Russian Marxist. And on June 18, 1956, they took time out to rule that it would no longer require their explicit permission *in each case* for the Party central committees at the republic level to start newspapers at factories, subject only to the reservation that such factories have at least two thousand workers, the newspaper have two printed pages half the size of *Pravda,* there be one issue per week with one copy for each three or four workers, and the paper have not more than one paid worker on its staff. This last decision was typical of a number which suggested that the overloaded central administrations of the Party were trying to devolve more routine responsibilities for guiding mass communications onto the local Party authorities. This contrasts with the policy of extreme centralization characteristic of Stalin's time.[8]

The major innovation in the administration of Soviet mass communications which followed Stalin's death, however, was the establishment of the Ministry of Culture. The new Ministry, established in March 1953, pulled together the former Ministry for the Film Industry and the scattered committees and special administrations for art, radio information, publishing, circuses, and other assorted activities. Wide as was the net thrown by this Ministry,* it seems far from sufficient to cover its realm or to manage it effectively. For some mysterious reason of Soviet administrative practice, the Ministry of Culture was given charge of book sales, but the Chief Administration for Distribution of Newspapers remained as of 1958 a part of the Ministry of Communications. In addition, persistent dissatisfaction with the Ministry's handling of radio broadcasting—apparently because it

---

* In 1957 it was possible to identify at least the following fifteen major functional subdivisions of the Ministry of Culture through references to them in the Soviet press: Book Sales, Cinemafication and Film Distribution; Cinematography; Circuses; Cultural and Educational Institutions (such as libraries and museums); Film Production; Pictorial Arts; Polygraphic Industry; Printing and Publishing Houses; Radio Broadcasting; Radio Information; Theaters and Musical Institutions.

offered weak competition with foreign broadcasts invading the U.S.S.R.—led the Council of Ministers once again to establish a State Committee on Radio Broadcasting and Television, answerable directly to it. Thus another hydra-head took its place along with the Ministry of Culture, the Ministry of the Radiotechnical Industry, and the Main Administration of Radiofication within the Ministry of Communications, all operating in the radio and TV field.[9]

Just as the official conception of the goals of mass communication has remained basically unchanged, so has the structure designed to effect the mobilization of public opinion in Soviet Russia. Ultimately the whole system of mass persuasion rests on the opinion leaders, the specialists in Communist politics and mass communication, trained in the higher Party schools. By 1956, 75 per cent of all "responsible Party workers" down to the district level had secured the equivalent of a completed or partial college education. Consequently, the special system of Party schools established a decade earlier to meet the training needs of the postwar period were declared to have fulfilled their mission. In the preceding ten years the Higher Party School trained 2,843 individuals, and more than 6,000 completed its correspondence courses. The republic and regional Party schools trained 55,000 in their regular three-year schools and more than 40,000 in correspondence courses. These schools are to be continued, but were reorganized in 1956 on a new basis. The new course requires four years, the schools are now inter-regional and are located only in the more important centers, and their emphasis has been shifted to technical and economic questions.[10]

The stress on technical economic questions in the Party schools reflects the strongly pragmatic quality of Khrushchev's thought. At the Twentieth Party Congress he expressed this orientation in more tempered language when he declared that lectures on Marxism, valuable as they might be, are not enough. He insisted that propagandists and agitators must give people "practical assistance . . . detailed exposition of advanced experience, sound advice on how to apply this experience . . . spoken not in generalities but with specific knowledge."[11] He expressed a similar view more bluntly and crudely a few months later when he said: "I know people who pose as theoreticians but whose theoretical 'wisdom' essentially boils down to the juggling of quotations. . . These sorry scholars cannot understand the important Marxist truth that people must first of all eat, drink, have homes, and clothe themselves. . . If Marx and Engels could rise again they would ridicule those pedantic quotation lovers who, instead of studying the life of modern society and developing theory creatively, try to find the proper classical quotation on what to do with a machine and tractor station. . ."[12]

In accord with the line laid down by Khrushchev, the Party reorganized its system of lower Party schools in August 1956. It preserved the political schools (*politshkoly*) as a way of giving the obligatory minimum two-year course for all Communists, particularly new members of the Party. For the study of Marxist-Leninist philosophy and for the study of the History of the Party there were to be the familiar seminars or circles (*kruzhki*). But a new type of circle was added for study of the current policies of the Party and government. Equally important, a separate and entirely new program was added for the "economic education of cadres." For more casual study there were to be seminars and circles on political economy. More serious students were to attend two-year evening schools on economics. These were based on the former Evening "Universities" of Marxism-Leninism, which were now reorganized to give more hours to political economy and the economics of industry and more attention to the concrete economic tasks of the local region.[13]

The new educational programs on the current policies of Party and government, and in economics, seem to have swept the field. The circles on current policy were by far the most popular, and in 1956 they were chosen by one fourth of the participating Communists and an additional one-half million nonmembers who participated. Together these two groups apparently made up more than half of all students in the Party's educational program. Economics captured 27 per cent of the participants, and an additional 10 per cent or so were enrolled in more theoretical courses on "political economy." The circles and seminars on Party history were attended by only 4 per cent of the trainees, and those on philosophy and dialectics by not more than 1 per cent!

The central authorities understandably became rather alarmed that some Party organizations were simply cutting down on the less popular circles for studying Party history and dialectical materialism. Such tendencies were labeled "abnormal" and "harmful." The central authorities also looked unfavorably upon the tendency to select the instructors for courses on economics mainly on grounds of their engineering experience, warning that after all "this is not a technical high school." Figures for the enrollment for the fall of 1957 suggested the balance had been somewhat redressed, since in Moscow 80,000 Party members were to study political economy and practical economics, but the enrollment in Party history and dialectics was up to a more respectable 60,000.[14] The spontaneous action of the participants in the Party's educational program in avoiding the tired old courses in Party history and dialectics and escaping into those on current affairs, political economy, and practical economics must be recognized as more than merely an obedient response to Khrushchev's command to study economics. Rather, it reflects the low level of interest in what can honestly be described only as the moribund science of Soviet Marxism-Leninism, which even the head of the Party Department of Propaganda and Agitation admits is often taught in a way that is "uninteresting, boring, and primitive."[15]

The system of Party schools has been supplemented by a vast program of popular lectures conducted by the All-Union Society for the Dissemination of Political and Scientific Information. This society works in that middle ground occupied by those not sufficiently active politically or advanced educationally to enroll in the system of Party schools, yet more advanced or active than the rank-and-file citizen reached by the usual system of oral agitation. The Society has over 400,000 members—scholars, scientific and technical workers, representatives of literature and the arts, and members of the rural intelligentsia. In 1956, they gave over two million lectures on such subjects as Marxist-Leninist theory, the history of the Communist Party, the materialist world view, the scientific and technological achievements of the Soviet Union, and the superiority of its forms of democracy over those practiced in bourgeois society.[16]

Backing up these lectures, the Soviet army of oral agitators continues its work. During the election campaign in February 1958 the city of Moscow alone boasted 30,000, and the Moscow region mobilized 100,000 to man its 3,240 agitation points. They produced prodigious feats of agitation on numerous occasions. For example, from the first to the twenty-fifth of March 1958 they organized 576, 879 general sessions with the people of the country to discuss Khrushchev's proposals for reorganizing the collective farms and machine-tractor stations, in which they reached 49,909,000 citizens who "came forward" with over three million comments and suggestions. So important is the agitators' work to the regime that it maintains a separate network of journals to keep them advised and briefed. The 176 "agitators' guides" published in 1956 accounted for fifty million journal issues per year, or 13 per cent of the total journal circulation.[17]

The more traditional means of mass communication have experienced very rapid growth over the past decade, reflecting the general expansion of facilities which characterized the economic development of Russia just before and after Stalin's death. As in the past, this growth was not spontaneous, but resulted from decisions adopted by the planning authorities in accord with their conception of the increased availability of resources and changing pattern of needs. This was dramatically illustrated in the spurt of growth in the Soviet press.[18] From 1949 to 1955 the number of newspapers fluctuated, from an initial 7,200 up to 8,300 in 1952, and down again to 7,100 in 1954. The regime then apparently concluded that there were new tasks for the press and new opportunities offered it on the newly consolidated collective farms. In 1956, consequently, 600 new newspapers were introduced on these farms. There was a further sharp spurt in 1957. Indeed, in that year 2,399 newspapers were launched. Circulation also jumped markedly, rising by four and a third million to a total of almost fifty-eight million copies for any single issue of the 9,936 papers published as of 1 January 1958.

There was, however, no danger that this growth at the lower levels would transform the basic structure of the Soviet press. The twenty-five central newspapers lost no ground. Indeed the giant dailies on the national level, such as *Pravda* with a circulation of 5.5 million, *Komsomolskaya Pravda* with 2.3 million, and *Izvestiya* with 1.5 million, combined to give the central press a circulation of over 18 million in 1958. This was 30 per cent of the total circulation, as against the 24 per cent these papers accounted for in 1947 (see Table 3 on p. 148). Neither did the increased importance of factory and farm newspapers challenge the dominance of the Russian language in the Soviet press. In 1958, Russian language papers were about 58 per cent of the total published, but they accounted for 79 per cent of the single-issue circulation. This was even more than their share in 1947 (see p. 146).

The growth of the press has been outstripped by the development of radiobroadcasting.[19] By 1957 there were 23 million wired receivers in operation, organized in almost 36,000 radio-diffusion exchanges (*radio-uzly*). A large part of this increase was in the rural areas. Indeed, of the 19 million receivers the Sixth Five Year Plan called for, 10 million were to be installed in farms and villages. This is a much higher ratio in favor of the countryside than existed earlier. It reflects the regime's intensification of its propaganda and agitation in the villages, a task greatly facilitated by the larger and better equipped units which emerged from the consolidation of the collective farms.

Regular wireless receivers were also vigorously produced after 1950, so that by 1957 there were 8 million registered. The new ratio of three wired sets to each regular set is much more favorable to the latter than was the ratio of almost 5:1 which prevailed in 1950. Despite the substantial growth of the Soviet Radio network, it continues to lag far behind the United States and the advanced countries of Western Europe. The United States, of course, vastly overshadows the Soviet development. Against the U.S.S.R.'s 130 stations (1956), there were in the United States 2,570 AM and 650 FM installations, and they served six times the number of radios operating in the U.S.S.R. The Soviet ratio attained by 1958 of one radio for every nine in the population now compares much more favorably with poorer European countries such as Italy, where the 1956 ratio was approximately 1:9, but still lags behind France where it was 1:5 and the United Kingdom which in 1956 had one set for each four inhabitants.[20]

Television has now joined the radio and film as a significant means of mass communication in the U.S.S.R. Two million sets, served by over 25 stations, were in operation by 1958. Considering the vastness of the Soviet Union and the size of its population, this was not a very impressive showing. Unesco data for 1956 credited the Soviet Union with 10 stations and 700,000 receivers, whereas the United Kingdom, with a minor fraction of the geographical area to cover and one fourth the population, had over four million receivers and the United States had 413 stations and thirty-five million receivers, about fifty times the number in the U.S.S.R. Even if the Sixth Five Year Plan were fulfilled, by 1960 there would be only 75 stations (supplemented by 300 low-powered re-broadcasting installations) and eight million receivers.[21] It is clear from Soviet sources that the planners are eager to avoid extensive capital outlays for the television network. The reason for this neglect may lie in the fact that the regime has not yet learned to use television effectively for propaganda purposes. It seems to be treated mainly as a form of amusement and as an adjunct to the theater and cinema. The TV network, therefore, suffers from the general neglect of the consumers' desires in the Soviet Union, without benefit of the priorities given to the press and radio which have proven their worth as instruments of propaganda and agitation.

In 1954 the Soviet Union still lagged far behind the leading film producers such as the United States, Japan, and India, which produced 354, 302, and 259 feature films, respectively. Indeed its output of 38 films placed it in the lower third of world producers, on a level with Argentina and Sweden.[22] An intensification of effort led to a marked advance over the next several years, and in 1957, ninety feature films were completed. In contrast to earlier years when the regime could augment its own meager production only by reshowing older Soviet films, the domestic output can now be supplemented by the relatively "safe" product of the people's democracies. In 1957 there were 70 such films shown on Soviet screens, drawn either from the satellites or nations such as Egypt currently being given especially friendly treatment by the Soviet Union.

The increased film output was facilitated by expansion of the studio network, particularly at a distance from the main bases in Moscow and Leningrad. Thirty-three studios were in operation in 1957. Those in republics other than the Russian made fifty-nine of the feature films, the Ukraine alone contributing twenty. The number of film projectors of all types rose to 63,000 in 1957, or twice the prewar number, but of these 26,000 were portable and mainly of the 16-millimeter type. The villages and other rural areas had the greater number of all installations, 78 per cent as against a prewar level of 64 per cent. More than half of the equipment in the rural areas, however, was of the portable type, and those areas possessed 94 per cent of the nation's portable projectors.

The problems of the Soviet film industry have not changed appreciably with the death of Stalin. The studios still work on a set of themes given to them by the political authorities. For 1958, there were thirty-three main and eighteen reserve themes on the "life and work of people." According to the Minister of Culture, who addressed a National Conference of Film Workers in Moscow in 1958, the Soviet moviegoer expects films which show "the reorganization of the management of industry and construction, the struggle of farm workers to outstrip the United States in per capita production of meat, milk, and butter . . . [and] the tremendous role of housing construction. . ." It is small wonder that at the same conference one film writer dolefully complained that the Soviet studios put out "very little in the way of comedy, and no satire at all." [23]

In 1950 the most problematic aspect of Soviet mass communications was its effectiveness. Even under the best conditions it is difficult to assess the effects of mass communication. In the face of the almost complete inaccessibility of the Soviet audience, the topic seemed to defy analysis. Since then we have recorded the testimony of many thousands of escapees from the Soviet terror who became refugees during and after World War II.[24] After 1955 it was possible for scholars and others to travel more or less freely in certain Soviet cities. Although neither of these sources is an adequate substitute for systematic opinion sampling under conditions of free communication, they do enable us to venture much further in assessing the effects of Soviet mass communications.

Our latest studies have given rather definitive results for an assessment of the patterns of exposure to Soviet mass communications. Soviet sources have always been noticeably silent about the audiences for the mass media, hinting that all segments of the population alike are avid consumers of the regime's communications. Numerous studies of other industrial countries, however, consistently reveal that there are marked differences in the "communications behavior" of individuals differing in education and occupation. Our data lead us to conclude that this is true for Soviet society as for other industrial countries. Among those working in the intelligentsia over 80 per cent read newspapers frequently, and more than 60 per cent "frequently" listened to the radio. By contrast, among skilled workers the comparable figures were only 43 and 36 per cent, respectively, and among peasants from the collective farms only 16 per cent were regular newspaper readers and only 7 per cent listened to the radio frequently. Obviously the regime was being very effective in reaching the well educated and responsible people, but was doing much less well among the middle ranks and apparently was hardly hitting the peasants at all with its main battery. Those who were escaping this first line of attack were not necessarily being caught on the second wave. On the contrary, we found that those who were often exposed to one type of official communication were also often exposed to other types, and vice versa. For example, those in the intelligentsia were reached by the more "personalized" communications, such as meetings and agitation sessions, as much as three times more often than the peasants and ordinary workers. A similar contrast prevailed with regard to the movies, which were attended "often" by 53 per cent of the intelligentsia as against 17 per cent of unskilled workers and 7 per cent of the peasants.[25]

Insofar as there is any connection between exposure to Soviet mass communication and acceptance of its message, we should expect a much higher proportion of convinced Soviet Communists among those with better education, holding more responsible positions. Such indeed was the finding in our studies of former Soviet citizens. This is not to deny the dramatic evidence of student discontent which from time to time has reached us from the Soviet Union. This more "political" and vocal segment of the population may generate the most vivid evidence of unrest while yet being the group which has been most shaped and molded to the main patterns of Soviet thought. Indeed, on the basis of our studies with Former Soviet citizens, my own travels in the Soviet Union, and the full accounts of my colleagues who were also there in 1955–56, I am led to eschew any one-sided estimate of the effectiveness of Soviet mass communications. The dominant impression I took away was of the imposing effectiveness of a completely controlled system of mass communications operating under virtually complete monopoly conditions. Yet at the same time I was filled with awe at the extraordinary persistence of the human drive for trustworthy information, and amazement at the capacity of individuals to work their way to a personal assessment of the truth even when they were surrounded on every side by an endless barrage of highly organized official propaganda.

With a few notable exceptions, the media of mass communication appear to have been extraordinarily effective in shaping the pattern of thought about public issues among Soviet citizens. This ranges all the way from matters of general ideology to matters of fact. It reveals itself in the strength of belief in such ideas as the welfare state or the notion that a society needs strong guiding hands such as the Communist Party provides; in the conviction that Soviet accomplishments in various economic fields are superior to those of other countries; and in estimates of the treatment of the Negro in the United States, or in the assessment of the British Labour Party's desire for peace. It seems clear that where the reporting of the regime's monopoly of mass communication does not run too patently counter to the direct experience of Soviet citizens or does not challenge their basic values, it has a powerful grip on the Soviet mind and shapes it pretty much to the official image. Very often the official line does, of course, run counter to the direct experience of Soviet citizens. This was especially true during the years of greatest hardship before the war and immediately afterward. It continues true today when the Soviet citizen can see in many areas, such as housing, how the large promises of the regime fall far short of the needs of the population. Although now more tempered in its attack, the Soviet press continues in many of its comments on religion, the family, friendship, ethnic loyalty and work, to urge a pattern not congenial to the traditional culture, and consequently one which finds little response in important segments of the Soviet audience.

The most serious weakness of the Soviet press and radio continues to lie in its being unfree, a mere agent of government policy rather than a medium for conveying news and expressing opinion. This forces it of necessity to be tendentious, repetitive, arid, and often palpably insincere and untrue. In the brief "thaw" before the regime cracked down again, we secured "from within" a few brief glimpses of this condition, as in the following comment by a writer in the *Literary Gazette:* "Sometimes the noisy rumble of the prepared text of speeches at the Young Communist League meetings has drowned out the worried voices of young consciences. At times a deadening formalism made the carrying out of important propaganda assignments meaningless. It was important to place 'jackdaws' [check-marks] in a column of assignments. 'Done.' How many good crops were picked clean by such jackdaws?"[26]

My contacts with Soviet citizens in the U.S.S.R. left me, as it did most of my colleagues, with a strong impression of their extraordinary hunger for honest and straightforward information about the world outside—especially about Western Europe and the United States. It is a strange anomaly that while continuing to jam the Voice of America and to make the free circulation of foreign non-Communist magazines almost impossible, the Soviet government nevertheless decided to permit more than half a million Soviet citizens to go abroad in 1956, a not insignificant proportion to visit Western Europe.[27] However carefully these tourists may have been selected on grounds of political reliability, their observations cannot fail to affect their opinions and the opinions of others they will talk to. There is, of course, nothing which can effectively prevent the regime from withdrawing the privilege of foreign travel and from restricting travel inside the Soviet Union by visitors from non-Communist countries. Unless the terror returns to dam up these new currents of information and ideas, however, they will act to constrain the freedom of the official monopoly from arbitrarily dispensing arrant nonsense instead of information and will press it toward greater frankness and honesty. This will hardly give the Soviet citizen a free press, but it may prove a step on the road toward the still-distant attainment of freedom of thought and communication in Soviet society.

NOTES

BIBLIOGRAPHY

INDEX

NOTES

All Russian works are first cited by Russian title followed by English translation in parentheses. For ease of reference, all subsequent citations and those in the Bibliography are by English title.

Chapter 1: The Study of Mass Communication

1. Vladimir Ilyich Lenin, *Sochineniya* (Works; 2d ed.; Moscow, 1927-1930), XXVI, 32.

2. In 1917 Lenin wrote: "The proletariat needs state power, the centralised organisation of force, the organisation of violence, both for the purpose of crushing the resistance of the exploiters and for the purpose of *guiding* the great mass of the population—the peasantry, the petty-bourgeoisie, the semi-proletarians—in the work of organising socialist economy." Lenin, *Collected Works* (London, 1927-1930), XXI(2), 169.

3. See Paul F. Lazarsfeld, Bernard Berelson, and Hazel Gaudet, *The People's Choice* (New York, 1948), pp. 150-158.

4. For recent general discussions of this field, see Wilbur Schramm (ed.), *Communications in Modern Society* (Urbana, 1948), and Lyman Bryson (ed.), *The Communication of Ideas* (New York, 1948).

5. Compare the analysis by Paul F. Lazarsfeld and Robert K. Merton appearing in Bryson, *The Communication of Ideas.*

6. For a detailed annotated bibliography, see B. L. Smith, H. D. Lasswell, and R. D. Casey, *Propaganda, Communication, and Public Opinion* (Princeton, 1946).

7. See Paul F. Lazarsfeld and Frank Stanton (eds.), *Communications Research 1948-1949* (New York, 1949), pp. xiii-xiv.

8. See below, Chapter 4, note 2.

9. For a fuller statement of this need, see Talcott Parsons, "Propaganda and Social Control," *Psychiatry,* vol. V, no. 4 (November 1942); Lazarsfeld and Stanton, *Communications Research,* p. xv.

Chapter 2: Leninist Theory and Public Opinion

1. For a criticism of Lenin's views on the relations of party and masses, see Rosa Luxemburg's famous articles from *Die Neue Zeit* which appeared in English as the pamphlet *Leninism or Marxism?* (Glasgow, [1935]).

2. Lenin, *Sochineniya* (2d ed.), XX, 342; see also V. I. Lenin, *Selected Works,* edited by J. Fineberg (New York, 1935-1939), II, 124.

3. Lenin, *Selected Works,* II, 53-56.

4. *Ibid.,* pp. 132-33.

5. *Ibid.,* pp. 51-74 and 115-168, *passim.*

6. *Ibid.,* X, 84, 88, 136; see also Lenin, *Collected Works,* XX(1), 129, 135; XXI(2), 169-70; XXIII, 404-05.

7. Lenin, *Selected Works,* II, 53 (italics mine).

8. *Ibid.,* pp. 132-33.

9. *Ibid.,* pp. 133-141; Lenin, *Collected Works,* XXI(1), 133.

10. Lenin, *Selected Works,* II, 136-139.

11. *Ibid.*, pp. 409, 457.

12. *Ibid.*, pp. 133-141.

13. For example, see Lenin, *Collected Works*, IV(1), 44-50.

14. Joseph Stalin, *Leninism* (New York, 1932-33), I, 163, 165.

15. See Lenin, *Collected Works*, IV(2), 65-67; XX(1), 97-98, 129, 135; Lenin, *Selected Works*, X, 84-96.

16. This was one of the major parts of Lenin's early thinking set forth in his well-known pamphlet *What Is To Be Done?*

17. Lenin, *Sochineniya* (3d ed.; Moscow, 1934-1935), II, 514.

18. Lenin, *Selected Works*, II, 55-56, 123; Lenin, *Collected Works*, IV(2), 67-68.

19. Lenin, *Collected Works*, IV(2), 69.

20. Stalin, *Leninism*, I, 95-96, 162 (italics mine).

21. Lenin, *Sochineniya* (3d ed.), XXVII, 47-49; Stalin, *Leninism*, I, 37; II, 219.

22. Lenin, *Selected Works*, X, 136.

23. *Ibid.*, pp. 91-92.

24. *Ibid.*, II, 137.

25. *Ibid.*, X, 84 (italics mine).

26. *Ibid.*, p. 95.

27. Stalin, *Leninism*, I, 45.

28. Lenin, *Selected Works*, X, 136; Lenin, *Collected Works*, XXI(1), 133; Stalin, *Leninism*, I, 44, 170.

29. Stalin, *Leninism*, I, 38.

30. *Ibid.*, pp. 40-41.

31. Lenin, *Collected Works*, XXI(1), 133.

32. Lenin, *Sochineniya* (2d ed.), X, 18; XI, 206.

33. Lenin, *Collected Works*, XX(1), 129; XXIII, 404-05; Lenin, *Selected Works*, I, 497-501; X, 91-92; Stalin, *Leninism*, I, 45; II, 285.

34. Stalin, *Leninism*, I, 38, 340.

35. This was most forcefully stated by Frederick Engels in *The Origin of the Family, Private Property and the State* (New York, 1942); see especially pp. 61-73.

36. Lenin, *Selected Works*, X, 84; Lenin, *Sochineniya* (2d ed.), XXVII, 37-52; XXII, 49, 459; XXVI, 92.

37. Stalin, *Leninism*, I, 170.

38. Lenin, *Selected Works*, II, 136-37.

39. *Ibid.*, X, 91; see also Stalin, *Leninism*, I, 45.

40. Lenin, *Sochineniya*, XVIII(1), 135, quoted in Stalin, *Leninism*, I, 46.

41. Stalin, *Leninism*, I, 42.

42. *Ibid.*, p. 163; in particular see Stalin's comments made in 1939 to the Eighteenth Party Congress in *Leninism: Selected Writings* (New York, 1942; hereafter referred to as *Selected Writings*), pp. 468-474.

43. See Percy E. Corbett, "Postwar Soviet Ideology," and Sergius Yakobson, "Postwar Historical Research in the Soviet Union," *Annals of the American Academy of Political and Social Science*, vol. 263 (May 1949), pp. 45-51 and 123-133.

44. This principle was reaffirmed by the late Mikhail Kalinin, then President of the Supreme Soviet, in his address to the Eighteenth Congress of the party. *Vosemnadtsaty (XVIII) S'ezd Vsesoyuznoi Kommunisticheskoi Partii (b): Stenograficheskii Otchet* (The Eighteenth Congress of the All-Union Communist Party [of Bolsheviks]: Stenographic Report; Moscow, 1939), p. 398. Hereafter cited as *Eighteenth Congress*.

45. For example, see the discussion in Lev M. Perchik, *Agitatsiya* (Agitation; Moscow, 1937), especially pp. 13, 35-53, 70-71, 81, 129-30.

Chapter 3: The Administration of Propaganda and Agitation

1. For a more detailed discussion of the structure, operations, and membership of the party, see Julian Towster, *Political Power in the U.S.S.R., 1917-1947* (New York, 1948), chapters vi-viii, and xiii.

2. The text of the Rules as adopted unanimously in 1939 may be found in *Eighteenth Congress*, pp. 677-687. An adequate English translation is included in *The American Quarterly on the Soviet Union*, vol. II, no. 1 (April 1939), pp. 59-73.

3. The Constitution of the U.S.S.R. refers to the party in identical terms as "the leading core of all organizations of the working people, both public and state." *Constitution (Fundamental Law) of the Union of Soviet Socialist Republics* (Moscow, 1947), Article 126.

4. For a brief review of the evolution of these units and a more detailed statement of their spheres of competence, see the article on the Central Committee in the *Bol'shaya Sovetskaya Entsiklopediya* (Large Soviet Encyclopedia; Moscow, 1926-1948), LX, 531-554. See also Towster, *Political Power*, pp. 159-175.

5. See Merle Fainsod, "Postwar Role of the Communist Party," The *Annals of the American Academy of Political and Social Science*, vol. 263 (May 1949), pp. 20-32.

6. The mandate of the Administration was set forth in detail in the special decision of the Central Committee promulgated in connection with publication of the new *History of the All-Union Communist Party, Short Course* in 1938. See *Resheniya Partii o Pechati* (Party Decisions on the Press; Moscow, 1941), pp. 184-186.

7. See the interesting comments made on this point in the Resolutions of the Eleventh Party Congress, *VKP (b) v Rezolyutsiyakh i Resheniyakh S'ezdov, Konferentsii i Plenumov TsK* (The All-Union Communist Party [of Bolsheviks] in the Resolutions and Decisions of its Congresses, Conferences, and Plenums of the Central Committee; hereafter cited as *The A.U.C.P. in Resolutions*), 2 vols. (Moscow, 1932-33), I, 508-511. For the early decisions on propaganda and agitation up to the end of the Civil War, see *ibid.*, pp. 33, 52, 302.

8. For a review of the measures taken for political indoctrination of military personnel, see D. Fedotoff White, *The Growth of the Red Army* (Princeton, 1944), *passim*.

9. For a brief description of these early developments, see "Agitprop," and "Agitpunkty," *Large Soviet Encyclopedia*, I, 420-426.

10. In 1926 the Department of Propaganda and Agitation included five sub-units: agitation, propaganda, the study of local experience, the distribution of literature, and national minorities. Control of the press was in the hands of a distinct Press Department which had been created in 1924. For a review of these early developments, see *Large Soviet Encyclopedia*, I, 420-423, and LX, 551-554. See also *The A.U.C.P. in Resolutions*, I, 360-362, 448-451, 615-618.

11. *Large Soviet Encyclopedia*, I, 420-423.

12. The Department of Agitation and Mass Campaigns consisted of four sectors: general agitation, mass campaigns of an industrial character, mass campaigns in agriculture, and mass work among women workers and peasants.

The Department of Culture and Propaganda had three sectors: scientific work, education, and art; propaganda of Marxism-Leninism; and the press, including newspapers and literature, the latter replacing the formerly independent Press Department. *Partiinoe Stroitel'stvo* (Party Construction), no. 2 (1930), pp. 70-72; nos. 3-4 (1930), p. 86.

13. See the discussion of these measures in the speech of Lazar Kaganovich to the Seventeenth Congress, reported in Stalin and others, *Socialism Victorious* (New York, 1935), pp. 226-231.

14. *Sputnik Agitatora* (Agitator's Guidebook), no. 10, 1935.

15. See *Vlast' Sovetov* (Soviet Power), nos. 6-7, 1937; *Agitator's Guidebook,* no. 6, 1937.

16. *Party Decisions on the Press,* p. 186.

17. *Eighteenth Congress,* p. 671. See also the comments by Zhdanov, p. 532.

18. *Party Decisions on the Press,* pp. 184-186.

19. A current official description of the formal organization of the Department is not available. This compilation is based on published reports of the activities of the various sectors which regularly appear in the Soviet press, notably in *Kul'tura i Zhizn'* (Culture and Life), the organ of the Department of Propaganda and Agitation under the Central Committee.

20. *Bol'shevistskaya Pechat'* (Bolshevik Press), nos. 17-18 (1940), p. 71.

21. *Eighteenth Congress,* p. 671.

22. The workings of this system of interlocking controls may be traced in detail in *Culture and Life.* Almost every issue reports in detail the activities of some superior unit in supervising the work of a lower propaganda and agitation organization.

Chapter 4: Communist Propaganda: The Schooling of Opinion Leaders

1. See Harold D. Lasswell, "Agitation," *Encyclopedia of the Social Sciences,* I (New York, 1930), 487-88; and Lasswell, "Propaganda," *Encyclopedia of the Social Sciences,* XII (New York, 1934), 521-528.

2. Smith, Lasswell, and Casey, *Propaganda, Communication, and Public Opinion.* The 1935 (Minneapolis) edition, Lasswell, Casey, and Smith, *Propaganda and Promotional Activities,* did have several references to agitation.

3. *Encyclopedia of the Social Sciences,* I, 487-88.

4. H. D. Lasswell, "Communications Research and Politics," *Print, Radio, and Film in a Democracy,* edited by Douglas Waples (Chicago, 1942), p. 106. A similar definition is offered by Paul Lazarsfeld and Robert Merton, "Studies in Radio and Film Propaganda," in *Transactions of the New York Academy of Sciences,* series II, vol. 6, no. 2, pp. 58-79.

5. Quoted by Lenin, *Selected Works,* II, 85.

6. *Ibid.,* pp. 85-86.

7. *Ibid.,* pp. 86-87.

8. See the general discussion of these issues in Perchik, *Agitation,* chapters i and ii, *passim.*

9. See the articles on "Agitatsiya" and "Propaganda" in the *Large Soviet Encyclopedia,* I, 420-423, and in the *Malaya*

Sovetskaya Entsiklopediya (Small Soviet Encyclopedia: 1st ed.; Moscow, 1928-1931), I, 102-03, and VI, 931.

10. See note 9.

11. *Politicheskii Slovar'* (Political Dictionary; Moscow, 1940), pp. 453-54.

12. *Ibid.,* p. 10.

13. This remark was made in his speech to the Plenary Session of the Central Committee in March 1937. *Soviet Power,* nos. 6-7 (1937), pp. 26-27. See also the supplementary remarks by Zhdanov to the Eighteenth Congress, *Eighteenth Congress,* pp. 524-25.

14. *Party Decisions on the Press,* pp. 182-184.

15. Stalin, *Leninism,* I, 207.

16. The classic formulation of this assertion was made by Lenin shortly before the Revolution: "We are not doctrinaires. Our philosophy is not a dogma, but a guide to action." Lenin, *Collected Works,* XXI(1), 133.

17. For a brief review of the characteristic difficulties this poses, see Yakobson, "Postwar Historical Research."

*18. These decisions may be found in *The A.U.C.P. in Resolutions.* See especially the decisions on propaganda of the Eleventh, Twelfth, and Thirteenth Congresses, pp. 529-533, 607-618 in vol. I, and pp. 50-59 in vol. II (1933).

19. For a concise review of the early membership problems of the party, see the *Large Soviet Encyclopedia,* XI, 428-502, *passim.*

20. *The A.U.C.P. in Resolutions,* II, 50.

21. See the report of L. M. Kaganovich to the Seventeenth Congress of the party in Stalin, *Socialism Victorious,* especially pp. 198-205.

22. *Ibid.*

23. For a brief discussion of these measures, see Alexander Baykov, *The Development of the Soviet Economic System* (New York, 1947), pp. 149-152, 174-182.

24. For an interesting discussion of the changing composition of Soviet technical and managerial industrial personnel, see the chapter on "Plant Managers" by Solomon Schwarz in G. Bienstock, S. Schwarz, and A. Yugow, *Management in Russian Industry and Agriculture* (New York, 1944), pp. 104-124. The hypothesis which Mr. Schwarz develops about the self-perpetuation of the intelligentsia can by no means be regarded as established and should be used with considerable caution. See Towster, *Political Power,* pp. 313-336.

25. A detailed breakdown by occupation of this intelligentsia was given by Molotov in his address to the Eighteenth Party Congress. *Eighteenth Congress,* p. 310.

26. Stalin, *Selected Writings,* pp. 206-07.

27. *Ibid.,* p. 384.

28. The text of Stalin's address may be found in *Soviet Power,* nos. 6-7, 1937.

29. *Agitator's Guidebook,* no. 6 (1937), p. 7.

30. "On the Establishment of Party Propaganda in Connection with the Publication of the *History of the VKP(b)*." The full text of the decision appears in *Party Decisions on the Press,* pp. 172-186.

31. This was further indicated in Stalin's address to the Eighteenth Congress. *Selected Writings,* pp. 465-468, 475-477.

32. *Party Decisions on the Press,* p. 178.

33. *Ibid.,* pp. 180-81.

34. Stalin, *Selected Writings*, p. 468.

35. *Party Decisions on the Press*, p. 177.

36. Stalin, *Leninism*, I, 456-57 (italics mine).

37. Stalin, *Selected Writings*, p. 467.

38. *Party Decisions on the Press*, p. 184. For more recent activities in this area, see the editorial in *Bol'shevik* (Bolshevik), no. 5, March 1947; and *Culture and Life*, no. 1, January 11, 1947; no. 9, March 30, 1947.

39. For a general discussion of this institution, see John S. Curtiss and Alex Inkeles, "Marxism in the U.S.S.R.—The Recent Revival," *Political Science Quarterly*, vol. LXI, no. 3 (September 1946). See also *Culture and Life*, no. 28, October 10, 1947; no. 13, May 11, 1948; no. 26, September 11, 1948; no. 15, May 30, 1949.

40. The establishment of this lecture system was ordered in the Central Committee's basic decision on propaganda in 1938. *Party Decisions on the Press*, p. 181. For reports of the current scope of this activity, see *Culture and Life*, no. 12, October 20, 1946; no. 15, May 30, 1947; no. 17, June 20, 1947.

41. See the discussion of the functions of the press in Chapter 11.

42. An informal and balanced discussion of the impact of ideology on Soviet science can be found in Eric Ashby, *Scientist in Russia* (London, 1947).

43. *Eighteenth Congress*, p. 677.

44. *Bolshevik*, no. 16 (August 1946), p. 3.

45. Set forth in a decision of the Central Committee on July 26, 1946: "On the Growth of the Party and on Measures to Strengthen Party Organizational and Party Political Work with those Newly Accepted into the VKP(b)." For a dis-cussion of these measures, see the lead article in *Bolshevik*, no. 16 (August 1946), pp. 1-11.

46. For detailed reports on the operation of this training apparatus, see *Culture and Life*, 1947: no. 17, June 20; 1948: no. 4, February 11; no. 15, May 30; no. 30, October 21; no. 33, November 21; 1949: no. 13, May 11; no. 16, June 11.

47. These propagandists are themselves instructed in special three-month seminars conducted by the district and regional party units. *Culture and Life*, no. 17, June 20, 1947; no. 24, August 31, 1948; no. 17, June 21, 1949.

48. *Party Decisions on the Press*, pp. 180-81.

49. For example, see *Culture and Life*, no. 2, January 21, 1947.

50. *Soviet Power*, nos. 6-7 (1937), pp. 26-27.

51. *Eighteenth Congress*, pp. 524-25.

52. *Bolshevik*, no. 16 (1946), p. 3.

53. *Party Decisions on the Press*, p. 178.

54. Stalin, *Selected Writings*, p. 466.

55. *Eighteenth Congress*, p. 526.

56. For a description of the system of schools for the Marxist indoctrination of party cadres, see the Resolutions of the Eighteenth Congress in the *Eighteenth Congress*; see also the decision "On the Establishment of Party Propaganda in Connection with the Publication of . . . the *History of the VKP(b)*," *Agitator's Guidebook*, no. 6, 1937. The postwar system was set forth in a decision of August 2, 1946, "On the System of Training and Retraining Directing Party and Soviet Personnel." *Culture and Life*, no. 6, August 20, 1946.

57. *Culture and Life*, 1946: no. 11,

October 10; no. 13, October 30; 1948: no. 22, August 11; no. 18, June 30.

58. *Ibid.*, no. 6, August 20, 1946; no. 25, September 10, 1947; no. 21, July 31, 1948.

59. *Ibid.*, no. 19, December 31, 1946, no. 18, June 30, 1947; no. 7, March 11, 1948.

60. *Ibid.*, 1946: no. 6, August 20; no. 14, November 7; no. 16, November 30; 1947: no. 25, September 10; no. 29, October 22; 1949: no. 11, April 21.

61. *Ibid.*, 1946: no. 7, August 30; no. 14, November 7; no. 16, November 30; 1947: no. 14, May 21; no. 32, November 20; 1948: no. 26, September 11.

Chapter 5: The Bolshevik Agitator

1. For a fuller discussion of the types of agitation, see the *Agitator's Guidebook*, nos. 20-21 (1932), pp. 37-42.

2. *Propagandist* (Propagandist), no. 10 (1942), p. 3.

3. Reported by the Chief of the Department of Agitation under the Central Committee. *Culture and Life*, no. 17, December 10, 1946.

4. Occasionally data are released on the number of agitators in particular areas of the country. Such information, available for eight major regions of the Soviet Union in the period 1939-1944, yielded the following results: total number of agitators, 257,285; total population of the regions according to 1939 census, 27,319,000; ratio of agitators to population, 1:106. Assuming a population of about two hundred million, this would yield a total of about two million agitators for the country as a whole. Since the "sample" of eight regions covered a wide variety of territory and population density, and represented about 15 per cent of the total population, this estimate is probably reliable. *Agitator's Guidebook*, no. 21 (1939), p. 40; *Propagandist*, no. 3 (1940), p. 14; nos. 19-20 (1942), pp. 34, 36-37, 42-43, 46-47; *Culture and Life*, 1947: no. 1, January 11; **no. 27, September 30.**

5. *Culture and Life*, no. 14, May 21, 1949.

6. O. Kremneva, *Opyt Politicheskoi Agitatsii Na Predpriyatii* (Experience with Political Agitation in the Plant; Moscow, 1948), p. 60.

7. *Agitator's Guidebook*, no. 6 (1937), p. 9; no. 10 (1940), p. 6.

8. *Culture and Life*, no. 27, September 30, 1947.

9. Lenin, *Collected Works*, XXI(1), 248; Lenin, *Selected Works*, X, 88-89, 95; Stalin, *Leninism*, I, 37, 164, 340.

10. Zhdanov reported in 1937, for example, that the local party committees compiled lists of complaints and questions on the basis of the work of the agitators. A. A. Zhdanov, *Podgotovka Partiiykh Organizatsii k Vyboram v Verkhovnyi Sovet S.S.S.R.* (Preparation of the Party Organizations for the Elections to the Supreme Soviet of the U.S.S.R.; Moscow, 1937), p. 24.

11. One of the four points in the Rules describing the member's duties states that he must "constantly strengthen the ties with the masses . . . and explain to the non-Party masses the meaning of the policy and decisions of the Party." *Eighteenth Congress*, p. 678.

12. *Agitator's Guidebook*, no. 10 (1938), p. 19; no. 16 (1938), pp. 12-13.

13. *Ibid.,* no. 15 (1936), pp. 58-62.

14. *Culture and Life,* no. 37, September 30, 1947.

15. *The A.U.C.P. in Resolutions,* I, 615-16.

16. For a brief description of the current pattern of activities of agit-collectives, see Kremneva, *Experience with Political Agitation,* pp. 57-67.

17. This was the number of agitators at the "Stalin" automobile plant in Moscow in 1948. The "Bolshevik" plant in Leningrad had 800 agitators in 1939. Kremneva, *Experience with Political Agitation,* p. 59; *Agitator's Guidebook,* no. 12 (1939), p. 24.

18. *Agitator's Guidebook,* no. 10 (1940), p. 6.

19. *Ibid.,* no. 15 (1936), pp. 58-62; no. 12 (1938), p. 19; no. 16 (1938), pp. 12-13; no. 3 (1940), p. 12.

20. *Agitator's Guidebook,* no. 16 (1934), pp. 1-5; Kremneva, *Experience with Political Agitation,* pp. 63-67.

21. *Agitator's Guidebook,* no. 24 (1937), pp. 41-42; no. 7 (1938), p. 31; no. 13 (1938), pp. 13-14; Kremneva, *Experience with Political Agitation,* p. 66.

22. *Agitator's Guidebook,* no. 10 (1937), pp. 43-44; no. 12 (1938), pp. 14-16.

23. Lenin, *Collected Works,* XXIII, 191.

24. *The A.U.C.P. in Resolutions,* I, 360-362; II, 50.

25. Quoted by Perchik, *Agitation,* p. 80.

26. *Ibid.*

27. *The A.U.C.P. in Resolutions,* II, 50.

28. Lenin, *Collected Works,* XXIII, 225-227.

29. Quoted by Perchik, *Agitation,* p. 71.

30. *Agitator's Guidebook,* no. 7 (1932), pp. 17-22.

31. *Ibid.,* no. 18 (1929), pp. 70-74.

32. *Ibid.,* no. 8 (1929), pp. 51-54; no. 22 (1931), p. 3.

33. *Ibid.,* no. 12 (1928), p. 7.

34. *Ibid.,* no. 6 (1934), pp. 4-5.

35. *Ibid.,* no. 24 (1929), p. 64; nos. 26-27 (1933), pp. 18-23; no. 6 (1934), p. 5; no. 16 (1934), pp. 1-5.

36. *Ibid.,* no. 16 (1933), pp. 35-42.

37. *Ibid.,* no. 24 (1929), pp. 53-60.

38. *Ibid.,* no. 18 (1934), pp. 22-29; no. 22 (1934), pp. 1-6.

39. *Ibid.,* no. 24 (1928), pp. 54-58; nos. 17-18 (1930), pp. 76-82; no. 22 (1931), pp. 1-4.

40. *Ibid.,* nos. 26-27 (1933), pp. 18-23; no. 5 (1934), pp. 1-5.

41. *Ibid.,* no. 8 (1939), p. 27; no. 1 (1940), p. 23.

42. *Ibid.,* no. 10 (1938), p. 19; no. 13 (1939), p. 2.

43. *Ibid.,* no. 7 (1937), pp. 20-21; no. 11 (1940), pp. 1-3; no. 21 (1940), pp. 12-14.

44. *Ibid.,* no. 16 (1940), p. 1; no. 20 (1940), pp. 17-18.

45. *Ibid.,* no. 11 (1939), pp. 12-14.

46. *Ibid.,* no. 3 (1940), p. 17; no. 11 (1941), pp. 21-22.

47. *Ibid.,* nos. 13-14 (1940), p. 32.

48. *Ibid.*

49. *Ibid.,* no. 2 (1941), pp. 34-35.

50. *Ibid.,* no. 10 (1940), p. 4; no. 18 (1940), p. 7.

51. *Propagandist,* no. 18 (1942), p. 14.

52. See Kremneva, *Experience with Political Agitation,* pp. 58-60.

53. Perchik, *Agitation,* p. 77.

54. The most extensive review of those functions is contained in the series

of fourteen pamphlets in "The Agitator's Library" series, published during 1948-1949 in 500,000 copies in accord with a special decision of the Central Committee. *Partiinaya Zhizn'* (Party Life), no. 22 (November 1947), p. 38.

55. Zhdanov, *Preparation of the Party Organizations*, p. 24. *Agitator's Guidebook*, no. 7 (1937), pp. 20-21; see also no. 4 (1926), pp. 35-36; no. 16 (1933), pp. 35-42; no. 10 (1938), p. 19; no. 11 (1939), pp. 12-14; nos. 13-14 (1940), p. 34.

56. For the question and the answer, see the article "Why Are the Stores Still Without Mass-Consumption Goods?" *Agitator's Guidebook*, no. 18 (1938), pp. 42-43.

57. Perchik, *Agitation*, p. 93.

58. *Ibid.*

59. *Agitator's Guidebook*, no. 9 (1935), p. 18.

60. *Ibid.*, no. 20 (1940), p. 18.

61. *Ibid.*, no. 16 (1940), pp. 1-3.

62. Perchik, *Agitation*, p. 69.

63. For recent evidence of this continuing problem, see the decision of the Central Committee, "On Deficiencies in and Measures for the Improvement of the Work with Agitators in the Stalingrad Party Organizations," *Party Life*, no. 22 (November 1947), pp. 35-38. See also *Culture and Life*, no. 17, December 10, 1946; no. 11, April 20, 1947.

64. *Agitator's Guidebook*, no. 21 (1939), pp. 42-44.

65. *Ibid.*, no. 15 (1939), pp. 39-40.

66. *Ibid.*, no. 6 (1938), pp. 7-8.

67. A similar but less marked defection was noted following the postwar elections. *Culture and Life*, no. 17, December 10, 1946.

68. This problem of competing role obligations is one that characterizes the situation of the "activist" or "volunteer" in any society in which these phenomena appear. For a full discussion of this problem, see Bernard Barber, " 'Mass Apathy' and Voluntary Social Participation in the United States," unpublished Ph.D. thesis, Harvard University, 1948.

69. For examples, see *Agitator's Guidebook*, no. 11 (1928), pp. 39-44; *Party Life*, no. 22 (November 1947), pp. 35-38; *Culture and Life*, no. 17, December 10, 1946.

70. *O Propagande i Agitatsii* (On Propaganda and Agitation; Leningrad, 1936), pp. 36-38.

71. *Agitator's Guidebook*, no. 10 (1936), pp. 1-2; no. 6 (1937), pp. 16-17.

72. *Agitator's Guidebook*, no. 10 (1935), pp. 11-12.

73. Perchik, *Agitation*, p. 83.

74. *Agitator's Guidebook*, no. 24 (1929), p. 64.

75. Perchik, *Agitation*, p. 105.

76. *Ibid.*; *Agitator's Guidebook*, no. 1 (1940), pp. 23-24.

77. *Agitator's Guidebook*, no. 17 (1934), pp. 21-31.

78. *Ibid.*, no. 3 (1941), p. 18.

79. *Ibid.*, no. 10 (1940), p. 13.

80. *Ibid.*, no. 17 (1940), pp. 7-8.

81. *Ibid.*, no. 11 (1940), p. 2.

82. *Ibid.*, no. 14 (1939), pp. 36-37; no. 20 (1939), pp. 17-19; no. 3 (1940), pp. 20-21. See also I. Ryabov, *Opyt Politicheskoi Agitatsii v Kolkhoze* (Experience with Political Agitation in the Collective Farm; Moscow, 1948), *passim;* and G. Shitarev, *Opyt Politicheskoi Agitatsii Sredi Naseleniya po Mestu Zhitel'stva* (Experience with Political Agitation among the Population at the Place of Residence; Moscow, 1948), *passim.*

83. *Agitator's Guidebook*, no. 12 (1938), p. 15.

84. See Bienstock, Schwarz, and Yugow, *Management in Russian Industry*, pp. 104-124.

85. See the section, "The Agitators are the Foremost People," in Kremneva, *Experience with Political Agitation*, pp. 58-60.

86. *Agitator's Guidebook*, nos. 13-14 (1940), p. 34.

87. For example, see Baykov, *Development of Soviet Economic System*, pp. 355-361.

Chapter 6: The Role of the Local Party Organization

1. The Rules of the Party, *Eighteenth Congress*, p. 684.

2. For example, see the decisions of June 1935, *The A.U.C.P. in Resolutions* (2d ed., 1936), II, pp. 666-67; of December 1935, *On Propaganda and Agitation*, pp. 36-38; of September 1944, *Agitator's Guidebook*, September 1944; and of November 1947, *Party Life*, no. 22 (November 1947), pp. 35-38.

3. For a description of this selection process, see the *Agitator's Guidebook*, nos. 26-27 (1930), pp. 53-57. See also no. 3 (1926), p. 33; no. 7 (1937), p. 20; no. 12 (1939), pp. 23-25.

4. *Ibid.*, no. 18 (1929), pp. 68-70.

5. *Ibid.*, no. 21 (1929), pp. 59-62; no. 15 (1936), pp. 58-62; no. 7 (1937), pp. 19-22; *Party Life*, no. 22 (November 1947), pp. 35-36.

6. *Agitator's Guidebook*, no. 24 (1929), pp. 53-60; no. 8 (1930), pp. 52-59); nos. 26-27 (1930), pp. 53-57.

7. *Ibid.*, nos. 8-9 (1931), p. 58.

8. *Ibid.*, nos. 11-12 (1932), pp. 1-4.

9. Stalin, *Socialism Victorious*, pp. 193-195.

10. For a discussion of these changes, see Chapter 7.

11. *Agitator's Guidebook*, no. 12 (1934), pp. 1-5; no. 8 (1935), pp. 1-4.

12. *Ibid.*, no. 7 (1937), pp. 20-21; no. 12 (1938), pp. 14-16.

13. *On Propaganda and Agitation*, pp. 36-38.

14. *Agitator's Guidebook*, no. 16 (1936), pp. 50-51; no. 6 (1937), pp. 11-17; no. 15 (1939), pp. 39-40; Perchik, *Agitation*, pp. 60-61.

15. *Agitator's Guidebook*, no. 9 (1935), pp. 18-21.

16. *Ibid.*, no. 22 (1938), pp. 33-34; no. 11 (1939), pp. 12-14; no. 22 (1940), pp. 1-3; no. 11 (1941), pp. 21-22.

17. *Party Life*, no. 22 (November 1947), pp. 35-38.

Chapter 7: The Development of Oral Agitation Policy

1. The emphasis on intensive propaganda rather than extensive agitation is unmistakable in the prerevolutionary resolutions and decisions of the party. See *The A.U.C.P. in Resolutions*, I, 33, 51, 302.

2. Lenin, *Selected Works*, X, 136.

3. *The A.U.C.P. in Resolutions*, I, 508-510.

4. *Ibid.*, p. 615.

5. Lenin, *Collected Works*, XXIII, 191.

6. For the complete text, see *The A.U.C.P. in Resolutions*, I, 360-362.

7. Lenin, *Sochineniya* (2d ed.), XXVII, 37-52.

8. *Ibid.*

9. *The A.U.C.P. in Resolutions,* I, 615-618.

10. For a description and discussion of the measure adopted, see the resolutions of the four party congresses which met between 1921 and 1924, in *The A.U.C.P. in Resolutions,* I, 448-451, 508-511, 533, 615-16, and II, 50-59.

11. For discussion of the considerations underlying the Plan, see Baykov, *Development of Soviet Economic System,* pp. 153-159; and Maurice Dobb, *Soviet Economic Development since 1917* (New York, 1948), pp. 172-260.

12. *Agitator's Guidebook,* no. 13 (1926), pp. 3-7.

13. *Ibid.,* no. 12 (1928), p. 7.

14. These remarks were made by Stalin in an address to a plenary session of the Central Committee in November 1928; see *Agitator's Guidebook,* no. 23 (1928), p. 14.

15. The text of the decision "On the Establishment of Agitation among the Workers," dated March 29, 1929, may be found in *Agitator's Guidebook,* no. 18 (1929), pp. 68-70.

16. *Ibid.,* no. 24 (1928), pp. 54-58; no. 13 (1929), pp. 79-83; no. 17 (1929), p. 46; no. 24 (1929), pp. 53-60.

17. *Ibid.,* nos. 20-21 (1931), pp. 1-4; no. 22 (1931), p. 3.

18. *Ibid.,* no. 27 (1933), pp. 18-23.

19. *Ibid.,* no. 66 (1934), pp. 1-5.

20. For example see *ibid.,* no. 24 (1929), pp. 13-14.

21. See the charges to be found in the stenographic report of the conference of the Moscow agitation department in the *Agitator's Guidebook,* nos. 31-32 (1930), pp. 54-64.

22. *Ibid.,* nos. 8-9 (1931), pp. 58-59, 60-61.

23. *Ibid.,* no. 10 (1931), pp. 62-64; no. 10 (1932), pp. 9-10; no. 25 (1932), pp. 21-23; no. 10 (1933), pp. 7-11.

24. See *ibid.,* nos. 20-21 (1931), pp. 1-4; no. 7 (1932), pp. 17-22; no. 9 (1934), pp. 1-4.

25. *Ibid.,* no. 6 (1934), pp. 1-5.

26. For example, see *ibid.,* no. 6 (1934), pp. 1-5.

27. Stalin, *Selected Writings,* p. 363.

28. *Pravda,* April 7, 1935, reprinted in *Agitator's Guidebook,* no. 8 (1935), pp. 5-6.

29. The call for greater emphasis on political agitation was sounded in a *Pravda* editorial of April 7, 1935, and in the decision of the Central Committee in December 1935, "On the Condition of Political Agitation in the Balakhninsk Cellulose-Paper Combine" (reprinted in *Pravda,* December 4, 1935). See also the *Agitator's Guidebook,* 1935: no. 8, pp. 3-4; no. 9, pp. 18-21; no. 10, p. 6; no. 12, pp. 15-17; 1937: no. 7, p. 21; 1938: no. 10, p. 19; no. 12, p. 15.

30. *Agitator's Guidebook,* no. 16 (1938), pp. 12-13. See also no. 10, p. 19; no. 12, pp. 14-16.

31. *Ibid.,* no. 16 (1938), pp. 12-13.

32. *Pravda,* December 4, 1935.

33. *Agitator's Guidebook,* no. 6 (1937), p. 9.

34. *Pravda,* December 4, 1935.

35. Perchik, *Agitation,* p. 13. The objection here was not so much concerned with the ideas expressed as with the words chosen. The Russian word *nataskivat',* for example, is not politely used with reference to persons, but rather explicitly refers to training animals.

36. *Pravda,* December 4, 1935.
37. *Agitator's Guidebook,* no. 16 (1938), pp. 12-13.
38. *Ibid.,* no. 13 (1939), pp. 1-2.
39. *Ibid.,* no. 13 (1939), pp. 1-2; nos. 13-14 (1940), pp. 32-34; no. 16,

pp. 1-3.
40. *Ibid.,* no. 11 (1940), pp. 1-3.
41. *Ibid.,* no. 8 (April 1946), pp. 24-25.
42. *Party Life,* no. 22 (November 1947), pp. 35-38.

Chapter 8: Oral Agitation and the Soviet System

1. See Chapter 16.
2. *Propagandist,* no. 18 (1942), pp. 3-10.
3. *Agitator's Guidebook,* no. 8 (1929), pp. 79-83; no. 8 (1930), pp. 52-59; no. 12 (1940), p. 22.
4. For brief reviews of research experience on this problem, see Herbert Hyman and Paul Sheatsley, "Some Reasons Why Information Campaigns Fail," *Public Opinion Quarterly,* XI (Fall 1947), 412-423; Bernard Berelson, "Communications and Public Opinion," in Schramm, *Communications in Modern Society,* pp. 167-185. Some of the concrete research findings may be found in Lazarsfeld, Berelson, and Gaudet, *The People's Choice,* especially pp. 73-136. For the most comprehensive research investigation yet undertaken into these problems, see the series of the Social Research Council, *Studies in Social Psychology in World War II,* vols. I-IV (Princeton, 1949-), especially vol. III, *Experiments on Mass Communication,*

Carl Hoveland (ed.).
5. The late Kurt Lewin and his associates were foremost in providing research evidence on the relatively greater effectiveness of group discussions as compared to "formal" attempts to change attitudes through devices such as lectures. See Lewin's pioneering study, "Forces Behind Food Habits and Methods of Change," in *The Problem of Changing Food Habits,* National Research Council, bulletin 108 (1943), especially pp. 55-64. A variety of demonstrations of the principle will be found in *The Journal of Social Issues,* vol. I, no. 3 (August 1945). See also Lazarsfeld, Berelson, and Gaudet, "The Nature of Personal Influence," in *The People's Choice,* pp. 150-158.
6. *Agitator's Guidebook,* no. 24 (1931), p. 3.
7. *Ibid.,* no. 4 (1926), p. 36.
8. *Ibid.,* no. 11 (1940), p. 2.
9. Perchik, *Experience with Political Agitation,* pp. 129-30.

Chapter 9: The Soviet Conception of the Press

1. The most complete picture of the role of the press in Soviet society is to be obtained by an examination of the basic collections of party and government regulations governing its operations: L. G. Fogelevich, *Osnovnye Direktivy i Zakonodatel'stvo o Pechati* (Basic Directives and Legislation on the Press; Moscow, 1935); *Party Decisions on the Press,*

1941. Before the war the Central Committee also published a special slick-paper journal, *Bol'shevistskaya Pechat'* (Bolshevik Press), devoted to transmission of decisions and the discussion of press problems.
2. Lenin, *Collected Works,* IV(1), 114.
3. The listings in *Party Decisions on*

the Press were under *informatsiya*. The headings searched in the alphabetical index in Fogelevich were *informatsiya, novosti, poslednie novosti, informatsionnoe soobshchenie,* and *soobshchenie.* Fogelevich does contain a section listed in the table of contents under the title "Procedure for Publishing Official Materials."

4. See the *Political Dictionary,* p. 422; *Small Soviet Encyclopedia* (2d ed.), X (1933-1940), pp. 289-292; *Pechat' Strany Sotsializma* (The Press in the Land of Socialism; Moscow, 1939), pp. 64-71.

5. Lenin, *Sochineniya,* VIII, 386-392.

6. *Constitution,* Article 125.

7. *Ibid.*

8. For example, see the exchange between Kent Cooper, then Executive Director of the Associated Press, *Washing-*ton *Post,* January 21, 1945, and the Soviet writer N. Baltiisky, "Freedom of the Press; A Frank Talk with Mr. Kent Cooper," *The War and the Working Class,* no. 1 (January 1945), pp. 8-15. The discussion of freedom of the press in the United Nations has followed very similar lines.

9. See the *Kratkii Filosofskii Slovar'* (Brief Philosophical Dictionary; Moscow 1939), pp. 198-99; *Small Soviet Encyclopedia* (2d ed.), VII, 634-35; and Dmitrii N. Ushakov (ed.), *Tolkovy Slovar' Russkogo Yazyka* (Explanatory Dictionary of the Russian Language; Moscow, 1940), II, 734-35.

10. *Opyt Gazety "Zarya Vostoka"* (The Experience of the Newspaper "Dawn of the East"; Moscow, 1940), pp. 75-76.

Chapter 10: The Structure of a Planned Press

1. See *Pyatiletnii Plan Pechati* (The Five Year Plan for the Press; Moscow, 1929). Where not specifically documented, material in this chapter is drawn from the following: *Tsifry o Pechati S.S.S.R.* (Figures on the Press of the U.S.S.R.; Moscow, 1940); *Kul'turnoe Stroitel'stvo S.S.S.R.* (Cultural Construction in the U.S.S.R.; Moscow, 1940), pp. 203-228; *Sovetskaya Pechat' v Tsifrakh* (The Soviet Press in Figures; Moscow, 1948); and *Pechat' S.S.S.R. v 1939 Godu: Statisticheskie Materialy* (The Press in the U.S.S.R. in 1939: Statistical Materials; Moscow, 1940).

2. *Bolshevik Press,* no. 5 (1939), p. 39. The "Chronicle" section of this magazine regularly carried notices of the creation, reorganization, and dissolution of papers at all levels according to the decisions of the Central Committee of the party. This also applied to the selection of editorial personnel.

3. *Figures on the Press,* p. 10.

4. See the decision of the Central Committee, "On the Immediate Tasks of the Party Organizations of the C.P.(b) of Byelorussia in the Sphere of Mass-Political and Cultural-Education Work among the Population," *Agitator's Guidebook,* September 1944, p. 17.

5. *Pravda,* May 5, 1947.

6. Of 3,613 papers at the district and city level in 1939, 3,293 served predominantly agricultural districts and were therefore defined as part of the agricultural-press network. *Sel'skokhozyaistvennaya Pechat' v Tsifrakh* (The Agricultural Press in Figures; Moscow, 1939), p. 16.

7. *Figures on the Press,* p. 17. The circulation on *Pionerskaya Pravda* had

reached one million in 1949. *The Soviet Press*, p. 107.

8. Reported to be 2,200,000 in 1947. *The Soviet Press*, p. 105.

9. *The Soviet Press*, pp. 107-08.

10. See the table in *The Press in the U.S.S.R. in 1939*, p. 84.

11. See the stenographic report of the address of T. Antropov to the conference of territorial, regional, and republican newspaper editors in *Bolshevik Press*, no. 14 (1940), pp. 2-7. See also the address by Georgi Alexandrov and P. Fedoseev, then Director and Vice-Director, respectively, of the Administration of Propaganda and Agitation, to a similar conference of provincial editors in 1946. *Culture and Life*, no. 17, December 10, 1946.

12. See note 11.

13. *Bolshevik Press*, no. 10 (1940), p. 1.

14. *Party Decisions on the Press*, p. 128.

15. *Figures on the Press*, pp. 17, 21.

16. *The Agricultural Press in Figures*, p. 16.

17. *Figures on the Press*, p. 17; *The Press in the U.S.S.R. in 1939*, pp. 83-85.

18. *Party Decisions on the Press*, p. 189. *Culture and Life*, no. 15, November 20, 1946; several articles on the district press appeared in that issue.

19. *Party Decisions on the Press*, pp. 189-90. See also *Culture and Life*, 1946: no. 15, November 20; no. 17, December 10; no. 18, December 20; 1947: no. 7, March 11.

20. *Figures on the Press*, p. 17; *The Soviet Press*, p. 107.

21. Of the total of 4,583 published in 1939, 622 were so located. *Figures on the Press*, p. 17; *Agricultural Press in Figures*, p. 24.

22. *Figures on the Press*, p. 17; *The Soviet Press*, p. 109.

23. See the decision of the Central Committee, "On the Factory-Plant Press," August 19, 1932, in *Party Decisions on the Press*, pp. 154-55; see also pp. 133, 163. *Culture and Life*, no. 10, April 10, 1947.

24. See *Party Decisions on the Press*, pp. 80-81, 87, 89. Detailed discussions of the structure, functioning, and control of the wall newspaper may be found in the journal *Pravda Raboche-Krestyanskii Korrespondent* (Worker and Peasant Correspondent's Pravda; hereafter referred to as *Worker and Peasant Correspondent*), which was published by the Central Committee at least up to the beginning of the war. More recent comments appear regularly in *Culture and Life*.

Chapter 11: The Functions and Content of the Press

1. This situation has been significantly changed by the recent launching of two publications devoted to presenting extracts from the Soviet press. See *Soviet Press Translations* (University of Washington, Seattle), and *Current Digest of the Soviet Press* (Washington, D. C.).

2. Lenin, *Collected Works*, IV(1), 114.

3. Lenin, *Sochineniya*, XXII, 412-417.

4. *Ibid.*; Lenin, *Collected Works*, XXIII, 225-227.

5. *Party Decisions on the Press*, pp. 22-25.

6. *Ibid.*, pp. 37-39, 53.

7. Fogelevich, *Basic Directives*, pp. 127-129; *Bolshevik Press*, no. 16 (1940), pp. 45-46.

8. *Pravda*, May 5, 1947.

9. See, for example, the instructions to the press, issued at the time of the completion of the Great Fergana Canal, on the treatment of that news event in such a way that it would support the program of drafting farm labor for work in road building. *Bolshevik Press*, no. 4 (1940), pp. 3-4.

10. *Party Decisions on the Press*, p. 53. See also pp. 22-25.

11. *Pravda*, May 5, 1947.

12. *Party Decisions on the Press*, pp. 80-81. See also pp. 110-11, 190; and *Bolshevik Press*, 1940: no. 4, p. 2; no. 14, pp. 2-7, no. 16, pp. 45-46.

13. *Party Decisions on the Press*, pp. 110-11, 190; *Experience of the Newspaper "Dawn of the East,"* pp. 32-37.

14. *Pravda*, May 5, 1947.

15. For a description of Soviet experience with problems of labor incentives, see Baykov, *Development of Soviet Economic System, passim;* and Maurice Dobb, *Soviet Planning and Labor in* *Peace and War* (New York, 1943), pp. 65-100.

16. *Political Dictionary*, p. 422.

17. *Early Decisions on the Press*, pp. 104-107.

18. *Ibid.*, pp. 182-83.

19. For detailed reports on the current propaganda activities of the press, see *Culture and Life*, 1946: no. 15, November 20; no. 17, December 10; 1947: no. 27, September 30.

20. For a discussion of this problem, see the address of T. Antropov to the 1940 conference of regional and republic editors. *Bolshevik Press*, no. 14 (1940), pp. 2-7.

21. See *Party Decisions on the Press*, pp. 101-02, 105-107, 168; Fogelevich, *Basic Directives*, p. 22; *Bolshevik Press*, no. 4 (1940), pp. 1-2.

22. For example, see the report on the activities of the newspapers published by the various units of the Ministry of River Transport. *Culture and Life*, no. 9, March 30, 1947.

23. See *Party Decisions on the Press*, pp. 189-191; *Bolshevik Press*, no. 14 (1940), pp. 2-7.

Chapter 12: Editors and Writers of the Soviet Press

1. *Eighteenth Congress*, pp. 681, 683-84; see also *Bolshevik Press*, no. 1 (1937), p. 34; and *Worker and Peasant Correspondent*, no. 7 (April 1940), pp. 23-25.

2. The "Chronicle" section of *Bolshevik Press* regularly carried long lists of the names of editors of all types of central and regional newspapers whose appointment or removal it formally confirmed. Many examples of similar control exercised by the regional organizations are to be found in the same journal, and of control by the local organizations in the journal *Worker and Peasant Correspondent*.

3. See *Party Decisions on the Press*, pp. 130-31; *Party Construction*, no. 9 (1940), p. 7.

4. *Party Decisions on the Press*, pp. 130-31.

5. See *ibid.*, pp. 19, 27, 60, 112-13.

6. *Ibid.*, pp. 130-31.

7. In addition to these higher schools there are special technical secondary schools (*tekhnikumy*), as well as cor-

respondence courses for training newspaper personnel. *Culture and Life*, no. 27, September 30, 1947.

8. *Bolshevik Press*, nos. 7-8 (1937), p. 10; nos. 11-12 (1940), pp. 47-48; no. 16 (1940), pp. 39-40; *Culture and Life*, no. 27, September 30, 1947; no. 14, May 21, 1949.

9. See *Bolshevik Press*, nos. 11-12 (1938), p. 41; *Agitator's Guidebook*, September 1944, p. 17; *Culture and Life*, no. 6, August 20, 1946; no. 17, December 10, 1946.

10. *Party Construction*, nos. 17-18 (September 1943), p. 47; no. 1 (1944), p. 47; *Bolshevik Press*, no. 4 (1940), p. 30.

11. *Bolshevik Press*, no. 4 (1940), p. 30.

12. *Party Decisions on the Press*, pp. 182-184.

13. *Culture and Life*, no. 6, August 20, 1946; no. 7, August 30, 1946.

14. *Bolshevik Press*, nos. 17-18 (1940), p. 60.

15. *The Experience of the Newspaper "Dawn of the East,"* p. 75.

16. *Party Decisions on the Press*, pp. 171, 192-93.

17. *Bolshevik Press*, no. 14 (1940), pp. 2-7; *Party Decisions on the Press*, pp. 166, 189-90.

18. *Bolshevik Press*, no. 10 (1940), pp. 1-6; no. 14 (1940), pp. 2-7; *Party*

Decisions on the Press, pp. 192-93; *Culture and Life*, no. 6, August 20, 1946; no. 15, May 30, 1947.

19. *The Experience of the Newspaper "Dawn of the East,"* passim.

20. *Party Decisions on the Press*, pp. 189-90.

21. *Ibid.*, pp. 166, 189-90, 192-93; *Culture and Life*, no. 15, May 30, 1947.

22. See the address by T. Antropov to the conference of editors of regional newspapers called by the Press Department of the Administration of Propaganda and Agitation in 1940. *Bolshevik Press*, no. 14 (1940), pp. 2-7. See also *Party Decisions on the Press*, pp. 166, 189-90, 192-93.

23. *Bolshevik Press*, no. 4 (1940), pp. 1-2. *Culture and Life*, no. 6, August 20, 1946.

24. For examples of this criticism, see *Bolshevik Press*, no. 14 (1940), pp. 1-7; *Culture and Life*, no. 15, November 20, 1946; no. 17, December 10, 1946; no. 27, September 30, 1947.

25. See *Bolshevik*, nos. 17-18 (1944), pp. 4-5, for a discussion of this incident.

26. *Bolshevik Press*, no. 14 (1940), p. 1.

27. Examples of such criticism can be found in *Party Decisions on the Press*, p. 168; *Bolshevik Press*, nos. 7-8 (1938), p. 11; and *Bolshevik*, nos. 10-11 (1944), pp. 94-96.

Chapter 13: Censorship and Supervision of the Press

1. Fogelevich, *Basic Directives*, pp. 124-25. For a brief discussion of *Glavlit*, see Vladimir Gsovski, *Soviet Civil Law* (Ann Arbor, 1948-49), I, 65-66.

2. *Party Construction*, no. 9 (1940), p. 7.

3. See *Party Decisions on the Press*, pp. 22-25, 37-39, 80-81; *Culture and Life*, no. 17, December 10, 1946; no. 27, September 30, 1947.

4. For examples of such press review articles, see *Culture and Life*, 1946: no.

6, August 20; no. 15, November 20; no. 17, December 10; no. 18, December 20.

5. *Sotsialisticheskii Vestnik* (Socialist Herald; New York), February 27, 1945, p. 40.

6. For example, see *Party Construc-*

tion, nos. 17-18 (1943), p. 47; no. 1 (1944), p. 47; *Culture and Life*, no. 17, December 10, 1946.

7. See the report of a meeting of editors of newspapers published by the Ministry of the River Fleet, *Culture and Life*, no. 9, March 30, 1947.

Chapter 14: Public Control, Self-Criticism, and the Press

1. *Political Dictionary*, p. 277.

2. Lenin, *Sochineniya*, VI, 161; VII, 307.

3. From an article in *Pravda* by Stalin, "Against the Vulgarization of the Slogan of Self-Criticism" (June 26, 1928), reprinted in *Party Decisions on the Press*, pp. 12-18.

4. *Party Decisions on the Press*, p. 115.

5. *Political Dictionary*, p. 497.

6. On the importance of self-criticism for the successful functioning of the party, see Lenin, *Sochineniya*, XXI, 219; XXV, 200; XXVII, 126.

7. Lenin considered practice in self-criticism a form of training for the masses in the art of leadership, and Stalin spoke of it in similar terms. *Ibid.*, XII, 303; Stalin, quoted in *Party Decisions on the Press*, p. 15.

8. For major references to the utilization of self-criticism to regulate and control the activities of the bureaucracy, see *Party Decisions on the Press*, pp. 12-18, 86, 115.

9. *Ibid.*, pp. 12-18.

10. *Ibid.*

11. *Ibid.*, pp. 5-9.

12. *Ibid.*, pp. 20, 123; Fogelevich, *Basic Directives*, pp. 8, 22-23.

13. For examples of corrective actions taken by government and other officials on the basis of criticism in the press, see

Vechernyaya Moskva (Evening Moscow) 1947: December 10, December 19; *Turkmenskaya Iskra* (Turkmen Spark), 1947: November 16, December 20.

14. See Silas Bent, *Newspaper Crusaders; A Neglected Story* (New York, 1939).

15. Fogelevich, *Basic Directives*, p. 8; *Party Decisions on the Press*, pp. 156, 162-63.

16. *Party Decisions on the Press*, pp. 5-9; Lenin, *Collected Works*, XXIII, 225-227.

17. See *Party Decisions on the Press*, pp. 22-25, 68, 114, 156; Fogelevich, *Basic Directives*, p. 18.

18. Quoted in *The Experience of the Newspaper "Dawn of the East,"* p. 54.

19. See the *Small Soviet Encyclopedia* (1st ed.), VII, 110-11; and Fogelevich, *Basic Directives*, pp. 35-37.

20. *Party Decisions on the Press*, pp. 130-31, 166.

21. *Small Soviet Encyclopedia* (1st ed.), VII, 110-11; Fogelevich, *Basic Directives*, pp. 35-37.

22. *Small Soviet Encyclopedia* (1st ed.), VII, 110.

23. *Bolshevik Press*, no. 14 (1940), pp. 34-35; *Worker and Peasant Correspondent*, no. 2 (January 1940), pp. 12-16.

24. See *Eighteenth Congress*, pp. 677-78.

25. Fogelevich, *Basic Directives*, pp. 35-37.

26. *Party Decisions on the Press*, p. 90; *Small Soviet Encyclopedia* (1st ed.), VII, 111.

27. *Large Soviet Encyclopedia*, Supplement, "Soyuz Sovetskikh Sotsialisticheskikh Respublik" (Union of Soviet Socialist Republics; Moscow, 1948), p. 1637. This figure was reported to be based on incomplete data. In any event, it represents a significant decrease from the figure of over three million given by Stalin in 1934. Stalin, *Socialism Victorious*, p. 80.

28. *Bolshevik Press*, 1940: no. 10, pp. 1-6; nos. 11-12, p. 23.

29. *Ibid.*, no. 14, pp. 59-61.

30. *Worker and Peasant Correspondent*, 1940: no. 1 (January), p. 44; no. 2 (January), pp. 12-16; no. 4 (February), p. 24; Fogelevich, *Basic Directives*, pp. 35-37; *Party Decisions on the Press*, pp. 90-92.

31. *Bolshevik Press*, no. 14 (1940), pp. 34-35; *Worker and Peasant Correspondent*, no. 2 (January 1940), pp. 5-7.

32. Quoted in Fogelevich, *Basic Directives*, p. 35.

33. *Ibid.*, pp. 35-37; *Party Decisions on the Press*, pp. 90-92.

34. *Pravda*, November 28, 1947; *Komsomolskaya Pravda*, December 13, 1946.

35. For an example of a letter criticizing a republic Ministry of Communal Economy, see *Bakinskii Rabochii* (Baku Worker), November 26, 1947, p. 2.

36. This statement is based on discussions with displaced persons from the U.S.S.R.

37. The party set this level as early as 1921. *The Party on the Press*, pp. 24-25.

38. In 1946, for example, the Uzbek republic-level paper *Pravda Vostoka* (Truth of the East) was receiving only from fifteen to twenty letters per day, and the district paper *Put' Il'icha* (Along the Path of Ilitch [Lenin]) was receiving at most four letters a day in 1940. *Culture and Life*, no. 6, August 20, 1946; *Worker and Peasant Correspondent*, no. 10 (May 1940), pp. 63-64.

39. *The Press in the Land of Socialism*, p. 73.

40. *Bolshevik Press*, 1940: no. 9, pp. 53-54; no. 19, pp. 1-5.

41. For examples, see *Evening Moscow*, 1947: November 21, p. 4; December 10, p. 4; December 19, p. 4; *Turkmen Spark*, 1947: November 16, p. 3; November 25, p. 4; December 20, p. 4.

42. *Party Decisions on the Press*, pp. 156, 162-63; *Bolshevik Press*, 1940: no. 2, pp. 39-42; no. 4, pp. 13-14; no. 9, pp. 53-54; no. 23, p. 5; *Worker and Peasant Correspondent*, 1940: no. 1, pp. 27-29; no. 2, pp. 12-16; no. 10, pp. 63-64; *Culture and Life*, no. 6, August 20, 1946.

43. *Experience of the Newspaper "Dawn of the East,"* pp. 47-60.

44. On some newspapers the letter office and the *rabsel'kor* office are joined in a unified department. *Worker and Peasant Correspondent*, no. 7 (April 1940), p. 62.

45. *The Experience of the Newspaper "Dawn of the East,"* pp. 47-60.

46. *Party Decisions on the Press*, pp. 156, 162-63.

47. See examples cited above in this chapter in note 41.

48. *Bolshevik Press*, no. 4 (1940), pp. 13-14.

49. *Ibid.*

50. *Experience of the Newspaper "Dawn of the East,"* pp. 47-60.

51. *Worker and Peasant Correspondent,* no. 1 (January 1940), pp. 27-29; no. 2 (January 1940), pp. 12-16.

52. Fogelevich, *Basic Directives,* pp. 18, 37-38; *Party Decisions on the Press,* pp. 141-42, 156.

53. *Ibid.; Bolshevik Press,* no. 4 (1940), pp. 13-14; *Experience of the Newspaper "Dawn of the East,"* pp. 47-60.

54. *Bolshevik Press,* 1940: no. 2, pp. 39-42; no. 4, pp. 13-14; no. 9, pp. 53-54; no. 23, p. 5.

55. See *Party Decisions on the Press,* pp. 162-63; *Culture and Life,* no. 6, August 20, 1946; *Worker and Peasant Correspondent, no.* 10 (May 1940), pp. 63-64.

56. Stalin's report to the Fifteenth Congress. *Report of the Fifteenth Congress of the Communist Party of the Soviet Union* (London, 1928), p. 65.

57. See Fogelevich, *Basic Directives,* pp 39-44.

58. Cf. Lenin, "The State and Revolution," *Selected Works,* VII, 91-94, 101-02.

59. For an excellent discussion of the relation of this element of Communist theory to Soviet practice, see Barrington Moore, Jr., "Some Readjustments in Communist Theory," *Journal of the History of Ideas,* vol. VI, no. 4 (1945), pp. 468-482.

60. See especially Stalin, *Selected Writings,* pp. 211-216, 382-384, 397-98, 475-477.

61. See John Dollard and others, *Frustration and Aggression* (New Haven, 1939).

62. For the affirmation of the principle that the party must be foremost in conducting criticism of the bureaucracy, see *Culture and Life,* no. 27, September 30, 1947.

63. For a discussion of the functioning of the Soviet electoral system which highlights both its elements of rigidity and flexibility, see S. N. Harper, *The Government of the Soviet Union* (New York, 1937).

64. *Party Decisions on the Press,* pp. 12-18.

Chapter 15: The Administration of Radiobroadcasting

1. "Radioveshchanie" (Radiobroadcasting), *Small Soviet Encyclopedia* (1st ed.), VII, 124.

2. *Pravda,* June 22, 1937; December 16, 1944.

3. A. D. Fortushenko, *Pyat'desyat Let Radio* (Fifty Years of Radio; Moscow, 1945), pp. 68-69. The Vice-Commissar omitted mention of the date on which American broadcasting began, although the *Small Soviet Encyclopedia* ("Radiobroadcasting") credits the United States with being first in the field.

4. I. E. Goron, *Radioveshchanie* (Radiobroadcasting; Moscow, 1944), pp. 13-14.

5. Arno Huth, *La Radiodiffusion-Puissance Mondiale* (Paris, 1937), p. 144.

6. *Izvestiya,* November 29, 1933.

7. *Radioezhegodnik: 1936* (Radio Yearbook: 1936; Moscow), p. 43. See also Rose Ziglin, "Radio Broadcasting in the Soviet Union," *The Annals of the American Academy of Political and Social Science,* vol. 177 (January 1935), pp. 66-72.

8. See, for example, *Radiofront* (Radio Front), nos. 7-8 (1940), pp. 2-4.

9. *Literaturnaya Gazeta* (Literary Gazette), December 16, 1944.

10. *Sovetskaya Muzyka* (Soviet Music), no. 1 (1946), pp. 97-98.

11. See the regulation of the Council of Commissars defining the responsibilities of the Radio Committee, *Izvestiya*, November 29, 1933.

12. *Verkhovny Sovet S.S.S.R., Vosmaya Sessiya, 1941, Stenograficheskyy Otchet* (Supreme Soviet of the U.S.S.R., 8th Session, 1941, Stenographic Report), pp. 286, 485, 524. In 1935 the Radio Committee received 27 million rubles in fees, but this constituted only one fourth of its total budget. *Govorit S.S.S.R.* (U.S.S.R. Speaking), no. 1 (1935), pp. 2-3.

13. See, for example, *U.S.S.R. Speaking*, no. 5 (1936), p. 50; *Radio Front*, no. 3 (1939), pp. 1-3; *Elektro-Svyaz* (Electrical Communication), nos. 5-6 (1940), pp. 2-4.

14. See the description of the regulations governing local broadcasting in *U.S.S.R. Speaking*, no. 5 (1936), p. 44. See also Article 7 of the *Sovnarkom* Regulation, *Izvestiya*, November 29, 1933.

15. *Large Soviet Encyclopedia*, Supplement, p. 1659.

16. Article 2 (1) of the *Sovnarkom* Regulation, *Izvestiya*, November 29, 1933.

17. *U.S.S.R. Speaking*, no. 5 (1936), p. 44.

18. *Radioprogrammy* (Radio Programs), no. 5 (1937), p. 7.

19. *U.S.S.R. Speaking*, no. 2, (1935), p. 13.

20. *Ibid.*, no. 2 (1936), p. 7.

21. *Ibid.*, no. 2 (1935), pp. 13-14 and 23-24; no. 6 (1935), pp. 33-35; no. 8 (1935), p. 4; and *Pravda*, June 22, 1937.

22. *U.S.S.R. Speaking*, no. 2 (1935), p. 23.

23. *Pravda*, June 22, 1937.

24. The head of the Radio Committee would not have a voting, but only a consultative, voice in meetings of the Council of Ministers. See Towster, *Political Power*, pp. 280-286.

25. See the comment in *Pravda*, May 7, 1947.

26. The Central Committee apparently must confirm the appointment of all responsible officials of the Radio Committee. For example, see its decision to free one man and confirm another as responsible editor of the "Latest News By Radio" section of the All-Union Radio Committee. *Bolshevik Press*, nos. 19-20 (1939), p. 63.

27. *U.S.S.R. Speaking*, no. 2 (1936), p. 1, presents a complete record of the impressive career of Kerzhentsev up to that point; this appears to be the only complete description of the career of a Radio Committee Chairman that is readily available.

28. *Culture and Life*, no. 17, December 10, 1946; no. 3, January 31, 1947.

29. Such control was provided for in the original decree establishing *Glavlit*. Fogelevich, *Basic Directives*, pp. 124-25. There was apparently some transfer of this authority to the Committee on Art Affairs in 1939, but control was shortly thereafter restored to *Glavlit*. *Sobranie Postanovlenii i Rasporyazhenii Pravitel'stva S.S.S.R.* (Collection of Decrees and Orders of the Government of the U.S.S.R.), no. 53 (October 19, 1939), art. 485; no. 32 (December 31, 1940), art. 811.

30. *Pravda*, June 22, 1937; *Trud*, May 7, 1946; July 14, 1943.

Chapter 16: Broadcasting and Radio Reception in the U.S.S.R.

1. *Large Soviet Encyclopedia,* Supplement, p. 1660.

2. See Llewellyn White, *The American Radio* (Chicago, 1947), pp. 27-67; and Robert J. Landry, *This Fascinating Radio Business* (New York, 1946), Chapters ii-iii.

3. Fortushenko, *Fifty Years of Radio,* pp. 53-54.

4. Rose Ziglin, "Radio Broadcasting in the Soviet Union."

5. *Pravda,* December 16, 1944. For later comments stressing this point, see *Culture and Life,* no. 17, December 10, 1946; *Izvestiya,* May 7, 1948; *Radio* (Radio), no. 1 (1948), pp. 1-2; no. 6 (1948), pp. 1-4.

6. *Sotsialisticheskoe Stroitel'stvo S.S. S.R.* (Socialist Construction in the U.S.S.R.; Moscow, 1936), p. 505, gives the figure of 23 stations for the end of 1928.

7. *Ibid.*

8. *Itogi Vypolneniya Vtorogo Pyateletnego Plana Razvitiya Narodnogo Khozyaistva S.S.S.R.* (Results of the Fulfillment of the Second Five Year Plan for the Development of the National Economy of U.S.S.R.; Moscow, 1939), p. 103. The planned figure for the end of the Second Plan is from *Proekt Vtorogo Pyatiletnego Plana* (Outline for the Second Five Year Plan; Moscow, 1934), I, 260.

9. *Pravda,* May 7, 1947.

10. *Ibid.*

11. *Ibid.*

12. *Ibid.*

13. "Law on the Five Year Plan . . . Adopted March 18, 1946," published by *Soviet News* (London, n. d.), p. 16.

14. *Izvestiya,* May 7, 1946; *Large Soviet Encyclopedia,* Supplement, p. 1659. Before the war central broadcasting ac-counted for only 64 hours of the daily total.

15. *Pravda,* December 16, 1944.

16. *Izvestiya,* December 16, 1944.

17. *Large Soviet Encyclopedia,* Supplement, p. 1659.

18. *Radio Yearbook: 1936,* p. 119.

19. *Izvestiya,* December 16, 1944.

20. *Pravda,* May 8, 1947.

21. There were ten thousand loud-speakers in the squares and streets of Soviet cities and settlements in 1947. *Large Soviet Encyclopedia,* Supplement, p. 1656.

22. *Pravda,* May 7, 1947; *Izvestiya,* May 7, 1947.

23. See editorial in *Electrical Communication,* nos. 5-6 (1940), pp. 2-4; also *Pravda,* May 8, 1947.

24. *Izvestiya,* May 7, 1946.

25. *Ibid.,* May 7, 1947; *Pravda,* May 7, 1947.

26. There were 864,000 wired speakers served by the main exchange and its substations, and 175,000 served by 188 unattached diffusion exchanges. *Radio,* no. 1 (1948), p. 14.

27. Fortushenko, *Fifty Years of Radio,* p. 74.

28. *Izvestiya,* May 7, 1946.

29. *Ibid.,* February 8, 1940.

30. *Large Soviet Encyclopedia,* Supplement, p. 1656; Fortushenko, *Fifty Years of Radio,* p. 77.

31. *Izvestiya,* December 16, 1944.

32. *Ibid.,* May 7, 1947.

33. *Pravda,* May 8, 1947.

34. See *U.S.S.R. Speaking,* no. 6 (1935), pp. 33-35; *Trud,* June 13, 1943; July 14, 1943; May 7, 1946.

35. *Izvestiya,* May 7, 1946.

36. *Radio Front,* nos. 21-22 (1940), p. 9.

37. *Pravda,* May 7, 1947. In 1948 the

Ministry of Communications still controlled less than half the total number of exchanges. *Radio*, no. 3 (1948), p. 1.

38. An estimate based on data given in *Pravda*, May 7, 1947; *Radio*, no. 1 (1948), p. 14; no. 3 (1948), pp. 5-6.

39. *Trud*, May 7, 1946.

40. In a basic technical manual on radiobroadcasting used as a college text, I. E. Goron, *Radiobroadcasting*, pp. 10-13, has set forth the following disadvantages of the system of aerial radio-receiving sets of the type which predominate in the United States and England: (1) each listener must have a complete receiving apparatus (aerial, tube, condensers, and so forth); (2) this apparatus becomes more complicated, and hence more expensive, as the distance of the receiver from the transmitter increases; (3) atmospheric and other interferences may make reception difficult and at times impossible; and (4) there are severe limitations on the number of broadcasting stations which can operate because of the limited number of channels available.

41. Goron, *Radiobroadcasting*, pp. 10-13; Fortushenko, *Fifty Years of Radio*, pp. 75-76.

42. In 1939 the initial cost of installing a wired speaker was given as 53 rubles; a battery set, 200 rubles; and a superheterodyne set on household current, 800 rubles. The comparable yearly operation costs based on an average of six hours of use daily were 33 rubles, 338 rubles, and 288 rubles, respectively. Goron, *Radiobroadcasting*, p. 10.

43. Reported by Fortushenko, *Fifty Years of Radio*, p. 76.

44. Goron, *Radiobroadcasting*, p. 11; *U.S.S.R. Speaking*, no. 5 (1936), p. 51.

45. *U.S.S.R. Speaking*, no. 5 (1936), p. 51.

46. *Culture and Life*, no. 17, December 10, 1946; *Izvestiya*, May 7, 1948; *Radio*, no. 1 (1948), pp. 1-2; no. 3, pp. 2-3, 12-13.

47. *U.S.S.R. Speaking*, no. 2 (1936), p. 46. It should be noted that the comparison between the U.S.S.R. and North America favored the Soviet Union. If the basis of comparison were radio sets in the United States alone, the contrast would be still sharper.

48. *Electrical Communication*, nos. 5-6 (1940), p. 2.

49. *U.S.S.R. Speaking*, no. 1 (1935), pp. 2-3; no. 2 (1936), p. 48.

50. *Radio Front*, no. 3 (1941), pp. 1-2.

51. *Pravda*, May 8, 1947.

52. *Ibid.*; *Radio*, no. 1 (1948), pp. 1-2. The problem was particularly acute in some of the formerly occupied areas like Kalinin and Smolensk Regions, in which only 4 per cent and 8 per cent of the collective farms, respectively, had access to radiobroadcasts. *Radio*, no. 3 (1948), pp. 12-13.

53. *U.S.S.R. Speaking*, no. 2 (1936), p. 48.

54. *Electrical Communication*, nos. 5-6 (1940), p. 2.

55. *Radio*, 1948: no. 1, pp. 1-2; no. 3, pp. 5-6; no. 4, p. 1; no. 8, pp. 3-4; *Izvestiya*, May 7, 1948; *Culture and Life*, no. 17, December 10, 1946.

56. *Pravda*, May 8, 1947.

57. Fortushenko, *Fifty Years of Radio*, p. 77.

58. *Izvestiya*, December 16, 1944.

59. Fortushenko, *Fifty Years of Radio*, p. 77.

60. *Izvestiya*, May 7, 1946.

61. *Pravda*, May 7, 1947.

62. *Ibid.*

63. *Ibid.*, May 8, 1947.

64. *Ibid.*, May 7, 1948; *Radio*, 1948: no. 1, pp. 1-2; no. 6, pp. 1-4.
65. *Pravda*, May 8, 1946.
66. *Ibid.*
67. See the party resolutions on the Third Plan, *Eighteenth Congress*, p. 659.
68. *Soviet News*, May 29, 1946.
69. *Pravda*, May 8, 1946, and May 7, 1947.
70. *Sotsialisticheskoe Sel'skoe Khozyaistvo S.S.S.R.* (Socialist Agriculture of the U.S.S.R.; Moscow, 1939), p. 142.
71. *Izvestiya*, May 7, 1947, and May 7, 1948.
72. *Trud*, July 11, 1944.
73. *U.S.S.R. Speaking*, no. 2 (1936), p. 46.
74. *Ibid.*, no. 1 (1936), pp. 2-3.
75. *Radio Front*, no. 23 (1936), p. 2.
76. *Electrical Communication*, nos. 5-6 (1940), p. 4.
77. *Radio Front*, no. 19 (1940), p. 2.

78. *Izvestiya*, February 8, 1940.
79. *Pravda*, May 8, 1947.
80. *Ibid.; Izvestiya*, May 7, 1947; *Radio*, 1948: no. 6, pp. 1-4; no. 7, pp. 14-15; no. 8, pp. 3-4.
81. *Trud*, May 7, 1946.
82. *Electrical Communication*, nos. 5-6 (1940), pp. 2-4.
83. *Pravda*, May 8, 1947.
84. *Ibid.*, May 7, 1947.
85. *Ibid.*, May 8, 1947.
86. *Ibid.*, May 7, 1947.
87. *Ibid.*, May 8, 1947.
88. *Radio*, no. 1 (1948), pp. 1-2. The Ministry of the Means of Communication Industry had produced only 30,000 of these sets in the last quarter of 1947. One other organization which was scheduled to produce 55,000 in the course of the year had built only 6,000 by midyear. *Radio*, no. 3 (1948), pp. 12-13.

Chapter 17: Program Policy and the Content of Soviet Broadcasts

1. *Pravda*, June 22, 1937; December 16, 1944; May 8, 1946; *Izvestiya*, May 7, 1946; *Trud*, May 7, 1946; *Literary Gazette*, March 17, 1945; *Culture and Life*, no. 17, December 10, 1946; *Small Soviet Encyclopedia* (1st ed.), VII, 124; *Large Soviet Encyclopedia*, Supplement, pp. 1653-1664.
2. *Izvestiya*, May 7, 1946. See also second footnote on page 236 above.
3. *Ibid.; Pravda*, May 7, 1948; *Culture and Life*, no. 3, January 31, 1947.
4. *Pravda*, leader, June 22, 1937.
5. *Literary Gazette*, leader, March 17, 1945.
6. Ziglin, "Radio Broadcasting in the Soviet Union," p. 72.
7. *Bolshevik*, nos. 19-20 (1944), p. 61.

8. *U.S.S.R. Speaking*, no. 2 (1935), p. 13.
9. *Izvestiya*, May 7, 1946.
10. Ziglin, "Radio Broadcasting in the Soviet Union," p. 66.
11. *Izvestiya*, December 16, 1944.
12. *Pravda*, December 16, 1944.
13. Ziglin, "Radio Broadcasting in the Soviet Union," p. 66.
14. *U.S.S.R. Speaking*, no. 2 (1936), pp. 28-29.
15. *Sovetskoe Iskusstvo* (Soviet Art), December 12, 1944, p. 1.
16. Ziglin, "Radio Broadcasting in the Soviet Union," p. 66.
17. *Literary Gazette*, December 16, 1944.
18. *Ibid.*
19. *Ibid.*

20. *Ibid.,* leader, March 17, 1945.
21. *Ibid.,* December 16, 1944.
22. *Izvestiya,* December 16, 1944.
23. *Literary Gazette,* December 16, 1944 (my italics).
24. *Ibid.*
25. *Ibid.*
26. *Radio Programs,* no. 2 (1938), p. 2.
27. *Literary Gazette,* March 17, 1945.
28. *Pravda,* December 16, 1944.
29. *U.S.S.R. Speaking,* no. 2 (1935), p. 14.
30. *Ibid.,* p. 23.
31. *Trud,* leader, May 7, 1946.
32. *Pravda,* May 8, 1946.
33. *U.S.S.R. Speaking,* no. 2 (1935), pp. 13-14.
34. *Ibid.,* pp. 14-17.
35. *Ibid.,* pp. 14-15.
36. *Ibid.,* p. 15.
37. *Ibid.*
38. *Ibid.*
39. *Ibid.*
40. Quoted in *Large Soviet Encyclopedia,* Supplement, p. 1654.
41. *Culture and Life,* no. 17, December 10, 1946.
42. Quoted in *U.S.S.R. Speaking,* no. 2 (1935), p. 15.
43. *Pravda,* May 8, 1947.
44. Ziglin, "Radio Broadcasting in the Soviet Union," p. 68.
45. For a more detailed discussion of the role of children's programs, see *Culture and Life,* no. 6, March 1, 1947.
46. *U.S.S.R. Speaking,* no. 18 (1935), pp. 36-37.
47. *New York Herald Tribune,* June 2, 1947.
48. *Small Soviet Encyclopedia* (1st ed.), VII, 124.
49. *Izvestiya,* December 16, 1944.
50. Ziglin, "Radio Broadcasting in the Soviet Union," p. 72.
51. *Literary Gazette,* March 17, 1945.
52. *U.S.S.R. Speaking,* no. 6 (1935), pp. 33-35. This order was followed by another on the sixteenth of August (*ibid.,* no. 18 [1935], pp. 36-37), and still another on the fifteenth of January 1936 (*ibid.,* no. 5 [March 1936], pp. 43-44), designed to tighten the control over exchange broadcasting.
53. *Izvestiya,* May 7, 1946; *Culture and Life,* no. 17, December 10, 1946; *Large Soviet Encyclopedia,* Supplement, p. 1659.
54. *Trud,* June 13, 1943. For other reports, see *Trud,* July 14, 1943, and May 7, 1946.
55. See *Rabota Agitatora s Gazetoi* (The Agitator's Use of the Newspaper; Moscow, 1943), especially pp. 42-45.

Chapter 18: The Radio Audience in the U.S.S.R.

1. *Trud,* July 14, 1943.
2. See editorial, *Radio Front,* no. 19 (1940), p. 1.
3. *Culture and Life,* no. 17, December 10, 1946; *Radio,* no. 3 (1948), p. 1.
4. *Electrical Communication,* nos. 5-6 (1940), p. 3.
5. Ziglin, "Radio Broadcasting in the Soviet Union," p. 71.
6. *U.S.S.R. Speaking,* no. 1 (1935), p. 3.
7. *Ibid.,* no. 2 (1936), p. 8.
8. *Izvestiya,* February 8, 1940.
9. *Large Soviet Encyclopedia,* Supplement, p. 1656.
10. *Small Soviet Encyclopedia* (1st ed.), VII, 124.

11. *U.S.S.R. Speaking*, no. 2 (1935), p. 17.

12. *Ibid.*, no. 6 (1935), pp. 33-35.

13. *Pravda*, December 16, 1944.

14. Ziglin, "Radio Broadcasting in the Soviet Union," p. 72.

15. *Radio Programs*, no. 50 (1937), p. 14.

16. *Soviet Art*, December 12, 1944, p. 1.

17. Ziglin, "Radio Broadcasting in the Soviet Union," p. 72.

18. See *U.S.S.R. Speaking*, no. 2

(1936), p. 11; *Radio Programs*, no. 4 (1937), p. 3; *Trud*, July 14, 1943.

19. Ziglin, "Radio Broadcasting in the Soviet Union," p. 68.

20. *U.S.S.R. Speaking*, no. 2 (1936), p. 11.

21. *Ibid.*, no. 6 (1936), p. 34.

22. *Ibid.*

23. *Ibid.*

24. *Time*, July 13, 1942, p. 64.

25. See *Culture and Life*, no. 17, December 10, 1946; *The Agitator's Use of the Newspaper*, pp. 42-45.

Chapter 19: The Soviet Film Industry

1. *Lenin, Stalin, Partiya o Kino* (Lenin, Stalin, and the Party on the Film; Moscow-Leningrad, 1938), pp. 7-8.

2. Nicolai A. Lebedev, *Ocherk Istorii Kino S.S.S.R.* (An Outline History of the Film in the U.S.S.R.; Moscow, 1947), pp. 33, 35; Thorold Dickinson and Catherine De la Roche, *Soviet Cinema* (London, 1948), pp. 9-11.

3. Lebedev, *Outline History of the Film*, pp. 64-68; Dickinson and De la Roche, *Soviet Cinema*, pp. 11-13; *Large Soviet Encyclopedia*, Supplement, pp. 1602-03.

4. The full text of the decree may be found in *Lenin, Stalin and the Party on the Film*, pp. 11-12.

5. Lebedev, *Outline History of the Film*, p. 72.

6. *Ibid.*, pp. 71-75; Dickinson and De la Roche, *Soviet Cinema*, pp. 14-16.

7. Dickinson and De la Roche, *Soviet Cinema*, p. 15.

8. Lebedev, *Outline History of the Film*, pp. 83-85.

9. *Lenin, Stalin, and the Party on the Film*, p. 50. This figure refers to the business year 1922-23.

10. See *Large Soviet Encyclopedia*, Supplement, pp. 1603-04; Lebedev, *Outline History of the Film*, pp. 76-82.

11. Lebedev, *Outline History of the Film*, p. 83; *Lenin, Stalin, and the Party on the Film*, pp. 12-13, 21-22; Dickinson and De la Roche, *Soviet Cinema*, pp. 15-18.

12. *Lenin, Stalin, and the Party on the Film*, p. 49.

13. *Ibid.*, pp. 19-20; Lebedev, *Outline History of the Film*, pp. 83-84.

14. *Lenin, Stalin, and the Party on the Film*, p. 21; Lebedev, *Outline History of the Film*, 84-85; Dickinson and De la Roche, *Soviet Cinema*, p. 17.

15. *Lenin, Stalin, and the Party on the Film*, p. 21.

16. *Large Soviet Encyclopedia*, Supplement, pp. 1604-05.

17. See the instructions sent by Lenin, in a letter written by the business manager of the *Sovnarkom* to the Commissar of Education, on January 27, 1922. *Lenin, Stalin, and the Party on the Film*, p. 20.

18. *Ibid.*

19. Dickinson and De la Roche, *Soviet Cinema*, p. 18.

20. Lebedev, *Outline History of the Film*, pp. 86-90.

21. *Ibid.*

22. *Lenin, Stalin, and the Party on the Film*, p. 30.

23. *Ibid.*, pp. 51-52.

24. *Ibid.*

25. *Ibid.*, p. 52.

26. Lebedev, *Outline History of the Film*, p. 140.

27. Dickinson and De la Roche, *Soviet Cinema*, p. 20. Their study of the Soviet film was made under the auspices of the British Film Society.

28. Lebedev, *Outline History of the Film*, p. 141.

29. *Ibid.*, pp. 141-42.

30. *Lenin, Stalin, and the Party on the Film*, pp. 64-67.

31. *Ibid.*, p. 64.

32. See George Reavey, *Soviet Literature Today* (New Haven, 1947), pp. 16-19.

33. *Lenin, Stalin, and the Party on the Film*, pp. 69-70.

34. *Ibid.*

35. *Ibid.*, pp. 33-35, 71-79.

36. *Ibid.*, p. 72.

37. *Ibid.*, p. 33.

38. See the article, "A False Film," *Pravda*, August 16, 1940; and the editorial, "Communist Morality and the Upbringing of Youth," *Pravda*, August 27, 1940.

39. See the public address given by I. Bolshakov on the twenty-fifth anniversary of the Soviet film, in I. V. Sokolov, *Istoriya Sovetskogo Kinoiskusstva Zvukovogo Perioda* (History of Soviet Film Art in the Period of Sound), vol. II: 1934-1944 (Moscow, 1946), pp. 201-204.

40. For example, see *Culture and Life*, no. 12, October 20, 1946; no. 19, December 31, 1946; no. 28, October 10, 1947; no. 18, June 30, 1948.

41. *Ibid.*, no. 12, April 30, 1947.

42. *Ibid.*, no. 18, June 30, 1948.

43. *Dvadtsat' Let Sovetskoi Kinematografii* (Twenty Years of Soviet Cinematography; Moscow, 1940), p. 169; I. Bolshakov, *Pyatiletnii Plan, Vosstanovleniya i Razvitiya Sovetskoi Kinematografii* (The Five Year Plan for the Restoration and Development of Soviet Cinematography; Moscow, 1946), p. 14.

44. *Twenty Years of Soviet Cinematography*, p. 12.

45. Bolshakov, *Five Year Plan*, p. 23.

46. *Pravda*, March 24, 1938.

47. Dickinson and De la Roche, *Soviet Cinema*, pp. 9-13.

48. *Lenin, Stalin, and the Party on the Film*, pp. 50, 52; *Large Soviet Encyclopedia*, Supplement, p. 1607; Lebedev, *Outline History of the Film*, pp. 143-44.

49. Lebedev, *Outline History of the Film*, p. 144.

50. *Ibid.*; *Large Soviet Encyclopedia*, Supplement, p. 1607. Of the 820 films produced, 120 were art films, 200 "cultural" films, and 500 newsreels and documentaries.

51. *Cultural Construction*, p. 197.

52. *Culture and Life*, no. 19, December 31, 1946.

53. Bolshakov, *Five Year Plan*, p. 14.

54. *Ibid.*

55. *Culture and Life*, no. 19, December 31, 1946.

56. *Ibid.*, no. 28, October 10, 1947.

57. *Ibid.*, no. 12, October 20, 1946; no. 28, October 10, 1947.

58. *Ibid.*, no. 19, December 31, 1946.

59. *Ibid.*, no. 28, October 10, 1947.

60. *Twenty Years of Soviet Cinematography*, pp. 161-62.

61. *Ibid.*, pp. 153-159.

62. Bolshakov, *Five Year Plan*, p. 17.

63. *Ibid.*, p. 18.

64. *Ibid.*, pp. 18-19.

65. *Culture and Life*, no. 14, May 21, 1948.

66. *Twenty Years of Soviet Cinematography*, p. 168.

67. *Ibid.*, p. 169.

68. Bolshakov, *Five Year Plan*, p. 19.

69. *Twenty Years of Soviet Cinematography*, p. 15.

70. *Culture and Life*, no. 9, March 30, 1947; no. 14, May 21, 1948.

71. *Ibid.*

72. *Twenty Years of Soviet Cinematography*, pp. 14, 169.

73. *Sotsialisticheskoe Stroitel'stvo S.S.S.R.* (Socialist Construction in the U.S.S.R.; Moscow, 1939), p. 130.

74. *Cultural Construction*, p. 196.

75. *Ibid.*, p. 192.

76. Bolshakov, *Five Year Plan*, p. 20.

77. *Cultural Construction*, p. 196.

78. Bolshakov, *Five Year Plan*, pp. 20-21.

79. *Culture and Life*, no. 9, March 30, 1947.

80. *Ibid.*

81. *Ibid.*, no. 14, May 21, 1948.

82. *Cultural Construction*, p. 193.

83. *Ibid.*, pp. 193, 195.

84. *Culture and Life*, no. 14, May 21, 1948.

85. *Twenty Years of Soviet Cinematography*, p. 14.

86. An estimate based on data for 1938 given in *Cultural Construction*, pp. 198-99.

87. Bolshakov, *Five Year Plan*, p. 20.

88. An estimate based on data for 1938 given in *Cultural Construction*, pp. 198-99.

89. *Culture and Life*, no. 14, May 21, 1948.

90. Ibid.

91. Quoted in *Lenin, Stalin, and the Party on the Film*, p. 26.

92. *Large Soviet Encyclopedia*, Supplement, p. 1605.

93. *Lenin, Stalin, and the Party on the Film*, p. 33.

94. *Ibid.*, p. 64. See also pp. 49-50, 51-52, 61, 72, and 87-101.

95. *Ibid.*, pp. 33, 61, 64; Lebedev, *Outline History of the Film*, p. 142.

96. This remark was made by the late President Kalinin in 1935. *Lenin, Stalin, and the Party on the Film*, p. 78.

97. *Large Soviet Encyclopedia*, Supplement, p. 1605.

98. Bolshakov, *Five Year Plan*, p. 4.

99. *Ibid.*, pp. 5-6.

100. *Ibid.*, pp. 7-10.

101. *Twenty Years of the Soviet Film*, p. 138.

102. Bolshakov, *Five Year Plan*, p. 13.

103. *Large Soviet Encyclopedia*, Supplement, pp. 1609-10.

104. *Ibid.*, p. 1610.

105. *Lenin, Stalin, and the Party on the Film*, pp. 61, 64.

106. Lebedev, *Outline History of the Film*, p. 142.

107. *Large Soviet Encyclopedia*, Supplement, p. 1609.

108. *Lenin, Stalin, and the Party on the Film*, p. 61; Lebedev, *Outline History of the Film*, p. 142.

109. Bolshakov, *Five Year Plan*, pp. 9-10.

110. See the article by S. Kovatev, then head of the Film Sector of the Department of Propaganda and Agitation, in *Propagandist*, no. 17 (September 1944), pp. 6-10.

111. *Ibid.*, pp. 11-12.

112. See, for example, the collection

of decisions in *Lenin, Stalin, and the Party on the Film.*

113. For the description of a recent conference, see *Culture and Life*, no. 12, October 20, 1946.

114. *Culture and Life*, no. 18, June 30, 1948.

115. *Lenin, Stalin, and the Party on the Film*, pp. 35-42, reports several such meetings.

116. *Culture and Life*, no. 12, April 30, 1947.

117. *Bolshevik*, no. 16 (August 1946), pp. 50-53.

Chapter 20: A Note in Conclusion

1. Lenin, quoted in *Party Decisions on the Press*, pp. 5-9.

2. Stalin, *Sochineniya*, I, 79, 96, 103.

3. I am indebted to Merle Fainsod for this analogy, which he applied to the Soviet system as a whole. It has been considerably elaborated here.

Chapter 21. Addendum: 1950–1960–?

1. See Leo Gruliow, ed., *Current Soviet Policies—II: The Documentary Record of the 20th Communist Party Congress* (New York: Praeger, 1957), p. 61.

2. *Kommunist*, no 12 (August 1957), p. 23. Krushchev's article was a condensation and collation of three separate talks which he gave on the general subject "For a Close Tie Between Literature and Art and the Life of the People."

3. Gruliow, *Current Soviet Policies.* p. 61.

4. *Partiinaya Zhizn'*, no. 23 (December 1956), pp. 73-74.

5. For a full report see *The Current Digest of the Soviet Press*, vol. X, no. 6 (March 19, 1958), pp. 3-7.

6. *Kommunist*, no. 12 (August 1957), p. 23.

7. The revised Party Statutes adopted at the Nineteenth Congress in 1952 no longer explicitly specified that there should be such departments, instead adopting the more flexible approach of authorizing the local organizations to have a certain number of secretaries

without uniformity as to portfolio. At all levels of the Party, without exception, however, a secretary or comparable official for propaganda and agitation is invariably appointed. See Boris Meissner and John S. Reshetar, *The Communist Party of the Soviet Union* (New York: Praeger, 1956).

8. For the text of these and other relevant decrees, see *Spravochnik Partiinogo Rabotnik* (Moscow, 1957).

9. *Izvestiya*, May 28, 1957.

10. *Partiinaya Zhizn'*, no. 14 (July 1956), pp. 3-10.

11. Gruliow, *Current Soviet Policies—II*, p. 60.

12. In *Kommunist*, no. 12 (August 1957), translated by *Current Digest*, vol. IX, no. 35 (October 9, 1957), pp. 3-5.

13. *Partiinanya Zhizn'*, no. 15 (August 1956), 10-16.

14. *Patiinaya Zhizn'*, no. 15 (August 1957), pp. 24-31; *Kommunist*, no. 13 (September 1957), pp. 40-45; *Pravda*, September 30, 1957.

15. *Pravda*, June 15, 1957.

16. *Pravda*, March 5, 1957; *Agitator*,

no. 7 (1958), pp. 43-46.

17. *Agitator*, 1958, no. 3, p. 50; no. 4, p. 63; no. 7, p. 4; no. 8, p. 3; *Pechat' SSSR za Sorok Let, 1917-1957* (Moscow, 1957), p. 108.

18. The following data on the press network are from *Pechat' SSSR za Sorok Let; Sovetskaya Pechat'*, no. 5 (1958), p. 32; *Rasprostraneniye Pechati*, no. 4 (April 1958).

19. Following data on the radio network are from *Bloknot Agitatora*, no. 12 (April 1957), pp, 12-19; *Pravda*, February 26, 1958; *Promyshlenno-ekonomicheskaya Gazeta*, May 24, 1957; *SSSR (Bolshaya Sovetskaya Entsiklopediya)*, 1957, pp. 415-417; *Current Digest of the Soviet Press*, vol. X, no. 13, p. 43; *Narodnoe Khozyaistvo SSSR* (Moscow, 1956).

20. Based on data given in *World Communications: Press, Radio, Film, Television* (Paris: Unesco, 1956).

21. *World Communications: Press, Radio, Film, Television* (3rd ed.; Paris: Unesco, 1956;) *Current Digest*, vol. X, no. 13, p. 43 (May 7, 1958).

22. *World Communication*, pp. 40-41.

23. Material on the film is from following sources: *Pravda*, February 28 and March 1, 1958; *Izvestiya*, March 4-5, 1958; *SSSR: Bolshaya Sovetskaya Entsiklopediya*, 1957. pp. 631-639; *Current Digest of the Soviet Press*, vol. IX, no. 24, pp. 24-25; *Narodnoe Khozyaistvo SSSR*, 1956, p. 238.

24. See Raymond Bauer, Alex Inkeles, and Clyde Kluckhohn, *How the Soviet System Works* (Cambridge, Mass.: Harvard University Press, 1956).

25. These and other data on the communications behavior of former Soviet citizens apply mainly to the prewar period, roughly 1940. There is little reason to assume great change in the class patterning we observed, although the average levels of exposure may well now be higher. See Peter Rossi and Raymond Bauer, "Some Patterns of Soviet Communications Behavior," *Public Opinion Quarterly*, vol. 16, (1952-53), no. 4, pp. 653-670.

26. Quoted in *Current Digest*, vol. IX (1957), no. 27, pp. 12-14.

27. *Pravda*, July 25, 1957.

BIBLIOGRAPHY

This bibliography does not purport to be a general reading guide to Soviet mass communication. Only those books directly cited in the text are included here; many valuable basic sources relevant to the field have of necessity been omitted. For ease of reference, all Russian works with no author designated, excepting familiar periodicals, are listed by the English title followed by the Russian title in parentheses.

BOOKS AND ARTICLES

The A.U.C.P. (All-Union Communist Party [of Bolsheviks]) in the Resolutions and Decisions of its Congresses, Conferences, and Plenums of the Central Committee (*VKP (b) v Rezolyutsiyakh i Resheniyakh S'ezdov, Konferentsii i Plenumov TsK*). 2 vols. Moscow: Partizdat, 1932-33; 1936.

The Agitator's Use of the Newspaper (*Rabota Agitatora s Gazetoi*). Moscow, 1943.

The Agricultural Press in Figures (*Sel'skokhozyaistvennaya Pechat' v Tsifrakh*). Moscow: All-Union Book Chamber, 1939.

Ashby, Eric. *Scientist in Russia*. London: Penguin Books, 1947.

Baltiisky, N. "Freedom of the Press; A Frank Talk with Mr. Kent Cooper," *The War and the Working Class,* no. 1, January 1945.

Barber, Bernard. " 'Mass Apathy' and Voluntary Social Participation in the United States." Unpublished Ph.D. thesis, Harvard University, 1948.

Baykov, Alexander. *The Development of the Soviet Economic System*. New York: Macmillan, 1947.

Bent, Silas. *Newspaper Crusaders; A Neglected Story*. New York: McGraw-Hill, 1939.

Bienstock, Gregory, Solomon Schwarz, and Aaron Yugow. *Management in Russian Industry and Agriculture*. New York: Oxford University Press, 1944.

Bolshakov, I. G. *Pyatiletnii Plan, Vosstanovleniya i Razvitiya Sovetskoi Kinematografii* (The Five Year Plan for the Restoration and Development of Soviet Cinematography). Moscow, 1946.

Brief Philosophical Dictionary (*Kratkii Filosofskii Slovar'*). Moscow: Ogiz, State Publishing House for Political Literature, 1939.

Bryson, Lyman (ed.). *The Communication of Ideas*. New York: Harper, 1948.

Collection of Decrees and Orders of the Government of the U.S.S.R.

(Sobranie Postanovlenii i Rasporyazhenii Pravitel'stva S.S.S.R.). Moscow, 1938—.

Commission on Freedom of the Press. *A Free and Responsible Press*. Chicago: University of Chicago Press, 1947.

Constitution (Fundamental Law) of the Union of Soviet Socialist Republics. Moscow: Foreign Languages Publishing House, 1947.

Corbett, Percy E. "Postwar Soviet Ideology," *The Annals of the American Academy of Political and Social Science*, vol. 263, May 1949.

Cultural Construction in the U.S.S.R. *(Kul'turnoe Stroitel'stvo S.S.S.R.)*. Moscow: Gosplanizdat, 1940.

Curtiss, John S., and Alex Inkeles. "Marxism in the U.S.S.R.—The Recent Revival," *Political Science Quarterly*, vol. LXI, no. 3, September 1946.

Dickinson, Thorold, and Catherine De la Roche. *Soviet Cinema*. London: Falcon Press, 1948.

Dobb, Maurice. *Soviet Economic Development since 1917*. New York: International Publishers, 1948.

—— *Soviet Planning and Labor in Peace and War*. New York: International Publishers, 1943.

Dollard, John, and others. *Frustration and Aggression*. New Haven: Yale University Press, 1939.

The Eighteenth Congress of the All-Union Communist Party (of Bolsheviks): Stenographic Report *(Vosemnadtsaty (XVIII) S'ezd Vsesoyuznoi Kommunisticheskoi Partii (b): Stenograficheskii Otchet)*. Moscow: Ogiz, State Publishing House for Political Literature, 1939.

Engels, Frederick. *The Origin of the Family, Private Property and the State*. New York, 1942.

The Experience of the Newspaper "Dawn of the East" *(Opyt Gazety "Zarya Vostoka")*. Moscow: Ogiz, State Publishing House for Political Literature, 1940.

Fainsod, Merle. "Postwar Role of the Communist Party," *The Annals of the American Academy of Political and Social Science*, vol. 263, May 1949.

Figures on the Press of the U.S.S.R. *(Tsifry o Pechati S.S.S.R.)*. Moscow: All-Union Book Chamber, 1940.

The Five Year Plan for the Press *(Pyatiletnii Plan Pechati)*. Moscow, 1929.

Fogelevich, L. G. (ed.). *Osnovnye Direktivy i Zakonodatel'stvo o Pechati* (Basic Directives and Legislation on the Press). Moscow: Ogiz, State Publishing House "Soviet Legislation," 1935.

Fortushenko, A. D. *Pyat'desyat Let Radio* (Fifty Years of Radio). Moscow: Svyaz'izdat, State Publishing House for Literature Concerning Questions of Communication and Radio, 1945.

Goron, I. E. *Radioveshchanie* (Radiobroadcasting). Moscow: Svyaz'izdat, State Publishing House for Literature Concerning Questions of Communication and Radio, 1944.

Gsovski, Vladimir. *Soviet Civil Law*. 2 vols. Ann Arbor: University of Michigan Law School, 1948-1949.

Harper, Samuel Northrup. *The Government of the Soviet Union*. New York: Van Nostrand, 1937.

History of the All-Union Communist Party (of Bolsheviks), Short Course. *(Istoriya Vsesoyuznoi Kommunisticheskoi Partii [Bol'shevikov], Kratkii Kurs)*. Moscow: Ogiz, Gospolitizdat, 1946. The first edition was published in 1938.

Huth, Arno. *La Radiodiffusion-Puissance Mondiale*. Paris: Librairie Gallimard, 1937.

Hyman, Herbert, and Paul Sheatsley. "Some Reasons Why Information Campaigns Fail," *Public Opinion Quarterly,* vol. XI, Fall 1947.

Kremneva, O. *Opyt Politicheskoi Agitatsii Na Predpriyatii* (Experience with Political Agitation in the Plant). Moscow: Ogiz, State Publishing House for Political Literature, 1948.

Landry, Robert John. *This Fascinating Radio Business*. New York: Bobbs-Merrill, 1946.

Large Soviet Encyclopedia *(Bol'shaya Sovetskaya Entsiklopediya)*. Moscow: Ogiz, 1926-1948.

—— Supplement, "Soyuz Sovetskikh Sotsialisticheskikh Respublik" (Union of Soviet Socialist Republics). Moscow: Ogiz, State Science Institute "Soviet Encyclopedia," 1948.

Lasswell, Harold D. "Agitation," *The Encyclopedia of the Social Sciences*. Vol. I. New York: Macmillan, 1930.

—— "Communications Research and Politics," *Print, Radio, and Film in a Democracy,* Douglas Waples (ed.). Chicago: University of Chicago Press, 1942.

—— "Propaganda," *The Encyclopedia of the Social Sciences*. Vol XII. New York: Macmillan, 1934.

Lasswell, Harold D., Ralph D. Casey, and Bruce L. Smith. *Propaganda and Promotional Activities*. Minneapolis: University of Minneapolis Press, 1935.

"Law on the Five Year Plan. . . . Adopted March 18, 1946." Published by *Soviet News*. London, no date.

Lazarsfeld, Paul F., Bernard B. Berelson, and Hazel Gaudet. *The People's Choice*. New York: Columbia University Press, 1948.

Lazarsfeld, Paul F., and Robert K. Merton. "Studies in Radio and Film

Propaganda." *Transactions of the New York Academy of Sciences,* series II, vol. VI, no. 2, December 1943.

Lazarsfeld, Paul F., and Frank Stanton (eds.). *Communications Research 1948-1949.* New York: Harper and Brothers, 1949.

Lebedev, Nicolai A. *Ocherk Istorii Kino S.S.S.R.* (An Outline History of the Film in the U.S.S.R.). Moscow: Goskinoizdat, 1947.

Lenin, Vladimir Ilyich. *Collected Works.* London: Martin Lawrence, Ltd., 1927—. New York: International Publishers, 1927—.

—— *Selected Works.* J. Fineberg (ed.). 12 vols. New York: International Publishers, 1935-1939.

——*Sochineniya* (Works). Moscow: Gosizdat, 2d ed., 1926-1932; 3d ed., 1935.

Lenin, Stalin, and the Party on the Film *(Lenin, Stalin, Partiya o Kino).* Moscow-Leningrad: State Publishing House on Art, 1938.

Lewin, Kurt. "Forces Behind Food Habits and Methods of Change," *The Problem of Changing Food Habits.* National Research Council, Bulletin 108, 1943.

Luxemburg, Rosa. *Leninism or Marxism?* Glasgow: Anti-Parliamentary Communist Federation [1935].

Moore, Barrington, Jr. "Some Readjustments in Communist Theory," *Journal of the History of Ideas,* vol. VI, no. 4, 1945.

On Propaganda and Agitation *(O Propagande i Agitatsii).* Leningrad: Lenoblizdat, 1936.

Outline for the Second Five Year Plan *(Proekt Vtorogo Pyatiletnego Plana).* Vol. I. Moscow: Partizdat, 1934.

Parsons, Talcott. "Propaganda and Social Control," *Psychiatry,* vol. V, no. 4, November 1942.

Party Decisions on the Press *(Resheniya Partii o Pechati).* Moscow: Politizdat, 1941.

Perchik, Lev M. *Agitatsiya* (Agitation). Moscow: Partizdat, 1937.

Political Dictionary *(Politicheskii Slovar').* Moscow: Ogiz, State Publishing House for Political Literature, 1940.

The Press in the Land of Socialism *(Pechat' Strany Sotsializma).* Moscow: All-Union Scientific Publishing Institute of Graphic-Pictorial Statistics, TsUNKhU, Gosplan, 1939.

The Press in the U.S.S.R. in 1939: Statistical Materials *(Pechat' S.S.S.R. v 1939 Godu: Statisticheskie Materialy).* Moscow: All-Union Book Chamber, 1940.

Radio Yearbook: 1936 *(Radioezhegodnik: 1936).* Moscow: State Publishing House on Radio Questions, 1937.

Reavey, George. *Soviet Literature Today.* New Haven: Yale University Press, 1947.

Report of the Fifteenth Congress of the Communist Party of the Soviet Union. London: Communist Party of Great Britain, 1928.

Results of the Fulfillment of the Second Five Year Plan for the Development of the National Economy of the U.S.S.R. *(Itogi Vypolneniya Vtorogo Pyatiletnego Plana Razvitiya Narodnogo Khozyaistva S.S.S.R.).* Moscow: Gosplanizdat, 1939.

"Rules of the All-Union Communist Party (of Bolsheviks)," *American Quarterly on the Soviet Union,* vol. II, no. 1, 1939.

Ryabov, I. *Opyt Politicheskoi Agitatsii v Kolkhoze* (Experience with Political Agitation in the Collective Farm). Moscow: Ogiz, State Publishing House for Political Literature, 1948.

Schramm, Wilbur (ed.). *Communications in Modern Society.* Urbana: University of Illinois Press, 1948.

Shitarev, G. *Opyt Politicheskoi Agitatsii Sredi Naseleniya po Mestu Zhitel'stva* (Experience with Political Agitation among the Population at the Place of Residence). Moscow: Ogiz, State Publishing House for Political Literature, 1948.

Small Soviet Encyclopedia *(Malaya Sovetskaya Entsiklopediya).* Moscow: 1st ed., 1928-1931; 2d ed., 1933-1941.

Smith, Bruce L., Harold D. Lasswell, and Ralph D. Casey. *Propaganda, Communication, and Public Opinion.* Princeton: Princeton University Press, 1946.

Social Science Research Council. *Studies in Social Psychology in World War II.* Vols. I-IV. Princeton: Princeton University Press, 1949—.

Socialist Agriculture of the U.S.S.R. *(Sotsialisticheskoe Sel'skoe Khozyaistvo S.S.S.R.).* Moscow: Gosplanizdat, 1939.

Socialist Construction in the U.S.S.R. *(Sotsialisticheskoe Stroitel'stvo S.S.S.R.).* Moscow, 1936 and 1939.

Sokolov, I. V. *Istoriya Sovetskogo Kinoiskusstva Zvukovogo Perioda* (History of Soviet Film Art in the Period of Sound). Vol. II: 1934-1944. Moscow: Goskinoizdat, 1946.

The Soviet Press in Figures *(Sovetskaya Pechat' v Tsifrakh).* Moscow: Publishing House of the All-Union Book Chamber, 1948.

Stalin, Joseph. *Leninism.* 2 vols. Translated by Eden and Cedar Paul. New York: International Publishers, 1932-1933.

—— *Leninism: Selected Writings.* New York: International Publishers, 1942. Cited as *Selected Writings.*

—— *Sochineniya* (Works). Moscow: Ogiz, State Publishing House for Political Literature. Vol. I—, 1942—.

Stalin, Joseph, and others. *Socialism Victorious.* New York. International Publishers, 1935.

Supreme Soviet of the U.S.S.R., Eighth Session, 1941, Stenographic Report *(Verkhovny Sovet S.S.S.R., Vosmaya Sessiya, 1941, Stenograficheskii Otchet).* Moscow, 1941.

Twenty Years of Soviet Cinematography *(Dvadtsat' Let Sovetskoi Kinematografii).* Moscow: Goskinoizdat, 1940.

Towster, Julian. *Political Power in the U.S.S.R. 1917-1947.* New York: Oxford University Press, 1948.

Ushakov, Dmitrii, N. (ed.). *Tolkovy Slovar' Russkogo Yazyka* (Explanatory Dictionary of the Russian Language). Moscow: Ogiz, 1934-1940.

White, D. Fedotoff. *The Growth of the Red Army.* Princeton: Princeton University Press, 1944.

White, Llewellyn. *The American Radio.* Commission on Freedom of the Press. Chicago: University of Chicago Press, 1947.

Yakobson, Sergius. "Postwar Historical Research in the Soviet Union," *The Annals of the American Academy of Political and Social Science,* vol. 263, May 1949.

Zhdanov, A. A. *Podgotovka Partiinykh Organizatsii k Vyboram v Verkhovnyi Sovet S.S.S.R. po Novoi Izbiratel'noi Sisteme i Sootvetstvuyushchaya Perestroika Partiino-Politicheskoi Raboty* (Preparation of the Party Organizations for the Elections to the Supreme Soviet of the U.S.S.R. in Accordance with the New Electoral System, and the Corresponding Reorganization of the Party Political Work). Moscow: Partizdat TsK VKP (b), 1937.

Ziglin, Rose. "Radio Broadcasting in the Soviet Union," *The Annals of the American Academy of Political and Social Science,* vol. 177, January 1935.

PERIODICALS

Agitator's Guidebook *(Sputnik Agitatora).* Journal of the Central Committee and Moscow Committee of the All-Union Communist Party (of Bolsheviks). Moscow.

Baku Worker *(Bakinskii Rabochii).* Organ of the Central and Baku Committees of the Azerbaidzhan Communist Party. Baku.

Bolshevik *(Bol'shevik).* Theoretical and Political Journal of the Central Committee of the A.U.C.P. Moscow:

Bolshevik Press *(Bol'shevistskaya Pechat').* Publication of the Central Committee of the A.U.C.P. Moscow.

Culture and Life *(Kul'tura i Zhizn').* Newspaper of the Department of

Propaganda and Agitation of the Central Committee of the A.U.C.P. Moscow.

Current Digest of the Soviet Press. Joint Committee of Slavic Studies, Washington, D. C.

Electrical Communications *(Elektro-Svyaz)*. Organ of the Ministry of Communications of the U.S.S.R. Moscow.

Evening Moscow *(Vechernyaya Moskva)*. Newspaper of the Moscow City Committee of the A.U.C.P. and the Moscow City Soviet. Moscow.

Izvestiya. Organ of the Soviets of Workers' Deputies of the U.S.S.R. Moscow.

Komsomol'skaya Pravda. Organ of the Central and Moscow Committees of the All-Union Leninist League of Young Communists. Moscow.

Literary Gazette *(Literaturnaya Gazeta)*. Organ of the Union of Soviet Writers of the U.S.S.R. Moscow.

Party Construction *(Partiinoe Stroitel'stvo)*. Journal of the Central Committee of the A.U.C.P. Moscow.

Party Life *(Partiinaya Zhizn')*. Journal of the Central Committee of the A.U.C.P. Moscow.

Pravda. Organ of the Central Committee and Moscow Committee of the A.U.C.P. Moscow.

Propagandist (Propagandist). Journal of the Central and Moscow Committees of the A.U.C.P. Moscow.

Radio (Radio). Organ of the All-Union Committee for Radiobroadcasting. Moscow.

Radio Front *(Radiofront)*. Organ of the All-Union Committee for Radiobroadcasting. Moscow.

Radio Programs *(Radioprogrammy)*. Organ of the All-Union Committee for Radiobroadcasting. Moscow.

Socialist Herald *(Sotsialisticheskii Vestnik)*. Organ of the Russian Social Democratic Workers' Party. New York.

Soviet Art *(Sovetskoe Iskusstvo)*. Organ of the Committee on Artistic Affairs under the Council of Ministers of the U.S.S.R. Moscow.

Soviet Music *(Sovetskaya Muzyka)*. Organ of the Union of Soviet Composers of the U.S.S.R. and the Committee on Artistic Affairs under the Council of Ministers of the U.S.S.R. Moscow.

Soviet News, London.

Soviet Power *(Vlast' Sovetov)*. Journal of the All-Union Central Executive Committee. Moscow.

Soviet Press Translations. Far Eastern and Russian Institute, University of Washington, Seattle.

Trud (Labor). Organ of the All-Union Central Council of the Trade Unions. Moscow.

Turkmen Spark *(Turkmenskaya Iskra).* Organ of the Central Committee of the Turkmen Communist Party and the Presidium of the Supreme Council of the Turkmen Soviet Socialist Republic. Ashkabad.

U.S.S.R. Speaking *(Govorit S.S.S.R.).* Organ of the All-Union Committee for Radiobroadcasting. Moscow.

Workers and Peasant Correspondent's Pravda *(Pravda Raboche-Krestyanskii Korrespondent).* Moscow.

INDEX

RUSSIAN RESEARCH CENTER STUDIES

* Out of print.
† Publications of the Harvard Project on the Soviet Social System.
‡ Published jointly with the Center for International Affairs, Harvard University.